Cities and the Making of Modern Europe, 1750–1914

ANDREW LEES

Rutgers University

and

LYNN HOLLEN LEES

University of Pennsylvania

CAMBRIDGE
UNIVERSITY PRESS

CAMBRIDGE UNIVERSITY PRESS
Cambridge, New York, Melbourne, Madrid, Cape Town, Singapore, São Paulo,
Delhi, Mexico City

Cambridge University Press
The Edinburgh Building, Cambridge CB2 8RU, UK

Published in the United States of America by Cambridge University Press, New York

www.cambridge.org
Information on this title: www.cambridge.org/9780521548229

First published 2007
3rd printing 2012

Printed and bound by MPG Books Group, UK

A catalogue record for this publication is available from the British Library

Library of Congress Cataloguing in Publication data
Lees, Andrew, 1940–.
Cities and the making of modern Europe, 1750–1914 / by Andrew Lees and Lynn
Hollen Lees.
    p.   cm. – (New Approaches to European History)
Includes bibliographical references.
ISBN 978-0-521-83936-5 (hardback) – ISBN 978-0-521-54822-9 (pbk.)
1. Cities and towns – Europe – History.   2. Urbanization – Europe – History.   I. Lees,
Lynn Hollen.   II. Title.   III. Series.

HT131.L44   2007
307.760994–dc22   2007032989

ISBN 978-0-521-83936-5 Hardback
ISBN 978-0-521-54822-9 Paperback

To friends and colleagues, past and present, at the
Centre for Urban History, University of Leicester

Contents

Illustrations

Maps

Tables

Acknowledgments

Inasmuch as this book builds on earlier books each of us has written about urban history, a full list of the people to whom we are intellectually indebted would be very long. Here, we thank in the first place William Beik for having suggested that we write it for the series he helps to edit and for his comments on our drafts along the way. Others have assisted us too, either by discussing our conception of the volume with us or by reading and commenting on parts of it. For such support, we thank Robert Fishman, Peter Jelavich, Heinz Reif (and participants in his colloquium at the Center for Metropolitan Studies of the Technical University in Berlin), Jürgen Reulecke, Marc Schalenberg, and Jennifer Sessions. Alan Allport and Ralf Stremmel have helped with illustrations. We wish to express gratitude also to the Camden Campus of Rutgers, The State University of New Jersey, and to the University of Pennsylvania for giving us the sabbatical leaves that enabled us to finish this volume. Our editors at Cambridge University Press, Michael Watson, Helen Waterhouse, and Elizabeth Davey have consistently smoothed the way for us, and we are also grateful for their assistance.

Introduction

Historians regularly and rightly refer to the great importance, particularly during the period between the late eighteenth century and 1914, of the process of urbanization. Between 1750 and 1910, the percentage of the European population living in communities numbering 5,000 or more inhabitants more than tripled, and between 1800 and 1900 the percentage living in "big cities" (defined at the time as cities of at least 100,000 inhabitants) more than quadrupled. Owing both to the overall growth of European population and to its changing distribution, the absolute numbers of city dwellers skyrocketed, from 14.7 million in 1750 to 127.1 million in 1910.[1] As Robert Vaughan, an English observer to whom we shall return at several points, observed around the middle of the period, this was "the age of great cities." In our volume, we seek to show where and how these rapidly growing collections of men and women arose and why the physical and demographic expansion of such places mattered.

Scholars justifiably regard the growth of cities as a major force behind democratization and industrialization, two processes they often label as "the dual revolutions" that marked these years, and as a crucially significant development in its own right. Neither the political upheavals that broke out in the late eighteenth century and recurred in 1830, 1848, and 1871 nor the industrial revolution, which began a few decades earlier and continued to accelerate even as expressions of political radicalism evolved from revolutionary to less violent manifestations, can be understood apart from the story of urban growth. Cities brought together energy, information, and human and financial capital in the critical mass needed for social transformation. New forms of transportation, communication, employment, family life, governance, and leisure within Europe, which signaled the change from the world of the mid-eighteenth century to that of the twentieth, were also closely linked to urban development. The rise of great cities, even more than the rise of the factory, transformed the

---

[1] For these and later remarks about the growth of urban populations, see Tables 1 and 2 below and, with regard to individual cities, Appendix A.

appearance of much of the European landscape and also, much more than any political events, dramatically altered the conditions under which sharply increasing percentages of Europeans (and, albeit to a lesser extent, non-Europeans) experienced daily life. Cities were the places where modernity began and where it reached its zenith, and they richly deserve a central place in general as well as in local historiography. Concentrating on the urban variable thus opens a window that enables us to look at and bring into focus many of the most important aspects of European history during the period between the pre-revolutionary "old regime" and the outbreak of the First World War.

Urban centers served as the focal points where not only the dual revolutions but also many other transformations occurred. Institutions located in cities brought together, employed, housed, and educated the social groups that produced these changes, and urban growth was in turn stimulated by them. Bankers, entrepreneurs, radical politicians, students, workers, political philosophers, and economists – all of whom sought to change their societies – worked primarily in cities and through urban organizations and networks. The nature of urban industries and cultural production made cities the sites where nation-states were imagined by members of the educated middle classes, and created and strengthened in no small part as a result of their efforts. Via newspapers, print shops, coffee-houses, theaters, schools, and other institutions, cities served as centers for communication and cultural innovation more broadly as well. They transmitted information, functioning both as laboratories and as command centers, whose examples and powers influenced not only rural areas within their own nations but also growing cities in European empires overseas.

Concentrating on the urban sector braids into one narrative rope many related threads, not in a narrowly determinist fashion but as a story of interconnections. Although urban growth seemed to be and in many respects really was disruptive, investments in the cities' physical and human capital made the towns exemplars of a changing order and also engines for the creation of that order. High levels of consumption by members of urban elites contributed to and reinforced sharp differences among social classes but also set standards for emulation. The cities experienced in a particularly acute fashion the contradictions of nineteenth-century society: squalid poverty and astonishing wealth, early death and growing longevity, ignorance and science, popular and high culture, and appalling chaos and impressive institutions of social control and betterment. The social and cultural history of cities mirrored and shaped the evolution of nineteenth-century society, both negatively and positively.

Four mutually reinforcing themes will recur throughout this book: the cities as milieux characterized by both freedom and discipline; cities as places of social and political diversity in an era of growing national unity; cities as concentrations not only of people but also of governmental functions; and cities as nodes in networks of exchange in Europe and in global economic and imperial systems. As we explore each of these aspects of urban history, we shall seek to provide answers to many questions of interest to historians of modern Europe. How were industrial and urban development linked? How did urban populations experience the impact of technological change and intensified city growth? How did urban governments respond to the challenges of populations divided by race, class, and gender? What roles did cities play in stimulating political democracy and the rise of nationalism? How did imperial networks shape cities in Europe and in its colonies?

Our volume focuses on the three countries whose cities, we argue, merit the closest scrutiny of historians who seek to link urban development and the making of modern Europe. European-wide trends and processes occurred here most visibly, dramatically, and influentially. The claims on our readers' attention of Britain, the clear leader in the area of urban development during the early and middle parts of the period we consider, and of Germany, where urban growth took place with particular rapidity toward the end of it, require no further justification with regard to the importance of what occurred there. Urban developments were less marked in France, but for a variety of reasons – perhaps foremost among them the role of its capital as a laboratory in which some of the most pronounced extremes of urban life asserted themselves with particular force and clarity – it, too, must be included. Inasmuch as what we offer is an interpretive synthesis, which depends heavily on work by others as well as our own research for earlier projects, there are other reasons in addition, of a practical sort, for focusing on Britain, Germany, and France. Our own research and teaching have centered on these three countries, and the scholarly literature on their cities is particularly rich, both in monographs and in broad treatments of urban change. Many bricks, some of which have already been cemented together by others, thus lay ready to hand for use in constructing the work we had in mind.

Almost all of the particular places to which we shall refer belong to a group of forty-eight cities that numbered 250,000 or more inhabitants in 1910 and were located to the west of what was then the Russian Empire (see Appendix A). The cities to whose histories we shall refer most frequently were very large places that came to be known as major "world cities." Each enjoyed, at the latest by about 1880, unquestioned pride of place among urban areas in the country in which it was located, and each in 1910 boasted a population of at least 2 million inhabitants. Not only because of their size but also for numerous other reasons, the British, French, and German capitals – London (far and away the largest city in the world, with more than 7 million inhabitants), Paris, and Berlin – figure prominently in what we have written. In the case of Britain, we refer also to such places as the port cities of Liverpool, Bristol, and Glasgow and the industrial cities of Manchester, Birmingham, and Leeds. In Germany, Munich (the capital of Bavaria), Frankfurt am Main (which was a major center of commerce), the northern port city of Hamburg (a city state until 1871), and the Ruhr Valley area in the west (which contains a number of industrial cities, most prominent among them Düsseldorf and Essen) have served as additional touchstones. Among French cities, Lyon, second only to Paris as a center of economic life of various sorts, the port cities of Marseille and Bordeaux, and the industrial cities of Lille and Saint-Étienne (although the last two were not large enough for inclusion in Appendix A) also deserve mention, here and later.

Only seventeen of the places on our list of forty-eight in Appendix A were located in European countries other than the United Kingdom, Germany, or France, none of which, except for Italy, contained more than two of the seventeen. Although we do not generally discuss them as exemplars of national trends, some of them require being referred to in their own right as important and interesting sites of urban life and development. Among the ones that have attracted the most attention by historians are Vienna, a fourth "world city," whose role both as the capital of the ill-fated Habsburg Empire and as a major center of cultural life has long fascinated writers and readers; Budapest, the capital of the Empire's Hungarian half; Brussels, the capital of heavily urbanized Belgium; Amsterdam, which, although it no longer enjoyed the standing it had possessed in the seventeenth century, remained the largest city in a country that had an extensive empire overseas; Stockholm, the leading city of Scandinavia; Barcelona, a major Spanish industrial city and a site of important initiatives in the area of city planning; and the industrial city of Milan, the largest city in northern Italy. Each of them will make at least an occasional appearance in what follows, and many more will be discussed in passing as well.

As this list indicates, we discuss various sorts of cities, and readers should bear in mind that our selection reflects, if only partially, the great heterogeneity of urban types. One must distinguish among national capitals, older centers of trade and commerce, port cities, resort cities, and newer factory towns. That said, we emphasize typicality rather than peculiarity and similarities that linked cities rather than differences that separated them. This perspective results partly from the book's brevity. But

Table 1 *Urbanization in Europe, 1750–1910*

Europe	Britain	France	Germany
1750: 12.2	1750: 24.2	1750: 14.8	1750: –
1800: 12.1	1801: 30.1	1801: 20.5	1816: 26.5
1850: 18.9	1851: 50.4	1851: 25.5	1849: 28.3
1880: 29.3	1881: 67.1	1891: 37.4	1880: 41.4
1910: 40.8	1911: 79.6	1911: 44.2	1910: 60.0

Numbers indicate urban populations at specified dates as percentages of total populations. The figures for Europe, which come from Bairoch, *Cities and Economic Development*, 216, pertain to the area west of the Russian Empire. They refer to municipalities or other administrative units that numbered 5,000 or more inhabitants. For the figures for individual countries, the threshold is generally 2,000 inhabitants. The figures for Britain in 1750 and 1801 come from Jan De Vries, *European Urbanization, 1500–1800* (Cambridge, MA, 1984) and apply to settlements over 2,500; the figures for France in 1750 also come from De Vries and tally settlements over 3,000. Percentages for Germany for the period before 1880 pertain to Prussia, the largest German state in the area that was unified in 1871. For comments on sources for other numbers in this table and on sources for all of Table 2, see Lees, *Cities Perceived*, 4.

Table 2 *The growth of the big cities, 1800–1910*

Europe	Britain	France	Germany
1800: 2.9 (21)	1801: 8.2 (1)	1801: 2.8 (3)	1816: 1.9 (2)
1850: 4.8 (43)	1851: 21.8 (11)	1851: 4.6 (5)	1849: 3.1 (4)
1900: 12.3 (143)	1881: 29.5 (24)	1891: 12.0 (12)	1880: 7.2 (14)
	1911: 40.7 (39)	1911: 14.6 (15)	1910: 21.3 (48)

For each area, the first numbers after dates indicate populations of cities that contained 100,000 or more inhabitants as percentages of an area's total population. Numbers in parentheses indicate total numbers of such cities. Percentages for Germany before 1880 are for Prussia.

it also reflects the fact that we deal with large cities (placing particular emphasis on the *largest* cities), in which, despite variations, multiple functions were inevitably intertwined.

Having acknowledged in a general way our indebtedness to other practitioners of urban history, whose many works of exemplary scholarship form the foundation on which and most of the building blocks with which this volume was constructed, we want to emphasize that it differs significantly from comparable work in the field. There are three major surveys in English that encompass urban developments during our period in the territory on which we concentrate: the classic jeremiad by Louis Mumford (in which modern cities are portrayed as appalling departures from earlier norms), the more recent and generally celebratory survey of over a dozen individual cities by Peter Hall, and the work by Paul Hohenberg and one of the present authors, Lynn Hollen Lees. More analytic than either Mumford's work or Hall's, it makes heavy use of concepts drawn from economics and other social sciences. What unites these volumes, despite their differences from one another, in comparison with the present work is the fact that all of them treat much longer periods and much larger territories than the ones on which we focus, so that anyone who wants to concentrate on the later eighteenth and the nineteenth centuries in the European heartland must sift through them with some care in order to find what she or he seeks. Not counting the classic work by Adna Weber, which is heavily statistical, only a single work other than the present one focuses comparatively on the period we treat: an excellent survey in French by Jean-Luc Pinol, which treats developments in Britain, France, Germany, and the United States.

Aside from its chronological and its geographic boundaries and the language in which it is written, our work also differs from the ones to which we have just referred by virtue of the way in which it has been constructed conceptually. We seek – despite all the diversity and complexity to which we shall refer along the way – to chart an overall trajectory. Although our approach is not primarily narrative, we do have a story to tell, a story that embodies an interpretation.

To state matters as simply as possible, we move from often appalling challenges to adaptive responses of varying adequacy. We take the reader in the first three chapters, which roughly treat the period 1750 to 1850, from relative stability through explosive growth and some of the concerns and conflicts that arose in connection with it. We treat not only commerce, industry, and migration but also the social geography of wealth and poverty, birth rates and death rates under the impact of overcrowding and poor sanitation, and illegitimacy and crime. We point in Chapter 3 to urban networks of revolutionary activity, which mobilized urban populations in several states. We also pay attention, in Chapter 4, to early nineteenth-century efforts to improve the urban scene, many emanating from churches and private associations, others from public authorities. Pressure for solutions centering on aesthetic improvement, philanthropy, individual moral reform, and institutional reform led, however, only to piecemeal results. A later wave of growth and popular mobilization followed in the second half of the century, prompting more aggressive action on the part of state and municipal governments. Here, too, we chart the challenges that convinced contemporaries of the need to deal with urban problems: challenges which emerged through growth and its environmental impacts. Big cities had turned into giant metropolises, compounding the difficulties of adequate housing, transportation, and sanitation. Newly armed with statistical information, contemporaries moved from unease over urban political movements and fears of slums and slum populations to the development of public policies with regard to urban social conditions. Their representations of the urban poor shaped the solutions they advocated. As the political forces unleashed by democratization intensified, the range of proposed solutions widened, as did the means at the disposal of growing local as well as state governments. After revisiting the subject of philanthropy, we consider a wide range of city services and other measures taken by public authorities to deal with the needs of urban populations. We also consider the varieties of urban cultures – elite, popular, and modernist – which greatly enriched big-city life. We turn in our last chapter to European influences on the cities of overseas empires and the networks which linked metropoles and colonial centers. During the last half of the century, European governments expanded their control of cities both at home and abroad.

There is, in the writing of good history, no such thing as a "happy ending," and it is not our intention to suggest that by 1914 city dwellers in the countries on which we concentrate – let alone city dwellers in colonial areas – lived in communities that were even close to being perfect. Just as cities were diverse, so too were the experiences of their inhabitants. Yet there are reasons to regard urbanization between 1750 and 1914 as a process that contributed overall, at least toward its end, to the prosperity and the wellbeing of the Europeans who experienced it. By 1914, average city dwellers lived longer, and they had higher incomes, more civil rights, and, if male, greater rights to political participation than their parents or grandparents had enjoyed earlier. More cultural choices were also open to them, although pressures for conformity also increased along with the power of central states.

A few words follow about bibliographies and citations. The following list includes all the works discussed above; additional ones that bear in a general way on the urban history during the nineteenth century of Europe as a whole, of Britain, of France, or of Germany; and several books that deal broadly with perceptions of cities. In general, neither they nor the works listed in Appendix B have been cited in bibliographies at the ends of individual chapters, even though a number of them have proved highly useful. We have generally not cited in footnotes any of the works listed in any of the bibliographies unless we have quoted or referred to them in the text, drawing on them instead without specific attribution. In cases in which a work is cited, but only in an abbreviated fashion, the reason is usually that full information appears in the relevant bibliography. Full information is provided in citations for most primary sources, only a few of which are listed in the bibliographies.

BIBLIOGRAPHY

Agulhon, Maurice, *et al.*, eds. *Histoire de la France urbaine, vol. IV: La ville de l'age industriel.* Paris, 1998.

Bairoch, Paul. *Cities and Economic Development: From the Dawn of History to the Present.* Trans. Christopher Braide. Chicago, 1988.

Bergmann, Klaus. *Agrarromantik und Großstadtfeindschaft.* Meisenheim am Glan, 1970.

Borsay, Peter, ed. *The Eighteenth-Century Town: A Reader in English Urban History, 1688–1820.* London and New York, 1990.

Briggs, Asa. *Victorian Cities.* Ed. Andrew and Lynn Lees. Berkeley and Los Angeles, 1996.

Clark, Peter, ed. *The Cambridge Urban History of Britain, vol. II: 1540–1840.* Cambridge, 2000.

Coleman, B. I., ed. *The Idea of the City in Nineteenth-Century Britain.* London, 1973.

Corfield, Penelope. *The Impact of English Towns, 1700–1800.* New York, 1982.

Daunton, Martin, ed. *The Cambridge Urban History of Britain, vol. III: 1840–1950.* New York, 2000.

Dyos, H. J., and Michael Wolff, eds. *The Victorian City: Images and Realities.* 2 vols. London and Boston, 1973.

Fraser, Derek, and Anthony Sutcliffe, eds. *The Pursuit of Urban History.* London, 1983.

Goodman, David, and Colin Chant, eds. *European Cities & Technology: Industrial to Post-Industrial City.* London, 1999.

Hall, Peter. *Cities in Civilization: Culture, Innovation, and Urban Order.* London, 1998.

Hohenberg, Paul M., and Lynn Hollen Lees. *The Making of Urban Europe, 1000–1994.* 2nd edn. Cambridge, MA, 1995.

Hunt, Tristram. *Building Jerusalem: The Rise and Fall of the Victorian City.* New York, 2005.

Krabbe, Wolfgang. *Die deutsche Stadt im 19. und 20. Jahrhundert: Eine Einführung.* Göttingen, 1989.

Le Roy Ladurie, Emmanuel, ed. *Histoire de la France urbaine, vol. III: La ville classique.* Paris, 1981.

Lees, Andrew. *Cities Perceived: Urban Society in European and American Thought, 1820–1940.* Manchester and New York, 1985.

Morris, R. J., and Richard Rodger, eds. *The Victorian City: A Reader in British Urban History, 1820–1914.* London and New York, 1993.

Mumford, Louis. *The City in History: Its Origins, Its Transformations, and Its Prospects.* New York, 1961.

Pike, Burton. *The Image of the City in Modern Literature.* Princeton, 1981.

Pinol, Jean-Luc, ed. *Histoire de l'Europe urbaine.* 2 vols. Paris, 2003.

Le monde des villes aux XIXe siecle. Paris, 1991.

Reulecke, Jürgen. *Geschichte der Urbanisierung in Deutschland.* Frankfurt a. M., 1985.

Sutcliffe, Anthony, ed. *Metropolis, 1890–1940.* Chicago, 1984.

Teuteberg, Hans Jürgen, ed. *Urbanisierung im 19. und 20. Jahrhundert.* Cologne and Vienna, 1983.

Weber, Adna Ferrin. *The Growth of Cities in the Nineteenth Century: A Study in Statistics.* Ithaca, 1899.

Zimmermann, Clemens. *Die Zeit der Metropolen: Urbanisierung und Großstadtentwicklung.* Frankfurt a. M., 1996.

Part I

1750–1850, an era of disruption

1   Urban worlds around 1750

Johann Pezzl loved Vienna. "Long live great cities! They make people out of barbarians," he proclaimed. His sketch of the capital of the Holy Roman Empire, written in 1786, boasted of fine theaters, green parks, and contented citizens. Sited on the Danube, the city had been a fortified place for centuries, defended by thick walls and trenches. St. Peter's Church lay at its center, not far from the emperor's castle. Elegant palaces owned by "a numerous, wealthy, and brilliant" nobility could be seen nearby. Monasteries, convents, churches, and multiple government buildings lay along narrow streets, crowded by carriages and foot traffic. Passing through the city gates, women brought food in from the countryside to sell in open-air markets. Immigrants from France, Italy, Switzerland, and Germany worked alongside the Viennese to produce goods for the city, as well as for an international clientele. Although no two cities are identical, much of what Pezzl experienced would have been familiar to residents of other European capitals in the eighteenth century. The streetscape of Vienna had been built over several centuries in forms and styles widespread throughout Europe; its mixed population, ranging from pauper to prince, exhibited the familiar inequalities of many old regime towns. Views of eighteenth-century Vienna emphasized walls, churches, and its medieval street plan. The legacy of the past was easy to see.

Christopher Friedrichs argues that in the two centuries before 1750, European cities remained remarkably stable.[1] Continuities in their institutional structures and governance reinforced existing social and political orders, and, outside England, the pressures of industrial change were limited. Yet stability was not stasis. Writing in the mid-1780s, Pezzl complained of challenges to older standards of behavior, which produced new "manners, attitudes, pleasures, life-style, dress, education, speech, religion, and pomp." While he approved of the ending of both the persecution of the Jews and the death penalty, he worried about mothers who

---

[1] Friedrichs, *The Early Modern City*, 331.

gambled and flirted, promiscuous teenagers, and miserly nobles, voicing standard complaints of conservatives who feared that times were changing for the worse. Pezzl found those things suggesting a "New Vienna" unsettling.[2] For the most part, however, he remained contented with the elitist, elegant, imperial city in which he lived.

Cities in eighteenth-century Europe mixed the old and familiar with a few tastes of the new. Since cities functioned to exchange information and ideas, as well as consumption goods, they were places where intellectuals and journalists sometimes attacked the status quo. They were places of relative freedom, where the aggressive and the self-confident could make their way, pushing at the restrictions which held them back. Nevertheless, powerful social and political disciplines dampened conflict. Monarchs and state bureaucracies worked to curb urban independence and to shape the many networks that linked one town to another. Cities did not exist as independent entities. This chapter explores the physical, social, and political organization of mid-eighteenth century cities, so that the urban contribution of later political and economic revolutions can be understood. Its emphasis is on the legacy of the past, whose rapid transformation is traced in following chapters.

The physical city

Travelers knew they had arrived at a particular town when they caught sight of its skyline. Arthur Young on his tour of France in the late 1780s recorded his early impressions of Reims: "The first view of that city from this hill, just before the descent, at a distance of about four miles, is magnificent. The cathedral makes a great figure . . . Many times have I had such a view of towns in France."[3] Visitors to Vienna admired the great tower of St. Stephen's Church and its multicolored tile roof as they approached the city from its suburbs, outside the wall. The twin onion-shaped towers of the Frauenkirche in Munich or the Baroque dome of St. Peter's in Rome were instantly recognizable. Religious buildings were meant to impress as well as to sanctify, and they fulfilled both functions effectively in the European cityscape. Cathedrals dominated central squares in Prague, Rome, and Venice, and parish churches acted as the social, political, and visual centers of neighborhoods. But cities were more than the sum of their individual parts and their largest public buildings.

Contemporaries defined European towns in common-sense terms: numbers and density of houses. Spatial organization and architecture

---

[2] Landon, *Mozart and Vienna*, 60, 63, 188.   [3] Young, *Travels in France*, 171.

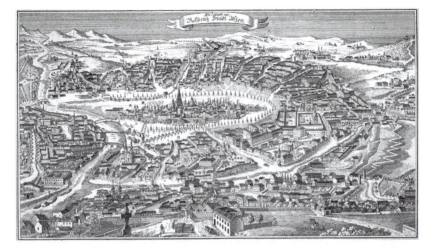

1. Vienna in 1750. The medieval city, dominated by St. Stephen's Cathedral, was surrounded by elaborate sixteenth- and seventeenth-century fortifications and growing suburban areas.

signaled the difference between urban and rural. In 1765, the *Encyclopédie*, described a town as "an agglomeration of houses, arranged in streets and with a shared enclosure, typically of walls and moats . . . It is a walled center, containing a variety of quarters, streets, public places, and other buildings."[4] Clearly, the author had in mind a relatively large, fortified settlement. Indeed, in the eighteenth century, many cities in Northern, Central, and Southern Europe kept the medieval barriers that encircled them, although cannon balls and gunpowder had long since made high, thin walls obsolete. As a result, those states that worried about invasions and enemy fire power had modernized and expanded the defensive structures of important cities and key border towns. During the late seventeenth century, Vauban surrounded Lille with a ring of deep, sloping walls and triangular bastions, large enough to hold a prison, barracks, arsenal, and chapel. Brussels, Leiden, Munich, and Naples invested in elaborate earthworks and ditches, sacrificing nearby suburbs to the need for a free field-of-fire. Venice and the Netherlands poured out vast sums to fortify border towns against their larger neighbors and enemies, and dozens of cities in the Holy Roman Empire rebuilt their defenses.

Walls brought control along with constriction. Visitors had to enter through elaborate gates, where they could be stopped, searched, and

[4] *Encyclopédie, ou Dictionnaire raisonné des sciences, des arts, et des métiers*, vol. XVII (Paris, 1765); quoted in Lepetit, *The Pre-industrial Urban System*, 45–46.

taxed, if the government chose to do so. Unwanted goods and people could be excluded, and citizens were confined when gates closed at night. Since the walls blocked the annexation of new land, growth had to be vertical or through the filling in of existing lots. In Barcelona, third and fourth stories had been added to most of the houses. By the late eighteenth century, the back streets of Naples and Vienna were narrow and dark, overshadowed by towering buildings. Arthur Young commented that however fine the skyline of many French towns, once a visitor ventured inside, all was "a clutter of narrow, crooked, dark, and dirty lanes." The older sections of Marseille, he judged, were "close" and "ill built."[5] Whatever the elegance of a town's public spaces, the private ones were often cramped and nasty.

Most of the housing in the larger cities, particularly that used by workers, was old. When wealthier owners wanted something more fashionable and moved on, their cast-off houses were subdivided and recycled for the poor. The stone houses in Scottish cities lasted for centuries, as did the solid brick houses of the Netherlands and northern Germany. Larger cities acquired multistory dwellings long before the era of the elevator. But as density mounted, light and fresh air decreased. Moreover, the absence of good water supplies and waste removal had predictable consequences in high density environments, producing high rates of death and disease.

It is worth considering the mixture of old and new in major European cities around 1750 in order to move closer to what contemporaries would have seen. The imprint of a city's past is difficult to destroy, even after fire or flood. In the absence of catastrophe, eighteenth-century towns tended to retain the public buildings that they had accumulated over the centuries, despite changes in architectural fashions. A medieval market hall and belfry loomed over central Ypres. Once a wealthy citizen had endowed a hospital, school, or orphanage, the institution remained to remind descendents of his benevolence and their public duties. Both the cost of replacement and the symbolic value of these properties discouraged innovation.

After the Great Fire in 1666, which burned out much of the City of London, town officials and the royal court considered modernizing street plans and giving the town a new look. Christopher Wren, the leading British architect of the day, borrowed Italian and French urban designs and produced a plan that cut wide, straight streets through winding alleyways, using strong geometry to produce visual order and symmetry. But property lines would have had to be redrawn, and owners would have had

---

[5] Young, *Travels in France*, 171, 229.

to delay rebuilding and to conform to formal restrictions. Economic pressures and individual rights won out easily over aesthetic considerations in the absence of a ruler prepared to force change. The rebuilt City kept its old street pattern, although a Baroque-style St. Paul's replaced the burned-out Gothic cathedral. For the individual house owner, rebuilding meant substituting brick for timber and abiding by certain restrictions on height. But while the architectural styles of individual buildings might change, their footprints on the ground, lot sizes, and street settings remained remarkably stable. The complexities of multiple ownership and vested rights meant that it was very difficult to make wholesale changes in existing areas of cities. Most locations of markets, public buildings, and palaces, as well as street names, stayed the same for centuries. Urban structures and spatial organization were remarkably stable over time. When more buildings were needed, contractors filled in back gardens or built upward.

Sites always constrained city rebuilding and produced stable urban geographies. Most of the larger European cities had originated on major rivers or coasts and depended heavily upon water transport for trade and travel. Ports like Liverpool, Bordeaux, and Hamburg grew up around their harbors and quays. A wall of city buildings faced outward to a line of ships in the ports of Bristol, Nantes, and Marseille. Stockholm, Venice, and Genoa fitted their cities into clusters of islands and mainland areas oriented toward water. When Amsterdam needed to expand in the seventeenth century, new circles of canals were added to the older core of the city, which faced the waterfront. Water constituted an important public space in many of Europe's largest cities, and it shaped overall growth and design.

Governments had to be willing to intervene to produce large changes in cityscapes. With the support of Louis XIV, Colbert worked to make Paris a model city during the late seventeenth century. Architects rebuilt the Louvre palace and designed new hospitals and a botanic garden, while improvements in paving, lighting, and water supply made the city cleaner and safer. Absolutist monarchs with deep pockets and a taste for the dramatic built Versailles, Karlsruhe, and Mannheim as new, residential cities for themselves and their courts. Long tree-lined streets led to gigantic Baroque palaces, which dwarfed even the churches. They made clear who was in charge.

The shift from closed to open cities accelerated in those states – principally England and France – where the danger of civil war was low during the late seventeenth and early eighteenth centuries. Officials allowed the walls of non-border cities to decay, permitting easy expansion. The French monarchy ordered the walls around Paris torn down, so that by

1715 tree-lined boulevards encircled the capital. In Bordeaux, walls and the fortress disappeared to be replaced by boulevards and a monumental square. New, elegant districts primarily for the rich were laid out in Edinburgh and Nancy. Private contractors accelerated the rebuilding of the richer towns by laying out new streets and erecting fashionable town houses or residential squares – for example, in the Faubourg St. Germain in Paris or Grosvenor Square in London. What at the time counted as suburban housing for urban elites spread around the larger British and French towns.

Growth and change took place in the cultural area too. Urban stocks of public, institutional, and commercial properties proliferated where there were funds for expansion. Innovation could be seen in new theaters built in Copenhagen, Vienna, and Moscow, as well as in dozens of French and German towns. Opera houses and concert halls multiplied in central and northern Europe. Entrepreneurs laid out racecourses and sports grounds, as well as dancing and amusement parks, for urbanites with time for fun. Clubs for wealthy London men provided wood-paneled retreats, and the opening of assembly rooms supplied venues for dances, lectures, and general sociability. Where people had surplus money and time, cities adapted to provide new playgrounds and opportunities.

The unusual qualities of big cities need, however, to be kept in mind. In the later eighteenth century, European towns came in many shapes and sizes, but most were small, having only a few thousand people. Citizens could stroll from one end to another of most towns in well under an hour. Shops, churches, markets, and town halls had been built compactly along major roads or in central spaces; simple houses and perhaps an inn or two lined the streets. Similarity of scale and building materials gave such places a uniform look, quite unlike the mixture of styles that characterized London or Paris. In 1750 in the lands from Ireland to Poland and Scandinavia to southern Italy, fewer than fifty settlements with populations over 40,000 can be identified. At that time, only thirteen cities, among them London, Paris, Amsterdam, Naples, and Vienna, had more than 100,000 inhabitants. The cities to be discussed in this book were atypically large and wealthy places – more complex in organization and function and better endowed with public buildings and institutions than small towns. They offered a wide variety of services to their regions and participated in far-flung networks of exchange. Some of their most important contacts were with urban settlements outside Europe.

By 1750, neo-European towns had appeared throughout the Americas. The Spanish government had pursued a conscious policy of urbanization in Mexico, Central America, Cuba, Puerto Rico, and most of South America, where it built over 800 towns by the mid-eighteenth century.

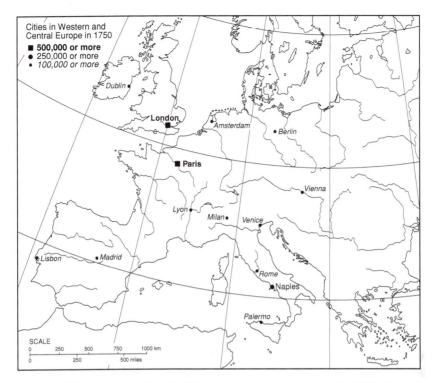

Map 1. Large cities in Western and Central Europe in 1750. In the mid-eighteenth century, the area west of Poland had fourteen cities with populations in excess of 100,000, three of which numbered more than 250,000. Only London and Paris broke the 500,000 mark. (Based on Tertius Chandler and Gerald Fox, *3000 Years of Urban Growth* [New York and London, 1974], 18.)

Conquest led to the building of a small settlement, which then became a site from which colonists dominated the surrounding territory and priests sought to convert its population. An administrative hierarchy stretched from Madrid to colonial capitals, such as Mexico City in the Vice-Royalty of New Spain, and then to regional centers, such as Guadalajara and Guatemala City, where courts, tax collectors, and other administrative offices could be found. Further subdivisions of those districts housed less important officials and smaller churches, but each provided important links to the colonial state. Lima, Bogota, and Buenos Aires served as the capitals of administrative regions to the south of New Spain. These towns brought European institutions and European styles into Latin America. Baroque cathedrals, palatial residences for the governor or major officials, and town halls dominated their central squares. The most important settlements acquired universities, libraries, and convents as they grew. Church celebrations and public ceremonies drew residents into a Hispanic-Catholic civic culture which included Amerindians as well as their conquerors. By 1750, the largest settlement in Latin America, Mexico City, had reached a population of 110,000, Lima housed 54,000 and Havana 28,000 people.

British overseas expansion depended heavily on urbanization, which became a royal strategy for control of a territory. Lord Ashley, a leading defender of the rights of the Stuart dynasty, declared in the 1670s "no concern of more consequence for the security and thriving of our Settlement, than that of planting in Townes, in which if men be not overruled theire Rashnesse and Folly will expose the Plantation to Ruin."[6] Governors of Virginia and Maryland were required to build a town by each river and to plan its space around a central square. From Upper Canada to the Caribbean, British officials lived in towns which had been designed as part of the settlement process. A rectangular grid, where north–south streets intersected east–west ones at regular intervals, was the most common form. Although boring, the plan had the advantages of simplicity, symmetry, and easy growth. The proprietors or the crown usually set aside land for markets, schools, churches, and public buildings, intending to duplicate in the Americas the institutions as well as the forms of European planned towns. Surveyors laid out Charleston, Philadelphia, and Savannah according to this model, and it was used as well in Jamaica and Canada. The Puritan settlers of Massachusetts also believed in towns, moving west from Salem and Boston in community units. Those who wished to go farther had to wait until enough neighbors to found a new church and town were prepared to go with them.

By 1715, three waves of migrants had settled along North America's Atlantic coast, bringing their religions, languages, material cultures, and technologies. European assumptions about gender, family, work, and time structured daily lives, and their attitudes to power and rights became part of the emerging American political order. Market towns and seaports, whose names echoed their English origins, dotted the landscape from Maine to Georgia. Boston (20,000), Philadelphia (14,000), and New York (13,300) had become substantial neo-European cities, weakly controlled by British monarchs. French towns – Montreal, Quebec City, and New Orleans – complicated the political and cultural geography of the Americas, as did the Spanish mission settlements of what would become California and Texas.

---

[6] Quoted in Robert Home, *Of Planting and Planning* (London, 1997), 8.

Farther afield, European merchants and trading companies had built port-forts along the Asian and African coastlines as sites from which to bargain for slaves and spices. In the mid-eighteenth century, Pondicherry, owned by the French, had become a major trading center on the east coast of the Indian peninsula, and, from the communes of St. Louis and Gorée, French merchants operated in West Africa in relative safety. The Dutch East India Company masterminded its vast trading interests from Batavia (now Jakarta) on the island of Java. Its walls and moats, brick Dutch-style houses, regular street pattern, and canals resembled Amsterdam's, although its population consisted mostly of slaves bought in Africa and in South and Southeast Asia or the Indies islands. Chinese, Malay, Indians, and Mardijkers (Christian, Portuguese-speaking ex-slaves) far outnumbered Dutch and Eurasians. In 1730, about 20,000 people lived inside the walls, within easy walking distance of the town hall, church, and hospital. An additional 15,000 spilled out into the suburbs, where Chinese and Malay sections developed. Dutch governors tried, but failed, to maintain ethnic segregation; too few Europeans migrated to the Indies. After the Battle of Plassey in 1757, the British East India Company gained tax-collecting rights and land in Bengal. Their ownership of the fortified cities of Calcutta (120,000), Bombay (70,000), and Madras (55,000) gave them rich enclaves from which to expand territorial control and trade in South Asia. Ships, sailors, soldiers, and guns had given Europeans by the mid-eighteenth century a visible presence in new towns along the coastlines of Asia and Africa. From a European vantage point, these were important places – signs of military strength, astute statecraft, and mercantile success. From an Asian and African standpoint, they looked insignificant and probably uninteresting. The great empires of Asia – Ottoman, Mughal, and Qing – centered in the magnificent cities of Constantinople, Agra, Delhi, and Peking. The Chinese capital, in fact, with its 900,000 people, was the largest city in the world in 1750. While European towns had reshaped the Americas by the mid-eighteenth century, they had made little impact on Asia and Africa.

Urban functions

All cities are multifunctional. Their size and dynamism derive from the many ways in which they operate within economic, political, social, and cultural networks, both in their regions and internationally. They are simultaneously markets, service centers, and sites of production. In contrast to villages or small towns, which normally have relatively homogeneous populations and few or no political or administrative functions, cities are the sites of institutions that attract resources, people, goods, and information from near and far. Consider Stockholm. In the eighteenth century, it was not only Sweden's political capital, where government offices, law courts, and political institutions could be found, but also a large port and the country's manufacturing center. Its iron export trade continued at a rapid clip, and the town's shipyards, textile workshops, and sugar and tobacco processing plants employed thousands of local workers. On the streets could be seen both teenage female servants, fresh from the countryside, and elderly army generals, living off their military pensions. Clubs and scientific societies catered to the capital's intellectual elite. Even this relatively small city on the northern fringe of Europe had linkages far beyond its borders.

As many towns have discovered in recent decades, multiple functions can cushion cities in hard times. Even when major industries declined, the service sector and administrative offices continued to provide jobs. Cultural institutions – universities, theaters, and churches – drew visitors even during periods of economic recession. Coffee-houses offered visitors hot information along with steaming beverages. Urban printers produced books, pamphlets, and newspapers that circulated well outside their borders. Italian and German musicians traveled a circuit of court cities and national capitals, in search of patrons who would pay. Capitals, in particular, drew the most famous writers, singers, and composers. Paris and Berlin set standards for music and theater, that were promptly copied elsewhere. Provincial companies all over France followed the lead of the *Comédie Française*, borrowing its plays and acting styles. Multi-functionality helps to explain why so few major cities lost regional or international importance over time. Diversification has been a source of urban strength.

Although all large cities have multiple functions, to thrive they require strong economic bases. Cities have to produce something to sell in return for food. The larger a settlement, the wider the variety of occupations represented in its labor force. Rich landlords moved to cities to spend rents collected from their rural properties and thus fueled urban production of luxuries. Because urban capitalists invested in local and more distant industries, cities' economic functions also included finance. They bankrolled not only trade but also manufacturing and agriculture. In addition, cities served as sites of exchange. Their locations made them important marketing centers. The larger trading towns still held periodic fairs and shipped goods through their ports overseas or along rivers and canals. In early modern Europe, merchant families from distant cities sent male relatives to other towns to sell and buy products, creating a network of trading places. Although all towns had markets, the larger ones had multiple sites for sales linked to particular goods and to sites of production in their hinterlands.

Administrative employment was also part of urban economies. As states grew in early modern Europe, the numbers of legal, military, and bureaucratic jobs multiplied. Courts, jails, tax offices, and army barracks were built disproportionately in towns. In Britain, towns housed tax collectors, workhouse masters, post offices, and clergymen, while in more centralized, heavily administered France, royal officials of many sorts watched over the realm from their various posts in provinces, towns, and rural districts. The consolidation of state governments in Europe during the early modern period operated through hierarchies of cities – market towns, county centers, and regional and national capitals – settlements at each higher level containing more services and institutions than ones at ranks below them. Before the French Revolution, thirty-three intendants administered France from important cities within their districts, working with staffs of clerks, secretaries, and copyists. Usually a university, a college for secondary education, a regional court (*parlement*), an office of the General Tax Farm (*ferme générale*), a financial court, and a cathedral could also be found in these same towns. Although not all French cities housed complete arrays of government offices and economic institutions, the larger towns had numerous services on offer. The fact that the French monarchy and the Roman Catholic church administered the French population through officials who resided in the towns had far-reaching implications for the nature of life in those places.

In Europe between 1600 and 1750, capital cities were the most rapidly growing towns in all parts of Europe, their irresistible dynamism overriding economic depressions and high death rates. During this period, Berlin, Copenhagen, London, Madrid, Paris, Stockholm, The Hague, and Vienna more than doubled in size. With tax money to finance opera houses and offices, kings and courts proved the steadiest source of urban growth in this period of absolutist government. On the Italian peninsula and in the Holy Roman Empire, where no single, strong state had yet developed, this impact was muted, but the primacy of capital cities emerged strongly where centralized kingdoms flourished.

Contemporaries noticed this growth and sought to explain it. According to Richard Cantillon in 1735, "If a prince or lord . . . fixes his residence in some pleasant spot and several other noblemen come to live there to be within reach of seeing each other frequently and enjoying agreeable society, this place will become a city." Their location would then attract others: artisans and tradesmen would move there to supply clothing and food. The building of law courts and other government departments would subsequently attract still more residents, including the wealthiest families in the state. The town where the king and the largest land-owners lived would become the capital, which functioned as "the center of fashion," and "a model" for all the rest. "The landowners who reside in the provinces do not fail to come occasionally to spend time [in it] and to send their children there to be polished."[7] Cantillon's emphasis on the link between governments and growth accurately describes the populations of political capitals. In Vienna during the early eighteenth century, court nobility and government officials accounted for about 60 percent of the working population. Military families made up about a quarter of the Berlin population around 1789. Royal officials far outnumbered the burghers or citizens of Stockholm.

Such cities attracted the human resources of the rest of the country, as well as an unending stream of food, drink, and raw materials. Berlin needed far more grain for its daily bread than could be produced in Brandenburg, and by the late eighteenth century its merchants toured Polish Silesia, as well as East and West Prussia, in search of supplies. Even in the sixteenth century, Paris drew meat, cheese, grain, and firewood from a 100-km zone around it, where many farmers specialized in the high quality vegetables, meats, and fruits wanted in the capital. In bad years, middlemen went farther afield. To supply Madrid's needs for grain, meat, and fuel for cooking, merchants scoured a 200-km radius that extended well beyond the boundaries of Castile. London's hinterland by the eighteenth century consisted of all England, although the capital's pull on people and goods weakened in the far north.

The extent to which the growth of political capitals benefited their regions has long been questioned. Adam Smith, in the *Wealth of Nations*, distinguished between trading or manufacturing towns and court or administrative cities. "Where the people are chiefly maintained by the employment of capital, they are in general industrious, sober and thriving," but where they are "chiefly maintained by the spending of revenue, they are in general idle, dissolute, and poor."[8] Madrid is one of the best examples of growth which had negative consequences for nearby towns and territory. The combination of wealth from the Americas, taxes, and rents meant that the Madrid elite could buy what it wanted from wherever it chose. Court officials commandeered transport services, grain, and wine supplies, outbidding merchants from other cities. Unfortunately, demand for food outstripped supply, leading to shortages and high prices.

---

[7] Richard Cantillon, *Essai sur la nature du commerce en géneral* (1735; repr. Boston, 1892), 17–21.

[8] Adam Smith, *An Inquiry into the Nature and Causes of the Wealth of Nations* (Harmondsworth, 1970), 435.

But local farmers proved unwilling to expand production because the gains from trade flowed primarily to wealthy landlords living in Madrid who spent their incomes on luxuries produced elsewhere. Moreover, a perverse combination of poor soils, harsh climate, and government controls and subsidies aggravated rural underdevelopment in central Spain. The net result was a decline of towns other than Madrid and economic stagnation in rural Castile during the seventeenth and eighteenth centuries. It can be argued that "while Spain was exploiting America, Madrid and its elites were exploiting Spain."[9]

The Madrid case was an extreme example of size and political clout drawing wealth parasitically from the surrounding territory and giving little back. In contrast, in Northern and Western Europe, the impact of urban growth during the seventeenth and eighteenth centuries was more favorable. Mixed regions of agriculture and small-scale manufacturing flourished in response to high metropolitan demand. Not only did regional transportation systems around London and Paris modernize, but they probably became cheaper. The small towns around Berlin, London, and Paris served as way-stations for migrants, easing their adjustment to the capital and providing jobs. Even if they remained small, the towns around the capitals became more functionally urbanized and tied to them as residents spent time there. A stable population size did not mean stagnation. Rather than suppressing economic activity in the surrounding area, the demands of most metropolitan economies encouraged the commercialization of nearby territories. By the later eighteenth century, European capitals reached far beyond their official boundaries to shape much wider regions.

During the seventeenth and eighteenth centuries, more specialized cities developed along with the growing wealth and power of states and citizens. Royal residential cities, such as Versailles, Potsdam, and Mannheim, were planned in part to glorify the rulers who had built them. Streets and parks flowed toward and away from the palaces, which dwarfed the surrounding structures. More important for their architecture than their urbanity, such towns testified to the extreme inequalities of wealth that shaped their societies. State-driven city construction could also be found in other forms. Monarchs who feared their neighbors built frontier fortress towns, which flourished until military threats ended. The French military engineer Vauban designed several towns in octagon and star shapes, geometry taking precedence over civilian needs. Scandinavian monarchs, not to be outdone, sited fort-towns to protect outlying

[9] Ringrose, *Madrid and the Spanish Economy*, 13–16, 312–16, 318.

2. The harbor in eighteenth-century Bordeaux. Trade with West Africa and the Caribbean made the Bordeaux port one of the busiest in France. Rich merchant firms built quayside warehouses and offices. (Thomas Bankes, *A New, Royal Authentic and Complete System of Universal Geography* [London, 1798].)

territories. State-sponsored urbanization served as a tool of centralizing kings.

Flourishing cross-Atlantic trade brought prosperity to port towns in Western Europe, which attracted workers and new investment. Protected by their countries' respective navies, Bordeaux, Bristol, and Liverpool participated in an Atlantic economy organized around sugar and slaves. From their ports, ships carried manufactured goods to the west coast of Africa, North America, and the Caribbean, bringing back to Europe sugar, rum, cotton, and other colonial products to be stored in quayside warehouses. Their leading families owned plantations and slaves, traveling between continents as part of their trade. The French crown, eager for a larger share of colonial commerce, poured money into Le Havre. Under Louis XIV, four new towns – Brest, Lorient, Rochefort, and Séte – developed to serve as ports, dry docks, and naval bases under government patronage. The Danish crown created the ports of Frederikssund and Frederickshaven. When the Atlantic routes outstripped Mediterranean ones as the quickest path to the best markets, sea-side towns with good harbors from Denmark south through Spain gained new importance and grew rapidly as a result.

To pay for the rising tide of imports coming into the Atlantic port towns, the European economy generated more and more industrial goods, many made in urban areas. Even in 1750, manufacturing towns could be found in several regions. Specialized textile towns, which produced silks, cottons, linens, and woolens, could be found from Italy north through Britain. Customers from all over Europe knew of Solingen sword blades, Maubeuge guns, and Sheffield knives. Manufacturing towns had already established themselves in western Europe by the mid-eighteenth century. They were most visible in England, where Leeds, Manchester, and Birmingham, as well as smaller centers in their regions, expanded dramatically as their export industries flourished.

By this time, rising wealth had also made possible the success of several tourist towns, most organized around mineral springs, where visitors could "take the waters" and pretend that the pursuit of health, rather than desire for a vacation, had lured them there. The most famous, the British town of Bath, grew along with its Mineral Water Hospital. The addition of elegant housing erected around squares, crescents, and greenery solidified its reputation with the fashionable, who came there to play and to find suitable husbands for their daughters. On the continent, Baden-Baden, Vichy, and Spa were destinations for wealthy travelers.

In Roman Catholic areas, pilgrimage towns continued to have a strong appeal. Thousands traveled yearly not only to Rome and to Reims, but also to an array of small towns from Częstochowa in Poland to Avila in Spain to pray in the company of fellow Christians. Their churches and shrines supported hotels, inns, cooks, and souvenir vendors. Where the demand for services rose, an urban supply was forthcoming.

Social groups

When tourists wanted to see Parisian society, they strolled along the city's boulevards. Courtesans and countesses shared these spaces with carpenters and coachmen, all gazing at one another and enjoying the view. City streets permitted promiscuous mixing of the dignified and the disreputable on relatively equal terms, but contemporaries knew well the many differences among those they saw. Pierre-Jean-Baptiste Nougaret commented in 1787 on one such scene: "Do you hear the sharp little voice of the impatient marquise blending with the awful swearing of a porter addressing Hell and Paradise? See in the glass carriage the ugly woman of title with her rouge, her diamonds, the paste shining on her face; whereas the ordinary girl just to the side in a simple dress is brilliantly fresh and

3. On a London street in 1751. This engraving by an unknown artist
shows how ordinary Londoners challenged a rich woman out shopping.
When her coachman was rude enough to park in a crosswalk, pedestrians
opened its doors and marched through. The artist commented: "Tis
hop'd the fair Ladies from hence will beware / How they stop a Free
Passage with such Haughty Air."

plump. Look at this wealthy canon sunken into his cushions dreaming of
nothing, while the old magistrate in his antique carriage reads some petition."[10] He described a sharply stratified society dominated by an elite
whose members monopolized property, political influence, and cultural
prestige.

Few contemporaries questioned the inevitability and the utility of social
hierarchies. Even if the souls of the saved were to be equal in an afterlife,
bodies in this realm were certainly not supposed to be so. Some argued
that a Great Chain of Being stretched upward from the lowly to royalty
and then to God. Nevertheless, the exact order of links in the chain
was open for debate, and all of the established rankings were regularly
challenged by the socially mobile. The concept of hierarchy was easier
for contemporaries to accept than any precise list of precedence. Because
modern censuses of occupations date from the mid-nineteenth century,
and because earlier city documents – tax, church, or insurance records for

[10] Pierre-Jean-Baptiste Nougaret, *Les historiettes du jour ou Paris tel qu'il est*, 2 vols. (Paris,
1787), II: 18–19; quoted in McClain, *Edo and Paris*, 297.

example – generally captured only part of an urban population, people did not have what we would call a reasonably accurate profile of economic and social categories. Even if a set of numbers existed, no eighteenth-century record described the complicated mix of family background, occupation, wealth, religious affiliation, age, gender, and personal reputation that together determined one's social position. The issue of how to combine and order them still would have to be solved.

Conceptualizing the social gradations within cities raises multiple issues. Which criterion ought to be used? Multiple, often conflicting, hierarchies existed, and a person's position varied according to the context in which he or she was being viewed. Divisions could be made in terms of political influence, property holdings, occupation, and religion; yet these alternative classifications did not necessarily coincide in their results. Louis-Sébastien Mercier sorted the Paris population into eight different groups: "princes and great lords (the least numerous), professionals, financiers, merchants or store owners, artists, artisans, manual laborers, servants, and the poor."[11] His finely graded scheme has to be measured, however, against the official, legal division of the French population into three estates – nobility, clergy, and all the rest. This third category lumped together hundreds of occupations and economic levels without sorting out any of the commonly recognized nuances of status. Then, too, it mattered whose labels were to be used. Some of the terms used by elites for the lowly – the mob, *popolo minuto*, *Pöbel*, *peuple* – were terms less descriptive of status than of anxiety. And what about the status of females? Although women derived their status from male relatives, should a woman be given her husband's status or that of her father? Marriage did not erase the reality of paternal ties and of family culture.

Some cities had their own official rankings, listed in so-called "golden books" or enshrined in law, but these systems varied considerably. The government of Frankfurt am Main divided the inhabitants into five groups: patricians, non-patrician town councilors and wealthier merchants, lawyers and substantial shopkeepers, craftspeople and small-scale retailers, and finally all the rest of the population. Yet these categories excluded Jews altogether and barred non-Lutheran Protestants and Catholics from the highest classes. Venetians proclaimed a simpler social hierarchy, consisting of three major groups: *nobeli*, *cittadini*, and *popolani*, the vast majority. Neither of these rankings captured very effectively the complex gradations of prestige, wealth, and function that divided an urban population in the eighteenth century. Then there is the

---

[11] Louis Sébastien Mercier, *Tableau de Paris*, 1783 (Paris, 1994), II: 1060.

issue of translation: social statuses do not have exact equivalents in multiple languages. A *bourgeois* was not exactly a *Bürger* nor a *burgués* nor a *cittadina*, although all these terms identified an urban male person of intermediate status who counted as a citizen of a town. Any sort of precise all-European urban social-status hierarchy is defeated by local and national differences, status ambiguities, linguistic nuance, and changes over time.

By aggregating the multitude of small distinctions recognized by contemporaries, one can nonetheless divide urban societies loosely into categories corresponding to high, middle, and low status. While the boundaries of elites, middling groups, and the poor might be fuzzy, their cores were clear enough and signaled major differences in modes of life, prestige, and entitlements.

In every city, a few families had sufficient prestige, money, and power to lord it over the rest. Their houses dominated elegant, central squares; their older, male members often became mayors, town councilors, or magistrates, while their silk-clad wives and daughters went visiting in family carriages. Political power demonstrated elite status most clearly. In the capitals, national elites of nobles and court officials co-existed with municipal worthies, drawn from the richer merchant or banking families. In Frankfurt am Main in 1760, merchants made up almost half of the elite, supplemented by patricians, officials, lawyers, and a small contingent of rich craftsmen from the guilds. Although these men rose into the elite through different routes, their paths intertwined and overlapped when relatives and marriages were taken into account. Strategies of intermarriage, family limitation, and clever investment helped most to maintain their social position over several generations, but turnover was normal. New families joined the ranks of the most prestigious, while those that lacked heirs or lost money faded from view.

Peter Burke has contrasted cities with closed and those with open elites, although in practice the two sorts faded into one another. Many towns which had maintained legally closed elites during the medieval period later admitted new families to positions of power. In Venice, the city with the best example of a closed elite, there was a "golden book" listing patrician families who had the exclusive right to hold city offices. The list remained unchanged between 1381 and 1646. Then in the eighteenth century, when Venice needed money to fight the Turks, the town council allowed very wealthy families to buy their way in, and many did so. Other Italian towns, Genoa and Bologna among them, imitated this system, as did several German towns. Ruling dynasties in Italy and Spain helped to create urban aristocracies by limiting urban offices to those of "pure blood" or acknowledged noble status. The expansion of Habsburg power in Italy increased the power of nobles within town governments. This strategy worked best in areas with stagnant economies and stable politics. Over time, however, any such list became obsolete as political revolution, demographic failure, and social mobility took their toll. When faced with a need for new men to staff town offices and support urban projects, cities added families to their lists.

The upwardly mobile found it easier in open towns, such as London and Amsterdam, to make it into the upper ranks, particularly in periods of expanding trade. Low birth rates made it hard for Dutch towns in the eighteenth century to maintain a stable upper class, while a constant stream of immigrants ensured a steady supply of wealthy newcomers. By the mid-eighteenth century, most town elites were relatively open. Even in Spain, where the crown kept a tight hold on municipal affairs, newcomers could buy their way into the top ranks through purchase of a title.

Central governments also helped to add new men to town elites. Purchase of a court office or a title was a sure ticket to high status, and royal need for money meant that many such tickets were offered for sale. Louis XIV's sale of offices in the early eighteenth century brought hundreds of families into the nobility of the robe, the titled caste of administrators.

By the eighteenth century, continental town elites had become more self-consciously aristocratic, as the pursuit of a title or landed estate became more common. Families moved money out of trade and into land, hoping thereby to increase their status. A coat of arms or a liveried servant enhanced one's reputation, as did a country house. The result was a growing social distance between the powerful and the middling groups, as wealthy men moved out of trade and craft production and lived on rents and investments.

The ranks of the privileged extended, however, far beyond a small elite. Some corporations, such as those of the goldsmiths, owned magnificent urban halls, which they used for meetings and fancy dinners. Around the Grand Place in Brussels, one can still see the elegant, stone mansions of the tailors, brewers, bakers, and butchers. People with a profession or a skilled trade counted as respectable. Those who were citizens participated in organized civic society, whatever their income or family wealth. Different types of work divided town populations along occupational lines. Many guild corporations that regulated production and access to a trade, first established in the Middle Ages, persisted well into the modern period. During the seventeenth century, craft organizations gained a new lease of life. To bring more crafts under the control of the state, the French kings multiplied the numbers of regulated trades, and the same process took place in Prussia during the early eighteenth century.

In the eighteenth century, guilds abounded in Italy, France, Germany, Spain, Britain, the Netherlands, Scandinavia, and Poland. In Vienna in 1770, well over one hundred corporations organized the workforce.

Professional corporations existed alongside those of the craftsmen. London lawyers belonged to the Inns of Court, where they learned their trade by osmosis and by eating dinners together in wood-paneled halls. But even less skilled and poorly paid trades organized for self-protection. Sailors, carters, and shepherds won the right in Hamburg to form associations similar to those of the sword smiths and cabinet-makers. A corporation brought status and some manner of economic safety to its members.

The economic purpose of these associations was monopoly, through which one group sought to protect its turf and to safeguard its members' incomes by dampening competition and avoiding change. Although guilds retained economic influence over wages, working conditions, and manufacturing methods among their members, their political power waned within the larger towns during the eighteenth century. Moreover, economic growth undermined their ability to control an entire industry, and newer trades organized outside their framework and outside city walls. Dual systems of production developed in industries such as tailoring and shoemaking: a high-wage guild sector co-existed with a low-wage sector, where informally trained, unprotected workers made cheaper goods. By 1750, more city dwellers in the largest towns probably existed outside the guilds than within them. Unlicensed workers abounded outside city limits, in suburbs and nearby villages. In France, guildsmen tried to block the employment of non-guildsmen, who took lower wages and took away market share. Independent workers, called "ground rabbits" (*Bönhasen*), who had a hard time in small German towns, did reasonably well in tolerant, free-market Hamburg. A range of highly capitalized London trades – brewers, distillers, sugar refiners, and soap boilers to name only a few – abandoned the ideals of the closed shop and limited production. Alongside these larger-scale, unorganized trades were a wide variety of laboring jobs and port activities, where strong backs and healthy bodies were the major requirements.

Guilds expressed and reaffirmed urban social inequality, particularly in their parades and public costumes. Trades had their social ranks, carefully worked out according to the prestige of raw materials and the age and power of their organization, which were carefully followed when artisans appeared in public. In civic ceremonies, each group took its assigned place, announcing its relative wealth and respectability through its banners and uniforms. Inequality was also firmly established inside the guilds. Internal divisions among masters, journeymen, and apprentices signaled hierarchies of age and skill, but also long-term prospects. The likelihood that an individual would progress from stage to stage during his lifetime had vastly diminished by the eighteenth century. Corporations no longer served effectively as channels for social mobility. For many, "journeyman" was a dead-end status, unless they were the sons of masters. Hereditary mastership went along with organizations of journeymen who began to see their interests as diverging from those of the masters in their trade. The corporations took on the job of exclusion. For example, they refused entry to those of illegitimate birth or dishonorable marriage. In Barcelona, purity of blood (*limpieza de sangre*), had to be proven before admission to a corporation.

Because females had been formally excluded from many occupations and from formal positions in most corporations, guilds were overwhelmingly male organizations. From the fifteenth century, women's opportunities as skilled workers narrowed significantly all over Europe. In some towns, girls were barred from apprenticeships and masters' widows lost the right to run husbands' businesses. Women could be officially banned from learning a particular trade or limited to menial status and low-skilled work. Even in the trades where they were still officially permitted, female artisans generally had fewer rights and lower status. The few female guilds that remained in the eighteenth century were generally in lower-paid branches of the clothing trades, and they gave their members limited protection. In general, journeymen and masters were assumed to be male.

The nearly total exclusion of women from artisans' organizations did not mean that women remained outside the urban labor force. Wives ran shops, kept accounts, and marketed produce. Women took on a growing share of urban industrial jobs in the eighteenth century, as they moved into newer, unregulated trades and expanded their share of clothing production and needlework. Women and children worked alongside male journeymen in unlicensed trades, helping husbands and fathers in family workshops. They made gloves and lace, processed food, and sold things in the markets. Among the most common urban workers were domestic servants, usually young women from rural areas who came into town as adolescents to earn money for their families or a dowry. Moving into the city from nearby areas, these women spent years cooking, cleaning, and sewing before moving on to marry and start their own families. Wage levels were such that wives and daughters had to contribute to a family economy, either as part of a household unit or by finding wage work elsewhere. Their low wages and lack of corporate organization made them a bargain for employers. The longevity and continued vitality of the guilds protected some people, while others were marginalized. The lucky had group or family resources, but many were only one illness or accident away from hard times.

The most problematic group of city dwellers were the poor, who sparked anxieties over their numbers and claims. The attraction of the destitute to the large cities worried contemporaries, who identified rag-clad bodies with criminality and prostitution. Bernardo Tanucci described the Neapolitan population in 1742:

> All the dregs of humanity produced in the provinces make up the population of this city, and in this lies its greatness: not in fine buildings, and not in great merchants and thinkers and men of letters, as make Paris, London, Lisbon, and Amsterdam great cities; but in servants, in courtiers, for the most part of the lowest behavior and dishonesty, in traders, barbers, whores, pimps, beggars, who, by intermarrying increase and multiply so that each generation is worse than the one before.[12]

Seeing the urban poor through such lenses distorts their images and identifies them with the abnormal. Urban poverty was, however, distressingly normal. In addition to the beggars on town streets who made destitution visible, attics and cellars sheltered even more of the needy. Fine gradations of income and solvency, however, distinguished those who could make do in normal years from those existing in deep poverty. Contemporaries often missed these important distinctions. When in 1787 welfare authorities in Hamburg investigated that city's lower classes, they found both "rascally beggars" and hundreds of those "fearful of leaving their hovels except cloaked by a merciful darkness which concealed their nakedness."[13] Their fluctuating ranks and shadowy appearance in town records made it virtually impossible to quantify the numbers of the poor, making it all the easier to fear a potentially vast crew of dirty, disease-ridden paupers. In the early modern urban economy, anyone who worked for a living was potentially poor in a depression year or after an accident or an illness. Self-sufficient when all went well, low-wage workers faced the inevitable hardships of bad winters, high prices, and seasonal lay-offs. Early death of a husband brought hardship to a household, while those lucky enough to survive into old age faced declining incomes and poor health. Life-cycle poverty hit a high proportion of the urban work force; others had to contend with normally inadequate incomes.

Alongside the respectable poor whose family and local standing gave them some protection were a mixed group of migrants and the miserable, who drifted into the larger cities to look for work. Ships that sailed into city ports and the roads that linked towns to their neighbors

---

[12] B. Tanucci, *Epistolario*, ed. R. P. Copini *et al.* (Rome, 1980), I: 635, quoted in Clark and Lepetit, *Capital Cities*, 149.
[13] Lindemann, *Patriots and Paupers*, 137.

brought thousands of newcomers. Louis-Sébastien Mercier thought he could study "the entire human race" by looking at migrants in Paris. He claimed to have found not only Quakers, Arabs, and Japanese, but also Eskimos, Hottentots, and South Asians. As he put it, "Paris can be thought of as a large melting pot" in which products and people from all over the globe mixed together. London was even more diverse. In the late eighteenth century, colonies of poor Irish clustered in central and south London near the river. French Protestant silk weavers settled in the East End, while thousands of Sephardic and Ashkenazi Jews lived in the City and its eastern fringes. Runaway slaves from the West Indies or North America had stowed away on British ships and settled in the capital near the Thames. An English court decision, which held in 1772 that "as soon as any slave sets his foot upon English territory he becomes free," was used by slaves as well as masters to dissolve unwanted dependence.[14] After 1783, many blacks who had fought with the British Army in the American colonies were sent to London as part of the resettling of Loyalists after the revolution. Small numbers of Asians moved to London too. At the end of a voyage, Chinese and Indian sailors came ashore and found work. Generally hostile to outsiders, London mobs sometimes attacked anyone looking "foreign" on the streets, most of whom were accused of being "French" – the ultimate insult at the time.

Urban economies created marginal people along with marginal jobs. Street sweepers and ballad singers, day-laborers and peddlers lived by their wits as much as their wages. They survived through makeshift arrangements, turning to neighbors, pawnbrokers, and charities for resources to fill their stomachs. Petty theft was another alternative. Many women whose normal wages were below subsistence level found prostitution one of their few options for extra earning. Most of the prostitutes arrested in Amsterdam during the eighteenth century were immigrants, women who had worked as domestic servants or in the clothing trades. By the eighteenth century, a highly differentiated commercial market for sex existed in the larger cities, satisfied by an assortment of sex workers who ranged from street walkers to high-priced mistresses. State-registered brothels had been eliminated in favor of free competition, and the trade had mushroomed. Mercier observed scores of Parisian women leaning out of windows or standing in doorways with a beckoning air, who he claimed could "be hired like hackney carriages at so much an hour." Another large group, whom he ranked as "amateurs," but "honest, decent girls," traded their bodies for a free meal or an evening's entertainment.[15] Since the police repressed the trade only intermittently, brothels were

[14] George, *London Life in the XVIIIth Century*, 135.
[15] Mercier, *Tableau de Paris*, II: 12, 15–16.

easy to find and tightly embedded in local economies. Tavern keepers, lodging-house managers, and madams worked together in this flourishing urban industry.

Power and police

For all the random movement on their streets and potentially chaotic social relations, cities were regulated environments, where individual actions were subject to control by a variety of constituted authorities. Urban communities were highly disciplined, not only by craft guilds and other occupational groups, but also by additional institutions. Some were ostensibly philanthropic, while others were more obviously repressive. Some were voluntary, while others embodied public authority, most notably in the form of a town council. What we think of today as police forces were still quite rudimentary, but contemporaries believed in the need to "police" many aspects of social behavior in the interests of good order. This belief, moreover, found expression in many organizations and practices that helped to maintain social control.

Discipline operated informally through charities, orphanages, and almshouses, where the "deserving" poor – the elderly, widows, and deserted children – could find aid, as well as through more directly repressive institutions. European cities began to centralize and to secularize aid to the poor during the sixteenth century, and by the eighteenth many had developed an array of specialized ways of dealing with the destitute. In 1764, the French crown ordered convicted beggars to be shipped to *depots de mendicité*, where they would be put to work. For the disreputable and unruly poor, the larger French, Italian, and German cities built "hospitals" intended to reform them through punishment. In Amsterdam and other Dutch towns, female beggars and prostitutes were locked up and made to spin thread or do other jobs. Destitute English men and women had more alternatives, but those ordered into workhouses faced a similar mixture of discipline and forced labor. Even if these brutal regimes reached only a small proportion of the poor, they had great symbolic significance. The unemployed counted as idle, and it was the duty of the state to put them back to work and teach them the error of their evil ways.

Surveillance also took place on city streets, prompted by widespread fears of mugging and petty theft. Henry Fielding, a magistrate who helped organize London's first efficient police force, sounded an alarm in 1751 about the safety of night-time travel: "The Innocent are put in Terror, affronted and alarmed with Threats and Execrations, endangered with loaded Pistols, beat with Bludgeons and hacked with Cutlasses, of which the Loss of Health, of Limbs, and often of Life, is the Consequence."[16] The City of London maintained its own small force to keep the peace, and two other police offices oversaw the river and parts of western London. But surveillance remained local, uncoordinated, and mostly amateur. In contrast, the French government had appointed a lieutenant general of police for Paris, who had wide powers over arrested prostitutes, inspected markets, and worried about street paving. His duties combined repression and regulation with sanitation and welfare services. The use of royal officials to maintain order was, however, more advanced in Paris than in the other capitals in Western Europe, where organization of a large, paid police force was a nineteenth-century innovation.

Local governments intruded in a wide range of ways into the lives of city dwellers. Men in positions of power in Hamburg specified the rules of the game with regard not only to public behavior on the streets, family quarrels, and poor relief, but also to economic transactions, medical practice, and public health. Weights and measures, taxation, statistics, and military service came within their purview too. Johann Klefeker, a Hamburg jurist, needed twelve volumes around 1770 to codify the laws that would ensure that "civil life will pass in a tranquil and Christian manner [and] according to the judicious rules prescribed by the magistracy."[17] To be sure, German towns intruded more aggressively into the lives of their citizens than did English or Dutch cities, but the ideal of regulation or effective "police" by local authorities in the interests of good order was common throughout Western and Central Europe in the eighteenth century.

Multiple institutions, most staffed by elected male citizens, arose to keep towns functioning and inhabitants in order. While the range of terminology was extreme, incorporated towns tended to have mayors, councils, magistrates, and assemblies, to which could be added neighborhood associations, special purpose committees, parish offices, and guild structures with varying jobs and influence. In Hamburg, the city council (*Rat*) shared power with three collegial bodies, the *Oberalten*, the Forty-Eight, and the One Hundred and Forty-Four, who represented the city's parish councils. Since metropolitan London combined several loosely associated, independent territories, its government was particularly complex. The Corporation of the City of London ran the square mile of streets between Temple Bar and the Tower, Southwark south of London Bridge, and the Port of London. This relatively small territory had an exceptional number of administrators – among them a

---

[16] Quoted in J. J. Tobias, *Urban Crime in Victorian England* (New York, 1972), 23.
[17] Quoted in Lindemann, *Patriots and Paupers*, 49.

Lord Mayor, Sheriffs, a Recorder, a Clerk, Remembrancers, and a Chamberlain. They worked with a Court of Aldermen, the Court of Common Council, the Court of Common Hall, and the Court of Wardmote to administer the City's wards. Dozens of minor offices in each parish gave a share of local governance to a large number of adult men. The rest of the metropolitan area was governed for the most part by elected parish officials and appointed Justices of the Peace.

The Paris government was very different. Unlike incorporated towns in the German states, Italy, or Britain, it had never been granted a charter that guaranteed rights of self-government. The French kings knew they had to control the capital to control the country, and they chose its officials. Elections were formalities, and the municipal government – housed in the Hôtel de Ville – shared administrative authority with the magistrates from the royal court and the lieutenant general of police. Although there was a council of men elected by male taxpayers and property owners, the king had the right to veto candidates and to block the elections. (The first freely elected Parisian mayor took office only in 1977.) Its members had to bend to the royal will.

Political participation in cities varied from state to state and city to city, but at its most extensive only a small minority of total urban populations had the right to vote and to hold civic office. Not only adult women but also Jews and sometimes other religious minorities were barred from the political process. Citizenship or guild membership was the next hurdle to jump, which excluded most immigrants, lodgers, servants, and unskilled workers. The most restrictive systems, such as those operating in Venice or Nuremberg, specified particular families or the pieces of property whose owners qualified for political office or a vote. Political rights resulted not from adult status, but from family position and wealth, and they did not necessarily persist. In fact, a narrowing of the groups with political influence took place in many European cities during the closing years of the old regime, when effective control in many towns passed to a small group of magistrates, often unelected and sometimes appointed for life.

Cities functioned within state administrations, which had a strong interest in controlling urban resources and populations. The growth of stronger states in Europe during the seventeenth and eighteenth centuries led to the curbing of urban independence. To fight one another effectively, states enlarged their armies and bureaucracies, expanding their control over territories within their borders. Only in the Netherlands, on the Italian peninsula, and in parts of the Holy Roman Empire, where fifty-one imperial free cities survived until 1803, did cities remain largely independent. Elsewhere the era of the powerful city-state was over, and monarchs made sure that their wishes were obeyed within town walls.

City rights could be revoked and new rules and institutions could be imposed. Royal officials who lived in the larger cities of France and Spain supervised local administration, but for the most part, indirect rule sufficed for their purposes. Even if towns kept their own laws, the election of friendly mayors and judges, combined with royal power to tax, meant that kings got what they needed most of the time. Objections and local riots accomplished little, for kings had armies, and cities did not. By the eighteenth century, territorial balances of power had shifted decisively away from cities toward the states that surrounded them.

Cities formed networks of central places upon which state governments, economies, and cultures depended, and they did so in accord with precedent. Their streets housed the physical capital of earlier centuries; their libraries and schools transmitted the intellectual inheritance of the past; and their oligarchical political elites had, for the most part, made their peace with monarchical regimes. Before 1750, with few exceptions, most of which were located in England, their growth was sufficiently slow to be contained within existing structures. Nevertheless, cities had (and have) a built-in capacity for innovation. Information moved quickly around an international urban network into individual towns. Print culture and conversation introduced inhabitants to things modern, foreign, and different. Town borders were far more permeable than stone walls suggested. Officials found it as hard to control migration as to stop central governments from intruding into their spaces. In the next three chapters, we survey some of the changes which swept over European cities between 1750 and 1850. Industrialization, rapid urbanization, and democratic revolution upset the stabilities of old regime cities, forcing urban elites to confront the forces transforming their societies.

BIBLIOGRAPHY

Andrew, D. T. *Philanthropy and Police: London Charity in the Eighteenth Century.* Princeton, 1989.
Benabou, Erica-Marie. *La prostitution et la police des moeurs au XVIIIe siècle.* Paris, 1987.
Bordes, Maurice. *L'Administration provinciale et municipale en France au XVIIIe siècle.* Paris, 1972.
Borsay, Peter. *The English Urban Renaissance: Culture and Society in the Provincial Town, 1660–1770.* Oxford, 1989.
Butel, Paul. *Vivre à Bordeaux sous l'ancien régime.* Paris, 1999.
Calabi, Donatella. *The Market and the City: Square, Street, and Architecture in Early Modern Europe.* Burlington, VT, 2003.
Clark, Peter, ed. *The Transformation of English Provincial Towns.* London, 1984.
Clark, Peter, and Bernard Lepetit, eds. *Capital Cities and Their Hinterlands in Early Modern Europe.* Aldershot, 1996.

Corfield, Penelope. *The Impact of English Towns, 1700–1800.* Oxford, 1982.

Cowan, Alexander. *Urban Europe 1500–1700.* London, 1998.

Friedrichs, Christopher R. *The Early Modern City, 1450–1750.* London, 1995.

Urban Politics in Early Modern Europe. London and New York, 2000.

Garrioch, David. *Neighborhood and Community in Paris, 1740–1790.* Cambridge, 1986.

George, M. Dorothy. *London Life in the XVIIIth Century.* London, 1925.

Hitchcock, Timothy. *Down and Out in Eighteenth-Century London.* New York, 2005.

Hufton, Olwen H. *The Poor of Eighteenth-Century France, 1750–1789.* Oxford, 1974.

Isherwood, Robert M. *Farce and Fantasy: Popular Entertainment in Eighteenth-Century Paris.* New York, 1986.

Kaplan, Steven Laurence. *Provisioning Paris: Merchants and Millers in the Grain and Flour Trade During the Eighteenth Century.* Ithaca, 1984.

Landon, H. C. Robbins. *Mozart and Vienna, Including Selections from Johann Pezzl's Sketch of Vienna, 1786–1790.* London, 1991.

Lepetit, Bernard. *The Pre-industrial Urban System: France, 1740–1840.* Trans. Godfrey Rogers. New York, 1994.

Lindemann, Mary. *Patriots and Paupers: Hamburg, 1712–1830.* New York, 1990.

Lynch, Katherine A. *Individuals, Families, and Communities in Europe, 1200–1800: The Urban Foundations of Western Society.* Cambridge, 2003.

McClain, James L., *et al.*, eds. *Edo and Paris: Urban Life and the State in the Early Modern Era.* Ithaca, 1994.

Mercier, Louis-Sébastien. *Panorama of Paris: Selections from Tableau de Paris.* Trans. Helen Simpson. Ed. Jeremy D. Popkin. University Park, PA, 1994.

Persson, Karl Gunnar. *Grain Markets in Europe, 1500–1900: Integration and Deregulation.* Cambridge, 1999.

Poussou, Jean-Pierre. *Bordeaux et le sud-ouest au XVIIIe siècle: Croissance économique et attraction urbaine.* Paris, 1982.

Ringrose, David R. *Madrid and the Spanish Economy, 1560–1850.* Berkeley, 1983.

Roche, Daniel. *The People of Paris: An Essay in Popular Culture in the 18th Century.* Trans. Marie Evans. Ed Gwynne Lewis. Berkeley, 1987.

Söderberg, Johan, Ulf Jonsson, and Christer Persson. *A Stagnating Metropolis: The Economy and Demography of Stockholm, 1750–1850.* Cambridge, 1991.

Soliday, Gerald Lyman. *A Community in Conflict: Frankfurt Society in the Seventeenth and Early Eighteenth Centuries.* Hanover, NH, 1974.

Van der Wee, Herman, ed. *The Rise and Decline of Urban Industries in Italy and the Low Countries (Late Middle Ages – Early Modern Times).* Leuven, 1988.

Walker, Mack. *German Home Towns: Community, State, and General Estate, 1648–1871.* Ithaca, 1971.

Young, Arthur. *Travels in France during the years 1787, 1788 & 1789.* Ed. Constantia Maxwell. Cambridge, 1950.

2 Industrial urbanization

When Arthur Young toured northern England in 1770, he traveled on horseback. Because so few boats were available for hire, he had trouble using local canals. Since his interest centered on fields and farms, Young paid little attention to towns and industrial sites. Contrast his experiences with those of Sir George Head, a retired British Army supply officer, who explored the same region in 1835 by stagecoach, steamship, canal boat, and train.[1] At that time, three canal routes and one railway linked Liverpool, Lancashire's international port, to Manchester, its financial and service center. Rivers had been deepened and locks had been added to permit long-distance barge travel throughout the north. Throughout the region, people and products were in motion, using several different modes of transportation. On his travels, Head visited a pin factory in Warrington, a plate-glass plant in St. Helen's, an iron foundry in Halifax, and a worsted-spinning mill in Leeds. He marveled at the many uses of steam engines, which provided the energy for combing wool, turning lathes, pumping water, moving coal, and pulling railway passengers. Head was fascinated by technology, particularly that of transportation, because he realized that industrialization could not take place without tight connections among production sites, markets, and services. Even before extensive railroad development, Lancashire had developed a diversified, specialized urban network that housed processing industries, spinning and weaving firms, coal fields, and smelting and engineering works, which drew both workers and visitors. The economic power of the industrial region added up to more than the sum of its well-articulated urban parts, drawing strength from the economies of agglomeration and of scale.

During the late eighteenth and early nineteenth centuries, new technologies of transport and manufacturing remade urban England,

---

[1] Arthur Young, *A Six Month Tour through the North of England: Containing, an Account of the Present State of Agriculture, Manufactures, and Population.* 2nd edn. 4 vols. (London, 1770–71); Sir George Head, *A Home Tour through the Manufacturing Districts of England in the summer of 1835.* 2nd edn (1836; New York, 1968).

producing new cities and transforming older ones. The results often distressed contemporaries who did not like having to abandon comfortable ways. Older routines of travel and production shifted, and existing social hierarchies were challenged by the newly rich. Growth – uneven, usually unplanned, and sometimes unwanted – soon accelerated in France, Belgium, and other regions of Western Europe too. Migration brought waves of newcomers into older settlements, looking for work and housing. The impact was disruptive and unsettling. Urban communities had to adapt to larger numbers, higher densities, and more diverse populations, often without effective governments and proven technological solutions. The dual impacts of industrialization and intensified urbanization between 1750 and 1850 launched European cities into a new world, one which this chapter surveys.

Engines of urban expansion

Between 1750 and 1850, Western Europe began to industrialize at an increasingly rapid pace. As it forged ahead of the Chinese, the Indian, and the Middle Eastern economies, it became the most economically dynamic and prosperous region in the world. Stories of why "the West got rich" vary with the politics of those who tell the tales, but cities have to be given prominent parts because of their role in European industrial and colonial development. Although cities were not the earliest sites of rapid industrial change, many cities had manufacturing sectors, and Atlantic ports served as gateways for colonial products and commerce. Urban entrepreneurs organized regional systems of production, and urban financiers bankrolled industrial expansion, as well as international trade. The story of European economic growth starting in the later eighteenth century weaves together three processes – industrialization, urbanization, and empire-building. Their impact, however, was regional and selective. Some areas adopted new technologies and products quickly, while others lagged behind and lost manufacturing for a time. The first phase of European industrialization rearranged European urban hierarchies, as new towns grew and some older ones stagnated. What Kenneth Pomeranz has called the Great Divergence took place between Europe and Asia,[2] but a similar process of differentiation occurred between technologically advanced districts and stagnating regions within Europe. Cities, as sites of capital investment and capitalist entrepreneurship, offer windows into this process.

[2] Kenneth Pomeranz, *The Great Divergence: Europe, China, and the Making of the Modern World Economy* (Princeton, 2000).

Manufacturing for export, which had expanded in the towns of the Low Countries and the Italian peninsula in the later Middle Ages, decentralized during the seventeenth and early eighteenth centuries under the pressures of rising competition and rising demand. The production of light woolen and mixed fabrics declined in Lille, Bruges, and Ghent, but it increased in rural districts of Flanders, parts of Brabant, and northern France. Silk spinning and weaving moved from Naples into the surrounding districts, while the Tuscan woolen industry shifted from Florence into smaller towns in the region. Urban production was relatively costly because of city taxes, guild labor regulations, and price controls. Entrepreneurs, eager to increase profit margins along with output, moved simpler types of manufacturing into the countryside, where peasant households were underemployed. Women and children could be given thread to spin, and men could be trained to weave plain cloths. Since human muscles provided the needed energy and machinery remained simple and cheap, it was easy to decentralize. Labor was the sought-after, scarce resource.

This so-called "proto-industry" could be found throughout Europe, particularly in poorer agricultural areas and along rivers, where mills provided additional power and the water ways permitted easy transportation of raw materials and finished goods. Forests near ore deposits proved good sites for metallurgical production, and mountainous regions of small farms and poor soil, near Zurich in central Switzerland or in the hills of western Ireland for example, provided workers for thread spinning and linen weaving. By the mid-eighteenth century, proto-industrial regions turned out textiles and small metal wares from Sweden south through Italy and from Ireland to Russia.

Proto-industry, although predominantly rural, had strong urban linkages. By the late eighteenth century, the town of Duisburg on the lower Rhine had become a center for light manufacturing; its textiles and tobacco products went to markets in the Netherlands, Switzerland, and the Holy Roman Empire. Almost a third of the males who were employed there in 1810 worked in industry or craft occupations, as did about seven percent of employed women. Larger towns, such as Lille, Lyon, Ghent, and Leeds, acted as central places for proto-industrial regions under the guidance of their merchants. Urban bankers and entrepreneurs had capital for investment, as well as knowledge of regional facilities and needs. Thread would be "put out," or given to a rural household to be woven and then collected and brought to town. Even if local workers took the initiative to produce a particular item, for example transforming home-grown flax into linen, marketing led to and through towns because of their better linkage to ports and to large cities. Someone had to ship goods and arrange for their sale in distant markets. Who better than urban merchants? Pleasing finicky and distant customers who wanted particular colors, patterns, and fabrics required knowledge that did not circulate in proto-industrial villages. Moreover, proto-industrial textile workers generally produced plain or unfinished goods and then turned them over to more highly skilled urban artisans who would bleach or dye them. Proto-industry often required regional divisions of labor to which both urban and rural workers contributed under the direction of merchants responsive to market demand. These regional systems of production, when flexible, adapted to early changes in technology and provided increasing amounts of employment to local workers in city and countryside.

Technological change, earliest in the textile and iron industries in Great Britain, triggered the transition to larger-scale production in concentrated units. The water frame, patented by Richard Arkwright in 1769, allowed one worker to spin multiple rather than single threads, but turning the frame required more energy than could be provided by hand. Arkwright set up a water-powered thread mill in the village of Cromford, where he found both cheap land and a stream. As others adopted similar machinery, thread production moved from cottages and small workshops into riverside factories powered by water wheels. Iron making also increased in scale after Abraham Darby's discovery of a way to use coke, a coal byproduct, as fuel. Early blast furnaces and rolling mills were developed in the mining areas of Staffordshire and South Wales to save on the transport costs of fuel. Entrepreneurs located these new factories and smelters in the countryside, where land was cheap and no guilds existed to monitor production techniques. The first wave of industrialization, therefore, took place in rural areas. Older cities, even those of manufacturing fame, were not the original sites of industrial innovation. Their contribution was initially indirect: cities furnished much of the demand for industrial goods, and some of the needed capital, and they helped to develop transportation infrastructures that permitted easy movement of output from rural sites to urban markets.

As technological changes continued at a rapid clip, they continued to reshape locations of production, increasingly stimulating urban growth. By 1790, entrepreneurs could use one of James Watt's steam engines to supply power anywhere that fuel could be found or imported. Economic growth soon created new urban places. On the chance of finding a job, newcomers rushed into the coal fields of South Wales, the Black Country, Yorkshire, the Belgian Borinage, and the Ruhr Valley. Along with the expanding mines came ramshackle housing, new streets, and shops. Villages turned into towns, and towns eventually became cities, as industrial development continued. New settlements, mostly in mining districts, transformed European patterns of urbanization, as rapid economic growth spread from Britain to France, Belgium, and Switzerland. Much early industrial urbanization was rapid, geographically concentrated, and dependent on natural resources. Coal fields became urbanized in regions where growing industries produced a rising demand for cheap fuel. Networks of new towns resulted, reorganizing regional patterns of migration, transport, and marketing.

Port cities and transport junctions soon proved good places for industrial expansion. Businessmen could site new firms in existing cities, where workers could be found easily and where housing, food, and customers were ready to hand. By the 1830s, Manchester housed dozens of factories, steam engines, and dye houses, where many members of its large and rapidly growing population worked. Its entrepreneurs and bankers had transformed south Lancashire into an industrial region, with an integrated set of transport facilities, financial institutions, and labor markets. Its accelerated expansion and manufacturing strength symbolized the modern age to contemporaries.

The transformation of Glasgow in Scotland illustrates well the meshing of new technology into the fabric of a small town that had grown up around a river ford and a medieval cathedral. In the eighteenth century, growing imports of sugar and tobacco from the Caribbean and North America sparked the building of rum distilleries and snuff mills as well as the dredging of the relatively shallow Clyde river, which became Glasgow's highway to international markets. Large scale internal change came along with the steam engine, which permitted greatly expanded textile production in the city. By the early 1830s, forty-nine cotton spinning mills operated in Glasgow, and a ring of nearby villages, incorporated by mid-century, housed handloom weavers. Slightly to the north of the old town, chemical plants developed alongside the Monkland canal, where barges brought coal to feed the steam engines. By 1825, the old town, which hugged the river and the major north–south road, had added new districts along the south bank of the Clyde, as well as new residential districts to the west. Mills, warehouses, dye shops, factories, and engineering works sprouted up on vacant land in central districts, as workers poured into the city hoping to find jobs. An outer ring of industrial areas linked by road to the city center gave large factories room to expand. After a local engineer designed an improved, cheaper way to produce pig iron, entrepreneurs built dozens of efficient blast furnaces to the east and south of the city. The development of steamboats and railways encouraged the production of locomotives, ships, and marine engines, at the same time that they improved the city's transportation system. Soon, the

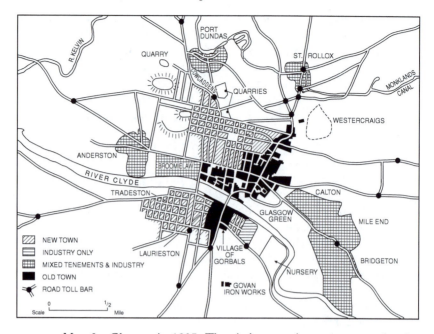

Map 2. Glasgow in 1825. The city's expansion to accommodate its growing trade and population included new residential areas on both sides of the river. Nearby villages became primarily industrial districts where workers' housing grew up around manufacturing plants and foundries. A network of toll roads improved local transportation.

riverbanks became industrial zones stretching far beyond the city limits to both east and west, while a ring of industrial districts circled the city to the north. In the hundred years between 1750 and 1850, the city's population leaped from 30,000 to 357,000, as Glasgow became the hub of development for the industrializing Clyde valley.

In the longer run, industrialization transformed older towns, as well as newer manufacturing centers. In Berlin between 1816 and 1846, the number of factory workers rose by almost 300 percent, as the size of the city as a whole approximately doubled. Liège in Belgium, Lyon in France, and Barcelona in Spain became centers of industrial regions organized around their major cities. Many towns famous for their artisanal manufacturing made a gradual transition to factory production, using their resources of skilled labor, capital, and marketing savvy. Lille served as the capital of a rich agricultural and industrial district, linked to the ports of Calais, Ostende, and Dunkerque. Already in 1800, its merchants imported cotton for spinning factories in the city and nearby towns, sending out thread to weavers in the region. Linen, lace, and ribbon making employed thousands of people in the city and surrounding communes. Breweries, sugar refineries, porcelain factories, and tanneries relied on raw materials imported either from the colonies or from the surrounding fields. By 1850, the construction of canals, railroads, and sidewalks cemented the links among local producers and Atlantic ports. Tourcoing specialized in wool, while Roubaix turned to cotton. Each of these towns anchored local divisions of labor with households in nearby villages, while Lille merchants acted as wholesalers and bankers. The region illustrates the complementarity of different styles of manufacturing. While Roubaix and Tourcoing spinning factories turned out mountains of cotton and woolen thread, handloom weaving continued, and linen making remained in small workshops. Entrepreneurs often adopted advanced technologies for part of a production process, combining them with artisanal methods. Cities anchored these complex divisions of labor because they had good access to needed transportation, information about marketing, and a supply of highly skilled labor.

By 1850, the map of industrial Europe was complex. It comprised pit head villages and brick towns marked by new factories and tall chimneys, "unnatural red and black, like the painted face of a savage."[3] In Prussia, early industrial development stimulated rapid growth in old and new towns in the Rhine and Ruhr valleys. Between 1810 and 1843, Duisburg's population expanded by about 75 percent, and manufacturing jobs more than doubled. Employment in crafts, trade, and transportation increased too, men being the primary beneficiaries. Industrialization had also spread to include hundreds of older towns of many sizes, where steam engines could be found powering sugar refineries, printing presses, and mills of various sorts. Leicester and Nottingham slowly turned from hand to factory manufacture of hosiery, bringing along with them a penumbra of tiny, industrializing places which supplied workers and small sites of production. Barcelona businessmen did the same for nearby parts of Catalonia where textiles were made, well before other parts of Spain industrialized.

By mid-century, signs of industrial growth and economic development had moved east through the Ruhr Valley to parts of the Austro-Hungarian Empire and to Berlin. Technology is essentially footloose: it can be bought and installed virtually anywhere, as long as fuel and power are available. But can it be maintained and can its products be sold? As the recent history of economic development shows, market access and the supply of skilled labor have proved more important than the supply of technology.

---

[3] Charles Dickens, *Hard Times* (1855), pt 1, ch. 5.

In the European case, cities with rich connections to skilled artisans and merchant networks proved adaptable over the long run. Human capital proved the decisive resource in the formation of industrial economies.

People in motion

Between 1750 and 1850, total population for the area west of Russia increased by approximately 83 million people, or 70 percent. Rates of growth were fastest in England and Ireland, but the German and the Italian states, Spain, and Sweden also expanded rapidly. In this period, not only did death rates decline, but fertility increased. From Scandinavia south to the Mediterranean, more and more people were born and more and more survived through their childbearing years, swelling the size of the next generation. Most of this growth took place, however, among those with little or no property and in rural areas. While a decline of death rates for adults and children is generally good news, for poor people in the countryside increased size meant increased economic burdens. How could the extra mouths be fed?

Where rural industry did not provide extra work and where landholdings were limited, families had to devise strategies for raising incomes. As a result, many peasant households, particularly in the widespread areas where access to land had become limited, had to send members elsewhere. People who had low incomes became wage laborers or proletarians, working for others either on large farms or in the towns. Joan Scott and Louise Tilly have described the shift of family economies to "family wage economies," in which the contributions of members to the survival of the group came not through joint production, but via earning power.[4] Throughout the year, parents disposed of their own and their children's labor, sending individuals to a variety of destinations. Since employers generally defined jobs as "male" or "female" work, appropriate places had to be found for members of both sexes and different ages. Adult males hired themselves out as soldiers or sailors. Where adult men traveled long distances to earn money as harvesters or construction workers, wives remained at home to care for young children, land, and animals. Single females could look for urban jobs as servants or textile workers. Household members of both sexes left seasonally or for longer periods, sending back money and information about a wider world. These family strategies gave adult women and adult men roughly equal responsibility for maintaining households and for planning ways to exploit local and more distant labor markets. Mary Hartman suggests that such households

---

[4] Joan W. Scott and Louise A. Tilly, *Women, Work, and Family* (New York, 1978).

gave women added independence inside and outside the family and that their "immense vitality" and flexibility helped to transform wider social institutions.[5] Changing rates of reproduction can be linked therefore to shifts in gender relations and to patterns of movement, which responded to the economic geography of the early industrial period.

Migration was a normal part of the life cycle for Europeans, women as well as men. The need to earn, to learn, and to find a viable place to establish a family pushed young people away from their birth families and communities. Merchants sent their sons to obtain training or to establish firms in other towns with which they had trading ties. Rural adolescents commonly left home for jobs in other households where they worked until marriage, and newlyweds often moved to new places. To train in a craft, boys would take up apprenticeships with a guild master, perhaps living in another community. Later, as journeymen, they traveled from town to town, practicing their trades. Around 1815, John O'Neill, a young Irish shoemaker from Cork, migrated to London in search of work. His father had made the same journey years before, and John knew of London's reputation as a center for clothing manufacture. Walking into the center of the metropolis, he asked directions to an Irish neighborhood. His queries quickly led him to an Irish tavern and the offer of a job in an Irish-owned workshop. After he had made enough money, he sent for his wife and children. O'Neill was part of a migration chain of shoemakers that reached from an Irish county town to the center of the British Empire. Such moves should be thought of as family strategies, designed to improve the position of the group by increasing access to wages, capital, and wider job options. Particularly where opportunities and resources were limited, migration gave families the chance to diversify their exposure to risk. Migration also helped families to build social and human capital through added training and ties to new people and places. Those with property or education had better chances than the poor; women on the road were more vulnerable than men, but a wider world beckoned to all.

Regional pressures for migration in Europe strengthened between 1750 and 1850, when economic prospects in rural areas worsened, increasing the incentives for young people to search for jobs in the towns. Agricultural employment became more seasonal, as the practice of year-long labor contracts declined in Western Europe. Farmers began to hire workers for planting and harvest only, letting them go off-season. When crops failed, as did the potato crop during the middle and late 1840s,

[5] Mary S. Hartman, *The Household and the Making of History: A Subversive View of the Western Past* (Cambridge, 2004), 240–41.

families found themselves lacking both food and wages. At the same time, rural manufacturing employment declined, as competition from factories killed the market for homemade products. Rural women's ability to earn money through spinning thread collapsed quickly in the later eighteenth and early nineteenth centuries, and rural weaving met a similar fate about fifty years later. Rural households, whose members had supported themselves through a variety of trades and part-time jobs, found few alternatives in nearby villages, and they heard stories of urban jobs and higher wages. Since they had time to spare and a growing need for cash, they tended to migrate toward cities. As the nineteenth century progressed, all the peripheral economies on the fringes of Western Europe – Ireland, Scandinavia, the Jewish areas of Poland and Eastern Europe, southern Italy, Spain, and Portugal – sent labor into the fast-growing industrial zones, as well as across the Atlantic to North America. Meanwhile, Europe's urban core from England east through France and Belgium to western Germany imported labor.

Migration, whether short or long distance, was not random movement. Labor market demand, available information, and local ties shaped destinations, routes, and times of travel. Ernest Ravenstein, using mid-nineteenth century census data, developed several "laws of migration," among them the assertion that most moves were short distance toward more attractive job markets.[6] Studies of individual city populations confirm that most migrants arrived from nearby villages and rural areas. Yet larger cities and ports also drew long-distance and foreign migrants. Their positions on transport routes, their reputations, and the size and diversity of their labor markets encouraged migrants to ignore intervening places of possible settlement and to move to the top of a regional or international urban hierarchy.

Scholars have described seasonal migration circuits and longer distance flows, distinguishing patterns of temporary residence from more permanent choices of destination. Migrants made choices, which can be described for the group if not predicted precisely in the individual case. Dirk Hoerder and Jan Lucassen have identified the impact of early industrialization on regional migration systems in northwestern Europe. In the later seventeenth and early eighteenth centuries, thousands of workers moved yearly into Sweden from around the Baltic region, into the Netherlands and to the North Sea coast from Norway, Scotland, and the German states, and into Spain from southern France. Principal destinations included Dutch towns, which needed soldiers, service, and textile

---

[6] Ernest Ravenstein, "The Laws of Migration," *Journal of the Statistical Society of London* 48 (1885): 167–235.

workers; Madrid, where foreign traders, artisans, and laborers were welcome; and Stockholm, where demand for construction laborers and servants ran high. Eastern European migration routes led German speakers into southern Russia, and northern Europeans of many sorts into St. Petersburg to work as artisans, administrators, and architects. When the Dutch and Swedish economies lost their vitality during the eighteenth century, other circuits of movement in Western Europe, especially to the towns of France and Britain, became more active. Paris and London drew newcomers most heavily because of their relative sizes and the strength of their manufacturing and construction industries. In the later eighteenth century, about 90 percent of the female servants and of the male day laborers in Paris had been born outside the city. Within Britain, young people flocked to the towns of Yorkshire and Lancashire as well as to the capital and to prosperous agricultural counties in East Anglia and Lincolnshire. Thousands of Irish moved during the summer and fall months from their small holdings to large farms in eastern Ireland and Britain to harvest grain. Some stayed on and moved into nearby towns.

Court cities, such as Milan, Madrid, and Rome, continued to attract young people from rural areas. In the 1820s, the French writer Stendhal described men from the Sabine Hills who came with their families to mass at St. Peter's on Ascension Day: "They wear ragged cloth cloaks, their legs are wrapped in strips of material held in place with string cross-gartered; their wild eyes peer from behind disordered black hair; they hold to their chests hats made of felt, which the sun and rain have left a reddish black color."[7] Mountain people appeared regularly in Mediterranean towns for short or longer stays. They traded, carried, built, begged, and served. Ridiculed for their clothes and their accents, some left quickly, while others slowly adapted to life in the cities.

After the French Revolution, political pressures to migrate compounded economic ones. Nobles fled revolutionary regimes, and weary soldiers deserted Napoleon's armies as they marched south into Spain and Italy and east to Russia. After 1815, when reactionary monarchs returned to power, middle-class reformers and republicans went into exile to escape jail. By the 1840s, Karl Marx and Giuseppe Mazzini in London and Heinrich Heine and Alexander Herzen in Paris helped to shape international dialogues about political change from their urban bases in Western Europe. London, Paris, and Geneva each housed thousands of political refugees, who plotted political change at home while settling in to support themselves.

---

[7] Quoted in Fernand Braudel, *The Mediterranean and the Mediterranean World in the Age of Philip II* (New York, 1975), I: 44.

Long-distance movement produced ethnic diversity. On the streets of Vienna could be heard the multiple languages of the Habsburg territories – German, Czech, Hungarian, Slovakian, Serbo-Croatian, and several more. Newcomers kept alive neighborhoods of Polish Jews, Italians, and Greeks. Southern port towns, such as Marseille, drew migrants from both shores of the Mediterranean, while Copenhagen and Stockholm attracted men and women from Baltic communities, the Russian Empire, and German territories. London drew Scottish administrators, Italian street sellers, Irish laborers, German sugar refiners, Jewish merchants, former slaves from Africa, South Asian sailors, and Chinese dock workers. In 1861, 2.4 percent of London's population was foreign-born, and an additional 5.1 percent came from Ireland or Scotland. European cities need to be recognized as vibrantly multi-ethnic.

Young women moved into cities in disproportionately large numbers. Although few skilled trades were open to them, the high demand for servants, textile workers, seamstresses, and prostitutes gave them a range of work opportunities, even if most paid poorly and were insecure. Because of sex-selective migration, most towns had more females than males. In 1831 and 1851, for example, Bordeaux's population was disproportionately female among residents over the age of ten. Women's migration patterns differed from those of men, in that they made fewer, but more permanent, moves. Leslie Moch argues that women did not go on the road from city to city in search of jobs. They targeted specific places and tended to stay longer, changing residence fewer times than men. A stream of young women left the villages and small towns of Languedoc for Nimes during the nineteenth century, following well-known paths that kin and neighbors had already explored. They knew where they were going.[8]

The nature of urban labor markets thus exercised much influence on women's places of settlement, as it did for those of men. Leslie Moch has identified demographic differences among migrants to commercial or administrative, textile-producing, and metalworking towns. Both textile cities and administrative centers drew high proportions of single women to work in factories and to take jobs as servants. Birth rates were relatively low, however, in administrative or commercial centers, such as Nimes or Cologne, because of heavy settlement by white-collar workers, who restricted family sizes early, and single servants living in employers' households. In contrast, towns specializing in heavy industry or mining, such as Sheffield, Duisburg, or Bochum, attracted disproportionate numbers of adult males. Having limited employment opportunities in these metal or mining areas, women married and had children relatively

[8] Moch, *Moving Europeans*, 131.

early; birth rates were high. Reproductive patterns, as well as life chances, changed with migration into cities.

Studies of the Ruhr area permit a detailed look at migration into its cities during the nineteenth century. Most astonishing is the sheer volume of migration into this area of rapid industrialization and heavy industry. In the Düsseldorf region, migration into both rural and urban areas intensified from the 1830s, continuing to rise until the end of the century. Around 1855, about eleven newcomers moved annually into industrial villages and towns for every hundred residents, and rates were higher in the large cities. If this sounds unimpressive, just multiply and keep in mind that almost as many people left in a given year as arrived. Within five years, even in small towns, the number of people who moved totaled more than half of the existing population! Most of this migration was temporary, resulting in short-term stays by young single men and women looking for work. Still, a significant proportion of migrants came as families, and these people generally stayed. As Steve Hochstadt concludes, "Family migration created urban growth; single migration was urban transience."[9]

The explosive growth of heavy industry in the Ruhr Valley transformed the small town of Duisburg, which grew from about 7,000 residents in 1831 to 92,500 in 1900, partly through migration and partly from natural increase. While most newcomers walked into town from nearby areas, a growing number of Dutch migrants and Poles traveled long distances to get there. About 70 percent of all in-migrants remained for only a year or less. The city was only a way-station for thousands of young, single people attempting to earn money for themselves and their families before marrying and setting up their own households. Nevertheless, James Jackson stresses the normality of social experiences among migrants.[10] Those who left town often returned to their birthplaces, either seasonally or permanently. Migration took place primarily in "years of major life-course transitions" during adolescence, at the time of marriage, or at the death of a spouse. Childhood years and married adulthood tended to be relatively stable. Most men and women who remained in the city married by their late twenties and had several children in quick succession. Even when Duisburgers changed their residences in the city, they settled near former neighbors and kin, and developed neighborhood ties. Although the city itself was transformed, family life and work brought continuity for individuals. His evidence contradicts the familiar picture of marginalized, rootless urban migrants. The social problems of industrial cities

[9] Hochstadt, *Mobility and Modernity*, 74, 102.
[10] Jackson, *Migration and Urbanization in the Ruhr Valley*, 24, 164, 170, 203.

arose primarily from sources other than the inability of newcomers to cope with urban life.

Migration into cities by Europeans took place outside Europe too. A continuing flow of Europeans moved across the Atlantic during the eighteenth and early nineteenth centuries, landing in the port cities of the Americas and the Caribbean. They came as indentured servants, convicts, soldiers, and paying passengers. English Quakers and Germans settled in Philadelphia, while Irish farmers and laborers tended to choose Boston, New York, and Toronto. French moved into New Orleans. Spanish and Portuguese sailed to Havana and Rio and took jobs as administrators in the towns of New Spain, Peru, and Brazil. Buenos Aires attracted a stream of British merchants and adventurers. Wartime victories gave the British control over the French towns of Quebec. Lord Dorchester, who served as Governor of Quebec, Nova Scotia, and New Brunswick from 1786, settled some of the loyalist refugees from the thirteen newly independent British colonies in newly planned townships, organized around town centers and public squares. Kingston, Jamaica, was the largest city in the British West Indies because of its position as a sugar exporter and the right of its merchants to trade with Spanish America and to export slaves there. In the late eighteenth century, the city was an important free port for manufactured goods and agricultural products. Its population of 17,000 in 1788 included white freemen (25 percent), slaves (63 percent), and an intermediate group of people of mixed heritage and status, which consisted of Sephardic Jews, free Blacks, and mulattos (12 percent). Each group enjoyed different rights and legal statuses, whites having a monopoly of political rights and government jobs. Havana, which claimed 96,000 inhabitants in 1800, far outstripped it in size and glamour, as did the major cities of Latin America.

In the century between 1750 and 1850, neo-European towns also sprang up in Australia under the control of the British. The British government's decision to send convicts there led directly to the founding of Sydney in 1788. Within five years, a small town of 3,000 people dominated by a military barracks and prison had been built. The main street led away from the harbor to Government House, one block inland. By 1850, Sydney had more than 50,000 people. Melbourne, founded in 1835, reached a size of 23,000 by mid-century, having grown in a few years from a collection of tents and mud huts to a substantial, planned town of brick and timber. An Anglican and a Catholic Bishop, as well as several Protestant clergymen, resided in the town, which also boasted a cricket ground, Masonic lodges, and a newspaper. Each new British colony in Australia had its capital city, carefully laid out and provided with government buildings, markets, and stores.

On balance, the colonial adventures of European states during the eighteenth century in the Americas, the Caribbean, and the South Pacific produced settler societies and neo-European towns. Emigrants attempted to reproduce abroad what they knew at home, and the ordered spaces of a new colonial town could be stamped with a European imprint fairly easily. The names, architectural styles, institutions, and imported material culture of places like New York and New Orleans announced both the hopes and the pedigrees of their founders.

This export of European culture was much less powerful in other areas. Entrepreneurial employees of the East India Company founded Penang off the Malayan coast in 1786 and Singapore in 1819. Wartime victories gave the British control of former Dutch ports – Capetown, Colombo, and Malacca. Defeating the Chinese in the first Opium War had led to the extra bonus of Hong Kong island, which quickly became a thriving center of free trade and a beachhead for expansion into China. Despite high hopes for riches through commerce in such settlements, relatively few Europeans chose African and Asian destinations, unless sent by the army or their employers for short stays. Such settlements co-existed uneasily with older territorial empires run from a rich and densely populated belt of cities stretching along the north African coast through the Middle East, Central and South Asia to China.

Most European-owned towns in Asia and Africa were small port-forts set up for trade. St. Louis in Senegal, Galle in Ceylon, and Amboyna in the Dutch East Indies typify such seaside settlements organized around merchants who were protected by a few cannons and soldiers. Ships left heavily laden with slaves and spices for sale in European and American markets. The urban network of ports adjusted along with the currents of international commerce. To encourage the ending of slavery and to accommodate newly freed slaves, the Sierra Leone Company, led by the abolitionist Granville Sharp, organized the development of a self-governing colony in West Africa in the late 1780s. Although African neighbors burned down the first settlement, Granville Town, in 1790, its successor, Freetown, established itself and grew to about 1,200 people in 1800. Sited on a good harbor near the sea, its defensive walls encircled a grid of several streets. Inhabitants, mostly farmers, owned land and animals, and they chose their own officials. Over 1,000 freed slaves migrated there in the later eighteenth century.

In the early nineteenth century, the small numbers of European migrants in Asia and Africa meant that they had limited cultural impact there. Outside of India, European-run towns in Asia and Africa were enclaves, certainly not command centers of thriving territorial empires. (The sizes of Calcutta, Bombay, and Madras, whose mostly Asian populations totaled 1.3 million people in 1850, made them exceptional, as did the growing territorial power of the East India Company.) In sub-Saharan Africa, Southeast Asia, and the islands of the Pacific, European trading posts remained most effectively linked via water back to Europe and to other port towns, not to the settlements of their hinterlands. Immigration was of limited importance, and they remained small in size. Their periods of explosive growth lay in the twentieth century.

Numbers and networks

In the century after 1750, demographic change resulted in Europe becoming much more urbanized than ever before. Table 1 in the Introduction sheds some light on this process, but we can understand it still better by referring to the following table. Raising the cut-off to 10,000 inhabitants and showing numbers of settlements of this size in broad regions of Europe, it reveals not only the enormous increase in the absolute number of towns but also the high degree of variation with regard to levels of urban development. The number of cities grew substantially, while the proportion of the total population living in cities of more than 10,000 jumped from 9.5 percent to 16.7 percent. The most spectacular growth took place in mining areas, where large numbers of small settlements passed the 2,000 mark and thereby became officially urban. Moreover, large cities became common, as figures in Appendix A indicate. By 1850, thirty-four cities in Europe had more than 100,000 inhabitants, and ten numbered more than 250,000.

These aggregate numbers hide, however, substantial regional and national variation, since they average rapid change and stagnation. Moreover, city development had been quite uneven in Europe for centuries. Italy and the Low Countries, which had acquired dense urban networks by 1600, later experienced urban decline during times of regional economic crisis. Growth for them merely replaced earlier losses of city populations. In contrast, towns were relatively few and far between in northern and Eastern Europe, and their eighteenth-century growth was sluggish. The British Isles were the only region to experience steady, substantial urbanization over a long period of time. It had the largest numbers of big towns too. Only after 1800 did rates of urbanization rise more generally, increasing very slowly in both southern and eastern regions. Both the pace of urbanization and its geographic weight varied greatly within Europe.

A city's importance depended on much more than its size. It depended in large part on the city's position in networks of other cities, which in turn influenced possibilities for urban growth. Individual cities gained

Table 3 *Urbanization in European regions, 1750–1850*

	Europe	Northwest	Central	South	East
1750	9.5 (261)	13.6 (65)	7.5 (95)	11.8 (94)	3.5 (7)
1800	10.0 (364)	14.9 (105)	7.1 (135)	12.9 (113)	4.2 (11)
1850	16.7 (878)	26.1 (246)	12.5 (306)	18.6 (292)	7.5 (34)

In each cell, the first number indicates populations of settlements with 10,000 or more inhabitants as percentages of total populations. Numbers in parentheses indicate total numbers of such cities.
Source: De Vries, *European Urbanization*, 29, 39, 45.

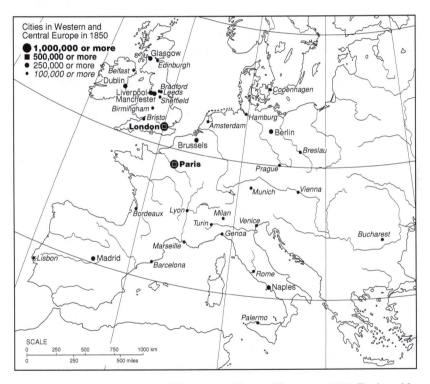

Map 3. Large cities in Western and Central Europe in 1850. By the mid-nineteenth century in the area west of the Russian Empire, which now included Poland, thirty-six cities had populations over 100,000, ten of which exceeded 250,000. Among them, London and Paris now broke the million mark. (Based on Tertius Chandler and Gerald Fox, *3000 Years of Urban Growth* [New York and London, 1974], 20, and Brian Mitchell, *European Historical Statistics, 1770–1970*, 2nd edn [London, 1981], 86–88.)

and lost in influence to the extent that they were part of wider urban networks. Fernand Braudel pointed to a succession of cities which dominated the European economy. By the eighteenth century, London had become the center of the European trading and financial system. It reaped many advantages from its easy access to large transatlantic markets. Jan De Vries has taken this insight a step farther, identifying zones with different intensities of urbanization. The largest cities, those with good access to water transport, and the most densely urbanized hinterlands had deeper potential fields of interaction, as computed on the basis of city sizes and relative distances one from another. In 1800, a date when London was the largest city in Europe and the center of the Atlantic economy, the most dense and most populous urban networks in Europe could be found in a large zone stretching from southern England through the Low Countries, Paris, and northwestern France. Urban concentration remained relatively intense from the Scottish lowlands south and east through the Rhineland and northern Italy, but beyond that circle, the potential for urban interaction dropped off sharply. By 1800, the urban core of Europe stretched from Britain to northern Italy. Beyond its boundaries, cities tended to be more geographically isolated, transportation links were less developed, and growth was generally slower. The accelerated urbanization of the later eighteenth century, therefore, not only revealed expansion but also highlighted contractions of the urban systems of southern Italy, Spain, and Eastern Europe, whose towns became less integrated into European systems of circulation.

Another way to conceptualize European urban systems is to track the relationships between small and large towns. "Central Place" theorists argue for a hierarchy of urban settlements, observable in terms of size and function, which develops from the differing sets of services available in towns of certain sizes and the distances that individuals are willing to travel to obtain them. Small towns, which house markets for the surrounding farms, have limited economic functions and lack complex political, social, and cultural institutions. Their capacity for growth is curbed by their limited functionality. Larger towns, however, offer a wider variety of services, acting as central places for smaller settlements in their regions and providing administration, complex services, and social institutions. Higher level centers, which tend to be larger, have links to multiple subordinate towns; states have one political capital, multiple regional centers, and then a large number of intermediate and smaller settlements.

History also shaped city distributions in Europe's regions in ways that had long-term consequences for their political and cultural organization. Some states, among them Portugal, Great Britain, France, the Austrian Empire, and Denmark, had atypically large capitals, called primate cities.

Lisbon, London, Paris, Vienna, and Copenhagen were many times larger than the next biggest cities in their states; they not only housed royal courts and political administration, but also dominated national cultural life and had many important economic functions as well. Migration streams and transportation networks centered on these capitals, which absorbed disproportionate shares of national resources. In contrast to these primate cities, the largest cities in the German states, northern Italy, and the Netherlands operated in 1800 more as ensembles of relative equals. State structures in these areas remained fragmented or relatively weak, and transportation systems looked more like nets than spider webs with a single center. Since the economic systems in which they participated did not coincide with national political networks, the pressures for growth on each individual place were less than in a centralized, primate system. These more egalitarian networks of cities carried into the industrial era political, cultural, and economic heritages that differed from those of the primate systems, which in combination with their regions' high rates of urbanization may well have retarded the growth of strong nation states.

Social problems

Particularly in the larger cities, the nasty results of rapid growth were obvious to all observers. Like other Scottish towns, as well as most European cities, Glasgow housed its citizens in high-rise, multi-apartment dwellings built to last a long time. When richer citizens left decaying buildings in the city center, workers moved in. Speculators added new construction in back gardens and courtyards, filling in all open spaces. Apartments were small; two-thirds of Glasgow's residents in 1861 lived in one- or two-room flats, most sharing their dwellings with at least five people. Low passageways led from narrow streets into strings of interior courtyards lined with wretched housing, their small central areas filled with dung heaps of household refuse and feces thrown there by inhabitants. Most of these buildings lacked privies, drains, and water. Smoke pollution came from blast furnaces, foundries, and coal-burning steam engines that powered local factories. A Parliamentary investigator commented in 1839: "I did not believe, until I visited the wynds [back alleys] of Glasgow, that so large an amount of filth, crime, misery, and disease existed on one spot in any civilized country."[11] He could have traveled a mile or two to the west, however, and found a new town of hill-top terraces and villas, complete with ornamental gardens, parks, and churches.

---

[11] J. Symons, quoted in Pacione, *Glasgow*, 86.

One result of Glasgow's growth was substantial social segregation, the poor crowded like canned sardines into slums on low-lying central land, while the better-off paid for more space, better sanitation, and cleaner air in western districts. Free-market provision of housing, water, and sanitation in an era of low incomes and little government regulation intensified social inequalities.

Housing problems for workers in Glasgow arose from pervasive difficulties. Rapid migration into the city meant that the demand for space increased much faster than the supply of dwellings. Overcrowding resulted. Moreover, the location of available buildings and their design did not suit the needs of the young workers who flooded into the city. They needed cheap, clean places in which to live near their work. What they found were old, dirty, badly ventilated, relatively expensive apartments, which they had to share in order to be able to afford them. Despite the need for new workers' housing, little was built in central Glasgow during the 1830s and 1840s. As the city grew and prospered, land prices rose, while construction costs did not fall. Given workers' low incomes, builders had little incentive to turn their attention to housing the poor. The same problems limited housing supplies in European industrial centers like Lille, Saint-Étienne, Liège, and Bochum, as well as older capital cities whose manufacturing sectors boomed. During the first half of the nineteenth century, when municipal governments largely ignored housing shortages, conditions worsened.

City dwellers with money could isolate themselves from some of the most severe consequences of rapid urbanization, but not from all of them. Since coal fires heated homes, even middle-class residents generated their own air pollution. Before the era of electric trolleys and underground railways, streets clogged with carriages and horse-drawn carts were also covered with manure. George Head, in his trip through Lancashire in 1834, noticed that "within a dozen miles of Manchester, the water of the canal is black as the Styx, and absolutely pestiferous, from the gas and refuse of the manufactories." In Leeds, he found that the burning of coal generated so much smoke that it obscured the sun.[12] Factory chimneys, rather than church towers, dominated northern town skylines, which were marked by separate columns of inky air. In Merthyr in Wales, many inhabitants used, for drinking and washing, river water into which sewage and industrial waste were poured.

These signposts of economic growth extorted a price paid with every breath drawn in their vicinity. In addition, middle-class people's tolerance for stink had decreased, as their standards of cleanliness rose. Slum

[12] Head, *A Home Tour*, 9, 172.

4. Factories in Manchester around 1850. George Godwin, the editor of the architectural magazine, *The Builder*, campaigned for better workers' housing in British cities. This picture of the Manchester skyline, which he entitled "Getting up the Steam," gave contemporaries clear evidence of industrialization's environmental cost. (George Godwin, *London Shadows* [London, 1854].)

visitors, whether in Rouen, London, or Berlin, complained about bad smells and feared their results. In the absence of a bacteriological or "germ" theory of diseases, most doctors believed that "miasmas" of sewage gas, decaying matter, and dirt produced fevers and infection, and they feared that contagion spread from the poorly ventilated, poorly drained, filthy homes of the poor. Edwin Chadwick, in his widely read 1842 *Report on the Sanitary Condition of the Labouring Population of Great Britain*, connected nasty smells and illness. French investigators of the cholera epidemic of 1832 focused obsessively on the scent of infection and covered their noses.

Because environments shaped exposure to risks, those living in cities during the first half of the nineteenth century had quite different life chances from those in rural areas. Big cities had long been death traps, well before the added burdens of industrial urbanization, and contemporaries knew it. Tolling bells, funerals, and filled cemeteries sent messages of high mortality. In many of Europe's largest cities during the eighteenth century, annual deaths normally outnumbered births. The most vulnerable city dwellers were the youngest: in Amsterdam around 1811, 251 of every 1,000 babies born died before the age of one. Rates were similarly high in large German and Russian cities. Moreover, smallpox and other infectious diseases produced intermittent crisis years, when already high death rates rose sharply. French urban babies, sent out by working parents to wet nurses in the countryside, died by the thousands and were probably not even included in the dismal, official statistics.

Although urban death rates declined in the later eighteenth century, they rose again in the nineteenth as rapid growth and pollution caused conditions to deteriorate. In Glasgow between 1821 and 1841, average life expectancy for those who reached age ten declined by five years for both men and women. Those who died in the city in 1843 had an average age of only twenty-seven! Death rates were proportional to size of settlement in most of Europe. In 1841 in Lancashire and Cheshire towns, the heart of industrializing Britain, 198 infants of every 1,000 born died before their first birthdays. At that time, infant death rates in northern English cities exceeded rural ones by about 50 percent. People who moved into towns from rural areas in Britain shortened their life expectancy by several years and lessened the chances of their children's survival. Inhabitants of Brussels faced a greater risk of early death than the people of Liège.

Although earlier deaths threatened all city dwellers, risks were not spread equally. Urban death rates varied considerably by occupation, income, and neighborhood. On average, clergymen living in large, warm houses had much longer lives than day laborers and servants packed into slum apartments. Differences in nutrition, working conditions, water supplies, and cleanliness gave the advantage to those with higher incomes. But money could not buy immunity from the risks of high-density living, which were compounded by poor sanitation and were scarcely alleviated by medical treatments that were quite primitive. Mortality rates generally rose with city sizes in the nineteenth century. Bacteria thrived in the unrefrigerated meats found in open-air markets and the animal feces on town streets. Urbanization, therefore, contributed directly to the high mortality of European populations.

Epidemic diseases, particularly those spread by dense living conditions and by polluted water, regularly devastated urban populations until sanitary reforms lessened their impact. During the 1830s, cholera had swept through European towns from Russia through Eastern and Central Europe before reaching the Netherlands, France, and Britain and then moving south into the Iberian peninsula and Italy. It terrified citizens from St. Petersburg to Amsterdam and Rome, hitting the poor the hardest and spreading fears of contagion and conspiracy. Cholera outbreaks in 1832, 1848–49, 1852–54, and 1866 killed thousands in Glasgow before improvements in the city's water supply lessened exposure to the bacillus in large districts of the city. Typhus, spread by body lice, struck young immigrants in Glasgow's filthy lodging houses particularly hard. Of the thousands who contracted it, at least a third died from the infection. Tuberculosis, a constant threat in overcrowded, damp housing, was that city's biggest killer, and smallpox continued to be a threat, despite the availability of free vaccinations. Smoky air exacerbated lung infections, and contaminated water brought typhoid bacteria into workers' homes. Glasgow's profile of ill-health was typical for large, crowded European cities in the first half of the nineteenth century, before the advent of filtered water supplies, extensive underground sewage disposal systems, and compulsory vaccinations.

Our knowledge of the problems of European cities during the industrial era is filtered through the perceptions of contemporaries, whose reports, drawings, and statistics fill the archives and libraries upon which historians depend. Their fears and accusations continue to shape our perceptions of the conditions of urban life. In their work, the idea of pollution had moved well beyond simple annoyance with dirty air and water, heightening their anxieties about promiscuity and perversion among the poor. When Eugène Buret published in 1840 an investigation of workers' living conditions in England and in France, he warned his readers: "If you venture into those accursed districts in which they live, wherever you go you will see men and women branded with the marks of vice and destitution, and half-naked children rotting in filth and stifling in airless, lightless dens. Here, in the very home of civilization, you will encounter thousands of men reduced by sheer besottedness to a life of savagery."[13] Similar charges, which linked poverty to barbarism, can be found in the books of dozens of doctors, officials, reporters, and reformers who toured urban slums during the nineteenth century. Accounts of street crimes and urban murders filled the pages of newspapers and novels, just as they today fill the television news. Historians now find these judgments more reflective of middle-class fears than working-class realities, but the conditions that helped to give rise to their suspicions deserve a more detailed look.

One needs to keep in mind the economic and social vulnerability of much of the urban population. Urban workers' families tended to be nuclear in organization, consisting of parents and their children. Katherine Lynch distinguishes between "plebian" and "patrician" households, the latter being much larger than the former because of the presence of servants and collateral relatives. Ordinary workers' households had relatively few children who survived into adulthood, and sizeable numbers were headed by a single parent, usually a widow or a deserted wife. Peter Laslett argued for the extreme exposure of such households

---

[13] Buret, quoted in Chevalier, *Laboring Classes and Dangerous Classes*, 360.

5. A slum dwelling in Paris around 1840. *The Mysteries of Paris* was one
of the most widely read novels published in France during the 1840s.
Written by a socialist reporter, Eugène Sue, it offered readers a melo-
dramatic portrayal of the capital's underworld and its poor inhabitants.
This illustration by H. Valentin appeared in several editions. (Eugène
Sue, *The Mysteries of Paris* [London, 1845], 192.)

to demographic accidents and economic hardship.[14] They had too few
resources to protect them against the pressures of disease, early death,

---

[14] Katherine A. Lynch, *Individuals, Families, and Communities in Europe, 1200–1800: The
Urban Foundations of Western Society* (Cambridge, 2003); Peter Laslett, "Family, Kinship,
and Collectivity as Systems of Support in Pre-industrial Europe: A Consideration of the
'Nuclear Hardship' Hypothesis," *Continuity and Change* 3:2 (1988): 153–76.

and economic downturn. Neighbors and friends could supply some additional help, but they lived under similar constraints. Urban workers had to scrounge and hustle to make do.

Before families began to limit fertility (a pattern adopted at different dates throughout Europe), the numbers of children born to married women during their lifetimes, as well as infants' death rates, were far higher than they are today. In French towns like Lyon, where working mothers sent infants to wet nurses and therefore lost the natural contraceptive protection of breast feeding, wives bore on average one child annually, although many died before their first birthday.[15] High fertility had the unfortunate consequence that every year hundreds of children were abandoned on Lyon streets or left at local hospitals when parents could not feed them. Their most likely prospects ranged from early death to life on the streets; the lucky made it into a dead-end job.

Many of these urban, abandoned children were illegitimate. During the later eighteenth century, pre-marital and non-marital pregnancy increased dramatically in many parts of Europe. Explanations of this change vary, but the most plausible ones center on the vulnerability of young, poor women away from home. When all members of a family had to earn in order to provide subsistence, many had to move to find a job. Young women became servants, textile workers, and street sellers, but they wanted companionship as well as protection in the cities. Sex, an accepted part of courtship, brought definite risks in a society with limited means of contraception. Moreover, sexual exploitation of servants by employers was far too common. In addition, marriage was expensive and sometimes incompatible with job requirements. Consensual unions became less stable in the later eighteenth and early nineteenth centuries, when wars, epidemics, and economic change destabilized communities and households. Men lost jobs and moved on, forgetting whatever promises they had made. Employers threw pregnant servants out on the streets, pushing young women into begging or prostitution. Cities, with their hospitals and charities for foundlings, attracted the poor and pregnant and made the problem more visible. The German demographer Wappäus calculated on the basis of census data from the major West European states around the middle of the nineteenth century that in almost all of them cities had higher illegitimacy rates than did rural areas. In France, 15 percent of urban births were illegitimate, in comparison with only 4 percent of children born in the countryside.[16] Women

---

[15] Garden, *Lyon*, 103.
[16] These figures are incomplete, however, and variations among countries were even greater than differences between urban and rural districts. See Weber, *The Growth of Cities*, 329.

who lacked local support systems – migrants and orphans, in particular – were most at risk of rearing a child without the help of a husband. They had the least bargaining power in local marriage markets. The high proportion of illegitimate births stems at least in part from the changed conditions within cities, where population turnover was rapid and much employment casual and seasonal.

Extreme poverty, combined with early death, desertion, and migration, meant that an unknown proportion of city dwellers lacked partners or living parents. Young workers in the cities had smaller family support systems than did their counterparts in the countryside or their wealthier neighbors. This lack of social support aggravated the prospects for young women, whose chances for skilled work, decent wages, and education were significantly less than those of young males. As a result, many young women turned to prostitution in order to survive. Although not legal, prostitution was essentially tolerated by European governments. As long as a woman was orderly and not too obvious and she avoided places considered out of bounds, she could usually ply her trade, either as a street walker or in one of the many urban brothels. Alexandre Parent-Duchâtelet, who studied public hygiene as well as sex for hire in Paris during the 1830s, argued that most of the women he investigated entered the trade only temporarily, because of poverty or homelessness. Pregnant servants who lost their jobs, women abandoned by their lovers, and young migrants who could not find other work found that the sex trade would pay the rent.

As cities grew, they became more socially and economically differentiated. While older city centers remained intact, the need for added space pushed industrial sites into peripheral areas where land was cheaper and more easily available. Homes and workplaces became distinct for more and more citizens, producing suburbs for middle-income families and slums for the poor, whether located in the older districts or in newer industrial areas. These spatial changes were well under way in British cities during the first half of the nineteenth century, and they continued thereafter, becoming increasingly noticeable in the large towns of Germany, France, Sweden, Austria, and northern Italy. Although not formally zoned for specific activities, urban spaces specialized as cities grew, and neighborhoods acquired reputations – respectable or rough, fashionable or squalid. Peripheral spaces beyond city walls attracted the illicit, the untaxed, and the disapproved to their poorly policed and badly lit streets. Police identified marginal districts, where threatening people were more likely to be found. In Lille, authorities worked to shift prostitution to the outskirts, even though their ability to regulate the trade declined with distance. In towns without walls, railways, canals, and factories created marginal areas, low-rent districts which attracted poor people, as well as sleazy taverns and cheap stores. Friedrich Engels commented on the contrasts he saw between the main streets of Manchester, which were lined by "shops of dazzling splendor," and the filthy riverside districts crammed with soot-blackened, crumbling buildings.[17] The wealthy, he charged, could avoid even looking at the poor because they had moved out of the city to large, single-family houses, surrounded by trees and gardens, and the poor were segregated into their own quarters. Industrial urbanization tore apart older neighborhoods where people of varied incomes and occupations had lived nearby or on different floors of the same building, producing much more economically and socially segregated areas. This process isolated both the rich and the poor, increasing social distances and a sense of mutual suspicion.

The Manchester example gave radicals, liberals, and conservatives evidence for their social analyses. Optimists praised its wealth and business successes while pessimists deplored the squalor of poor neighborhoods. Alexis de Tocqueville, the French social analyst who visited Manchester in 1835, described it as a medieval town with modern additions. He was fascinated by its extreme contrasts: Manchester was a town where "humanity attains its most complete development and its most brutish; here civilization works its miracles, and civilized man is turned back almost into a savage."[18] Industrial urbanization shocked contemporaries, whose response to the new cities remained deeply ambivalent. How could so much wealth co-exist with so much poverty? This question contributed to the protest activity explored in the next chapter.

BIBLIOGRAPHY

Anderson, Michael. *Family Structure in Nineteenth-Century Lancashire.* Cambridge, 1971.
Bairoch, Paul. *Cities and Economic Development: From the Dawn of History to the Present.* Trans. Christopher Braide. Chicago, 1988.
Berg, Maxine. *The Age of Manufactures: Industry, Innovation, and Work in Britain, 1790–1820.* Oxford, 1985.
Chevalier, Louis. *Laboring Classes and Dangerous Classes in Paris During the First Half of the Nineteenth Century.* Trans. Frank Jellinek. New York, 1973.
De Vries, Jan. *European Urbanization, 1500–1800.* Cambridge, MA, 1984.

[17] Engels, *The Condition of the Working Class*, 54, 60.
[18] Quoted in Asa Briggs, *Victorian Cities*, ed. Andrew and Lynn Lees (Berkeley and Los Angeles, 1996), 111–12.

Dennis, Richard. *English Industrial Cities of the Nineteenth Century: A Social Geography*. Cambridge, 1984.

Engels, Friedrich. *The Condition of the Working Class in England*. Trans. and ed. W. O. Henderson and W. H. Chaloner. Stanford, 1958.

Garden, Maurice. *Lyon et les Lyonnais au XVIIIe siècle*. Paris, n.d.

Garrioch, David. *The Making of Revolutionary Paris*. Berkeley and Los Angeles, 2002.

Gauldie, Enid. *Cruel Habitations: A History of Working-Class Housing in Britain, 1780–1918*. New York, 1974.

Goodman, David, and Colin Chant, eds. *European Cities & Technology: Industrial to Post-Industrial City*. London, 1999.

Hochstadt, Steve. *Mobility and Modernity: Migration in Germany, 1820–1989*. Ann Arbor, 1999.

Hoerder, Dirk. *Cultures in Contact: World Migrations in the Second Millennium*. Durham, 2002.

Hohenberg, Paul M., and Lynn Hollen Lees. *The Making of Urban Europe, 1000–1994*. 2nd edn. Cambridge, MA, 1995.

Jackson, James H. *Migration and Urbanization in the Ruhr Valley, 1821–1914*. Atlantic Highlands, NJ, 1997.

Kellett, J. R. *The Impact of Railways on Victorian Cities*. London, 1969.

Kudlick, Catherine J. *Cholera in Post-Revolutionary Paris*. Berkeley and Los Angeles, 1996.

Lees, Lynn Hollen. *Exiles of Erin: Irish Migrants in Victorian London*. Ithaca, 1979.

Lepetit, Bernard. *The Pre-Industrial Urban System: France, 1740–1840*. Trans. Godfrey Rogers. Cambridge, 1994.

Lucassen, Jan. *Migrant Labor in Europe, 1600–1900*. London, 1997.

Matzerath, Horst. *Urbanisierung in Preussen, 1815–1914*. Stuttgart, 1985.

Merriman, John. *The Margins of City Life: Explorations on the French Urban Frontier, 1815–1851*. Oxford, 1991.

Moch, Leslie Page. *Moving Europeans: Migration in Western Europe Since 1650*. 2nd edn. Bloomington and Indianapolis, 2003.

  Paths to the City: Regional Migration in Nineteenth-Century France. Beverly Hills, 1983.

Pacione, Michael. *Glasgow: The Socio-Spatial Development of the City*. New York, 1995.

Poussou, Jean-Pierre. *Bordeaux et le sud-ouest au XVIIIe siècle: Croissance économique et attraction urbaine*. Paris, 1982.

Ringrose, David R. *Madrid and the Spanish Economy, 1560–1850*. Berkeley and Los Angeles, 1983.

Roth, Ralf, and Marie-Noëlle Polino, eds. *The City and the Railway in Europe*. Burlington, VT, 2003.

Schwarz, L. D. *London in the Age of Industrialisation: Entrepreneurs, Labour Force, and Living Conditions, 1700–1850*. Cambridge, 1992.

Sewell, William H. *Structure and Mobility: The Men and Women of Marseille, 1820–1870*. Cambridge, 1985.

Söderberg, Johan. "Real Wage Trends in Urban Europe, 1730–1850: Stockholm in a Comparative Perspective." *Social History* 12 (1987): 155–76.

Thomson, J. K. J. *Distinctive Industrialization: Cotton in Barcelona, 1728–1832.* Cambridge, 1992.

Van der Wee, Herman, ed. *The Rise and Decline of Urban Industries in Italy and the Low Countries (Late Middle Ages – Early Modern Times).* Leuven, 1988.

Weber, Adna Ferrin. *The Growth of Cities in the Nineteenth Century: A Study in Statistics.* Ithaca, 1899.

3 Varieties of urban protest

Writing in the 1840s and 1850s, a Scotsman by the name of Archibald Alison who served as a sheriff in rural Lanarkshire voiced a set of complaints that pertained not only to urban behavior at the personal level but also to urban politics. In his view, the spread of sexual misbehavior, excessive drinking, and crime among city dwellers was accompanied by greater rebelliousness against governmental authorities. Seeking to link political developments to social ones, he argued that townsmen, "among whom numbers, closely aggregated together ha[d] awakened a feeling of strength, and increasing wealth ha[d] engendered the desire for independence," exhibited a passion for democratic leveling. Throughout Europe, it seemed to him as he considered developments since 1815, that the rise of cities had been central to the outbreak of revolutions. In Spain and France as well as in Britain, "the great towns ha[d] become the rulers," because their increasingly prosperous inhabitants had risen to positions of dominance. Alison's anxieties arose from competing perceptions. On the one hand, he was troubled by behavior among the urban masses that seemed to result from poverty; on the other, by an increasingly self-confident and assertive middle class. But such distinctions did not greatly concern him. What mattered was to paint cities as sources of disorder, both moral and political.[1]

Alison's views had been anticipated and were echoed not only by numerous conservatives but also, in a way, by liberals and radicals. These observers wrote much more sympathetically about at least some of what Alison condemned, but they accepted his basic premise that cities acted as solvents of traditional hierarchies in the area of politics. The Congregationalist clergyman Robert Vaughan celebrated cities in his book *The Age of Great Cities* as centers of political progress. Because town life fostered "just and enlightened views in relation to political science" and encouraged citizens to familiarize themselves with public affairs, it

---

[1] On Alison, see Andrew Lees, *Cities Perceived: Urban Society in European and American Thought, 1820–1940* (Manchester and New York, 1985), 32.

strengthened popular rule at every level of government. "The principles of self-government," he wrote, "have ascended from the borough to the senate, from the councilmen of the city to the councilmen of the nation. Such is the natural course of things." Shortly thereafter, the young Friedrich Engels, who was later to become famous as Karl Marx's comrade in intellectual arms, wrote from a position far to Vaughan's left. In a way, he provided even stronger support for Alison's arguments. In his famous work on *The Condition of the Working Class in England* (1845), Engels not only condemned cities (Manchester in particular) as places where manual workers suffered under the yoke of capitalist oppression but also welcomed them as places that served as "the birthplaces of the working-class movement," which would eventually bring about a political and a social revolution.[2]

Alison, Vaughan, and Engels were right in their belief that urban growth tended to disrupt established attitudes toward authority and the distribution of political power. The rise of cities did work to undermine an older order in which deference to traditional authorities, whose bases of power centered on landed and agricultural wealth, had long prevailed. Moreover, within urban settings, there was much contention among representatives of competing classes of city dwellers. The rest of this chapter deals with these processes, situating particularly salient examples of protest activity within the broader context of the rise of urban society. It will first survey key instances of protest activity, which occurred most notably in Britain and France, during what historians often refer to as "an age of revolution" that stretched from the 1760s through the 1840s (the most dramatic events of which occurred in Paris between 1789 and 1793). It will then turn to various features of cities that helped to precipitate such activity, paying attention both to grievances and goals and to networks of information and organization. These networks were central to the history of public protest. As has been argued most forcefully by Charles Tilly, protest did not result directly from discontent among aggrieved individuals but rather from organization and mobilization, which were greatly facilitated by urban environments.

Where, when, what, and who?

City dwellers who lived through the late years of the Old Regime and the era of the French Revolution or through the third of a century that

[2] Robert Vaughan, *The Age of Great Cities: Or, Modern Society Viewed in Its Relation to Intelligence, Morals, and Religion* (London, 1843), 119; Friedrich Engels, *The Condition of the Working Class in England*, trans. W. O. Henderson and W. H. Chaloner (Stanford, 1968), 137.

followed the downfall of Napoleon Bonaparte in 1815 witnessed (and in many instances participated in) rising tides of public protest. Much of what occurred entailed challenges to constituted authorities or others in influential positions. These challenges emanated from multiple sectors of urban society: representatives of urban-based elites, people of "the middling sort," and people of much lower rank. From the standpoints of landed aristocrats and others who spent the bulk of their time in the countryside, a great deal of what happened in cities clearly pointed toward threats either to their positions or to their values, but upper- and middle-class urbanites had growing reason to feel beleaguered too. Popular demonstrations frequently led to violent conflicts between what were pejoratively known in the eighteenth century as "mobs" (and known later as "crowds") and defenders of the status quo – whether local or state officials or other citizens who were relatively well off. These occurred repeatedly in cities and towns, most notably in the largest ones.

Starting in 1763, the British capital experienced political turmoil that lasted over a decade as a result of popular support for John Wilkes, a sharp critic of King George III. Arrested and then expelled from Parliament on account of his writings in a newspaper he edited, he ran successfully for Parliament again in 1768 and 1769 in Middlesex. This borough was inhabited by 700,000 Londoners who enjoyed much broader voting rights – and suffered from much less aristocratic interference in their political life – than most Englishmen elsewhere. Running under the slogan "Wilkes and liberty," he gathered support not only from tradesmen and manufacturers of the "middling sort," who voted for him in large numbers, but also from thousands of impoverished weavers, who helped keep supporters of his opponents from casting their votes. His victories led to riotous celebrations, in which many windows in houses of Londoners who had refused "to put out lights for Mr. Wilkes" were smashed, and when he was again denied his seat and again imprisoned there were more demonstrations. These resulted in one instance in eleven deaths and dozens of injuries as military men fired into large crowds. The formation of a Society of Supporters of the Bill of Rights led to still more mass meetings on his behalf, which came to an end only after he was elected to Parliament yet again, in 1774, and finally permitted to take his seat. Struggles by large numbers of politically conscious city dwellers had led to significant breakthroughs for the principles of freedom of expression and the rights of "the people," in this case adult male voters, to choose their own representatives.

The most violent example of urban disruption to occur in Britain at any point during the period under discussion here occurred in 1780, when Protestants protested against parliamentary repeal of legal restrictions on

British Catholics. After violent rioting in Edinburgh and Glasgow led to abandonment of the new law as it would have applied to Scotland, resistance spread to England. It was spearheaded in London by a Protestant Association, led by Lord George Gordon, who was said to be supported by "the better sort of tradesmen." Parliament's refusal to receive a petition signed by 60,000 opponents of legal equality for Catholics resulted in the Gordon Riots. Lasting a week, these disturbances led to the damage or destruction of numerous Catholic chapels and schools, other buildings belonging to Catholics, and half a dozen prisons, whose inmates were released. The riots ceased only after military intervention, which led to the deaths of 285 rioters, marking the end of the most violent disturbances in the history of the British capital.

Disruptiveness made itself felt in other ways as well. Labor disputes, albeit not overtly political, could easily spill over into activities that threatened to undermine respect for law and order. Not yet channeled through formally organized and legally recognized trade unions, protests by workers with regard to wages and working conditions often took the form of direct action against opponents. In 1763, journeymen coopers in Liverpool sought to intimidate a master cooper by carrying him around on the streets of the city on a pole, while, in the same year, 2,000 journeymen weavers in London broke into the homes of fellow workers who had refused to join them in a dispute with their masters, smashing their looms and wounding several of them. Despite repressive legislation that made destruction of looms a capital offense, such activities broke out again in the years 1767–69 and then once more in 1773.

Meanwhile, Paris too was marked by rising levels of agitation. Already in 1750, widespread rioting broke out as a result of the arrest of a large number of children on charges of vagrancy, many Parisians having believed that children of the poor were being shipped to colonies overseas. In 1775, at a time of high grain prices, acts of violence against prosperous farmers and millers that began in the countryside spread to the capital. Numerous Parisians from the lower classes swung into direct action against the owners of bakeries, with a view to seizing the bread that was a staple of their diets. Although less violent, strike activity recurred repeatedly. Between 1750 and 1789, five major disputes erupted between masters and journeymen in the baking trade, and seven similar conflicts affected the printing trade. Although such incidents may be viewed as harbingers of later industrial clashes, other disputes were more significant politically at the time. Demonstrations that occurred in support of the *Parlement* of Paris, a law court dominated by aristocrats that was acquiring a reputation as a defender of liberty as a result of its opposition to monarchical absolutism, stand out in this respect. Minor disturbances took place on six occasions between 1753 and 1786, and major ones broke out in 1787 and 1788, when journeymen and other craftsmen demonstrated both to support the *Parlement* after it was exiled and to celebrate its later return to the capital.

Urban-based protest reached new levels of intensity in the spring of 1789 and persisted thereafter for over half a decade. During this time, Paris served as the headquarters of the French Revolution and inspired activists in cities elsewhere in France and outside France as well. To be sure, the Revolution arose from discontent with the rule of the Bourbon monarchy among many citizens of the French kingdom. But its course must be understood in large measure in relation to events in the French capital, where revolutionary upheaval was especially violent and – owing to the capital's centrality – especially influential.

Between late April and early October, Paris experienced three major outbreaks, each of which involved a combination of discontent based on economic issues (mainly the high cost of bread, which had already led to serious disturbances in 1775) and support for revolutionary politics. In the first of these incidents, the Revéillon riots (named after one of the men against whom the rioters directed much of their wrath), wage-earners from the working-class Faubourg St. Antoine pillaged houses of wealthy merchants whom they suspected of wanting to reduce wages. Fighting between the rioters and national guardsmen resulted in a massacre, during which members of crowds proclaimed their support for representatives of the nation (i.e., "the third estate") who were about to meet in an assembly (the Estates General) that had been called into session by the king. On 14 July, at a time when relations between these representatives and the royal government seemed to have reached an impasse, a still more violent outburst tipped the balance of power in their favor. This event began in front of the Bastille, a prison dating from the Middle Ages from whose superintendent a crowd attempted to obtain weapons for struggles elsewhere in the city. Through a series of misunderstandings, the crowd turned into a mob. With the help of several trained soldiers and five cannon, the rioters induced the superintendent to surrender, but only after nearly 100 of their number had been killed. Consequently, they murdered six soldiers of the garrison, the superintendent, and the mayor, decapitating the latter two and marching through the city with their heads held aloft on pikes. A few months later, a large contingent of Parisian women who were angry over another crisis in the supply of bread marched to the royal palace at Versailles, just outside Paris. While there, they broke into private apartments of the king and queen, whom they then compelled to accompany them back to the capital. Under the watchful eyes of ordinary Parisians, the monarch was to be prevented

6. The storming of the Bastille in 1789. Seizure of this ancient prison in Paris by representatives of the bourgeoisie and the city militia stands out as a classic example of revolutionary activity on city streets. This illustration was one of many from the period that depicted what contemporaries perceived as a major turning-point in the history of France.

from withdrawing concessions he had made earlier to the revolutionaries. At the same time, the National Assembly that had emerged during the summer from the earlier Estates General, also moved from Versailles to the capital.

During the next few years, in conjunction with the rapid rise of political radicalism, popular violence broke out in Paris repeatedly. The climactic events took place in the late summer of 1792. On 10 August, crowds from working-class quarters, stirred up by soldiers from the city of Marseille, once again invaded a royal palace. This time it was the Tuileries, into which the royal family had moved after its forced return from Versailles. The number of those who lost their lives rose greatly. Over 600 of the king's bodyguards were massacred, many after they had surrendered. Within little more than a month, the result was the abolition of the monarchy itself and the proclamation of a republic. Later insurrections, which occurred in 1793, strengthened the hand of revolutionary leaders from the middle classes known as Jacobins. Supported by Parisian workers known as *sans-culottes*, radical politicians were able to wage a campaign of terror against actual and imagined opponents, thousands of whom were guillotined or executed in other ways.

Although the most significant and best-known events of the French Revolution occurred in Paris, revolutionary pressures came to a head in other cities in France too, such as Lille, Bordeaux, Lyon, and Saint-Étienne. In each of them, combinations of bourgeois elements and of workers succeeded during the Revolution's early phase in compelling municipal authorities to give way to new leaders. Bordeaux, Lyon, and Saint-Étienne were distinctly less radical in their politics than the capital, and they later revolted against it in the interests of a greater degree of local autonomy than the Jacobin leadership was willing to give them. In each case, as Parisian revolutionaries reasserted their authority over the country as a whole, these cities subsequently became scenes of retributive and repressive terror, carried out by a local minority aided and abetted by the national regime.

Revolutionary impulses in France set an example that inspired activists elsewhere on the continent, whose support for France was matched by French support for them. Here we see abundant evidence of international networks that linked cities, through which revolutionary impulses traveled from the main center of revolution to lesser ones. In Mainz, in the German Rhineland, German "Jacobins" who had formed a secret club early in 1792 warmly welcomed French forces upon their entry into the city in October of that year, hoping to establish a revolutionary republic. Such republics did in fact emerge later in the decade elsewhere in Europe as a result of the combination of French and local urban influences, contributing greatly to the magnification of French power outside France's borders. In Amsterdam, thirty-four Jacobin clubs helped to pave the way for the establishment of a Batavian Republic. Revolutionaries in Geneva performed a similar role in helping to found a Helvetic Republic. On the Italian peninsula, the creation of Roman and Neapolitan Republics also bore witness to the triumph of revolutionary forces in urban areas.

In Great Britain, London and other cities also spawned efforts to build support for the French in ways that would push the country as a whole along the path that French men and women had marked out. In 1791, middle-class radicals established a Society for Constitutional Information, and the following year artisans and other workers came together in the London Corresponding Society (LCS), headed by the shoemaker Thomas Hardy. Both of these societies communicated closely with similar organizations elsewhere, the links between the LCS and affiliated bodies in cities such as Sheffield, Manchester, and Leeds having been particularly close. All of these organizations helped to disseminate Thomas Paine's *Rights of Man* (1791), a political tract that celebrated the French

Revolution and urged emulation of the French example. Members of the LCS (labeled by the conservative Edmund Burke as "the Mother of all Mischief") and their counterparts elsewhere pushed for a wide range of reforms. They called for, among other measures, alleviation of harsh features of the penal system, elimination of unfair taxes, and measures intended to make an aristocratically dominated Parliament more representative of the nation as a whole. Meanwhile, in Edinburgh and Glasgow, reformers established a society known as The Friends of the People. Broadly based, with representation from among the business, professional, and working classes, each branch, by the end of 1792, had approximately 1,000 members. Less radical than members of groups such as the LCS, Scottish activists emphasized their loyalty to the king and their reliance on peaceful petitioning rather than intimidation, but they contributed nonetheless to an overall pattern of urban agitation for political change.

Meanwhile, Church and King Riots that reflected hostility to the Revolution arose in several cities. Like the Gordon Riots that had occurred in 1780, they embodied conservatism rather than radicalism. The first such outbreak occurred in Brussels in 1790, when the houses of wealthy "Vonckists" ("democrats" and "patriots" who were pro-French) were pillaged and destroyed. A later one occurred in Vienna in 1793, when members of the poorer classes rioted in protest against the execution of Louis XVI. They identified as their enemies not only Jacobins and their supporters but also anyone who possessed what they regarded as excessive amounts of property. In England, similar outbursts occurred in Birmingham in 1791, when mobs whose members had been egged on by Tory clergymen and justices of the peace destroyed the homes of many reformers, among them that of the scientist and Unitarian minister Joseph Priestley. They took place also in 1792 in Manchester, and in 1794 in Nottingham.

Largely suppressed by the forces of established order during the late 1790s, political protest gained a new lease on life in Britain after victories by radical candidates in Westminster at a general election in 1807, and it mushroomed a few years later. Following military victory over France in 1815, it broke out in several cities during a span of a little under two decades. Urban-based agitation for expanded rights of political participation occurred most notably early on among radicals in London. Many of them, under the influence of the journalist William Cobbett, pushed in vain for democratic political change. In 1819, just outside Manchester at Peterloo Field, an address to 60,000 listeners by the radical orator Henry Hunt – against taxes and corruption and in favor of democracy – led magistrates to order his arrest. In the charge on horseback by troops and the confrontation with the crowd that followed, eleven demonstrators died. Demonstrations elsewhere in Britain a little over a decade later led to at least partial victories for those who took part in them. Efforts by liberal politicians to broaden the representativeness of the House of Commons, by expanding a highly restrictive suffrage and assigning more seats to urban areas at the expense of rural ones, were supported by a torrent of organized protest against attempts by the House of Lords to thwart a reform bill the lower house had approved. In 1831 and 1832, many cities witnessed the births of "political unions," whose members demonstrated and sometimes rioted in favor of the bill. Birmingham stood out. The banker Thomas Attwood took the lead there in founding a Political Union of the Lower and Middle Classes of the People, under whose banner up to 200,000 people demonstrated at one time. Activists in Nottingham, Leeds, Bristol (where many government buildings were set afire), Glasgow, and London eventually entered into the fray as well.

The victory by British reformers, which took shape in the Reform Act of 1832, occurred as a result not only of agitation in British cities but also of events in cities elsewhere. The overthrow of the restored Bourbon monarchy by revolutionaries who had taken to the streets once again in Paris, in July of 1830, seemed to foretell the fate that might await men who failed to assuage popular discontent – or who, as was the case in France, provoked unrest via reactionary policies. Crowds of artisans and other skilled workers had risen up against a king who had sought to overturn the results of recent elections, in part by reducing the voting power of members of the bourgeoisie, and to tighten censorship of the press. Barricades went up in many parts of the capital, fighting between soldiers and civilians ensued, and over 600 Frenchmen (more than three-quarters of them civilians) lost their lives. During the disturbances, Charles X fled the country, and he was replaced as king by Louis-Philippe, who was expected to function in a more limited fashion as a constitutional rather than as a would-be absolute monarch. Another French-speaking city, Brussels, had also experienced political violence. Here, less than two months after the aforesaid events in Paris, fighting broke out between civilians and troops as a result of disputes that in many respects resembled those that had arisen in France. The conflicts were exacerbated by the fact that, as a result of decisions made at the Congress of Vienna in 1815, Belgium was ruled by a Dutch monarch. His rule there soon came to an end, as an independent Belgium – with Brussels as its capital – emerged on the European map.

Throughout the rest of the 1830s and beyond them, despite increasingly conservative efforts by the French government to maintain order, French cities remained hotbeds of radicalism. Men who sought to keep alive what they regarded as the great tradition of 1789 mingled with other individuals who set their sights on a much broader reconstruction of industrial and urban society, the rise of which was continuing to push the remnants of the Old Regime still further into the shadows of the past. Reacting against what they viewed as a "bourgeois" monarchy, which was primarily dedicated to defending the status of a well-to-do minority, radical workers plotted and agitated in favor both of republicanism and of redistribution of supposedly ill-gotten property. Their activities led to recurrent disturbances in the capital. Early in 1832, an outbreak of cholera – attributed by radicals to governmental hostility to the poor – that led to a death toll of over 18,000 fanned discontent in the city. This contributed to an uprising in which, after soldiers and police emerged victorious, almost 800 people had been killed or wounded. A paramilitary organization of radical republicans known as The Society of the Rights of Man and of the Citizen, founded later in 1832, had three to four thousand members by 1834 and was well positioned to help orchestrate another uprising in April of that year. This time the insurrection was briefer and the death toll was lower: "only" sixty-nine people were killed. But five years later, under the leadership of a new organization that called itself The Society of the Seasons, a third post-1830 uprising in the capital against the government resulted in an increase in the death toll, which rose to almost 100. In the meantime, in the industrial town of Lyon in February of 1834, an eight-day work stoppage by silk weavers had led to severe fighting there that lasted for six days. Soldiers and police eventually defeated strikers who had temporarily gained control of the center of the city, but when the fighting stopped about 300 people were dead and at least 200 more were wounded.

Beyond the major incidents described above, French cities experienced large numbers of strikes, which broke out in small as well as large towns. They occurred in the industrial city of Limoges in 1833, in Reims in 1834, and in many other towns around the same time or slightly later. In 1840, at least 30,000 and perhaps as many as 100,000 workers staged a series of mass walkouts in Paris as a result of disputes over wages, hours, and other work-related issues, and five years later a big strike by carpenters broke out there too, leading to judicial intervention by the government on the side of the employers. In order to avoid any taint of republicanism, a strike leader in 1845 proclaimed, "We are not political men," and it is true that the strikes here as elsewhere (except in Lyon in 1834) did not lead to overt efforts to seize power from the existing regime. But they strengthened nonetheless a growing impression that cities were places in which the social as well as the political status quo was under attack.

Parisians once again set a revolutionary example of major proportions in 1848. For a third time in little more than half a century, they drove a king from his throne. The decisive events occurred late in February. After the government had decided to suppress demonstrations by liberals in favor of political reform, large numbers of workers took to the streets, erecting an estimated 1,512 barricades in order to defend themselves in their battles with soldiers and policemen. As in 1830, after three days the insurgents emerged victorious on the field of battle. The casualties were somewhat fewer than two decades earlier, amounting to "only" 361 deaths (about four-fifths of them from the ranks of the opponents of the monarchy), but the end result was more dramatic. This time, as in 1792, they brought about not merely a change of dynasties but the establishment of a republic. After continuing demonstrations throughout the spring – directed against the country's new leaders by men who sought social and economic as well as political rights – a decision by the government to eliminate a make-work program that had attracted over 100,000 unemployed persons to the capital led to one of the century's most severe episodes of domestic violence. Between 24 June and 26 June, street fighting between workers and national guardsmen who fought in defense of a middle-class regime led once again to the construction of barricades and to many casualties. Deaths were measured this time not in the hundreds but in the thousands. The insurrection was suppressed, but "the June days" stood for over two decades, until the suppression of the Paris Commune in 1871, as the outstanding instance of urban violence in nineteenth-century Europe. Class warfare far bloodier than earlier conflicts of a political sort seemed to some observers (among them Karl Marx) to indicate the shape of things to come in industrial-urban society.

In the meantime, urban crowds had extracted major concessions from royal governments in several other countries. On 13 March, stimulated by news from Paris, working men and students rose up in revolt in Vienna, the political center of the multinational Habsburg (Austrian) Empire. They erected barricades, invaded the imperial palace, and forced the chief statesman of the empire, the conservative Clemens von Metternich, to resign his office and flee to England. Shortly thereafter, the emperor promised to convene an assembly for the purpose of writing a constitution for his realm. Within a few months, he fled the city, which soon came under the control of the forces that had compelled Metternich to leave earlier. Developments in Vienna had already helped to shape the course of events in Berlin, the capital of Prussia, where popular pressures on the monarch to make concessions to liberal leaders had been on the rise for several years. His decision, as conflicts between demonstrators and

7. Barricades in Berlin in 1848. Soldiers and ordinary citizens fought on opposite sides of hastily erected barricades in the Prussian capital in March of a year during which revolutionary upheavals broke out in many cities on the European continent. Hundreds died in the violence depicted in this illustration.

troops began to break out on 15 March, to announce a conciliatory policy of reform might have nipped revolutionary tendencies in the bud, except for the fact that at least one soldier fired on members of a crowd that had assembled to greet the royal proclamation. The shots provoked a melée in which at least twenty soldiers and more than 200 civilians died. The king then backed down, ordering his troops to return to their barracks and appointing liberals to his government to replace the conservatives on whom he had formerly relied.

Narrating all the other instances in which urban upheaval occurred on the European continent during the period of about a year between early 1848 (often called "the springtime of nations") and early 1849 is neither possible nor necessary at this point. Suffice it to say that although violence on the scale of what occurred in Paris, Berlin, or Vienna did not occur elsewhere, many cities served as nuclei of and staging grounds for efforts either to push existing governments in more liberal directions or to establish new regimes. Munich, where demonstrators forced the king of Bavaria to abdicate in favor of his son shortly after the "March days" in the capital of Prussia, was one of many cities in Germany in addition to Berlin that took the first route. Milan and Venice, in which uprisings against foreign rule by Austria occurred in March, and Rome, where a Roman Republic was proclaimed in early 1849, were major cities in Italy that took the second route.

Between the late 1830s and 1848, Britain too experienced an upsurge of popular radicalism, which took shape most notably in cities and industrial areas near them. Hundreds of thousands of people agitated for adoption of the "The People's Charter," a document drafted in 1837 by members of the newly founded London Working Men's Association. With its clear demands for universal male suffrage and secret balloting, which would have extended the size of the political nation far beyond the still modest dimensions arrived at in 1832, the Charter served as the focal point for a national movement. This took off at a convention of working men's organizations in Birmingham in 1838. Giant processions and mammoth meetings, numbering in the tens of thousands, soon took place there, in Manchester, and in Glasgow. In 1839, the first of three efforts to gather support for the Charter led to the submission of a petition with well over one million signatures to Parliament. Rejection of this document resulted in formation of a National Charter Association in Manchester and the submission in 1842 of a second petition, this one bearing more than twice as many signatures as the first one. Radical agitation reached one of its peak levels in Britain in that year. It came to a head not only in the Chartists' political efforts but also in the form of much labor unrest, expressed in numerous strikes, demonstrations, and riots. Many of these

8. A Chartist march in 1848. This engraving from the *Illustrated London News* (15 April 1848), a popular London newspaper, shows lines of demonstrators marching through the capital carrying a copy of the People's Charter, which demanded universal adult male suffrage and other democratic reforms. Their plan to present to Parliament a petition with several million signatures listing their demands was blocked by the government.

efforts won support from Chartists, who hoped that by forging alliances with men whose aims were primarily economic they could add significant force to their political demands. Rejection of their second petition led to a lull in Chartist agitation for half a decade. But during an economic downturn that began in 1847 a third petition drive took place. According to Chartist leaders, six million signatures were gathered this time. Thousands of demonstrators assembled in London with a view to carrying the petition to the Houses of Parliament, but en route they were blocked by much larger numbers of special constables who had been recruited for the purpose of safeguarding public order. Subsequently, mass agitation for political change fizzled out in Britain, during the very period when liberals and radicals on the continent were striding forward with seemingly unstoppable force.

The fact that in 1848 and 1849 not only in Britain but also on the continent the forces of popular radicalism (and on the continent the forces of middle-class liberalism too) were once again defeated does not detract from their significance in the history of urban Europe. Their activities had contributed greatly to the images of urban restlessness and instability with which this chapter began. In addition, they stimulated efforts by urban reformers, who sought to eliminate conditions that gave rise to revolutionary discontent. But before taking up this last theme, to which we shall turn in later chapters, let us look more thematically at some of the interconnections between protest and urbanity.

Some reasons why: grievances and goals

Having rapidly surveyed the most salient incidents of protest activity, we now turn to some of the underlying conditions from which they arose. In this context, we need to focus first on what city dwellers disliked and what they wanted. What irked them and what did they seek? How were their grievances related to urban experiences, and what sorts of measures did they have in mind as the hoped for results of their protest activities? Urban environments served in numerous ways as incubators of dissatisfaction and restlessness, markedly accentuating grievances among many of their inhabitants in ways that contributed to the disruptive protests discussed above. They also functioned as breeding grounds for ideas and movements whose supporters sought to rectify what they disliked. Sites of unhappiness but also sites of hopefulness, cities were marked by many characteristics that predisposed them to become centers of protest and turmoil.

Numerous members of the middle classes – referred to as "the middling sort" in Britain, the *bourgeoisie* in France, and the *Bürgertum* in Germany – resented the lack of social recognition and political power they thought should accompany their successes in the economic realm or in the learned professions. These individuals, to whom the conservative Scot Archibald Alison referred in a passage cited at the start of this chapter, were over-represented in cities. There, increasingly dominant elements consisted of men who stood out on at least one of two counts. Men of property, particularly in Britain and France, enjoyed a certain pre-eminence on the basis of growing incomes they received as bankers, financiers, overseas merchants, or other sorts of businessmen, among whom large-scale manufacturers were to become increasingly significant under the impact of the industrial revolution. One thinks, for example, not only of the men who frequented the Royal Exchange in London but also of others, who engaged in overseas commerce in Liverpool and Bordeaux and the increasing numbers of industrialists in the Ruhr Valley. At the same time, educated men stood out on the basis of their qualifications as lawyers, medical doctors, or professors (although university teachers tended to live in medium-sized cities, where most universities were located rather than in large ones). In towns in Central Europe, which long lagged economically behind areas to its west, a *Bildungsbürgertum* (educated middle class) enjoyed a particularly prominent position. For representatives from all of these groups, gains in some areas whetted their appetites for gains in others. In their view, political change should enable them to enjoy a greater share of the power and prestige that were still enjoyed by the titled nobility in France until 1789 and by landed aristocrats elsewhere well into the nineteenth century. To be sure, historians no longer talk about a "rising middle class" as the prime motor behind the outbreak of the great French Revolution. The existence of such a "class" as a politically cohesive force for changing the old order either during the late eighteenth century or subsequently cannot be demonstrated. Used carefully, however, the concept of status discrepancies, which prompted ascendant groups centered in cities to challenge landed groups that were viewed as still too privileged in relation to their actual worth, helps us nonetheless to make sense of much of what was going on politically in Europe between the 1760s and 1848. At any rate, it is difficult to see how historians of "modernity" can make do without it.

In other cases and at other levels, urban-centered discontent resulted not so much from hopes for greater recognition and power among the already prosperous as from experiences of hardship. Some educated men sought to undermine the status quo for reasons that had to do with their perception that they lacked status and opportunities for making a living commensurate with the knowledge they had so painstakingly acquired, or at any rate with the intelligence they were sure they possessed. In France and Germany, there was what many perceived to be, in the words of Lenore O'Boyle, an "excess of educated men,"[3] with substantially more graduates from institutions of higher education than there were opportunities for such graduates to work as professionals, particularly in the public sectors in which many of the best positions were to be found. Such men frequently turned to journalism or to work as independent publicists, usually eking out at best quite modest livelihoods through this activity. Consequently, they often attacked what they regarded as the unfairness of a society in which their knowledge and competence were so badly undervalued.

Then, too, there was the economic and physical deprivation among city dwellers who lived at still lower levels of urban society, reference to which has been made both in Chapter 1 and in Chapter 2. For the entire period with which we are concerned here, only a small portion of any city's population can be classified as having been solidly "middle

---

[3] Lenore O'Boyle, "The Problem of an Excess of Educated Men in Western Europe, 1800–1850," *Journal of Modern History* 42 (1970): 471–95.

class." In the eighteenth century, substantial majorities consisted of journeymen, artisans, household servants, day laborers, or vagrants, most townspeople having belonged to what were called "the lower orders." Poverty was endemic in European societies, among urban as well as rural populations, and as a result of population growth it was on the rise. It was still widespread throughout the first half of the nineteenth century (and was to remain so long thereafter, although poverty rates did decline during the century's second half). Even among those who could afford to purchase basic necessities, there was only a small margin of safety, and many who seemed secure might easily become poor. Overcrowding and environmental degradation imposed heavy penalties that paralleled and exacerbated low incomes, leading not only to lack of comfort but also, via pollution of air and water and via contagion in close quarters, to excessive disease and premature death, particularly among members of the urban masses. Such conditions inevitably exacerbated discontent with the political and social status quo. Whether as a result of cholera in Paris in 1832, unemployment in British towns in the "hungry" 1840s, or any one of a vast number of hardships there and elsewhere, at least a certain proportion of the urban population became available for purposes of protest. Perhaps even more significantly, glaring inequalities, which became all the more readily apparent under conditions of residential density, provided factual bases on which critical ideologists could draw in constructing the theories and programs that helped to guide protest activities – ideas to which we shall return toward the end of this chapter.

To say this is not to endorse a simplistic view of economic suffering among the down-and-out as the root cause of revolutionary upheaval. In this connection, it must be borne in mind that the poorest of the poor have seldom played a significant role in seeking to change existing conditions. Accordingly, it was not usually misery as such that led to disruptive outbreaks by ordinary city dwellers during the period under discussion here. Often, pronounced changes for the worse in their conditions mattered much more than absolute levels of deprivation or discomfort. Take, for example, the case of food riots, which antedated the year 1750 but continued well beyond it. Such disturbances reminded authorities, particularly in Paris, of the dangers posed to their power by ordinary men and women who felt aggrieved as a result of increases in the price of grain and thus of bread, a staple element of the ordinary person's diet. Having to spend the bulk of their incomes on what they ate, many of them reacted sharply and violently to being forced to pay still more in order to buy it. As Edward Thompson argued, ordinary people clung to the idea of a "moral economy" in which wages and prices remained at a "just" level, and that they were prepared to defend on the basis of what they considered their traditional rights.[4]

Agitation against established authorities arose repeatedly among artisans, such as the silk weavers who revolted in Lyon in 1834 and various craftsmen who took to the streets in German cities in 1848. They revolted not simply because they were experiencing hardship but rather because they felt that difficult circumstances were becoming worse, as was the case also among the weavers who had risen in protest in rural areas of Silesia earlier in the decade. In all of these cases and many more, grievances were aroused less by circumstances themselves than by evidence that conditions had deteriorated and the prospect that in the absence of remedial action they would deteriorate still further.

It would be misleading to suggest that all protest was (to use language that emerged only after 1815) "leftist" (or to use still later terminology, "progressive"). Much of it, even if it was disruptive, was also defensive, reflecting deep strains of popular conservatism and looking backward to supposedly better conditions instead of toward a new polity or a new society. Political instability arose in urban settings out of a wide range of concerns and situations that characterized urban life, and it pointed toward widely varying goals, some of which seemed to involve the restoration of earlier conditions rather than the creation of something novel. Take for instance the example of people who engaged in food riots in eighteenth-century Paris. Their resentments over rises in the price of bread rose to a fever pitch when they believed that such increases resulted from the greed of unscrupulous merchants, who had in their view violated the traditional tenets of a "moral economy." Later artisanal agitation in German towns, which reached a crescendo in 1848, also exemplified a radicalism that was deeply tinged with conservatism. Craftsmen frequently took to the streets in opposition to princely governments to defend the sources of their livelihoods against threats posed by the onslaught of industrialism and laissez-faire liberalism. One can offer still clearer evidence of conservative tendencies by recalling some of the events discussed earlier that took place in London. Both the Gordon Riots of 1780s and the Church and King Riots a decade later manifested explicit and sharp opposition to the forces of change, while at the same time clearly threatening public order. In subsequent years, as Mark Harrison has shown, crowds often assembled in cities such as Liverpool, Manchester, Bristol, and Norwich at the behest of members of the upper classes who sought to deploy them in ways that would affirm and embody solidarity among all groups in the

[4] E. P. Thompson, "The Moral Economy of the English Crowd in the Eighteenth Century," *Past and Present* 50 (1971): 76–136.

local community.[5] Here, too, one sees evidence of mass mobilization in urban settings that was not at all revolutionary.

Despite the examples just cited, one can argue that popular mobilization was increasingly associated with tendencies best described as liberal or egalitarian, pointing toward breaks with rather than reversions to the past. In so doing, one inevitably places ideology at the center of attention. Articulate criticism of existing conditions, combined with express belief in the necessity and the possibility of a better future, enabled grievances to become politically significant. Intellectuals could not whip up a sense of inequity out of thin air. Discontent had to be grounded in tangible aspects of daily life. But it had to take shape doctrinally if it was to become an operative force, capable of moving the discontented to act collectively.

Several outlooks, which partly overlapped and partly conflicted, indicated a set of urban beliefs that tended on the whole to promote not only discontent with the status quo but also a spirit of innovation. All of these doctrines were rooted in the eighteenth-century Enlightenment. Liberalism, which was most pronounced among solidly established members of the middle classes, came to the fore in documents such as "The Declaration of the Rights of Man and the Citizen," adopted by French members of the Constituent Assembly who met in Paris in 1789, and "The Basic Rights of the German People," adopted by the Frankfurt Parliament in 1849. Politically, these documents called for the sharing of governmental power between hereditary rulers and elected representatives and limitation of all such authority by means of written constitutions, which were to contain explicit guarantees of the civil rights of individuals. Such pleading reflected a desire to expand and secure freedom to express opinions and to learn about new ideas, freedom of a sort to which city dwellers were especially accustomed and attached.

Moving from the center of the spectrum to the left, one encounters the more egalitarian ideologies of popular sovereignty and democracy. Harking back to the thought of Jean-Jacques Rousseau, men such as the French Jacobins, their English admirer Thomas Paine, and the British Chartists of the 1830s and 1840s preached a kind of leveling that was broadly democratic, and sometimes – as in the case of the "terror" that beset Paris in the mid-1790s – quite illiberal. This leveling tendency, as George Rudé pointed out, became more and more pronounced among workers during the period between 1789 and 1848, revealing a percolation downward of democratic ideas that were first expressed by intellectuals.[6]

Political egalitarianism became intermixed with social and economic movements that pointed still further in the direction of lessening

---

[5] Harrison, *Crowds and History*, 27, 317.   [6] Rudé, *The Crowd in History*, 164–65.

9. A meeting of the Frankfurt Parliament in 1848. Elected representatives from over three dozen German states met in Frankfurt am Main between the spring of 1848 and the late winter of 1849 in order to draft a constitution for a united Germany. Although their debates included support for several political positions, the dominant one was moderate liberalism.

differences between privileged minorities and the majorities that enjoyed much less in the way of both power and wealth. Beginning with the thought and the agitation of the revolutionary François-Noël Babeuf during the 1790s, one can trace a rich history of socialist doctrine and endeavor in France that centered on Paris, where a highly visionary and prophetic form of social thought took shape in subsequent decades. Some of the men who expressed it – such as Henri de Saint-Simon and Charles Fourier – were much more intent on serving up designs for social utopias than they were in politics. But others sought to link their calls for public planning and ownership of the means of production with pursuit of power, whether by calling for peaceful reform or by calling for working-class revolution. Louis Blanc played a prominent part in the French capital in the late 1830s and the 1840s as a gradualist advocate of a system of national workshops that were intended to guarantee the "right to work" (i.e., full employment). Karl Marx, who along with many other émigrés from Central and Eastern Europe spent considerable time in Paris during these years, absorbed much from the thinking of socialists such as Blanc. In contrast, however, Marx developed a revolutionary theory according to which sharp conflicts among classes would result in accession to power by "proletarian" workers. This turn of events would in turn prepare the way for a transition to communism. Far less well known at the time than any of the other men discussed here, Marx deserves mention nonetheless as a symptomatic (and later extremely influential) contributor to a positive discourse of political and social upheaval – a discourse that thrived among networks of urban-based ideologists and would-be leaders of fellow city dwellers who stood on the lower rungs of the social hierarchy.

Some more reasons why: organizations and opportunities

City dwellers' discontents and their hopes for greater political and social justice had to be mobilized in order to produce significant impacts. Townspeople needed to become conscious of complaints that united them with other city dwellers, and they needed opportunities not only to think about but also to engage in collective action. Fortunately from the standpoint of proponents of such activity, not only dissatisfactions but also the will and the ability to seek to overcome them were greatly fostered by city life. Urban settings promoted mobilization to a high degree. They provided numerous spaces and places and encouraged the growth of numerous institutions in which displeasure with the social and political status quo could take shape and spread. What counted much more than either unhappiness or hope as such was the presence in cities of multiple opportunities for joining forces with fellow citizens with whom one could share grievances, with a view to seeking desired remedies. As historical sociologist Charles Tilly has argued repeatedly and persuasively, it was networks of urban solidarity rather than whatever traumatic consequences ensued from the process of urban growth that contributed most decisively to rebelliousness and what he calls "popular contention."[7] Not only in Britain but also elsewhere, it was not whatever disorienting experiences may have resulted from urbanization but instead the condition of urbanity, with its manifold possibilities for cooperation and networking among city dwellers, that lay behind collective protest.

Broadly speaking, one can point to cities as central sites for the emergence of what the German philosopher Jürgen Habermas famously

---

[7] See Tilly, *Popular Contention in Great Britain*, 30–32, 35–36, 144–45, 377–78.

identified as "the public sphere."[8] In his view, this process got under way in the eighteenth century. It arose in tandem with the accelerated growth of an urban society that was increasingly marked among its leading elements by prosperity, leisure, and the diffusion of information and opinion. Concentrations of wealth in densely populated areas, according to Habermas, went hand in hand with a wide variety of institutions in which sociability fostered the free exchange of ideas through open discussion. Such discourse pertained not only to group-centered affairs that concerned men largely as members of particular associations but also to "public" affairs more generally. It often entailed spirited criticism of established hierarchies and their powers, in contrast to which voluntary groups stood out by virtue of their openness and liberality. This criticism became increasingly widespread as a result of the parallel proliferation of newspapers and journals, in which public opinion was more and more influentially voiced.

Coffee-houses flourished during the eighteenth century both in British towns and in their counterparts on the continent, emerging as increasingly vital centers of a new urban sociability. They fostered not only contact with friends but also mixing with people from diverse circles and the cultivation of knowledge, and they thus encouraged critical thinking about the political and social status quo. London took the lead, boasting over 500 coffee-houses by mid-century. Other cities in England followed suit later in the century, and Scottish cities acquired them too after around 1800. In Paris, according to a contemporary observer, there were 600–700 in the 1780s. Cities in Central Europe had them as well, albeit in numbers somewhat lower than even their smaller populations would have suggested: sixty-four in Vienna in 1784, twelve in Berlin about the same time; and twenty in Hamburg in 1800.[9] Open to all who had the leisure to spend time and the means to spend money there, they mainly attracted members of the middle classes, but at least in England artisans and shopkeepers patronized them too. Coffee-houses thus encouraged a degree of social mixing that contrasted markedly with what took place in more formal associations, which often were limited to members of a particular profession, trade, or religion. Open-mindedness and a questioning spirit (i.e., "enlightenment") thrived in particular as a result of the omnipresence of newspapers – not only local ones but also, in many German cities, journals from foreign countries. Available for customers to read for free,

[8] See Jürgen Habermas, *The Structural Transformation of the Public Sphere*, trans. Thomas Burger (Cambridge, MA, 1989).
[9] On Central Europe, see Hans Erich Bödeker, "Das Kaffeehaus als Institution aufklärerischer Geselligkeit," in François, ed., *Sociabilité bourgeoise*, 65–80.

these publications vastly enhanced consumers' familiarity with the societies in which they lived. They also enabled them to engage in robust exchanges of opinion with fellow patrons. Discussions of current events touched on many subjects. Much of the conversation was nonpolitical, focusing on literature, the arts, commerce, and judicial proceedings, but by the 1780s opinions having to do with ways to improve government, which had been a staple of coffee-house culture in London for decades, became more and more widespread, in Paris and elsewhere.

Although the coffee-house was not itself an association, its physical and intellectual space fostered the formation of a rich array of other organizations. The leading historian of early modern towns in Britain, Peter Clark, has analyzed large numbers of these organizations – which flourished within coffee-houses and elsewhere as well – under the overall rubric of "club" life. He and R. A. Houston estimate that during the eighteenth century as many as 12,000 clubs were established in English towns, that another 3,000 were established in Scottish ones, and about 750 more were founded in Wales.[10] These organizations focused on a wide range of activities, some purely recreational, some philanthropic, others literary and philosophical. But many also fostered debates about political conditions and possibilities. In particular, members of literary and philosophical clubs and also members of debating societies sought to acquire and spread enlightenment in ways that pointed toward critical assessments of the status quo. Such groups grew greatly in importance in the early nineteenth century. As literary and philosophical societies spread, working-class versions of these societies, known as "mechanics institutes" came onto the scene as well. In Britain, they numbered over 100 by 1826 and over 300 by 1841. Combining emphasis on public improvement with pursuit of respectability through self-improvement, the mechanics institutes were far from revolutionary. They helped nonetheless to raise workers' desires and demands for influence in the area of public affairs.

What about the continent? France similarly experienced an upsurge of associational activity, which took shape quite rapidly after about 1770 in the form of reading groups, philosophical societies, and other clubs, many of whose members pursued broadly political objectives. Later, although the rise of clubs tapered off during the conservative Restoration after 1815, it resumed during the years between 1830 and 1848. Groups known as *cercles*, in which middle-class men (but not women) mixed on a far more egalitarian basis than had been possible in aristocratic salons, emerged on a wide scale, increasingly tending to support liberal and even

[10] Peter Clark and R. A. Houston, "Culture and Leisure, 1799–1840," in Peter Clark, ed., *The Cambridge Urban History of Britain*, vol. II (Cambridge, 2000), 587.

radical causes. Meanwhile, in Germany, coffee-houses in Hamburg functioned as recruiting stations for the Hamburg Patriotic Association, and there as well as in Vienna and other cities coffee-houses served as meeting places for members of masonic lodges. These men (like masons in England and France) stressed both the need for overall enlightenment and the more specifically civic values of free debate, tolerance, and equality. Later, during the 1840s, coffee-houses such as the Rote Stube (Red Room) in Berlin became gathering places for liberals and radicals, whose associations helped to prepare the way for the revolutions that broke out in Central Europe as well as France in 1848.

A specifically working-class sociability thrived in a setting where, as in the coffee-house, drinking served as the ostensible *raison d'être*. Particularly well studied in the case of Paris, the café offered not only coffee but also wine, beer, and other alcoholic beverages. It too provided a place in which to combine conviviality and concerns about public issues. Drink shops there, which numbered 3,000 in 1789 and 4,500 by the late 1840s, were not only places of boisterous enjoyment but also "cauldrons of conversation and thought," enabling Paris to function as "both a center of revolutions and a birthplace of modern leisure and helping to give rise to both republicanism and socialism."[11] During the 1790s, a "revolutionary proletarian café sensibility" found expression in works by writer-agitators such as Jean-Paul Marat, the editor of the radical newspaper, *L'ami du peuple*. It provided a running commentary on debates in places such as the café Le Procope, a central meeting place for Parisian sans-culottes and a staging area for one of the several massacres through which they asserted their political power. Reading of similar newspapers in cafés in later years helped to fan dormant sparks of radicalism back into life, making cafés centers of political and social protest between about 1820 and the mid-century revolution. Particularly just before and during 1848, café-based festivity assumed political dimensions of great importance. Working-class habitués translated egalitarian doctrines into easily comprehensible songs in which they celebrated proletarian comrades who drank together while raising toasts to international unity. One singer prophesied a future in which all would enjoy "bread, work, and good wine." More militantly, at the outset of the June Days, café-goers played leading roles in stirring up protest against the government's plans to close the National Workshops, and during the violence that ensued many cafés stayed open so as to provide refreshment for the insurgents.

In London, too, taverns functioned as breeding grounds for groups whose members sought to discredit people in positions of political power.

---

[11] Haine, *The World of the Paris Café*, 1, 2.

Informal debating clubs, such as the Athenian Lyceum and the Robin Hood Debating Society, and a multitude of so-called "free and easy societies" met there in order to combine hard drinking with political singing, ridicule hurled at the political elite, and serious discussion of possible reforms. The radical leader John Cartwright, for example, used the Crown and Anchor Tavern in 1817 as the initial venue for organizing a convention of about seventy fellow radicals that launched a nationwide petitioning campaign in favor of universal manhood suffrage.

Against the urban backdrop sketched here, a whole host of additional organizations–some of them referred to in the first part of this chapter – also emerged. These too were quintessentially urban. Whether one is talking about the Society of Supporters of the Bill of Rights that was formed in the 1760s in order to bolster John Wilkes's efforts to secure a seat for the borough of Westminster in Parliament, the pro-revolutionary London Correspondence Society as well as the Jacobin clubs during the French Revolution, or the "political unions" that emerged in Birmingham and elsewhere in the early 1830s, one is talking about organizations that arose in city centers. So too with regard to the French Society of the Seasons, the London Working Men's Association, and other organizations that were established later in the 1830s and in the 1840s in places such as Lyon and Manchester for the purpose of asserting the political and economic rights of manual laborers as well as members of the middle classes. The German scene was particularly noteworthy for the presence of artisanal organizations. Members of such groups agitated at meetings in a number of cities in 1848 – among them Cologne, Mainz, Hamburg, and Frankfurt am Main – with a view to pressing political leaders (such as the men who were meeting simultaneously in Frankfurt in order to write a constitution for a unified Germany) to provide protection for endangered crafts. Also in 1848, the German city of Cologne experienced the growth of a Workers' Association. Seen by its founders as an extension of the Communist League that had recently been established in London and Brussels, it provided a forum for Karl Marx when he returned to his native country in the spring of that year in order to help organize the forces of proletarian revolution. Whether or not such groups took shape in coffee-houses or taverns, their growth was rooted in the same public sphere in which coffee-house and café culture and the social life it promoted also arose.

The mobilization that occurred among members of such organizations drew important strength from another institution, referred to in passing above in connection with coffee-houses and cafés: the periodical press, which became an increasingly significant force on the urban scene. In an environment of growing literacy and declining censorship, newspapers and magazines served as the essential signposts and channels of communication within the public sphere. Building on the examples of magazines printed in London under titles such as the *Spectator* and the *Tatler*, which began to appear in the early eighteenth century, publishers there were, by about 1780, producing 160 periodicals aimed at a general public, many of which appeared daily. Between 1801 and 1832, annual sales of newspapers almost doubled, rising from 16 million to 30 million. The best known and most radical publications were weeklies, such as William Cobbett's *Political Register* (starting in 1806) and Richard Carlisle's *The Republican* (starting in 1817), but these journals represented only the tips of large icebergs of constant commentary, often critical, on current conditions. The *Journal de Paris*, founded in 1777, was selling 5,000 copies each day by 1782 and more than twice as many in 1789. Far fewer newspapers and magazines appeared in the French than in the British capital, but their number – already thirty-five in 1780 – was to increase sharply, rising by the end of 1789 to 169. During the French Revolution, periodical publications increased in number exponentially, both reflecting and intensifying the politicization of French life. At least 1,500 of them, mostly originating in Paris, appeared between 1789 and 1800, as extremist journals such as the *Révolutions de Paris* took their places next to the more widely circulated *Journal des débats* and the *Moniteur universel*. Half a century later, a legacy of mass readership persisted, with the daily circulation of nearly two dozen newspapers amounting to nearly twice that of their London counterparts. The one with the largest circulation, *Le siècle*, stood for reform within a monarchical system, but others, such as *Le national* and *La réforme*, advocated republicanism.[12] In German-speaking countries, the leading newspaper of a general sort in the eighteenth century was the Swiss *Neue Zürcher Zeitung*, founded in 1780, but many other papers appeared elsewhere too, albeit on a much smaller scale. Although newspapers that reflected distinctly partisan views did not get started in a big way until after the middle of the nineteenth century, some did emerge before then, among them the *Rheinische Zeitung*, which Karl Marx edited in Cologne during its brief lifetime between 1842 and 1843.

Popular mobilization was fostered not only by urban organizations and publications but also by other aspects of the urban scene. Some cities were particularly prone to protest activities by virtue of their status of capitals. As seats of national or state governments, they contained spaces and institutions of high value from both a strategic and a symbolic standpoint,

---

[12] See André-Jean Tudesq, "Le journal: Lieu et lien de la société bourgeoise en France pendant la première moitié du XIXe siècle," in François, ed., *Sociabilité bourgeoise*, 261–74.

thus tempting protesters to concentrate their energies there for maximum effect. The convergence between capitals and revolutions became most clearly apparent in Paris. Because of its administrative centrality in France and because of its stock of national political institutions, it was no accident that the revolutions of 1789–92, of 1830, and of 1848 – all of which resulted in regime changes – began there. Elsewhere, the linkage between capital-city status and revolution was less clear-cut. On the continent, the revolutionary potential of capital cities other than Paris was not realized until the very end of the period discussed here. But it did come to the fore, not only in Berlin and Vienna but also in lesser capitals, such as Munich and Milan. Britain did not experience any revolutions, and so the question of London's role as a revolutionary center does not really present itself. Still, London's importance as a center of radical politics cannot be denied.

Not only Paris but also other cities experienced popular insurgencies both because protesters regarded them as sites where insurrectionary activities were likely to yield maximum gains and also because of their vulnerability. Despite attempts by baroque city planners and their successors to fashion cityscapes marked by order and regularity, life on city streets still largely eluded governmental control. The crookedness and narrowness of many thoroughfares, paved as many of them were with cobblestones and crowded as many of them were with carts and wagons, made it rather easy for urban radicals to erect the barricades that became such widespread symbols of urban revolt, particularly during the latter part of the period under discussion here. The control of urban space enjoyed by the city dwellers who built and fought from behind them, although only temporary, resulted also from institutional weaknesses that beset the traditional forces of order. Governing authorities suffered not only from a perceived lack of legitimacy but also, as William L. Langer pointed out long ago, from a lack of – or at least hesitancy to use – effective force in order to impose their will before matters got out of hand.[13] Stridently denounced by their radical opponents for their supposed repressiveness, the men in charge of major cities where popular upheavals erupted between the mid-eighteenth and the mid-nineteenth centuries thus found themselves repeatedly on the defensive.

We can thus see how a multitude of factors worked together to make cities sources and focal points of a wide range of protest activities. Insurrections and riots in particular, but also more peaceful agitation for political change by middle-class liberals – whether in newspapers, in coffeehouses, or in assembly halls – contributed to an image of the city as a

---

[13] Langer, "The Pattern of Urban Revolution in 1848," 476–77.

center of public unruliness. Dealing with the whole range of responses to this perception would carry us far beyond the bounds of this book, into the history of political change at the level of nation states. In the following chapter, we shall instead consider a variety of specifically urban-oriented efforts to improve city life, for which a variety of protests provided an important part of the overall backdrop.

BIBLIOGRAPHY

Aminzade, Ronald. *Ballots and Barricades: Class Formation and Republican Politics in France, 1830–1871.* Princeton, 1993.

Belchem, John, ed. *Popular Politics, Riot, and Labour: Essays in Liverpool History, 1790–1940.* Liverpool, 1992.

Bezucha, Robert. *The Lyon Uprising of 1834: Social and Political Conflict in the Early July Monarchy.* Cambridge, MA, 1974.

Bossenga, Gail. *The Politics of Privilege: Old Regime and Revolution in Lille.* New York, 1991.

Briggs, Asa, ed. *Chartist Studies.* New York, 1967.

Cage, R. A., ed. *The Working Class in Glasgow, 1750–1914.* London, 1987.

Clark, Peter. *British Clubs and Societies, 1580–1800: The Origins of an Associational World.* Oxford, 2000.

Corbin, Alain, Jacqueline Lalouette, and Michele Riot-Sarcey, eds. *Femmes dans la cité, 1815–1871.* Grane, 1997.

Forrest, Alan. *Society and Politics in Revolutionary Bordeaux.* New York, 1975.

Foster, John. *Class Struggle and the Industrial Revolution: Early Industrial Capitalism in Three English Towns.* London, 1974.

François, Étienne, ed. *Sociabilité bourgeoise en France, en Allemagne et en Suisse (1750–1850).* Paris, 1986.

Fraser, Derek. *Urban Politics in Victorian England: The Structure of Politics in Victorian Cities.* Leicester, 1976.

Garrioch, David. *The Making of Revolutionary Paris.* Berkeley and Los Angeles, 2002.

Haine, W. Scott. *The World of the Paris Café: Sociability Among the French Working Class.* Baltimore and London, 1996.

Harrison, Mark. *Crowds and History: Mass Phenomena in English Towns, 1790–1835.* New York, 1988.

Harsin, Jill. *Barricades: The War of the Streets in Revolutionary Paris, 1830–1848.* New York, 2002.

Hone, J. Ann. *For the Sake of Truth: Radicalism in London, 1796–1821.* Oxford, 1982.

Hummel, Karl-Joseph. *München in der Revolution von 1848/49.* Göttingen, 1987.

Kramer, Lloyd S. *Threshold of a New World: Intellectuals and the Exile Experience in Paris, 1830–1848.* Ithaca, 1988.

Langer, William L. "The Pattern of Urban Revolution in 1848." In Langer, *Explorations in Crisis: Papers on International History,* ed. Carl E. Schorske and Elizabeth Schorske. Cambridge, MA, 1969.

McDougall, Mary Lynn. "Consciousness and Community: The Workers of Lyon, 1830–1850." *Journal of Social History* 12 (1978): 129–45.

Melton, James Van Horn. *The Rise of the Public in Enlightenment Europe.* Cambridge, 2001.

Merriman, John. *The Margins of City Life: Explorations on the French Urban Frontier, 1815–1851.* New York, 1991.

The Red City: Limoges and the French Nineteenth Century. New York, 1985.

Morris, Robert J. *Class, Sect, and Party: The Making of the British Middle Class: Leeds, 1820–1850.* New York, 1990.

Pickering, Paul. *Chartism and the Chartists in Manchester and Salford.* New York, 1995.

Rudé, George. *The Crowd in History.* New York, 1964.

The Crowd in the French Revolution. Oxford, 1959.

Paris and London in the Eighteenth Century: Studies in Popular Protest. New York, 1973.

Sheehan, James J. "Liberalism and the City in 19th-Century Germany." *Past and Present* 51 (1971): 116–137.

Stearns, Peter N. "Patterns of Industrial Strike Activity in France During the July Monarchy." *American Historical Review* 70 (1965): 371–94.

Tilly, Charles. *The Contentious French.* Cambridge, MA, 1986.

Popular Contention in Britain, 1758–1834. Cambridge, MA, 1995.

Tilly, Charles, Louise Tilly, and Richard Tilly. *The Rebellious Century, 1830–1930.* Cambridge, MA, 1975.

Tilly, Charles, and Lynn Hollen Lees. "The People of June." In *Revolution and Reaction: 1848 and the Second French Republic,* ed. Roger Price. New York, 1975.

Traugott, Mark. "Capital Cities and Revolution." *Social Science History* 19 (1995): 147–68.

4   Pursuits of urban improvement

Starting in the later 1820s, an information revolution transformed awareness of urban social problems. Statistics combined with social reporting
revealed with shocking clarity troubling aspects of city life. C. Turner
Thackrah, a physician in the industrial city of Leeds, contributed to this
development, if only in a small way, in a book in which he documented the
awful toll taken there by urban conditions on the health of city dwellers.
He wrote, "We may say that every day of the year is carried to the grave
the corpse of an individual whom nature would have long preserved in
health and vigour; every day we see sacrificed to the artificial state of society one, and sometimes two victims, whom the destinies of nature would
have spared."[1] Such statements clearly indicated a belief in the need
for remedial action. Although Thackrah himself focused on the need to
reduce pollutants in the air breathed by workers in the flax trade and
to combat intemperance, the discourse of which his writing was a part
pointed increasingly toward the urgent necessity of drastically improving
the urban environment.

Not all observers of the city painted so somber a picture. In 1843, a
London-based Congregationalist clergyman, Robert Vaughan, expressed
a much more optimistic view of urban prospects. While he recognized the existence of bad conditions and behaviors, he firmly believed
that cities fostered progressive action among their inhabitants, and he
applauded the ways in which "voluntary combinations of the virtuous in
the cause of purity, humanity, and general improvement" had arisen in
cities. No doubt with efforts such as the public health movements in mind,
he believed that the growth of civil society and local self-government
would permit cities to solve whatever problems arose in the course of their
expansion.[2] Vaughan was a Christian liberal, who believed that good will,

[1] C. Turner Thackrah, *The Effects of the Principal Arts, Trades, and Professions, and of Civic
States and Habits of Living, on Health and Longevity: With a Particular Reference to the Trades
and Manufactures of Leeds* (London, 1831), 3–5, 37ff., 84–85, 113–14.
[2] Robert Vaughan, *The Age of Great Cities: Or, Modern Society Viewed in Its Relation to
Intelligence, Morals, and Religion* (London, 1843), 296–98.

religious piety, and moral sensibility operating under conditions of free-dom were equal to the challenges posed by urban growth. Still, exposés of the sort written not only by Thackrah but also by many others inevitably called into question Vaughan's apparent satisfaction. It would take many years and it would require public as well as private intervention for his optimism to be validated.

As medical doctors, clergymen, philanthropists, and government offi-cials thought about how to deal with the repellent conditions and behav-iors that they condemned, they had various, rather limited strategies at their disposal. Governments in Europe between 1815 and 1848 were fun-damentally conservative. They sought to re-establish social discipline and the rule of elites after the turmoil of the French Revolution and the Napoleonic years. They did not have much money to spend, and the theories of Adam Smith recommending laissez-faire or non-intervention in markets enjoyed great support in increasingly influential sectors of society. Poverty was generally accepted as a mark of the human condi-tion, which could be overcome in individual cases by the lucky and the competent, but certainly not by the mass of the population. Adminis-trators generally believed that they could not and should not intervene massively to change social circumstances, and they decisively rejected the programs proposed by French radicals in their pursuit of equality. In the first half of the nineteenth century, medical, economic, and polit-ical theories gave inadequate guidance to those worrying about cities, and European engineers had not yet developed effective technologies of sanitation for high-density living. Before 1850, responses to the urban challenge were limited intellectually and practically. We shall survey in this chapter four clusters of responses: architectural approaches; reli-gious and philanthropic approaches; institution building; and public health reform and planning. Despite the variety among these efforts, they all shared one feature in common: inability to master the difficul-ties that had arisen as a result of the rapid and uncontrolled growth that had occurred in European cities since the mid-eighteenth century. More effective answers to urban questions would have to await the years after 1850.

Royal avenues

Power can be expressed in many ways, but the use of architecture to signify authority and superiority is a familiar tactic of governments of many sorts. Consider the size and placement of state buildings in Washington, DC along the Mall. Urban design to impress citizens emerged well before the early nineteenth century. Already in the course of the seventeenth and eighteenth centuries, European monarchs used palaces and other structures to enhance their prestige. One can point in this connection to the imposing layouts of streets and buildings that emerged in large measure as a result of directives by Louis XIV during the late seventeenth century in Versailles, just outside Paris, and to similar albeit less imposing schemes that took shape later in Potsdam, just outside Berlin, under the influence of Prussian monarchs. Lesser rulers also sought to place their imprints on the towns in which they lived, the small city of Karlsruhe having served as a particularly good example of what historians often refer to as "Baroque" planning, which sought to project images of grandeur and power.

Aesthetic solutions were a favored response to the problems of growing capital cities by monarchs, who had sufficient money and political power to force change in patterns of land use in cities where they resided. Both in Britain and on the continent, royal sponsorship of planning in capital cities led to efforts to implement grand designs for majestic spaces in urban centers. Imposing ensembles of buildings, streets, and squares would bear witness to an ongoing determination to substitute organized splendor for chaotic ugliness and to do so in a way that would add to the luster and the prestige of the sovereigns.

The first projects of this sort were launched in Paris under the aegis of Napoleon Bonaparte early in the century's first decade, shortly after he had seized power and established an imperial regime. While Napoleon fostered practical measures that pertained either to the provision or the control of water – constructing canals and underground aqueducts that more than tripled the amount of water brought into the city and several embankments that helped to prevent flooding – his most symbolically charged and historically significant contributions occurred on dry ground. An open area where King Louis XVI had been beheaded in 1793 (known since 1792 as "la Place de la Révolution") was expanded and renamed "la Place de la Concorde." Toward the north, along the Rue Royale, Napoleon ordered construction of the Church of the Madeleine, for which he chose the neoclassical design himself. Looking northwest from another side, down the already grand Avenue of the Champs-Élysées, he planned at first to place at the far end a statue of an elephant in order to recall the ancient conqueror Hannibal but then decided on a massive Arc de Triomphe (1806–36) in order to celebrate his own victories. Meanwhile, in 1801, he had authorized construction of a new avenue, the Rue de Rivoli, in order to link the Place de la Concorde to the Palais-Royal. Lined with buildings of uniform height and continuous balconies and accompanied by other new streets in its vicinity, it served as the nucleus for the most important achievement in the area of architectural development in Paris since the seventeenth century.

The Prince of Wales, who had become British regent in 1811 for the mentally ill King George III, sponsored an ambitious building project of his own that got under way well before he became King George IV in 1820. Desirous of embellishing London in ways that would rival Napoleon's plans for Paris, he worked closely with the architect John Nash for the purpose of redesigning much of the area between St. James Park and the much larger Marylebone Park – land that either belonged to the Crown already or was purchased by the Crown so as to permit realization of Nash's plans. A new avenue, named Regent Street, began in front of Carlton House, the Regent's London residence. Lined by shops, offices, and houses, some of which Nash designed himself, it proceeded north through Piccadilly Circus, and after making a graceful curve it terminated at the base of a vast new park, Regent's Park, which also bore Nash's imprint. Lined by upscale residences on one side and a new canal on the other, this creation as well as the new thoroughfare by which it could be reached testified both to the ambitions and to the power of the ruler after whom it was named. The king and his favorite architect also had plans to build another Regent Street. It was to link Trafalgar Square with Bloomsbury, where the British Museum was being built, but these plans fell through after the king's death in 1830.

Crown Prince Ludwig of the reigning Wittelsbach dynasty in Bavaria, who became King Ludwig I in 1825, ordered royal building projects of a sort quite popular among numerous rulers of independent principalities in politically fragmented Germany, who competed with one another by using architecture to burnish their prestige. Between 1812 (while still the crown prince) and his forced abdication in 1848, Ludwig strove with great success to enhance the already considerable charm of Munich, the Bavarian capital. The architects Leo von Klenze and Friedrich von Gärtner oversaw the planning for a new avenue, named after the monarch, that ran north from the city center for almost half a mile. Bounded by midcentury at both ends by monuments that commemorated feats of Bavarian soldiers, it was lined not only by a new headquarters for the war ministry but also by other newly constructed buildings that proclaimed the virtues of the Bavarian state in times of peace as well as of war: the Bavarian State Library, the Ludwig Church, and the main building of the University. Klenze worked at Ludwig's behest to improve the city elsewhere too, particularly in the area around a Royal Square just to the west of the Ludwig Street. For this part of the city, Klenze designed the Glyptothek as a museum for the king's collection of sculptures and the Propyläen, which served as a gateway at the square's west end. He further enhanced

10. A royal avenue in Munich. The Ludwigstrasse and the buildings along it were developed in Munich in the 1830s and 1840s with a view to enhancing the image of King Ludwig I of Bavaria as well as that of the Bavarian state.

Ludwig's image both as a patron of the arts and as a champion of the virtues of his people by conceiving of a massive statue of a female figure that represented Bavaria. It arose in front of a Bavarian Hall of Fame, also commissioned by Ludwig, construction of which began in 1843. Meanwhile, Gärtner supervised important projects in the capital elsewhere as well.

Construction projects of this type, although they stood out by virtue of their scale and their aesthetic pretensions, had little effect on the city as a whole and on the lives of most of its inhabitants. Planning of a more practical sort, which would depart much more radically from leaving the shape of the urban environment to the unregulated play of market forces, was therefore called for in the view of an increasing number of reformers. They believed that construction of cities worthy of their inhabitants' affection and loyalty entailed going far beyond – and beneath – the relatively superficial projects that were designed to boost the reputations of royal rulers. But before we consider some of their efforts, let us turn first to another response to perceived problems of urban disorder that appealed to, among many others, hereditary monarchs.

Piety and philanthropy

Not only monarchs, many of whom sought after 1815 to cement an "alliance between throne and altar," but numerous others believed in the need for a reawakening of religious faith. Efforts to master the challenges posed both by the supposed immorality of individuals and by political revolt frequently reflected a strong belief among frightened conservatives that chaotic and destabilizing conduct required active intervention by agents of God. Without an intensification of their ministry in urban areas, growing numbers of city dwellers would inevitably tend to stray from Christianity in ways that would result in selfishness, crime, and revolutionary upheaval. This message emerged quite clearly from a sermon preached and published in 1844 by the Anglican clergyman James Shergold Boone, minister of St. John's Church in the Paddington district of London. "The very extent of edifices, and the very collection of vast masses of human beings into one spot, humanity remaining what it is," he complained, "must be fraught with moral infection." Cities, he continued, were "the centers and theatres of human ambition, human cupidity, human pleasure," and they naturally tended to taint and defile their inhabitants' character. In these places, only energetic campaigns to bring back the influence formerly enjoyed by churchmen would make possible the restoration of decency and order.[3]

Such anxiety, although it contrasted sharply with the optimism voiced by Boone's fellow clergyman Vaughan, reflected and contributed to a movement of the sort Vaughan welcomed. In Britain and elsewhere as well, the first half of the nineteenth century witnessed widespread agitation in favor of a religious revival in urban areas. Feeling themselves to be on the defensive not only because of the evidence of anticlericalism during the era of the French Revolution but also as a result of plummeting church attendance in the burgeoning towns, churchmen and their supporters made pronounced efforts to reassert their presence in their countries' urban areas.

The mixture of challenges and responses in urban England may be described as follows. Leaders of the Church of England felt apprehensive not only over the general trends referred to above but also over the rising numbers of men and women who chose to belong to dissenting chapels, rather than to the established Church. These congregations consisted most frequently of Methodists, who had broken away in the late eighteenth century from the religious establishment and had gone on to make their most significant gains in urban areas. In response, leaders

---

[3] James Shergold Boone, *The Need of Christianity to Great Cities* (London, 1844), 1, 3–15.

of the Church of England mounted a vigorous counteroffensive. A central part of their program for asserting and defending the established faith pointed toward the construction of new church buildings, in order to accommodate townspeople for whom there was insufficient space in existing places of worship. In 1818, Parliament passed a Church Building Act, which provided funds for erecting thirty-three churches in London and sixty-three elsewhere in England. Because the perceived need was greatest in the large towns, expenditure there was disproportionately large. Consequently, the number of churches in Birmingham more than tripled during the first half of the century. In Leeds, between 1831 and 1851, the number of church buildings rose from twenty-one to thirty-six. As a result, the number of inhabitants there per Anglican church fell from 6,000 to 5,000. At the same time, there was great pressure for a revival of faith, with a view to ensuring that parishioners would fill the spaces that were opening up for them. At one level, the period witnessed a vigorous effort to promote Sunday Schools. By 1850, they enrolled about 2 million children, most of whom came from the working classes. In Birmingham, in the 1830s, approximately 40 percent of children from working-class families attended such schools. At a loftier level, prominent Anglicans sought through the Oxford Movement (named after Oxford University, where the movement began) to strengthen the Church via re-emphasis of traditional liturgy and ritual, which in their view had been dangerously undermined by the forces of liberal rationalism. The clergyman John Henry Newman, who had come from a middle-class family in London before going to Oxford to study, stood out in this campaign, but many others joined him.

Although competition by religious dissenters as well as urban growth and declining rates of attendance at places of worship seemed less significant on the continent, here too the one-third of a century after 1815 witnessed determined efforts to re-Christianize urban areas. In Germany as in Britain, established churches – whether in the mostly Protestant north or in the mostly Catholic south – received strong support from men who regarded organized religion as a primary means of buttressing the political and social status quo. Monarchs such as Friedrich Wilhelm III in Prussia and Ludwig I in Bavaria favored theological conservative clerics not only in their countries' churches but also in their universities, in part out of a conviction that a strengthening of religious orthodoxy would benefit hierarchical authority more generally. Their reigns coincided with the naming of the orthodox Protestant Ernst Wilhelm Hengstenberg to a chair of theology in Berlin and of Joseph von Görres, a publicist who had converted to Catholicism, to a professorship of history in Munich. Here, a conservative circle of intellectuals soon formed around the new arrival.

In both cities, there was also, as in British cities, an impressive process of church construction. Much of what arose in Berlin reflected the designs of the noted architect Karl Friedrich Schinkel, who contributed significantly to other building projects during these years. Not surprisingly, one of the more impressive buildings to be built in Munich during the period was the richly decorated Ludwig Church, which conveniently referred to the Bavarian monarch as well as to his patron saint.

France too experienced a religious revival, particularly during the years between 1815 and 1830. To be sure, although a number of new churches were built in Paris, the great wave of church building did not begin until around the middle of the century. (Thereafter, during a period of four decades, 310 churches were constructed in the diocese of Bordeaux.[4]) But the coronation in 1824 of a king, Charles X, who sought, with the support of a conservative pope, to reinvigorate the idea of a divine-right monarchy was both preceded and followed by growing numbers of men who entered into the secular clergy and of men and women who entered into religious orders. Bordeaux, for example, witnessed the establishment in 1820 of the Sisters of the Holy Family, which subsequently served as an umbrella for groups such as the Sisters of Saint Joseph, the Ladies of the Immaculate Conception, and the Sisters of Hope. Lyon experienced comparable developments, with the reconstitution after 1815 of the Sisters of Saint Charles, the Ursulines, and the Carmelites for women and, in the 1830s, the return of organizations for priests that had been banned during the Revolution, among them the Jesuits and the Dominicans.

Discussion of religious activism leads to the subject of philanthropy, to which Vaughan alluded when he referred to "voluntary combinations of the virtuous." Although religiously based charity reflected in many instances genuine desires to do good works for their own sake, neither it nor other philanthropic efforts resulted from purely disinterested altruism. Charitable voluntarism functioned in the urban arena, it must be emphasized here, in no small part as an enlightened means of doing battle with the perceived forces of destruction that Boone denounced and many others feared. It embodied a soft form of social discipline, through which generosity toward people who suffered and consequently misbehaved in urban settings would encourage among them an ethic of personal and social responsibility and of conservatism. Although the concept of "social control" has been much over-used by historians who seek to detect nefarious purposes in the minds of upper- and middle-class people who sought to enhance their reputations for righteousness through

---

[4] Gérard Cholvy, *Etre Chrétien en France aux XIXe-siècle, 1790–1914* (Paris, 1997), 66.

"good works," charity clearly functioned in part as an element of a broad strategy of combating social disorder.

Urban philanthropy thrived not only on a religious but also on a secular basis. Its institutions served as highly visible components of a vast array of voluntary associations that operated independently from (although, in the case of charitable organizations, often in collaboration with) religious organizations. Demonstrating the vitality of what has come to be known as "civil society," they functioned as essential foundations for the "public sphere" discussed in Chapter 3. Associational activity among activists comprised not only efforts to bring about political change but also nonpolitical attempts to ameliorate many of the grievances that underlay discontent, especially among city dwellers of the lower classes. Such efforts, it must be emphasized, occurred predominantly in urban areas. It was here that critical masses of educated men and women, information, and wealth intersected in ways that stimulated the most vigorous efforts to address social problems by concerned citizens.

Philanthropically minded men and women were particularly visible in Britain. A leading politician with strong ties to the Evangelical movement in the Church of England, William Wilberforce, joined forces with the Bishop of Durham and others who shared their religious convictions to take the lead in establishing the Society for Bettering the Condition and Improving the Comforts of the Poor. Founded in 1795, it provided soup and other nourishment for the indigent in times of need, but it also sought to base philanthropy on a rational footing, giving benefits only to the well-behaved and trying to show recipients of aid how to feed themselves as healthily and economically as possible. As Donna Andrew has put it, "An added advantage of the power such charity would give the rich was that they could use their influence to educate the willful and ignorant poor into becoming providential, self-regarding, and morally responsible adult-citizens."[5]

Numerous additional initiatives that stemmed from religious impulses followed in later years. The 1820s and 1830s saw a proliferation of "visiting societies," which originated most frequently under religious auspices. Consisting of men (and increasingly of women) who went into the homes of the poor in order both to determine their needs and to offer advice, these associations sought to combine material help with moral reform. Many of them came together in 1843 in London to form the Metropolitan Visiting and Relief Association, a basic purpose of which was to remove "the moral causes which create or aggravate want; to encourage prudence, industry, and cleanliness . . . and to promote kindly feelings

---

[5] Andrew, *Philanthropy and Police*, 176.

between those classes of society which are kept so far asunder by the difference of their worldly conditions."[6] In addition to the Sunday Schools mentioned above, religious groups supported the establishment of thousands of additional schools, many of them located in manufacturing towns and dedicated to the education of working-class children on a charitable basis. (At this time, in Britain, education was not yet provided by public authorities free of charge.) Finally, one must also note the leading role of churchmen in founding refuges, asylums, and orphanages for needy children. Andrew Reed, who preached in a Congregational chapel in East London between 1811 and 1861, established six charities in the metropolis, among them the East London Orphan Asylum and Working School, the London Orphan Asylum, and an Infant Orphan Asylum, the last of which accommodated 600 children under the age of seven. Although Reed opposed the introduction of denominational teaching, his supporters disagreed, insisting that the orphans be taught the catechism of the Church of England.

In other cases, charitable activity owed more to secular impulses than religious ones, but the overall objective of encouraging social harmony remained central. London saw the establishment in 1818 of a Society for the Suppression of Mendicity. Stemming largely from the efforts of secular radicals, among them the laissez-faire liberal economist and member of Parliament David Ricardo, the Society sought to reduce impersonal transfers from the rich to the poor, substituting for them direct gifts that would, in the words of Michael Roberts, serve "as a moralizing force in the lives of both givers and receivers."[7] The ultimate goal pursued by members of the group was to strengthen "that good feeling, which is so important to maintain amongst all Classes of Society." Subsequently, a four-decade period between 1820 and 1860 saw a sharp upswing of openings of specialist hospitals, most of them funded by charitable donations. One of the best known of these institutions, the Great Ormond Street Hospital for Children, resulted from a campaign led by a famous literary proponent of such "good feeling," Charles Dickens. Elsewhere too, charitable activity flourished. An 1842 handbook for visitors to Manchester by Benjamin Love contained entire chapters on "Benevolent Institutions" and on "Education and Educational Institutions," many of which reflected charitable as well as educational impulses. An article by the Manchester clergyman Robert Lamb that appeared in *Fraser's Magazine* in 1853 congratulated the citizenry of his home town for establishing not only infirmaries and hospitals, among them one for orphans, but also schools and "a Library of 10,000 volumes for the free use of the people."

---

[6] Quoted in Owen, *English Philanthropy*, 141.   [7] Roberts, *Making English Morals*, 104.

We are particularly well informed about middle-class life in early nineteenth-century Leeds. R. J. Morris has shown clearly how charitable activity arose there out of anxieties not just about poverty but also about begging, disease, and the threat of political radicalism. Not only the founding in 1804 of a House of Recovery a few years after a typhus epidemic, but also the later establishment of a Mechanics Institution (for the purpose of promoting adult education among workers) arose out of desires to improve the overall health of that city, as did the provision of soup kitchens and of garden allotments for workers. In Liverpool, Birmingham, Glasgow, and a host of other cities, comparable activity took place on a similar scale.

As regards France and Germany, urban-based philanthropy has left much less of an imprint on the historical record than in the case of Britain. Partly because urbanization still lagged in these countries, less in the way of organized charities seems to have marked the life of their cities – at least in ways that might have led scholars to pay attention to them. If one looks, however, here too one can find indications of charitable activity that stemmed both from religious and from more worldly impulses.

Among Frenchmen and French women, members of religious organizations and religiously inclined individuals played quite prominent parts in helping others. Voluntary sisterhoods in Bordeaux and Lyon of the sort referred to above, which became increasingly numerous after 1815, cared for the sick, supported schools, and established orphanages. Places of refuge designed for homeless children grew in number with increasing rapidity in the 1830s and 1840s, often supported by members of Catholic women's religious congregations but also by Protestants, as in the case of the Protestant Beneficent Society in Bordeaux, whose leaders worked with municipal officials there to establish an asylum for children in 1834. Various charities that operated under the direction of Catholic women in Paris focused throughout this period on providing help for poor females who were pregnant or who had infant children. In 1833 eight Catholic laymen in Paris, in response to charges by socialists that Christians did not care about social problems, founded the Society of Saint Vincent de Paul for the purpose of visiting the poor and sick and distributing alms. The Society went on, by 1846, to extend its work to include soup kitchens, holiday camps, and a bank where workers could get bonuses if they saved money there to pay for rent. Other Parisian Catholics began in the 1840s to take up housing problems. Some of them came together under the leadership of Count Armand de Melun, who in 1845 established the journal *Les Annales de la Charité* and in 1847 a Society of Charitable Economy.

What about Germany? Religiously based charitable work in an urban setting can be seen quite clearly in the case of Protestant Hamburg. Two individuals stood out. One was Amalie Sieveking, a pious daughter of a prosperous merchant. She played a pioneering role in drawing women into philanthropic activity via establishment in 1832 of a Women's Association for Care of the Poor and the Sick. Her group combined material assistance, such as the provision of low-cost housing, with efforts to spread the Evangelical faith among the people they sought to assist. While Sieveking opened new paths for women, her influence was exceeded by that of the clergyman Johann Hinrich Wichern, whose upbringing in a petit bourgeois family sensitized him early in life to the harmful impact of material need. Increasingly familiar, starting in the mid-1820s as a Sunday school teacher, with the plight of children who lived in slums, he played a leading role, with help from Sieveking's father, in the establishment in 1833 of the Rauhe Haus. A place of residence and instruction, both practical and religious, for homeless, destitute, and in many cases wayward boys, it also functioned as a training center for Wichern's assistants, many of whom went on to apply what they had learned there as welfare workers in other cities. In addition, it served as a springboard for Wichern's own rise in later years on the national scene. In 1849, at his urging, the Central Committee for the Inner Mission of the German Evangelical Church came into being as a means of coordinating hundreds of charitable and educational institutions that had sprung up in recent decades under Protestant auspices. A staunch supporter of monarchical as well as religious conservatism, Wichern made it clear in his mid-century writings that a central purpose of the Inner Mission was to combat not only material need but also moral disorder of a sort that had become particularly widespread in cities. Revolutionary activity as well as juvenile delinquency needed to be opposed.

Meanwhile, a secularly based group, the Central Association for the Welfare of the Working Classes in Prussia, had emerged in that country in 1844 as a result of a movement under the leadership of a pair of Berlin educators. Their efforts picked up support from businessmen there and in urban areas to the west, as well as from several high-ranking civil servants. Local branches quickly formed, not only in the capital but also in other cities, such as Elberfeld and Cologne. The Association neither concentrated on the plight of youngsters nor distributed alms. It sought instead to encourage savings and insurance programs, consumer cooperatives, and initiatives in the area of adult education. Members of the middle classes who understood the need for organized benevolence as a means of alleviating social tensions were expected to contribute time, effort, and money voluntarily. As the leading scholar of modern German cities, Jürgen Reulecke, has put it, the Association stood for "an idea of harmony that largely ignored class differences," and in this sense it may be regarded as backward-looking, but it also pointed the way toward a good deal of the welfare legislation that made its way onto the books in later decades.[8]

The purposes and the functions of charitable giving in an urban context have been incisively analyzed by Marco Van Leeuwen, whose study of Amsterdam discusses both religious and nonreligious organizations and the people who belonged to them. At a time when national authorities still played a minimal role in the provision of poor relief, which they largely left to local authorities and other groups, Amsterdam could boast of a large number of philanthropic organizations. Every religious denomination ran one or more such institutions. The major ones were the Reformed Charity, the Lutheran Charity, and the Dutch-Israelite Charity. Each generally maintained one agency for outdoor relief and several agencies for indoor relief, such as an orphanage, a hospital, a home for widows, and a home for old persons. There were in addition a publicly supported Municipal Charity and a multitude of private charities. Regarding the men who led these groups, Van Leeuwen writes, "Members of the elites could play a variety of roles: as employers who paid low wages, as citizens anxious to maintain law and order, as scions of patrician families who had to legitimize their standing in the eyes of other patricians or of the poor, and as believers in a God who commanded them to look after their impoverished fellow-men." In all of these ways, in Van Leeuwen's analysis, the philanthropically inclined did good with the ulterior motive of stabilizing social hierarchy and defending the status quo.[9] They, like philanthropists elsewhere, coped as best they could with an urban world that benefited from but also required a great deal more than what they could accomplish on the basis of voluntary action.

Public authority and policing

Proselytizing and philanthropy were accompanied (and eventually superseded) by the rise of other means of seeking to preserve urban order, which involved the extension and strengthening of public authority. Much of this enhancement was to occur at the level of the state, but both in Prussia, the largest of the German states, and in Britain significant strides forward also took place at the local level, leading to the creation of

---

[8] Jürgen Reulecke, "Die Anfänge der organisierten Sozialreform in Deutschland," in Rüdiger vom Bruch, ed., *"Weder Kapitalismus noch Kommunismus": Bürgerliche Sozialreform in Deutschland vom Vormärz bis zur Ära Adenauer* (Munich, 1985), 32.

[9] Van Leeuwen, *The Logic of Charity*, 182, 187.

institutional structures that would serve as the bases for greatly increased responsibility and activity by municipal officials in later years. While the French remained in thrall to a strongly centralized system of government, Germans and Englishmen who lived in cities gained significant new opportunities to manage their own affairs in the communities where they resided.

Although it was motivated less by any desire to cope with incipient growth than by a desire to foster greater loyalty to the state among subjects of the Prussian king, the "city ordinance" (*Städteordnung*) promulgated in 1808 by the king's leading minister, Baron Karl vom Stein, laid an important foundation for coping with urban expansion in later years. Stein had no wish to turn back the clock in ways that would resurrect the urban independence that had been such a marked feature of medieval Germany, before the rise of princely absolutism. But he wanted, as part of an overall agenda of reforming the Prussian state, to give city dwellers enhanced rights of self-administration. Stein's decree ordered the introduction of a constitutional system in which local power was to be divided between legislative chambers of deputies who were elected on the basis of a fairly broad franchise and executive branches, consisting of mayors (*Bürgermeister*) and town councilors. Councilors were in most cities indirectly elected by the chambers of deputies, rather than by voters themselves. Local autonomy was carefully limited. In larger cities, mayors were named by the state government from among candidates suggested by local representatives. Law enforcement remained, moreover, within the purview of central authorities, with local police chiefs reporting to state officials and the Berlin police force being administered directly by the Prussian government. In 1831 and 1845, additional ordinances extended the introduction of new institutions of local government to western areas (most importantly in the Rhineland) that had been added to Prussia since 1808. In some ways, they reduced the level of local independence in core areas of the kingdom, taking back rights that had been bestowed earlier, but city governments retained control of local budgets and taxation. They could also take out loans, acquire real estate, care for the poor, provide for elementary education, and look after public health. In Germany, Prussia led the way, but in many of the other German states the powers of city governments looked roughly similar as a result of early nineteenth-century developments. Edicts that strengthened local government were issued in 1818 in Bavaria and in 1822 in Württemberg, and comparable measures followed elsewhere.

In England, the establishment of new institutions of town governance also occurred during a period of broader reform. Amendments in 1832 by the British Parliament to the ways in which members of Parliament were elected had expanded the size of the political nation by a little over half – hardly a revolutionary change, but one that nonetheless stimulated the introduction of other liberal reforms after 1832. The major moment with respect to cities came in 1835, with the passage of a Municipal Corporations Act. This legislation was designed to rectify a situation in which many towns were governed by highly exclusive bodies. Members of these "corporations" held their positions as a result of co-option and therefore possessed no moral authority among their fellow townsmen and only quite limited ability to deal with urban problems. The act also resulted from the fact that other towns, Manchester being the most notable example, lacked incorporated status altogether and thus limped along without any sort of a formal city government. The act of 1835 marked a major milestone in the history of local institution building. It abolished 178 corporations and created 178 town councils in their stead. In contrast to the highly variegated franchises of the past, every male occupier of a household who had resided in a town and had paid taxes there for three years enjoyed the right to vote in council elections. The proportion of the male population entitled to vote amounted to only a small minority, but in any case the people who ran town governments were no longer accountable only to themselves. Town councilors were in turn to elect mayors and other officials known as aldermen. Great emphasis was placed on transparency. Debates were to be open to members of the public, and financial accounts were to be publicly audited. As Derek Fraser put it, "Free, open, representative town government replaced self-elective, close oligarchy in the corporate towns."[10] The act also established procedures through which unincorporated towns could seek to qualify for its benefits, and as a result by 1854 twenty-two non-municipal boroughs gained charters. All but four of these places were industrial cities of the Midlands or the north of England, among them Birmingham and Manchester (1838), Sheffield (1843), and Bradford (1847). The city that stood most notably apart from the incorporation process was London, which continued to lack a cohesive government until 1888.

For the purposes of combating misconduct on city streets and other urban ills, increasing use was made of professional policemen, who emerged increasingly as agents for the enforcement of social discipline via hard rather than soft power, but the record of such development was quite variable. Much more progress took place in some areas than in others. London, despite its lack of status as a municipality, became the site of a path-breaking innovation in 1829 as a result of the passage by Parliament of the Metropolitan Police Act. Under the terms of this legislation a

[10] Fraser, *Power and Authority*, 11.

11. Policemen in London in the 1830s. Members of the recently formed Metropolitan Police Department appear here in an illustration from *Knight's London* (London, 1837), marching in disciplined formation on a city street.

hodgepodge of local forces that operated in quite small jurisdictions, their members having little or no training and in many cases receiving no pay, was superseded by a uniformed (albeit unarmed) force that soon numbered over 3,000 men. The head of this force, whose authority extended over a vast area that radiated seven miles from the center of London (fifteen miles after 1839), reported to a national official, the Home Secretary, there being no municipality as such. In this sense, its establishment contributed to the strengthening of central rather than local government. But it did so in a way that clearly fostered stability at the local level, as London experienced considerably greater tranquility in 1832 and again in 1848 than cities that lacked similar means of enforcing obedience to laws. Other towns moved toward more professional policing during the 1830s and 1840s, partly as a result of the example of what had happened in London but also under the impact of legislation that gave them power to exercise more autonomy than was enjoyed by Londoners. Birmingham, Bradford, Bristol, Leeds, Liverpool, Manchester, Wolverhampton, and dozens of other towns took advantage of new authority given them by the Municipal Corporations Act and subsequent legislation either to establish or to substantially reform municipally based police forces.[11]

Municipal policing lagged on the continent. In both France and Germany, central power still counted for a good deal more than it did in Britain, even if one takes account of developments in London. In both countries, there was accordingly a high degree of reliance either on mounted gendarmes or, in case of extreme need, on regular troops, backed up by volunteer militias, for the purpose of maintaining order. Policemen who worked in cities operated under the direction of chiefs who reported to state officials. Some French cities did experience growth in the numbers of their policemen relative to their overall populations. Between 1806 and the middle of the century, for example, the ratio of policemen to total numbers of inhabitants rose in Toulouse from 1 per 2,200 to 1 per 1,144 and in Saint-Étienne from 1 per 4,000 to 1 per 1,305. These ratios remained, however, quite low in comparison with the ratio of 1 per 416 that already obtained in London. In Germany, despite recognition by burghers that the need for order in their cities required more effective policing, a rising tide of liberalism militated against any growth in the numbers of policemen there, which also remained relatively low. Precisely because policing was associated in the minds of many city dwellers not just with fighting crime but also with an intrusive *Polizeistaat* whose officials excessively regulated all too many aspects of their lives, members of the urban middle classes remained reluctant to see police forces grow in number, and they consequently remained quite small.[12]

Public health and planning

The problem of urban disorder was perceived to be not only a matter of city dwellers' conduct but also a matter of the physical settings in which they lived and acted, and dealing with it therefore necessitated public attention to physical as well as moral environments. City dwellers in positions of power increasingly realized that neither preaching, nor charity, nor repression would suffice for the purpose of controlling urban disruption among the lower classes. In addition, they wanted their cities to be characterized by higher levels of healthfulness, efficiency, and attractiveness for reasons having to do with their own comfort and pleasure as

---

[11] Ibid., 24, 59, 89–90, 113, 132; Clive Emsley, *Crime and Society in England*, 3rd edn. (London, 2005), 230–32.

[12] Cohen, *Urban Government and the Rise of the French City*, 79–88 (87 for statistics); Elaine Glovka Spencer, *Police and the Social Order in German Cities: The Düsseldorf District, 1848–1914* (DeKalb, IL, 1992), 5–23.

well as for reasons having to do with the maintenance of order. There thus arose, on several grounds, a gradually heightened awareness of the need for city planning, or what the Germans later referred to as *Städtebau* ("city building"). Intended to serve as a means of imposing public controls over decisions that would otherwise have resulted simply from the often conflicting desires of individuals, such activity began to move into a new phase as a result of urban growth. Like many of the other efforts to achieve urban mastery, city planning reached only modest levels of effectiveness during the period discussed here. It deserves attention nonetheless as early evidence of a movement that was to become increasingly prominent as the century wore on.

One of the primary impulses that lay behind the planning movement in the nineteenth century was a growing consciousness of the dreadful impact of the urban environment on public health. The need to combat the bad effects of urban living on city dwellers' bodies was made quite clear by medical doctors and other investigators, who exposed urban ills of the sort discussed in Chapter 2 with a view to stimulating remedial action. The impact of their warnings and their admonitions having been greatly strengthened by the widespread experience of cholera in 1832 and its return in 1848, the men who broadcast them made a major contribution to the idea that urban welfare and city planning had to go together.

The study of public health made its first big breakthroughs in Paris in the 1820s, largely as a result of the work of Louis-René Villermé and A. J. P. Parent-Duchâtelet. They teamed up in 1829 to establish the influential *Annales d'hygiène publique et de medicine légale* and became widely known abroad as well as in France for their urban research. Villermé showed that in the French capital the poorer the district, the higher the death rate. In a study of living conditions in French manufacturing towns, he reported on areas inhabited by poor workers. In Lille, he informed his readers, residences were badly lit and crowded, and they contained only the barest minimum of furniture. As a result, many of the city's inhabitants lived literally on top of one another. In numerous beds, "fathers, mothers, old people, children, [and] adults crowd[ed] together, heaped up." Alluding to incest, he added, "The reader will complete the picture [and] . . . his imagination must not recoil from any of the disgusting mysteries that take place on these impure couches, in the heart of darkness and intoxication." Similar if somewhat less shocking situations were in his view readily observable in other industrial cities, such as Lyon, leading him to conclude that textile workers who lived on the land, where they could combine weaving with agricultural work, enjoyed a much healthier life than those who had flocked to the towns.[13] Some of what Villermé wrote suggested that the filth and degradation from which members of the lower classes suffered resulted from poor choices and poor habits, indicating that moral reform needed to precede improved hygiene, but on the whole he supported an environmental explanation of moral deficiency.

Parent-Duchâtelet, a medical doctor and a member of the Board of Health in Paris, came to similar conclusions. He wrote a good deal about poor sewerage, the omnipresence of dead horses on city streets, and poor health among factory workers. He made his best-known contributions to knowledge of urban unhealthiness in a path-breaking study of Parisian prostitution. In this work, he depicted moral filth and material filth as being inextricably intertwined, comparing prostitutes' bodies with polluted drains. Still, it was the urban environment rather than the behavior of the people who inhabited it that most concerned him – real sewers rather than figurative ones, and also a host of other sources of filth, such as polluted rivers, slaughterhouses, and a huge garbage dump from which in his view poisonous "miasmas" spread infectious disease. His research as well as that of Villermé directed the attention of contemporaries to environmental problems in growing cities.

Agitation for sanitary reform took off from many bases and attracted many adherents, particularly in Paris but also elsewhere. Advances in the systematic collection of statistical data by governmental officials, starting in the early 1820s with the first four volumes of the five-volume *Recherches statistiques sur la ville de Paris* and continuing in the 1830s with the first several volumes of the multivolume *Statistique générale de la France* (thirteen volumes of which appeared by 1852) led to a vast database on which legions of critics of current conditions could draw. A multitude of medical doctors, pharmacists, other men with scientific training, and administrators, many of whom operated within key institutions, rose to the task. The Royal Academy of Medicine, founded after 1815, was one such nodal point. At the local and regional level, there were growing numbers of health councils, which advised mayors and prefects on hygienic matters. A health council had been established for Paris in 1802. By the 1830s, Nantes, Lyon, Marseille, Lille, Strasbourg, Bordeaux, Rouen, Troyes, and Toulouse all had health councils of their own. In Lyon, where uprisings in 1831 and 1834 had called attention to substandard living conditions endured by workers, hygienists argued that improvement of workers' morals required paying attention to poor

[13] Louis-René Villermé, *Tableau de l'état physique et moral des ouvriers employés dans les manufactures de cotton, de laine et de soie* (Paris, 1840), I: 82–83, 445–46.

dwellings, poor ventilation, lack of clean water, and inadequate provision for sewage disposal, and the litany of concerns expressed by health council members elsewhere was much the same.

All of this publicity work and advocacy led, by mid-century, to a mixed bag of tangible improvements. Scarcely adding up to anything like what the reformers desired, the outcomes of their campaigns reflected the continuing strength throughout the period of laissez-faire doctrines, which militated against public interventionism at all levels of government. Standing in the way of factory legislation at the national level (which progressed much less rapidly in France than in Britain), such thinking also inhibited efforts to sanitize cities. Nonetheless, the supply of water to the French capital was increased fivefold, the length of the underground sewer system was tripled, the sewers began to serve as conduits for liquid waste, and disinfection of cesspools at the time of cleaning became mandatory. The butchering of horses was moved out of areas where the filth it produced threatened public health, and the city's most noxious dump was resituated as well. In Lyon, the city council decided in 1846 on a plan to increase the supply of water and improve its quality, but the plan was shelved during the revolution of 1848 and implemented only later. Bordeaux made plans to build an aqueduct from the Taillan stream to the city, but putting them into practice was also delayed until after mid-century. Marseille, on the other hand, completed by 1849 construction of a canal 87 kilometers long that carried water to the city from the Durance River, giving it a reliable water supply for the first time. Finally, one may add to the plus side by mentioning a law of 1848 that set up health councils at the departmental and arrondissement levels, whose members were well positioned to agitate for further improvements in years to come.

Despite the fact that the public health movement first acquired prominence in Paris, it quickly gained still more traction in Britain. In 1832, the medical doctor James Phillips Kay, who had played an important part earlier that year in coordinating the work of several boards of health in Manchester during the cholera epidemic that afflicted that city and many others, reported in a widely read pamphlet on his visits to areas that disproportionately experienced the ravages of illness. Working-class Mancunians suffered to be sure from "prolonged and exhausting labour," which resembled "the torment of Sisyphus," and from wretched diets, but Kay particularly emphasized the bad consequences of living "in cottages separated by narrow, unpaved, and almost pestilential streets, in an atmosphere loaded with the smoke and exhalations of a large manufacturing city." The lack of sewers beneath the streets and of privies in the houses that lined them further exacerbated the inhabitants' plight, as

12. A protest against water pollution in the 1830s. This caricature, by George Cruickshank, appeared in 1832. It points to the connection between cholera and the dumping of sewage and refuse in the Thames river from which the Southwark Water Company supplied water to thousands of houses. It depicts Neptune offering a drink to enraged Londoners who shout to him from the shore pleading for clean water. "Salus populi suprema lex" translates as "The health of the people is the supreme law."

did the animal wastes that lay about because of the absence of properly regulated slaughterhouses. These ills, Kay argued, were in no way intrinsic to the manufacturing and commercial system itself, for which Kay expressed great admiration. They had to do not with industry per se but with the industrial city.[14]

Although Kay framed his indictment for the most part qualitatively, basing it on anecdotal observations rather than on numbers, what he wrote pointed up the need for accurate and comprehensive statistics that would enable him and others who shared his misgivings about urban conditions to make their arguments more systematically and authoritatively.

[14] James Phillips Kay, *The Moral and Physical Condition of the Working Classes Employed in the Cotton Manufacture in Manchester*, 2nd edn (London, 1832), 21–22, 24, 27, 42, 79.

Toward that end, statistical societies quickly sprang up in at least eight cities, starting with Manchester, where Kay again played a leading role, in 1833. The reports issued by these organizations repeatedly focused on public health, pointing to urban crowding and the consequent lack of proper sanitation as basic causes of excessive disease and death. So too did the reports issued by a General Register Office set up for England and Wales in 1837, which was led for three decades by William Farr, a physician – trained both in Paris and in London – who had practiced medicine for several years in the metropolis before becoming a bureaucrat. National in scope, his reports cast a good deal of light on urban conditions, consistently pointing to the inescapable conclusion that mortality increased directly in proportion to density of habitation.

Another national institution that contributed, to an even greater extent, to exposure of the ill effects of urban life was the Poor Law Commission, which had been entrusted by the New Poor Law of 1834 with the task of coordinating public assistance to the indigent. In connection with their obligations to supervise "outdoor" medical relief for people under their care, the Poor Law commissioners enlisted several physicians in the late 1830s for the purpose of carrying out further studies of deleterious conditions in British cities. One was James Kay. But the most influential among them was Thomas Southwood Smith. His "Report on Some of the Physical Causes of Sickness and Morality . . . Exemplified in the Present Condition of Bethnal Green and Whitechapel Districts" (both in London), and his "Report on the Prevalence of Fever in Twenty Metropolitan [Poor Law] Unions or Districts during the Year Ended 20th March 1838" stood out as major milestones in the evolving awareness of the prerequisites for healthy life in urban settings. The sanitary economy of the town, he showed, resulted from a constant interaction between living organisms and the environments in which they functioned. Like the individual bodies of the human beings who inhabited them, healthy cities depended on the free circulation of fluids and air and on the efficient elimination of waste products. Neither of these processes was occurring, and city dwellers suffered greatly in their absence.

Such writing set the stage for the appearance, in 1842, of the enormously influential work by Edwin Chadwick, a former Poor Law official who stood out unmistakably as the most influential advocate of public health anywhere in the nineteenth century. His *Report on the Sanitary Condition of the Labouring Population of Great Britain* (which was informed by wide reading both in the works of Villermé and Parent-Duchâtelet and in the writings of British experts) surveyed hygienic conditions in Scotland as well as in England and Wales. Appalled by excessive numbers of deaths that resulted from "epidemic, endemic, and contagious diseases, including fever, typhus, and scarlatina, amounting to 56,461 [in one year], the great proportion of which are proved to be preventable," Chadwick recognized that poor health and disease plagued the countryside as well as the towns, but they were clearly most acute among city dwellers, where they stemmed in large measure from defective drainage, inadequate water supplies, and overcrowded housing. Like Kay, and his French predecessors, Chadwick also linked the physical and physiological conditions he deplored to moral defects. But by asserting that "wretchedness and vice" were greatly exacerbated by an unfavorable environment and the sickness to which it gave rise he clearly emphasized the environment rather than morality as the more independent of the two variables.

The half decade that followed publication of Chadwick's *Report* witnessed a rising tide of agitation in favor of addressing the problems he had so convincingly identified. Publicists such as Robert Seeley, a promoter of evangelical and philanthropic movements, took up the cause of sanitary reform. He wrote in 1844, "Manchester and Glasgow . . . cannot keep up their own populations. Cut off supplies of labourers from without, and these towns, in sixty years, would be without inhabitants." Remedying this deplorable situation necessitated four things: "paved streets, covered sewers, ventilation, and a supply of water."[15] Many others chimed in, whether as members of a Health of Towns Association, which began to press for reform in 1844, or as members of a parliamentary Health of Towns Commission, which issued reports of its own in 1844 and 1845.

Under the impact of these studies and reports, governing bodies adopted various measures for the purpose of improving urban conditions from a sanitary standpoint. At the local level, a number of towns passed legislation that regulated housing: Leeds and Liverpool in 1842, Birkenhead in 1843, London in 1844, Manchester in 1844 and 1845, Nottingham in 1845, Newcastle in 1846, and so on. Parliamentary legislation further strengthened municipalities' powers in this area. The Nuisances Removal and Diseases Prevention Act of 1846 included in its definition of "nuisances" run-down dwellings, and the Towns Improvement Clauses Act of 1847 empowered authorities to demolish residences they considered to be dangerous to neighbors. Some towns acquired wider authority to introduce measures that pertained to city sanitation. The Leeds Improvement Act of 1842 vested all sanitary authority in the city in the town council, authorizing it to pave, light, and cleanse streets and to construct a system of sewerage and drainage. The Liverpool council obtained passage in Parliament, in 1846, of the Liverpool Sanitary Act,

---

[15] Robert Seeley (anon.), *The Perils of the Nation: An Appeal to the Legislature, the Clergy and the Higher and Middle Classes*, 3rd edn (London, 1844), xxi, 143.

which established a Health Committee of the Council as an executive agency that controlled health-related administration in the city. It also authorized appointment of medical officers of health as well as other officials, who were charged with enforcing the council's policies. Dr. William H. Duncan, Liverpool's (and the nation's) first "M. O. H.," served his city with distinction for many years, working diligently to clean up England's least healthy town.

The impulses that led to such legislation came to a climax with the passage of the Public Health Act of 1848. Its members' minds focused by the looming outbreak of another epidemic of cholera, Parliament enacted legislation that marked a major milestone in the evolution of sanitary policy. The law was, to be sure, hardly revolutionary. In contrast to what Chadwick had called for earlier, it did not establish a national system of public health commissions. It relied instead primarily on local boards. These boards were compulsory only in places other than London (to which the legislation did not apply) where the annual death rate exceeded twenty-three per thousand, which was well above the national average. Elsewhere, their establishment depended on petition by rate-payers. Such boards were permitted but not required to appoint medical officers. Similarly, they were empowered but not compelled to pave and clean streets and to provide sewerage and clean water. But doing so became easier by virtue of the fact that they gained new rights to borrow money in order to pay the costs incurred in taking such steps. Also, the act stated that no new houses were to be built within the jurisdiction of a local board without suitable provision for disposal of sewage. Finally, the local boards were to operate under the overall supervision of a Central Board of Health, two of whose three members were veterans of the public health movement: Thomas Southwood Smith and, unsurprisingly, Edwin Chadwick. Bureaucratic infighting between Chadwick and others in government led to the demise of the Central Board in 1854, but the pace of sanitary reform continued unabated. By 1858, 219 places had formed local boards in accord with the law of 1848, and they busily attended to the mundane but essential tasks of providing for inflows of clean water and outflows of waste, regulating the construction of housing and otherwise striving to maintain conditions that would be favorable to health.

The Germans lagged in this area, failing to exhibit anything like the vigor they would display later in the century. Still, there were already straws in the wind to which one can point. In Hamburg, where a disastrous fire destroyed much of the city center and rendered 20,000 people homeless in 1842, policy makers quickly decided to engage an English civil engineer, William Lindley, for the purpose of designing a number of infrastructural improvements. The most important ones in the present context had to do with water. In the first place, the city fathers desired a more dependable water supply to facilitate fighting future fires. At the same time, they also decided to upgrade the city's sewage system, a task for which Lindley was particularly well suited on the basis of close association with Chadwick and familiarity with ideas about sanitation in Britain. As a result of Lindley's work, Hamburg received the first comprehensive water and sewage system on the continent, one which included both provision for piped water and drainage both of streets and of toilets in private houses. In 1848, a medical doctor by the name of S. Neumann, who was closely connected with the Central Association for the Welfare of the Working Classes, wrote a pamphlet about public health that grew out of his work on the public census. He demanded an interventionist approach by government. In the same year, Rudolf Virchow, who was later to gain great recognition as an epidemiologist, began to propagate similar ideas in Berlin in a new journal, *Medicinische Reform*.

In addition to the steps men took as participants in more or less organized movements to promote public health, they and others in positions of public authority at the local level implemented a variety of other measures to extend the range of governmental activity with respect to the physical fabrics of urban life. Greater authority for local officials to determine street layouts as built-up areas expanded on the outskirts of city centers became an important tool for would-be planners. It helped them to shape urban growth, with a view to managing density, ensuring adequate amounts of light, air, and space for traffic, and providing a basis for necessary improvements of urban infrastructure. Prussia led the way in 1808 by placing such authority in the hands of local police officials and also by requiring each municipality to set up a building committee that would take responsibility for paving and draining streets and for maintaining walkways. Similar arrangements were introduced in other German states during the following few decades. They were followed in 1845 by a law in Prussia that added to the regulatory powers of police officials. It empowered them to supervise work at building sites with a view to protecting the community from dangers that might arise there. In Britain, where ownership of urban land in large parcels meant that private developers usually made adequate provision on their own for new streets to serve new buildings, public intervention occurred later. In 1845, a Lands Clauses Consolidation Act allowed municipalities to acquire land compulsorily in order to widen old streets and build new ones, and in 1847 a Towns Improvements Clauses Act added to these powers.

In France, where Paris already by 1783 had the most comprehensive building code in Europe, Napoleon proclaimed that all towns should draw up citywide plans, specifically authorizing them to design layouts for streets and other public places and to require buildings along them to conform to prescribed height limitations. Such powers were not used in France to anywhere near the extent that they were in Germany, and a court decision in 1837 that required officials to pay heavy indemnities if they needed to acquire land for street building made it much more difficult for them to do so. A number of French towns made significant structural breakthroughs nonetheless. Between 1807 and 1830, the Bordeaux city council enlarged 200 streets. During the 1830s and 1840s, Saint-Étienne and Marseille also underwent new street construction and broadening, as did Paris, where the activities of the prefect Claude Rambuteau set the stage for the much better known transformations that took place not long thereafter.

Beyond the piecemeal initiatives enumerated here, a vast planning literature pointed the way toward much more comprehensive approaches to the problems of the big city. Recently brought to light by Nicholas Papayanis, numerous writings produced by engineers and others between the 1820s and the 1840s made the case for a comprehensive approach to solving the physical problems of the French capital. Although lacking counterparts in the urban literature published in other countries (they reflected a distinctive readiness among French thinkers to propose large-scale solutions to social problems), they merit attention not only in their own right but also as intellectual precursors of the much better known work by Baron Haussmann, who would, in the 1850s, soon start to implement much of what they proposed. Influenced in many cases by the technocratic utopianism of Henri de Saint-Simon and the egalitarian utopianism of Charles Fourier, Parisian visionaries combined broad perspectives with careful attention to detail. Seeking to make the French capital safer, healthier, and more efficient, they called for far-reaching programs of reform that comprised but went well beyond what even the most insistent advocates of public hygiene had in mind. Their proposals for enhancing the city's infrastructure entailed measures designed to enhance not only cleanliness, through better circulation of water and waste, but also circulation more generally. They advocated improved street layouts, the construction both of sidewalks for pedestrians and of a system of underground transport, and many other changes as well. The city they had in mind would be easier for public authorities to control, more hospitable for businessmen, and more congenial as a place in which to live for most if not all of its inhabitants.

We must emphasize that the efforts discussed in this chapter had quite limited effects on urban life itself during this period. Fertile though they were with regard to reformist ideas and aspirations, the decades dealt with here saw little in the way of transformations that would have markedly changed urban conditions for the better. To be sure, there were important legal gains with regard to the powers of local governments in Germany and Britain, and there were some improvements in the area of public health in France and Britain. But tangible accomplishments paled in comparison with what was to take place in later decades.

BIBLIOGRAPHY

Aisenberg, Andrew R. *Contagion: Disease, Government, and the "Social Question" in Nineteenth-Century France*. Stanford, 1999.

Andrew, D. T. *Philanthropy and Police: London Charity in the Eighteenth Century*. Princeton, 1989.

Benevolo, Leonardo. *The Origins of Modern Town Planning*. Trans. Judith Landry. London, 1967.

Bullock, Nicholas, and James Read. *The Movement for Housing Reform in Germany and France, 1840–1914*. Cambridge, 1985.

Chadwick, Edwin. *Report on the Sanitary Condition of the Labouring Population of Great Britain*. Ed. M. W. Flinn. Edinburgh, 1965.

Cohen, William B. *Urban Government and the Rise of the French City: Five Municipalities in the Nineteenth Century*. New York, 1998.

Coleman, William. *Death Is a Social Disease: Public Health and Political Economy in Early Industrial France*. Madison, 1982.

Cullen, M. J. *The Statistical Movement in Early Victorian Britain*. New York, 1975.

Davidoff, Leonore, and Catherine Hall. *Family Fortunes: Men and Women of the English Middle Class, 1780–1850*. Chicago, 1987.

Evans, Richard J. *Death in Hamburg: Society and Politics in the Cholera Years, 1830–1910*. Oxford, 1987.

Finer, S. E. *The Life and Times of Sir Edwin Chadwick*. London, 1952.

Fraser, Derek. *Power and Authority in the Victorian City*. New York, 1979.

Hamlin, Christopher. *Public Health and Social Justice in the Age of Chadwick: Britain, 1800–1854*. Cambridge, 1998.

Harsin, Jill. *Policing Prostitution in Nineteenth-Century Paris*. Princeton, 1985.

Hennock, E. P. "The Urban Sanitary Movement in England and Germany, 1838–1914: A Comparison." *Continuity and Change* 15 (2000): 269–96.

Hitchcock, Henry-Russell. *Architecture, Nineteenth and Twentieth Centuries*. 4th edn. New York, 1977.

La Berge, Ann. *Mission and Method: The Early Nineteenth-Century French Public Health Movement*. Cambridge, 1993.

Leeuwen, Marco H. D. van. *The Logic of Charity: Amsterdam, 1800–1850*. New York, 2000.

Lindemann, Mary. *Patriots and Paupers: Hamburg, 1712–1830*. New York, 1990.

Mandler, Peter, ed. *The Uses of Charity: The Poor on Relief in the Nineteenth-Century Metropolis*. Philadelphia, 1990.

Morris, R. J. "Civil Society and the Nature of Urbanism: Britain, 1750–1850." *Urban History* 25 (1998): 289–301.

Class, Sect, and Party: The Making of the British Middle Class: Leeds, 1820–1850. Manchester, 1990.

"Voluntary Societies and British Urban Elites, 1780–1850: An Analysis." *Historical Journal* 26 (1983): 95–118.

Owen, David. *English Philanthropy, 1660–1960.* Cambridge, MA, 1960.

Papayanis, Nicholas. *Planning Paris Before Haussmann: Ideas and Proposals for a New City.* Baltimore, 2004.

Petit, Jacques-Guy, and Yannick Marec, eds. *Le social dans la ville, en France et en Europe (1750–1914).* Paris, 1996.

Prelinger, Catherine M. *Charity, Challenge, and Change: Religious Dimensions of the Mid-Nineteenth Century Women's Movement in Germany.* Westport, CT, 1987.

Prochaska, F. *Women and Philanthropy in Nineteenth-Century England.* New York, 1980.

Richards, Paul. "R. A. Slaney, the Industrial Town, and Early Victorian Social Policy." *Social History* 4 (1979): 85–101.

Roberts, M. J. D. *Making English Morals: Voluntary Association and Moral Reform in England, 1787–1886.* Cambridge, 2004.

Shanahan, William O. *German Protestants Face the Social Question, 1815–1871.* South Bend, IN, 1954.

Shapely, Peter. *Charity and Power in Victorian Manchester.* Manchester, 2000.

Sheard, Sally, and Helen Power, eds. *Body and City: Histories of Urban Public Health.* Burlington, VT, 2000.

Sutcliffe, Anthony. *Towards the Planned City: Germany, Britain, the United States, and France, 1780–1914.* Oxford, 1981.

Vaughan, Robert. *The Age of Great Cities: Or, Modern Society Viewed in Its Relation to Intelligence, Morals, and Religion.* London, 1843.

Wach, Howard. "A 'Still, Small Voice' from the Pulpit: Religion and the Creation of Social Morality in Manchester, 1820–1850." *Journal of Modern History* 63 (1991): 425–56.

Wohl, Anthony S. *Endangered Lives: Public Health in Victorian Britain.* Cambridge, MA, 1983.

Part II

1850–1914, an era of reconstruction

5   The challenge of the big cities

In 1898, Adna Ferrin Weber finished a statistical study of city growth in the nineteenth century, which quickly became a classic of comparative urban analysis. Having studied mathematics at Cornell, political science at the University of Berlin, and economics at Columbia, he looked at cities from multiple perspectives. The entire world was becoming, in his opinion, "a single industrial society." Because efficient industrial organization depended upon concentrated population, economic forces were pushing a "drift to the cities," throughout Europe, North America, and Australia. In the second half of the nineteenth century, rapid urbanization had spread well beyond Britain and Belgium. Weber judged that urbanization had become normal: because greater challenges and opportunities could be found in cities than elsewhere, anyone with ambition would move toward an urban center. Political and social pressures reinforced economic processes. The net impact was strongly centralizing, for big cities grew faster than small ones, and this process, Weber believed, would continue. When London could draw on the entire world for its food supplies, no limits remained on its expansion. Still, although Weber was an optimistic American, even he worried about possible negative consequences of the spread of big cities, which he identified as class antagonisms, extreme individualism, and governmental corruption.[1]

It is useful to compare Weber's analysis of urbanization with that of his contemporary Paul Meuriot, a French scholar who specialized in the areas of economics and demography. Meuriot also saw urban growth as an inevitable result of technological and economic changes. Coal, industry, steam power, and new means of transportation had all helped to bring about "this economic revolution, which explain[ed] the formation of the urban areas." Men and women migrated from the countryside to the cities for good reasons, he thought, and he pointed approvingly to many consequences of their decisions. Urban workers were more productive than

---

[1] Weber, *The Growth of Cities in the Nineteenth Century*, 181, 225, 446. For Weber and other contemporary social scientists, "big" cities were those with 100,000 or more inhabitants.

rural ones and thus earned more. In addition, their demand for food resulted in higher wages for farm laborers. Urban expansion could thus be viewed as a natural and positive process – one that enabled countries to absorb a rural surplus of men and women who thereby avoided emigration. And yet, Meuriot displayed strong concern about social and cultural problems in the big cities, which he thought were caused by the economic changes he described. Unlike his American counterpart, Meuriot was a demographic pessimist. Living in a society whose slow population growth prompted fears of national decline, Meuriot worried about health conditions in cities, which experienced relatively high death rates and low birth rates. If all France became like Paris, the nation would die out, he claimed. Even if demographic disaster could be avoided, he thought city life undermined religious faith. Worse still, it fostered crime, illegitimacy, alcoholism, suicide, and working-class radicalism. The urban masses had "a more tumultuous character" than other social groups. A spirit of "desire" moved them, in contrast to the spirit of "conservation" evident among peasants and villagers.[2] Behind Meuriot's general approval of urbanization lurked fears of social revolution and of social change. While technology enabled the multiplication of large cities, it had neither provided the means for the mastery of their problems nor supplied the imagination and will needed to tackle them effectively.

Liberals as well as conservatives worried about the potentially destabilizing impact of huge cities, although they differed in their diagnoses of problems. Urban diversity, anonymity, and freedom on a giant scale were frightening. City size, wealth, and political importance gave national impacts to events within metropolitan borders. If Paris sneezed, people in Provence caught cold.

This chapter takes up the themes of city growth and its consequences, both real and imagined, during decades when the balance between rural and urban tipped decisively toward the urban side in Western and Central Europe and when the numbers of large cities exploded. Growth increased the diversity of the urban population and widened the networks within which cities functioned. Moreover, urban scale shaped social life along with the urban environment, influencing group relations, neighborhood organization, and demographic patterns. The processes of political, economic, and cultural modernization developed in the large cities and then spread to towns and smaller settlements. In addition, the metropolis and other big cities posed mounting environmental and political challenges, straining the technological, organizational, and imaginative capacities of

---

[2] Paul Meuriot, *Des agglomerations urbaines dans l'Europe contemporaine* (Paris, 1897), 29, 412–14, 451–52; see 344–54, 407, on social and political consequences of urbanization.

towns and states. Their freedoms and multicultural populations frightened conservatives and excited the young and adventurous. The study of urban growth illuminates the challenge of the big cities, as they transformed European society during the second half of the nineteenth century.

The relentless pace of urban growth

Urbanization occurred rapidly in Europe between 1850 and 1900. Swift growth in the size of urban populations spread well beyond Britain and Belgium to include the German states, Switzerland, France, the Netherlands, Italy, Spain, and Sweden. The most highly urbanized nations still lay in northwestern Europe, in England, Belgium, and the Netherlands, where by 1850 over one-third of the population lived in settlements of more than 5,000 people. But the quickened pace of urban development in Germany, Italy, Denmark, Switzerland, and Spain raised substantially the proportion of city dwellers in those countries too. As parts of Northern, Central, and Southern Europe experienced the full impact of industrial change in the late nineteenth century, already established cities in those areas mushroomed in size.

Not only did more people live in towns, but for the first time very large cities dominated the urban landscape. While in 1850 in Europe there were only ten cities which numbered more than 250,000 people, by 1910 there were forty-eight. By the early twentieth century, twenty-three towns had more than 500,000 inhabitants and five had broken the million mark. Moreover, big cities could be found in every country, from Spain to Scandinavia. By the end of the nineteenth century, the giant metropolis had become a reality in Western and Central Europe. More than seven million people lived in London in 1910, almost three million had settled in Paris, and over two million resided in Berlin and Vienna. (See Appendix A.)

Sharply rising levels of overall urbanization conceal big differences in national and regional patterns. In France, urban growth was episodic throughout the nineteenth century: heavy in the 1850s and mid 1870s, years of political consolidation of new regimes, but relatively slow between 1846 and 1851 and during the 1880s and early 1890s. In contrast, urban growth in the states which would become the German Empire remained low before 1850 and then accelerated fast in the second half of the century, during the period of unification and industrial growth. In Italy too, national unity accelerated urbanization. Cycles of change could operate regionally. The rush cityward in Denmark, Norway, and Sweden revealed roughly similar patterns, as did the rhythms of urbanization in Italy and

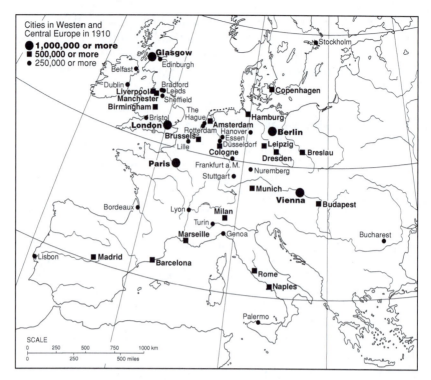

Map 4. Large cities in Western and Central Europe in 1910. By the early twentieth century in the area west of the Russian Empire, forty-eight cities had populations over 250,000, nineteen of which numbered more than 500,000, and five of which exceeded the million mark. Compare with Maps 2 and 5. Cities with more than 100,000 but fewer than 250,000 inhabitants were now too numerous to be included here. (Based on Brian Mitchell, *European Historical Statistics, 1770–1970*, 2nd edn [London, 1981], 86–88.)

Spain. Migration varied in strength according to the structure of opportunities – responding to economic cycles and political conditions, which could be regional as well as national.

Rising urbanization produced multi-ethnic cities, as peasant populations moved to towns to look for industrial or service jobs. By 1850, around half of the people in European cities had been born outside of the places where they lived. Poles, Russians, Italians, and Americans lived in Paris, as did thousands of artisans, servants, and laborers from Brittany, Auvergne, and Alsace. Because of low national birth rates, the French government encouraged immigration, and after 1889 it gave French

Table 4 *National levels of urbanization in Europe, 1800–1910*

Country	1800	1850	1910
Belgium	20	34	57
England	23	45	75
France	12	19	38
Germany	9	15	49
Italy	18	23	40
Netherlands	37	39	53
Portugal	16	16	16
Spain	18	18	38
Sweden	7	7	23
Switzerland	7	12	33
Europe	12	19	41

Percentages of populations in centers with 5,000 or more inhabitants.
Source: Bairoch, *Cities and Economic Development*, 221.

citizenship to those born on French soil. Entrepreneurs in the cities of the Ruhr Valley recruited thousands of Polish laborers after 1880 to keep their mines and smelters in operation. Glasgow attracted Irish, Lithuanians, Italians, and Highland Scots. Even though most movement took place within a single state or empire, pluralist, multilingual populations resulted from the mixing of migrant groups in the towns.

Urban expansion was driven by more motors than migration. Long-term shifts in urban birth rates and death rates made it possible for cities to grow by natural increase, as well as through movement into their territories. Generally during the nineteenth century, death rates were lowest in rural areas and increased with city size, but contemporaries knew this and had some success improving urban health conditions, as will be discussed in detail in Chapter 6. In most places, adult urban mortality declined slowly, making city life ever more survivable – even though high infant and child mortality continued throughout the century. At the same time, the large numbers of young people who migrated into the cities produced relatively high birth rates, thereby swelling the numbers of home-grown city dwellers. Individual cities differed in the balance between their birth rates and death rates because local age and ethnic mixes, as well as public health conditions, helped to produce highly variable urban demographic profiles. By the second half of the nineteenth century, over 80 percent of London's growth came from natural increase, the surplus of births over deaths. Scandinavia, Germany, and the Low Countries also shifted to positive demographic balances in the cities after 1850. In contrast, around

1890, Marseille, Lyon, and Bordeaux had higher death rates than birth rates, in part because of early, widespread fertility decline in France. In Paris, 80 percent of population increase came from migration and territorial annexation. The impact of declining birth rates and death rates, "the demographic transition," which slowed European population increase substantially, hit Europe's states and its cities differentially.

Where growth rates differed among types and sizes of cities, urbanization rearranged national urban networks. Before 1850, northern Italy, the Netherlands, Belgium, and the German states did not have primate cities, but instead relatively dense networks of medium-sized towns. Multiple places offered similar political and economic opportunities. Then in the second half of the century in Germany, national unification and Prussian economic development brought new centrality to Berlin, which by 1881 broke the million resident mark. The creation of new nation-states and, later, overseas empires, lifted Rome and Brussels from the ranks of sleepy, regional centers to the rank of imperial capitals. The fortunes of states and cities were strongly linked. Continuing centralization of political, economic, and cultural services in France, Austria, and Portugal reinforced the urban dominance of Paris, Vienna, and Lisbon. In Scandinavia, the primacy of Copenhagen became greater too. In contrast, the rapid development of northern English and Scottish cities undercut London's hegemony, and the capital's overwhelming cultural and economic importance diminished during the second half of the nineteenth century.

Growth could benefit existing settlements, or it could be channeled into new areas, where the labor demand was rising. New cities were most numerous in regions where coal was mined. Industrial settlements grew around pitheads, as factories, forges, and furnaces started up to make use of cheap fuel. Along the Ruhr River in western Prussia, iron entrepreneurs moved into local towns as deep shafts were dug in adjoining fields and hillsides. Bochum, Essen, Duisburg, and Dortmund, no longer small towns, became sprawling cities. By 1880, newly urbanized, industrial regions could be found in Silesia, northern Spain, northern Italy, Sweden, and southern Russia, as well as in the mining areas of Britain, southern Belgium, western Germany, and northern France. In new, undergoverned places, the impact of growth could be environmentally brutal: unplanned, unregulated, shoddy buildings spread out in all directions, with minimal provision of water, sanitation, and other services. Demand shaped land and housing markets, driven by immediate costs rather than longer run concerns for health and safety. Rapid industrial urbanization was chaotic and usually ugly.

Great changes also took place in older European cities into which factories moved slowly and unevenly as industrialization progressed. Bypassed in the early stages of industrial growth in favor of rural sites near streams and coal fields, cities became favored places for mass production after coal and food became cheaply transportable. Across Europe, the railroads helped spread the techniques of mass manufacturing by making possible long-distance transport of machines, raw materials, food, and fuel. Then the development of electric power and internal combustion engines in the second half of the nineteenth century permitted an even wider array of production sites, well away from pit-heads, ports, and railway stops. Factories no longer had to be placed alongside waterways or railway tracks so that they could receive raw materials and so that finished products could be moved from them to distribution centers. Technological change made possible the decentralization of production from coal fields to a wider array of urban places. The long-term marriage of town and industry was made possible by the automobile and portable power.

Where economies grew, cities became favored sites of investment because of their large local markets and their ready access to abundant sources of labor. A belt of industrial suburbs grew up around Paris, and iron, steel, and textile manufacturers moved into Stockholm. Around Milan, cotton production and engineering prospered in a penumbra of small, provincial towns. Knowledge-based industries – engineering, electricity, and chemicals, for example – thrived in cities, where schools could train technical personnel and where secondary education was well developed. Regionally important cities, such as Lyon and Milan, took advantage of local human capital to adapt their economies to newer industries. Their entrepreneurs continued to direct regional systems of production, utilizing well-developed marketing and transportation networks.

The railway sped travelers to the largest towns, channeling migrants toward central cities and station stops. Fixed routes privileged a minority of settlements, targeting ports, administrative centers, and prosperous industrial sites. Other towns, where prospects for profit were relatively dim, slumped into stagnation when deprived of direct rail connections. The primacy of Paris, the hub of the French railway system, grew along with the construction of five radial lines, which by 1860 linked the capital to the largest provincial cities. The railways' speed diminished distances and shrank time, bringing Paris much closer to Lyon, Bordeaux, Marseille, and Lille. In the following decades, goods depots, workshops, and new suburban stations turned green fields on the Parisian periphery into acres of pavement. Inside the city, the mainline stations concentrated noise, smoke, and human bodies. Thousands of passengers disembarked daily from around the country, while others rushed to the station, many by horse-drawn trams, to hop on the trains of their choice. By 1910, electrified trolley lines, metropolitan underground trains, and suburban rail stops integrated the flow of commuters and travelers into national and international rail systems. Urban growth flowed along the channels created by intra- and inter-urban travel.

When railways could deliver abundant food and fuel cheaply, constraints on city sizes dropped along with transport costs. At the same time, centralization of government services, the rising scale of manufacturing, and the development of mass leisure industries also stimulated the growth of the biggest cities. Construction spilled over urban boundaries, replacing pastures and woods with seemingly endless streets, lined by similar houses.

The development of Berlin illustrates the processes which created giant cities throughout Europe. Its expansion rested on the political fortunes of the Prussian state and its army, which transformed a modest, north German monarchy into a Central European superpower over a period of 150 years. Beginning as a small, fortified court city on the River Spree, Berlin grew rapidly as Prussia consolidated its influence over other German states. Its expanding size and royal patronage encouraged manufacturing in the capital, which soon became the center of the north German transportation network, as Prussia pushed the development of paved roads and, later, a railway system. Linked rivers and canals gave easy access also to the North Sea and the Atlantic. After Prussia drew the other German states in 1871 into an empire under its leadership, Berlin became the imperial capital and political center of the territory between Poland and the Rhineland. Its universities, theaters, museums, and publishing houses signified cultural leadership, while the movement of banks into the city made Berlin Germany's financial capital. By the end of the century, the city also housed important engineering, chemical, ammunition, textile, and electrical firms, all of which depended on the capital's well-developed network of railways and electrified trolley cars to move raw materials, workers, and goods from place to place throughout the region.

Migrants rushed into Berlin from all over Germany and other parts of Europe, expanding both the city population and that of its metropolitan region. Shanty towns and unplanned neighborhoods multiplied, until adjoining territories grew even faster than the capital. Berlin's population and its territory expanded rapidly, as the town annexed outlying areas in 1841, 1861, and 1920. Big cities cannibalized their neighbors, capturing them physically and incorporating them into the body of the metropolis. Starting from the city center, a traveler would have to walk or ride between fifteen and twenty kilometers to reach the outer ring of suburbs by 1910. Greater Berlin exceeded 3.7 million people by the time of the First World War.

Megacities took multiple forms. London remained a low density city, where small towns in several counties coalesced via seemingly endless lines of single family homes along new streets and highways. Mass transit made possible suburban residence for workers as well as middle-class families. In contrast, Paris remained much more centralized. The French capital developed a circle of relatively poor industrial suburbs around a high density core that combined apartment living and the central business district. Berlin's large territory contained both elegant, tree-filled suburbs and tightly packed industrial neighborhoods, where multistory housing surrounded factories. In the Ruhr Valley, multiple, medium-sized cities combined into one highly urbanized region linked by water, railways, and roads. "Randstad," or ring city, linked Amsterdam, The Hague, and Rotterdam into a core urban district. Together they provided the Netherlands with its economic center, political capital, and major port. Earlier patterns of settlement combined with transportation options, income levels, and housing preferences to give a local twist to each particular urban expansion. Cities remained astonishingly diverse in their economic, cultural, and spatial organization.

Contemporaries looked anxiously at "world cities," which for them embodied modernity in its many forms. Writers worried about the unknown faces and the endless press of bodies on the boulevards at rush hour. "Berlin was storming homeward from its work," wrote one observer in 1914. "Solid masses crossed the pavements, a stream of trams and crowded motor buses clamoured along the street. The *Stadtbahn*, or city railway, thundered across its arches overhead. The *Untergrund* [Underground] engulfed rivers of humanity in the side streets. Shop-girls, clerks, petty bureau-officials, tradespeople, typists – fresh eager faces, restless and nervous bodies"[3] Cities, like stormy weather, could threaten and engulf human beings, upsetting their equilibrium. Ernst Ludwig Kirschner painted Berlin streets filled with angular, anonymous, alienated adults walking toward unknown destinations. (See Illustration 20 in Chapter 7.) A metropolis seemed uncontrollable and unfamiliar. The scale of its diversity overwhelmed contemporaries, who worried about the physical and political problems generated within urban environments.

Technology, transportation, and disease

Technology had dramatic impacts on the ways in which cities looked and functioned. Like American pioneers cutting down trees, construction companies selectively leveled the older cityscapes, before they laid out new streets, underground sewers, and subway tunnels. Orgies of creative destruction substituted new for old. Innovative products and inventions

---

[3] Quoted in Anthony McElligott, *The German Urban Experience, 1900–1945* (London, 2001), 170.

changed methods of building, and architectural styles sometimes shifted to signal the modernity of the structure. The pell-mell growth of European cities went hand in hand with the technological upgrading of towns. The first industrial revolution brought gas lighting, cast-iron pipes and girders, and plate-glass panels for roofs and walls. Steam engines pumped, turned, and pulled. The second industrial revolution, which occurred late in the nineteenth century, brought electric power into cities and along with it electric lighting, telephones, trolley cars, and elevators. Internal combustion engines soon found practical uses in city buses and automobiles. Structural steel and reinforced concrete permitted higher and wider buildings, tunnels, and bridges. But talking about size, strength, speed, and more modernity captures only one part of a more complex story of social and cultural change. Industrial technologies made possible the reorganization of urban space and patterns of circulation in ways that altered social relationships and ways of life.

The most important technological agent of change in the nineteenth-century city was the railroad. For the most part, it concentrated settlement around production sites and city stations, moving migrants to places along the lines of the tracks. Designed for long-distance travel, railways primarily moved people between cities, channeling migrants to towns on the railway grid. But the multiple rail lines which entered major cities could also be used by short-distance commuters after local stations opened. The vast spaces of metropolitan London made it economically viable for train companies to add suburban stops and to build new lines designed for local traffic. As early as the 1850s, 6,000–10,000 people moved daily by railway into the capital. In Paris, the major railway companies built two circular lines, the Petite Ceinture in the 1850s and 1860s and the Grande Ceinture between 1875 and 1882, to transport goods and people among the several stations that ringed central Paris. At the end of the century, the Petite Ceinture moved 30 million passengers yearly around the region. By 1914, multiple suburban stops dotted the area around Berlin, giving people within a 20-km radius easy access to central districts. A new circle line allowed suburban passengers to reach much of the central business district easily. Because residents no longer had to walk to go to work or to shop, suburban railway networks permitted the decentralization – and thus the spatial as well as the demographic growth – of the larger cities. Mass transit allowed people to work in a central district but to live at a distance.

Over time, local transit options increased and became cheaper. The rich had always been able to use private coaches, and cabs for hire enabled those with money to avoid walking, but now many others could afford vehicular traffic too. As cities grew in size, so did the demand for

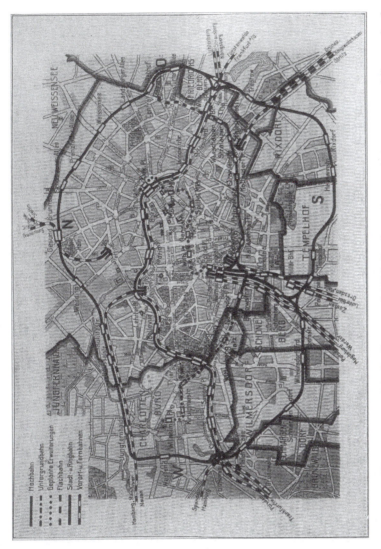

Map 5. The railway network in Berlin around 1900. By the early twentieth century, public transit of several types made travel easy in the German capital. Solid lines show both underground and elevated routes that operated only within the city. Alternating white and black lines show long-distance lines. Dotted lines show tracks planned for later construction. (Robert Wuttke, ed., *Die deutschen Städte: Geschildert nach den Ergebnissen der ersten deutschen Städte-Ausstellung zu Dresden 1903*, vol. II [Leipzig, 1904].)

transportation. During the later 1820s, entrepreneurs discovered they could make money from horse-drawn buses traveling set routes, and services started in Nantes, Bordeaux, Lyon, Paris, and London, soon spreading to other towns. Until the 1870s, middle-class passengers made heavy use of the "omnibus" to move around major European towns, but it was relatively slow and expensive. Because reduced friction meant that teams of horses could pull larger carriages, the addition of iron rails set into city streets made the service much faster and more efficient. In the 1870s, local transit companies multiplied in Western and Central European cities. Street railways carried passengers to and from major railway stations, and expanding services soon criss-crossed metropolitan areas, permitting thousands more people to move longer distances for lower fares. Using horses for power, however, had many disadvantages. Not only did horses pollute city streets, but they also had limited working lives and cost a lot of money to maintain.

Technology soon made horses obsolete for purposes of urban transport. As soon as cheap electric current became available, inventors on both sides of the Atlantic rushed to adapt it to mass transit. Change came after 1888, when Frank Sprague, an engineer who worked briefly for Thomas Edison, designed and introduced a trolley powered from overhead lines via poles and swiveling gears. Within a few years, when investors realized that the new system permitted faster, larger-scale, cleaner, and cheaper services, "electrification shot through the American street railway industry like current through a copper wire."[4] German and French engineering companies, working on their own, installed similar systems during the early 1890s, as soon as they worked out methods of powering the cars from underground circuits in central areas, where city governments usually vetoed overhead wires on aesthetic grounds. British companies followed suit during the next decade. By 1900, brightly colored trolleys cruised city streets from Glasgow to Budapest. The average citizen in a large German or a British town took about 200 tram trips a year, as walking cities expanded into riding cities. Street congestion pushed an additional change, the shifting of mass transit underground, which became an attractive option in the biggest cities after railway engines were adapted to electric power. London's Metropolitan Line circled the central business district by 1884, the first section of the Paris Métro opened in 1900, and an east–west line cut through Berlin by 1902. Well before workers, shoppers, and sales clerks had access to automobiles, electric trolleys and subway systems permitted them to move within decentralizing, metropolitan regions, which transportation knit into coherent systems.

[4] McKay, *Tramways and Trolleys*, 50.

As they remade journeys to work, railroads and other forms of mass transit transformed urban geography. First and foremost, railways meant destruction of large parts of the city to build tracks and depots, since companies wanted to bring their stations as far as possible into the centers of the bigger towns. Cutting across existing streets and neighborhoods, tracks turned isolated spots into slums, while they turned areas near the new stations into prime real estate. Street layouts changed as tracks blocked older traffic flows and privileged sites near stations. Demolitions encouraged new uses of land, and property values fell or rose, depending upon distances from tracks and stations. In city centers, construction companies leveled acre upon acre of housing, whose owners had to sell and whose tenants had to relocate. Although the British Parliament in 1885 legislated a requirement that railways build substitute housing for displaced workers, few new units were actually constructed. In any case, time lags between demolition and reconstruction made such programs ineffective. Economic and demographic growth of cities thus generally came at the expense of those living near rail lines, although not at the expense of those who owned property near stations.

Although many citizens equated new technology with progress, its introduction into urban environments that were crowded brought many indirect costs. Those who were not displaced still paid a penalty. Density rose along with rents in adjoining areas because of increased crowding. People living in some neighborhoods found themselves on "the wrong side of the tracks," where engine noise and coal smoke degraded the territory. Coal-powered steam engines spewed particles and sulfur dioxide into the air. Railways, steam hammers, and iron machinery chugged, thumped, whirred, and clacked. Industrial by-products attacked noses, ears, eyes, and intestines. Although people had for centuries been fouling air, earth, and water, the vast scale of industrial pollution and its proximity to large numbers of people produced disastrous results.

Long before global warming aroused growing concerns about the future of our planet, there was good reason to worry about the impact of new techniques of production and movement through space on the bodies of men and women who lived in urban areas. To be sure, rising standards of cleanliness and middle-class unease magnified awareness of the pollution problem. Contemporaries who had servants to fill baths and wash clothes wrote obsessively about filthy streets and tainted air. The chance of infection came in multiple forms. Mary Douglas's suggestion that the bourgeoisie worried about dirt particularly in periods of cultural upheaval helps to explain the mounting fear of pollution during the turmoil of industrial urbanization. Dirt can be defined as "matter out of place," and certainly growing cities were filled with multiple things

13. Housing in London around 1870. In a well-known set of illustrations, the French artist Gustav Doré depicted workers' neighborhoods
as vastly different from fashionable districts in London. This picture
of monotonous row housing shows his awareness of the environmental
impact of the railway and of the growing density of the city. (Blanchard
Jerrold and Gustav Doré, *London: A Pilgrimage* [London, 1872].)

and people out of place who threatened the orderly lives of the comfortable.[5] Worries about "dirt" had psychological, as well as physical,
roots. Nevertheless, environmental problems were real and threatened
the health of citizens.

Consider, for example, conditions within the city of Lille, about which
contemporaries complained loudly. Elegant brick and stone buildings
there had by the 1860s turned black from the smoke of the 200 textile factories operating within the city limits. Acid rain corroded metal
roofs and turned green trees brown. Tanners, dyers, butchers, and distillers dumped chemicals and waste directly into the city's canals, while
untreated sewage and household waste drained into the Deûle river,
where dead fish floated alongside industrial garbage. Yet housewives still

[5] Mary Douglas, *Purity and Danger* (London, 1984), 35.

used its water for washing clothes and dishes. Since even local wells were heavily polluted by industrial and human waste, cleaner water was in short supply. Mud, animal manure deposited by wandering cows and horses, cinders, and household trash littered city streets. Lille was a grey, sad-looking city – earth, sky, and water blending into a leaden hue. Its high mortality testified to the human costs of industrialization combined with urbanization and poor infrastructures. Children found local conditions particularly lethal: during the 1850s, a quarter of those born in Lille died before the age of three. They fell ill from lung and gastro-intestinal diseases, croup, diphtheria, and measles. Cholera swept through the city in 1832, 1849, 1854, and 1866, killing thousands of adults as well as many children. When military recruiters in 1858 examined workers in the poor Saint-Sauveur district, they rejected more than two-thirds of the registered males because of their size and their weak and deformed bodies. Life expectancy in the city at that time was only twenty-four years and eight months![6] To be sure, industrial technology does not deserve all the blame. Artisanal methods of production combined with high-density living contributed their share too. Improvement would depend on changed technologies of water provision, waste disposal, building, and public health.

Two diseases endemic in cities during the nineteenth century show some of the close connections between environmental conditions and illness. Typhoid spreads from the feces of those infected to others via water and food, commonly through contamination by sewage. Anyone was vulnerable, therefore, in towns which did not have effective public health systems and clean water. Typhus, on the other hand, is carried by body lice, whose feces and bites spread a micro-organism that enters the blood stream of people exposed to it. Typhus thrived particularly in overcrowded workers' districts, where bad housing and the lack of water supplies for bathing and laundry fostered body lice. It was a disease of the poor. The two diseases together killed annually over 100 people per 100,000 residents in Belfast, Dublin, Hull, Leeds, Sheffield, Manchester, and Newcastle, and over 200 persons per 100,000 in Liverpool during the 1860s. Death rates from these two diseases gradually declined later in the century, as more towns invested in clean water and effective sewage removal and as living standards gradually rose, but not all had learned this lesson as we shall see from the example of Hamburg.

Disease mortality rates help answer the question of who suffered the most from environmental degradation. In Birmingham during the 1880s, suburban areas experienced virtually no deaths from infectious diseases such as scarlet fever or measles, which killed many in crowded,

[6] Pierrard, *La vie ouvrière*, 136, 138–39.

inner-city workers' areas. In London, mortality rates during the 1870s and 1880s were much higher in east and central workers' districts than in the middle-class West End or in southern suburbs. Moreover, London's infant mortality from all causes was highest in the poorest districts. In Lille too, the highest death rates from a variety of diseases were to be found in the most crowded, dirtiest parts of the inner city and industrial suburbs. Even though smoky air, polluted water supplies, and defective drainage affected citizens of all sorts, the affluent could insulate themselves somewhat from the worst environmental hazards by purchasing better housing, food, and clothing. Their houses were the most likely to be connected to city sewer systems and to have running water. In the urban marketplace, money bought a good deal of protection from environmental hazards and early death. Consider, for example, the life expectations at birth of Sheffield residents in 1860–62. In professional and managerial families, men commonly lived to the age of forty-seven and women to the age of fifty, but the figure for men was only twenty-eight and for women thirty years of age among low-skilled and unskilled workers.[7] In the same town, the upper middle class lived on average twenty years longer than did the laborers and servants who worked for them.

Even the safety of the middle and upper classes, given the feeble state of medical knowledge at the time, rested on shaky foundations. With the exception of smallpox, doctors could provide no effective therapies against many diseases that afflicted all sectors of urban society to a much greater extent than is the case nowadays. Moreover, they lacked the drugs and vaccines which have proved potent against, for example, tuberculosis, measles, pneumonia, and scarlet fever. Although they could recognize many illnesses and knew that certain ones were highly infectious, without clear theories of transmission doctors' advice on how to stay healthy was contradictory and often useless. Medical practitioners and public health experts disagreed about what caused diseases. Some argued in terms of internal imbalances in the body induced by moral or psychological failings. Others attributed disease to bad air or miasmas, which arose from rotting plants, ground water, or sewage stink. The idea that microorganisms, or "germs," caused diseases spread slowly after 1868, when Louis Pasteur, a French chemist, isolated a bacterium from diseased silkworms and then formulated both an explanation and a strategy for preventing contagion. Support for germ theory spread slowly later in the century only after other researchers established links between particular illnesses and specific bacilli. Dr. John Snow's mapping of London cholera deaths and water supply systems in 1855 suggested that contaminated

---

[7] Woods and Woodward, *Urban Disease and Mortality*, 25, 28, 103–04, 108–10.

water spread that disease, but not until Robert Koch isolated the cholera bacillus in 1884 was it possible to identify the infectious agent and to confirm its method of transmission.

Before the late nineteenth century, medical knowledge and practices did little to lower urban mortality rates. Existing technologies for environmental improvement were in their infancy, and civil engineers argued about materials and design. Public health reforms could have unforeseen consequences. For example, underground sewage systems commonly drained into rivers, adding disease-producing micro-organisms to potential sources of drinking water and urban food supplies. When faced with alternative recommendations and unproven technologies, inexperienced town governments moved cautiously and sometimes ineptly. Christopher Hamlin argues on the basis of English examples that "urban improvement really was a matter of staggering complexity."[8] It occurred slowly and did not correlate easily with wealth, civic-mindedness, or urban scale. Technology transformed urban spaces and economic production faster than it changed public health conditions and the quality of everyday life. As a result, cities remained less healthy than the countryside and their populations more susceptible to epidemics through the nineteenth century.

The fact that nineteenth-century cities still had multiple public health problems can be clearly illustrated by a look at Hamburg around 1890. One of Germany's wealthiest cities, Hamburg was self-governing, self-confident, and self-satisfied. Its affluent amateur officials ruled the town in the interests of its merchants and declared the German Kaiser a "foreign monarch," rather than their sovereign. The growing Prussian public health bureaucracy was among the many German novelties they disdained. Despite its general prosperity, the city was very dirty: thousands of privies remained unconnected to its sewer system; smoke from numerous chimneys blanketed the city with a grey fog; and countless horses, pigs, and cattle walked the streets. Overcrowded tenements swarmed with roaches, rats, fleas, and lice, and without running water or bathrooms, poor inhabitants fought a losing battle against dirt.

Such conditions by themselves produced high death rates, but Hamburg also had to deal with the problem of diseases imported into the city through its extensive trading and transportation network. In 1892, Russian emigrants who had been exposed to cholera came by train to Hamburg en route to the United States. While waiting for their transatlantic steamers, they lived in barracks and lodging houses, whose latrines drained directly into the harbor or into canals which cut through older

---

[8] Christopher Hamlin, "Muddling in Bumbledom: On the Enormity of Large Sanitary Improvements in Four British Towns, 1855–1885," *Victorian Studies* 32 (1988): 83.

quarters of the city. Soon the city's source of drinking water was infected by the cholera bacillus from the migrants' feces, and within a few months approximately 18,000 people had contracted that disease and 9,000 of them had died. The great majority of those who fell ill were from low-income families who lived in overcrowded housing in the central part of the city, but residents of more prosperous neighborhoods died in great numbers too. Early efforts to ignore and to conceal the sickness only worsened the epidemic, which spread from Hamburg to hundreds of other places in north Germany. Because cholera epidemics had ceased to be a problem in Western Europe and elsewhere in Germany, where cities normally filtered their water to remove bacteria or located clean sources of supply, the severity of the epidemic that began in Hamburg was shocking. But it should not have come as a surprise. Disputes over who would pay for a filtration system and doubts about the need for it had delayed the construction of one in Hamburg, where officials remained skeptical about the need for state actions to improve public health. The city had also moved away from the practices of quarantine, disinfection, and compulsory inspection, which had slowed the spread of epidemics earlier in the century. Richard Evans, who has studied the 1892 Hamburg epidemic, calls it "a disease of human agency"; politics more than bacteria conditioned its spread. He blames Hamburg's government, run on the cheap by wealthy, part-time amateurs, for closing its eyes to the unsanitary conditions and overcrowded housing, which permitted the rapid spread of the disease.[9] More interested in healthy commerce than in healthy people, they expected individuals to take care of themselves.

The obvious failure of this strategy in 1892 forced major changes both in city government and in public health practices. If large, growing cities were to be healthy places in which to live, they required expensive infrastructures, sanitary housing, and environmental controls. Liberals' preferences for self-help and individual freedom might be viable on a personal level, but they were not adequate strategies for modern urban governance. The problems of the urban environment, as they came to be perceived, challenged contemporaries' political ideologies and undermined the position of middle-class liberal parties. Problems that could be ignored or tolerated in a village became unavoidable on the scale of the metropolis, reforms in which will be discussed at greater length in Chapter 6.

Conditions and conduct

Contemporaries were quick to merge the topics of physical and moral contamination, arguing that environmental problems led directly to

[9] Evans, *Death in Hamburg*, 565.

behavioral ones. Seth Koven comments that after the cholera outbreak of 1866 writers linked the slums of East London "with every form of literal and figurative impurity: contaminated water and fallen women; insect- and incest-riddled one-room tenements; rag pickers and rag wearers."[10] Anxieties about the condition of the urban poor, which had been acute during the 1840s, resurfaced in the 1880s in a large literature linking wretched housing to crime, corruption, and illicit sex in the city. Andrew Mearns's *The Bitter Cry of Outcast London* (1883) set the tone of alarm with the charge that "seething in the very centre of our great cities, concealed by the thinnest crust of civilization and decency, is a vast mass of moral corruption, of heartbreaking misery and absolute godlessness." He painted a lurid picture of slum dwellers – irreligious, hostile to marriage, drunken, and predisposed to crime. Living in "pestilential human rookeries . . . where tens of thousands are crowded together amidst houses which call to mind . . . the middle passage of the slave ship," they were pushed by a bad environment into dangerous and degrading behavior.[11] The novelist George Gissing forced readers to acknowledge the ugly misery within slum walls and to confront "those brute forces of society which fill with wreck the abysses of the nether world."[12] In addition to British writers who flooded the reading public with discussions of London's poor, Zola's novels about the Rougon-Macquart family during the Second Empire in France gave the public alarming pictures of urban slums and their inhabitants. Reporters, photographers, artists, and novelists regularly focused attention on the sharp outlines of human misery, which looked threatening and possibly contagious.

Moralists feared that city size and living conditions had a behavioral impact and led the poor into crime and irreligion. Images of criminal neighborhoods, juvenile gangs of pickpockets, and predatory beggars circulated via print and picture after 1850, just as they had in earlier decades. Henry Mayhew investigated Londoners "who would not work." German conservative newspapers charged that violent crime was on the rise during the later nineteenth century. Thieves who lurked in urban alleyways, knives in hand, appeared on stage and in novels. Victor Hugo warned that "Cities, like forests, have their dens which hide all their vilest and most terrible monsters. But in cities, what hides thus is ferocious, unclean, and petty."[13] Along these lines, French journalists and artists created the figure of the "apache," ready to strike out at his victims.

---

[10] Koven, *Slumming*, 185.
[11] Andrew Mearns, *The Bitter Cry of Outcast London* (London, 1883), 7.
[12] George Gissing, *The Nether World*, 2nd edn (London, 1890), 392.
[13] Victor Hugo, *Les Misérables*, trans. Charles E. Wilbour (New York, 1992), 644.

14. A view of crime in Paris in 1907. After journalists compared the brawling of urban gangs to the fighting of Native American Indians, contemporaries used the term "Apache" to describe the criminals and muggers who lurked on city streets. This illustration from a popular illustrated newspaper asserts, "The Apache is the plague of Paris." (*Le Petit Journal*, 20 October 1907.)

Anxieties about urban crime and immorality rested on suspicions that urban communities were drifting out of control of the institutions and elites that had predominated earlier. Clergymen expressed these opinions most strongly, linking half-empty churches and moral decay. Arthur F. Winnington-Ingram, an Anglican vicar in East London and a future Bishop of London, thought that the huge cities had too few clergymen to keep workers from succumbing to competing attractions and straying into unbelief. In his opinion, immorality and distance from organized religion went together. Otto Dibelius, a German Protestant clergyman who worked in Danzig, complained of low church attendance and urban disinterest in church weddings, baptisms, and burials. "Morality and communal life, which sustain the individual in smaller places, fall away in the big city . . . As a result, one support after another is removed from piety, until it finally collapses."[14] Many saw religious indifference leading to riot and rebellion as well as to crime, for example in the case of the Paris Commune of 1871. Both Pope Pius XI, who deplored the event, and the communist Friedrich Engels, who welcomed it, argued that workers had lost their faith and abandoned their churches. Contemporaries worried about the fate of religion in the cities because they feared the political implications of its decline, but most had little direct information about the problem.

It is worth examining these charges in some detail because they circulated so widely and for such a long period. Middle-class fears did have a material basis: urban slums were unhealthy, wretched places in which to live, and many poor people lived in the cities. Some city dwellers did break the law, and some stayed away from churches. The interesting question is whether these conditions were causally linked. Contemporaries had limited knowledge of the conditions they deplored, and they made large imaginative leaps between single cases and large groups. To what extent does the evidence as reconstructed today bear out their attacks?

The starting point of many critical analyses was the wretched condition of many buildings in workers' neighborhoods, which were well documented in the contemporary press. The defects of workers' housing are easily summarized: it was too often overcrowded, dark, dirty, damp, and in disrepair; it also usually lacked connections to gas, water, and sewer pipes, which were becoming standard for new, middle-class housing. One ordinary Budapest workers' area consisted in 1911 of wooden shacks and one-story "rental barracks," described by one observer as a line of "cells in a prison." In one such building, ninety-seven people

---

[14] Quoted in Andrew Lees, *Cities Perceived: Urban Society in European and American Thought, 1820–1940* (Manchester and New York, 1985), 158–59.

shared two privies. A typical apartment consisted of one room and a windowless kitchen.[15] Such conditions were products of both past and present construction in combination with the recycling of urban buildings and land that took place as cities grew, people moved, and economies changed. Edinburgh and Naples had centuries-old, multistory stone tenement buildings without running water, gas, electricity, or sewage connections. Newcomers crowded into pre-modern structures, which neither city governments nor landlords moved quickly to upgrade. As the wealthy moved out of central London, their older townhouses became multi-unit apartments. New construction was not necessarily better. In Brussels and Budapest, builders filled back alleys with rows of tiny, substandard, squalid dwellings. Multistory tenement blocks, most newly constructed, dominated the larger German cities. Four- or five-story buildings led back from streets through series of small courtyards. In the early 1880s a Berlin city missionary, Herr Böckelmann, visited one such building that housed 250 families. Paper, wood, or cloth, rather than glass, filled window frames, and many families shared a single room with lodgers.[16] But perhaps these families were among the relatively lucky ones; in periods of housing shortages, newcomers lived in tents and shacks on the outskirts of the city. Workers in Belgium, England, and Wales generally lived in self-contained cottages or terraces, but these could be built back-to-back without water and sewer connections. Many immigrants into Paris settled in shanty towns in the industrial suburbs that ringed the French capital. Observers found appalling conditions, whatever the outside physical form.

Workers' neighborhoods gained in notoriety as the contrast between them and middle-class areas deepened and as bourgeois romanticism about family life intensified. Those who could afford to do so tried to create "homes" in newly developed areas. At a time when central business districts expanded, many had to move because land prices and rents rose. Builders found it more profitable to design new districts for the middle classes, initially the only group able to afford to commute to work, than to rebuild in older areas. Since the eighteenth century, dozens of villages on the London periphery had acquired new villas, shops, and streets, as merchants and professionals fled the metropolis. Looking for a "bourgeois utopia," where harmony with nature and privacy would protect women and children from the pollution of the city, less affluent families also exchanged mixed-class neighborhoods in the center for

[15] Gábor Gyáni, "Budapest," in Daunton, ed., *Housing the Workers*, 165.

[16] Quoted in Nicholas Bullock and James Read, *The Movement for Housing Reform in Germany and France, 1840–1914* (Cambridge, 1985), 54, 60.

strings of monotonous terraced housing in the suburbs, inhabited by people like themselves.[17] Cities became more class segregated as they grew
larger, and the market for land gave desirable space to those who could
pay for it. Moreover, physical distancing brought emotional distancing
from older neighborhoods, increasingly perceived as squalid and threatening. Whatever sense of a united identity had existed in the past was
weakened greatly by growth. Focusing on the separation of urban space
into slum and suburb ignores, however, the ways in which each of these
environments helped to produce the other. The removal of the wealthy
changed the social composition and social functioning of decaying areas
and determined that of newly built sections, while lurid representations
of slum populations and their neighborhoods shaped social policies and
intensified segregation.

The suburbanization of London and other large English towns preceded the same trend on the continent, but the class segregation of other
major cities accelerated too during the second half of the century as
urban areas became more homogeneous because of building decisions
and migration streams. Elites remained concentrated in central areas in
Paris, Vienna, Budapest, and Brussels, but rising rent levels, industrial
relocation, and slum clearance forced workers to move farther out. By
1900, Paris had acquired its "red belt" of industrial suburbs, and outlying sections of metropolitan Berlin and Vienna had become workers'
neighborhoods. When new land came on the market, housing to be built
on it could be designed for a particular social group with room sizes and
amenities pegged to potential rent levels. By 1900 there were fewer mixed-
class districts than had existed a century earlier, a fact which intensified
the sense of class differences. Even if cities were becoming more diverse
through migration and growth, they were also becoming more socially
segregated through choice and through the combined impacts of land
markets and transportation costs.

Contemporaries found the contrast of suburb and slum frightening. As
the physical distance between middle-class and predominantly workers'
neighborhoods increased, so did fears of the poor and suspicions about
their political desires and social habits.

Although little in the way of systematic information about the extent of
urban poverty or about income distribution was available through most
of the nineteenth century, British investigators published major studies
of urban incomes around 1900. During the late 1880s, a wealthy businessman, Charles Booth, investigated standards of living in London to
see whether or not the shocking accounts of the starving poor were true.

---

[17] The phrase was coined by Robert Fishman in *Bourgeois Utopias*.

With a small team of assistants and the aid of local school board visitors, Booth spent years amassing data on the *Life and Labour of the People of London*, which he published in a partial form in 1889 and then fully in 1902. Aiming for a solid statistical analysis of London standards of living, he surveyed the capital by district, by trade, and by income level. His categories for the London population mixed income levels and judgmental descriptions, but they gave contemporaries for the first time a plausible quantitative portrait of city dwellers. Class A, "the lowest class of occasional labourers, loafers, and semi-criminals," and class B, "the very poor – casual labour, hand-to-mouth existence, chronic want," together accounted for only 8.4 percent of Londoners, but when classes C and D, people who worked irregularly or who were badly paid and were poor by any reasonable standard, were added the total of those living just at or below a subsistence level rose to 30.7 percent. Booth concluded that society had little to fear from "barbarians" at the bottom, who were not numerous enough to be a real danger. But by calling attention to the distressingly large number of workers who lived at the margins because of family circumstances and the nature of the job market he both sounded an alarm and pointed away from blaming the poor for their own plight.[18] A similar study of living standards in the northern town of York done by a Quaker businessman, Benjamin Seebohm Rowntree, which was published in 1901, gave almost identical results. Rowntree concluded that between 25 and 30 percent of city dwellers in the United Kingdom around 1900 lived in poverty, which he defined as having a family income that could not purchase enough food and clothing to maintain "physical efficiency." His calculations of wages, food expenses, and needed calories make depressing reading, as do his subsistence-level budgets, which allowed nothing for newspapers, tobacco, beer, transportation, or medical care.

Because no contemporary studies similar to those of Booth and Rowntree were done of French or German cities, less quantitative information was available on continental populations at the time. But the Association for Social Policy in Germany gave the public alarming pictures of urban slums, as did Paul Göhre's descriptions of Chemnitz workers' apartments. The British Board of Trade looked broadly at European urban rents, wages, and prices in 1908–09, enabling researchers to point to places where standards of living were lower than in England or Scotland. Since French and German urban workers paid higher rents in relation

---

[18] Charles Booth, *Life and Labour of the People of London, First Series: Poverty* (London, 1902), I: 39, 173–74; II: 20.

to their wages, on average British workers were better off.[19] Historians have recently found material in archives which allows some estimates of urban standards of living. Richard Evans concluded that around 1890, over two-thirds of the Hamburg population could be considered poor. Many families required multiple wage-earners to cover their rent and food costs, even though the economy was in relatively good shape. In France, according to André Gueslin, the picture was similarly grim. Late in the nineteenth century, between 63 and 70 percent of the populations of Lille, Nancy, and Clermont had no property to leave to heirs when they died. Those same cities at about the same date reported between 5 and 16 percent of their populations as receiving poor relief during a bad year. (This figure, of course, is a better measure of levels of public generosity than of need.) A plausible estimate of the proportion of poor citizens, which would have varied annually according to economic cycles, lies somewhere between these two sets of figures.

Precise levels of urban poverty are difficult to determine because poverty is difficult to define. Is it a state of absolute or relative deprivation? The destitute qualified on both counts, but what of the propertyless who managed to survive on a meager budget and who lived in slum housing? However such questions are answered, an exact number for the urban poor is less useful than a sense of how contemporaries viewed them and of their position in particular cities. Gareth Stedman Jones argues that fears of "outcast London" diminished after Booth published his analysis and after the London dock strike of 1889 established an image of a respectable working class, which far outnumbered and could be isolated from the relatively few troublemakers who hid in the urban slums.

The evidence that supports linkages between urbanization and rising crime is mixed. "Crime" is an all-purpose term that covers many activities from vagrancy to murder to rioting. It does not have a standard definition either among societies or over time, making generalizations difficult. Governments chose selectively which laws to enforce rigorously, and decisions changed over time, as did the list of offenses that constituted "criminal" activity. Focusing on particular kinds of illegal activity, rather than total amounts of crime, avoids some of these classification problems. Judicial statistics probably captured a higher proportion of town than country illegal activity since cities were better policed. Yet no one knows what percentage of total criminal activity was actually reported and prosecuted. Charles Tilly and his research collaborators argue that increased policing produced at least part of the rise in criminal activity reported in

---

[19] Daunton, *House and Home*, 80–81.

Europe during the early to mid-nineteenth century.[20] Michel Foucault also linked trends in crime patterns to changes in enforcement, which he blamed on hardening bourgeois attitudes. For all these reasons, it is difficult to prove that criminal behavior changed significantly over time, whatever its setting.

While noting these complications, we must nevertheless point out that statistics collected in Europe in the nineteenth century generally reported higher rates of theft and assaults in urban than in rural areas when relative sizes of population are taken into account. In 1899, Adna Weber referred to British government statistics for all indictable offenses to argue that cities in England had "double or even quadruple the amount of crime that rural communities have."[21] Yet when he examined statistics for individual crimes, the urban component varied. London had high amounts of theft and assault but low rates of reported rape. Seaports had a higher incidence of crime than did the capital, while spas and vacation towns scored almost as low as agricultural counties in terms of assaults, murder, and other sorts of violent attacks. Different types of cities had different types and rates of crime.

Information on the Marseille population between 1850 and 1870 helps to explain some of the links between cities and crime. Most people arrested in that city for the common crimes of theft, assault, and vagrancy were young, probably single men in their late teens and twenties, the category of residents most likely to have moved recently into town (and most likely even today to commit crimes). Immigrants, particularly those coming from distant places, were more likely to commit crimes than the native born. Occupations made a big difference in crime rates too. Sailors and the unskilled were particularly likely to find themselves hauled into court. Most of those arrested were one-time offenders, caught by the law as they passed through the city. William Sewell argues that temporary migrants, whom he calls a "floating" population, made a disproportionate contribution to Marseille crime. He points to their lack of social ties, to particular occupational cultures, and to the impact of life in the lodging houses, where the down-and-out met others like themselves. Most crime took place in the slums near the port, where newcomers congregated.[22]

Cities attracted a great many young people with few resources and skills. Some had relatives who would house and feed them, while others had to fend for themselves. Petty theft and begging, both punished harshly, were plausible, if risky, survival strategies. Those on the margins

---

[20] Charles Tilly et al., "How Policing Affected the Visibility of Crime in Nineteenth-Century Europe and America" (Ann Arbor, 1982).
[21] Weber, The Growth of Cities, 404.   [22] Sewell, Structure and Mobility, 214–33.

of a city's society sometimes did not play by its rules, but they scarcely constituted a criminal class and most of them left the city quickly. It is important to remember the diversity within cities. Multiple urban groups operated semi-independently, following their own cultural norms and opportunities. The relative anonymity and freedom of urban life gave opportunities to those who chose to commit crimes, but the overwhelming majority of inhabitants were law abiding.

Modern researchers linking cities and crime point to the complexities of making any simple linkage between growth of the two. On the basis of the German Empire's judicial statistics, Eric Johnson argues that there was no linkage in Germany between urbanization and rising rates of theft. Although proportionally more property crimes took place in cities – where there were more visible goods to steal – violent crimes such as assault and battery were more common in rural areas and villages. German cities, moreover, varied greatly in the reported amounts of crime. Region mattered more than the size of a settlement, crime rates being much higher in the northeast and in Bavaria than along the northwestern German border. Port cities and Rhineland towns experienced significantly more crime than did Berlin. Johnson points to economic conditions, poverty in particular, as the best explanation of why some areas and cities had higher crime rates than others. Above average crime correlated directly to relatively high death rates and large populations of minority ethnic groups, who tended to have the worst paid and the most insecure jobs. From his point of view, poverty rather than city living pushed people to flaunt the law. Crime was indeed an urban problem, but it was a rural one too – rooted in inequality and general social circumstances, not in the city itself. Urban crime was not a single phenomenon with a single set of explanations. While some types of crime were related to urban poverty, law-breaking rested on a much wider set of social conditions and experiences.

The linkages between urban residence and rejection of church membership are also complex. Overall, as the great German sociologist Max Weber argued, one can note a certain "disenchantment of the world" that resulted from growing rationalism and the expansion of bureaucracies, both of which were closely linked to urban development. More specifically, two pressures that had begun to build in earlier years intensified an urban drift away from religion during the period under consideration here. Challenges to organized religion from intellectuals and modernizing monarchs had emerged two centuries earlier. Governments in Britain, France, Austria, and Hamburg granted religious toleration; monarchs banned or expelled religious orders, and uncensored publications critical of the clergy multiplied. During the era of the French Revolution, political radicals popularized deism and atheism, as they put anticlerical policies into practice. In the nineteenth century, the numbers of those who had abandoned religious faith multiplied, particularly among urban intellectuals, their skepticism given additional ammunition by biblical criticism and scientific attacks on a literal interpretation of the book of Genesis. The continued institutional power of state-supported religion in Britain, France, Prussia, Italy, the Netherlands, Sweden, and Spain did not prevent the general loss of privileges for European churches as governments cut subsidies, diminished church monopolies of education and charity, and restricted the special benefits of membership. During the 1870s, the German government expelled the Jesuits, took control of clerical education, required civil marriage ceremonies, and curbed Roman Catholic church disciplinary authority. The challenge to the churches was particularly pointed in cities, where religious pluralism and alternative systems of belief, such as socialism and spiritualism, had institutional grounding.

The physical processes of urban growth also undermined the hold of orthodox religion. If rates of church attendance and of participation in church rituals in cities are looked at over time, virtually every European country shows a decline in these numbers. Particularly in Germany, parishes became too large for clergy to provide basic services. In Berlin in 1890, each Protestant clergyman ministered to over 9,500 parishioners. Protestant churchgoing in German towns reached a low point in the 1870s and 1880s, when between 1 and 5 percent of members attended services. London figures were higher, but definitely in decline. The proportion who went to a church service in metropolitan London on Sunday stood at 28.5 percent in 1886 and 22 percent in 1902. Rates were highest in white-collar suburbs and wealthy districts and significantly lower in central workers' neighborhoods. Scholars agree that urbanization broke the hold of the churches on the mass of the population, many of whom had migrated recently from rural areas. Not only did movement into the cities outrun the ability of contemporaries to build enough new churches, but the high mobility of newcomers undermined the clergy's efforts to form stable religious congregations. The high hopes of evangelicals and other religious reformers were smashed on the rocks of rapid migration, which also undermined religious homogeneity. Large Jewish minorities moved into Vienna, Berlin, and London from Eastern Europe; Catholic populations became divided ethnically and linguistically as Poles, Italians, and Irish went to manufacturing cities outside the areas where they were born.

Although there was no mistaking an overall decline in religious observance, a simple picture of uniform abatement of religious faith and practice in European cities fails to take into account diverse forms of popular loyalty to religious traditions. Many scholars have noted significant differences among places and social groups and offered alternative definitions of popular religiosity. Not all countries and cities moved away from formal religion. Roman Catholic practice remained high in Belgium and in Ireland; northern industrial towns in Britain had a religious boom in the late nineteenth century; and even in Germany, Protestant churches increased their appeal between 1880 and 1900 as they added new buildings and welfare services. Women remained more active in church congregations generally than did their husbands, and income mattered too. Many members of the middle classes and elites remained within religious congregations. Declines in attendance varied by gender, social class, and denomination. In any case, attendance is a poor guide to faith. Hugh McLeod argues that "most nineteenth-century working-class people . . . would have loudly insisted that they were Christians, or Jews, and indeed better Christians or Jews than those who were apparently more pious."[23]

Even if not in church on Sundays, large proportions were christened, married, or buried in a religious ceremony and held to a religious world view; they simply refused to be active in religious groups dominated by middle- and upper-class people. McLeod argues that class conflicts and hostilities blocked their participation in socially mixed congregations and that they turned to different forms of religiosity. Religious alienation in his opinion went through three stages: 1) a distancing from ties to a specific church because of migration or shifts in work; 2) development of a working-class identity and a retreat from participation in mixed-class congregations; 3) a shift into secularism and an active refusal of church rites of passage. While most workers throughout Europe went through stage one, and the majority experienced stage two, only in a minority of places, such as Berlin and Hamburg, did a majority move as far as stage three. In those two cities, socialism offered an alternative faith that was militantly secular. Workers' disenchantment with organized religion came in various forms, which varied by national context and denomination. It represented, however, a radical shift in the relationship between workers and elites, which went together with changes in political ideologies and political practice. It was another aspect of the fracturing of urban communities that followed explosive growth and migration.

Lurid depictions of the urban poor, such as those by Andrew Mearns, need to be weighed against alternative interpretations and much more extensive evidence. Today, social historians picture workers not as the dangerous classes or the rioting masses but as low-income people who struggled to survive with the tools at hand. Children went to work early

[23] McLeod, *Piety and Poverty*, 206.

to earn money. Women worked at home, making clothing or taking in lodgers. Older children and grandmothers took care of infants, and neighbors served as childminders when necessary. Wives negotiated with charities, schools, or state relief agencies for temporary help. The Irish, Jews, Poles, and south Italians moved into districts crowded with others like them, many using a local Catholic parish or synagogue as a community center. If one looked closely, one could see in workers' districts a variety of religious and secular institutions, as well as informal groups, which created social capital. Pubs and cafés served as meeting places and labor exchanges. Local squares and courtyards gave children places to play and mothers space to congregate. Urban neighborhoods could function as face-to-face societies, spreading needed information and limited resources. Walter Besant described East London as "a city of working bees." He added, "As we linger and loiter among the streets . . . we hear, as from a hive, the low, contented murmur of continuous, patient work . . . The children work at school; the girls and boys, and the men and women, work in factory, in shop, and at home, in dock and in wharf and in workhouse; all day long and all the year round, these millions work."[24] For Besant, low wages produced discipline and toil, not depravity.

When urban poverty was conceptualized not as moral laxity but in terms of imperfect labor markets, demographic structures, and low wages, workers looked different. Cultural representations were weapons of great consequence in late nineteenth-century political struggles. The focus of public attention remained on cities, sharply divided by class, neighborhood, ethnicity, religion, and ideology. As nation states sought to create common identities and a disciplined citizenry, urban populations posed many challenges. How could the desires and goals of all be accommodated in one space and political framework? How would the growth of democracy shape urban communities?

Active citizens

Although attempts at democratic revolution had fallen flat in Europe after 1789 and 1848, the concept of equality had spread far beyond its original champions. Notions of natural rights that transcended gender, ethnicity, religion, income, and class gave ammunition to groups of women, workers, and religious minorities who wanted improvements in their legal, political, social, and economic statuses. Moreover, revolutions in the Americas and Europe showed that monarchical regimes were vulnerable. Even failed revolutions left important legal and institutional legacies:

---

[24] Walter Besant, *East London* (London, 1903), 115.

after 1848, universal suffrage in France, the memory of a "social republic," which provided jobs for the unemployed, and individual equality
before the law. Voting rights and political participation widened in Britain
after 1867 and in the German Empire in 1871. Meanwhile, industrialization and urbanization transformed the settings in which people lived
and worked. Information flowed faster and farther where there were giant
cities, railroads, telegraph lines, a relatively free press, and mass literacy.
During the second half of the nineteenth century, Europeans confronted
the memories and legacies of earlier political battles on transformed terrain, but basic political questions continued to be asked. Who ought to
have the right to vote, to organize, to strike, to work, to attend school,
to hold property, to divorce, to control children? Should these rights be
universal or limited by gender, age, literacy, wealth, religious confession,
or birthplace? These were hotly debated issues, with strong defenders of
the status quo as well as of change, particularly because recent history
showed that laws and constitutions could be rewritten, and new rules
enforced. Power could be challenged, transferred, shared, or regained.

Groups mobilized in their self-interest, defending their views of rules
and rights. Yet they did so in very different ways, employing tactics that
ranged from voting or holding public meetings to rebelling. Disturbances
of the political peace could be merely verbal or symbolic, or they could
escalate into full-scale riots and general strikes. The shape of rights campaigns depended upon several factors: local legal structures, tactics and
beliefs of active groups, and responses of those in power. Peaceful protests
could turn violent if the army or the police attacked a meeting or a march.
Despite this range of possibilities, however, the trend in the second half of
the nineteenth century led away from national revolutions toward protests
that accepted current regimes, if not all the rules of the game. Symbolic
demonstrations, strikes, and electoral campaigns proved more attractive
tools than barricades or bombs. As nation-states became solidly established, activists became more interested in reforming them than in rejecting their authority.

Demands for change could be strident and threatening, nevertheless.
Charles, Louise, and Richard Tilly have called the period from 1830 to
1930 "the rebellious century," because of high levels of collective action,
both violent and non-violent. Even within the shortened time span to
be covered in this chapter, 1850–1914, hundreds of thousands of people
mobilized in order to pursue one or another political objective, provoking others to criticize and counter-attack. The Tillys also argue that the
targets and aims of these mass actions changed during the later nineteenth century – after 1851 in France, the 1860s in Germany, and the
1870s in northern Italian industrialized regions. After those dates, most

mobilized groups became "proactive" in their claims, attempting to control new resources of property, rights, or status, such as the right to strike or to vote. The change, they argue, resulted from "the growth of complex organizations" and from the expanded frameworks within which people lived their daily lives. As urbanization, industrialization, and state-making enlarged the networks of "production, distribution, and power," those who felt themselves excluded from participation made "bids for places in the national structures."[25] Demands for rights came from national and local political parties, trades unions, women's associations, churches, and special interest groups. They could be printed in newspapers, debated in clubs and legislatures, or shouted on the streets, and cities were prime places for these activities. Urban associations, public spaces, and media offered multiple sites for political expression and discussion. As central places through which information flowed, they offered their diverse populations a rough-and-tumble arena within which to operate politically and to assert their identities and claims.

The transformation of European society under the impact of ongoing urbanization encouraged political action on a larger scale than previously, as organizations expanded their reach and national identities grew stronger. State electorates expanded – universal suffrage for adult males starting in France in 1848, in the German Empire in 1871, and in Italy in 1912. The Scandinavian states moved to universal manhood suffrage between 1898 and 1907, and Britain permitted adult male urban taxpayers to vote after 1867. This increasing democratization of the national political process excluded women until after 1918, except in Finland (1906), and Norway (1913), making them a constituency ripe for mobilization in favor of rights claims. Urban franchises expanded too, enlarging the groups able to vote for town councils and, in some states, mayors. After 1869, the British municipal electorate included not only adult males but also widows and unmarried women who paid local property taxes. Although European governments were by no means run democratically, ultimate power remaining in the hands of elites, such changes greatly energized political life and pointed the way toward further equalization after the First World War.

From the 1860s through the 1880s, the loosening of legal limits on organization permitted the founding of workers' political parties, which pushed for greater democracy via electoral campaigns and demonstrations, frightening conservative politicians. In the 1870s, socialist or social democratic parties were founded in Portugal, Germany, Denmark, Czechoslovakia, and Spain. During the following decade, similar groups

---

[25] Tilly, Tilly, and Tilly, *The Rebellious Century, 1830–1930*, 253–54.

emerged in Hungary, France, the Netherlands, Poland, Britain, Belgium, Switzerland, and Norway. Such parties used the language of class to attract respectable, largely unionized male workers, who constituted sizable portions (albeit minorities) of their countries' populations. They fared best in Scandinavia and Central Europe. Here, around 1914, over a quarter of all voters chose these mass democratic parties over their more conservative competitors. Their appeal was less in Britain and France, where many workers had Liberal and Republican loyalties, as well as in Mediterranean states, such as Italy and Spain, where anarchist and syndicalist commitments to direct action weakened interest in elections and conventional parties. While most party energy went into national campaigns, socialists, liberals, and conservatives also faced one another in local contests for town councils, where voters could see immediate consequences from their choices. Campaigns brought citizens to the ballot box, as well as into the streets.

Big cities fostered militant behavior through their scale, their symbolic importance, and their networks. Urban density brought critical masses of people together and gave them organizational models; urban institutions created occasions for self-assertion. To be effective, demonstrations had to have an audience, and capital cities where governments could be picketed and traffic stopped with reporters watching from the sidelines were ideal sites for attracting attention. The groups which fostered mass political action in the later nineteenth century – socialist parties, federations of unions, special interest groups, and voluntary associations – had their national headquarters in capitals and regional centers, where they could be close to the political decision makers and institutions they wished to influence. Both allies and opponents were nearby. From central places, the politically active reached down the urban hierarchy to intervene when they chose to do so. When the glassworkers of Carmaux, a small town in southwest France, organized a union, they drew on the platform of the Socialist Party. When they went on strike in 1895, Jean Jaurès, a Socialist deputy in Parliament who had been elected to represent the region, traveled from Paris to give encouragement and coach local leaders about tactics. Networks of ideas, individuals, and resources reached from small towns to the center and back to the towns.

A brief survey of European conflicts between 1850 and 1914 shows why city populations and associations could seem politically threatening. In France, Paris, Marseille, Lyon, and Lille led the list of most politically active places, as the biggest cities had the largest and most frequent demonstrations and strikes. The story of the Paris Commune shows how a city population could be mobilized around demands for local rights and social changes – with disastrous local results. After the defeat of

French forces by the Prussian Army in 1870 and the ending of the Second Empire, activists of all sorts wanted to shape a new French government. Political clubs, newspapers, and conspiratorial groups mobilized the population, reviving memories of Parisian radicalism during earlier French revolutions. Parisian militants formed "vigilance committees," and workers rushed to join the National Guard for the purpose of safeguarding the new regime in the city. When elections for a National Assembly returned a strongly conservative majority whose efforts to disarm the Parisian National Guard and arrest its leaders failed, the stage was set for violent conflict. After government ministers and the army left the city to better attack it, voters in Paris elected a communal council dominated by Jacobins, anarchists, and Proudhonian socialists, who were determined to defend the city and to institute reforms that socialists and workers had been demanding for decades. A nasty, nine-week military siege of the city followed, ending in street battles, mass executions, and a city in flames. Possibly 20,000 Communards were killed by the soldiers and 45,000 more jailed or exiled. Rebellions also took place in Marseille, Lyon, Toulouse, and several industrial towns, but they ended the series of large-scale urban uprisings in France. Thereafter, popular politics shifted to other, less violent forms.

Strikes constituted an important tactic for workers' rights claims in France, as well as the rest of Europe, in this period. In 1864, strikes and, in 1884, trade unions became legal in France, making it easier for workers to organize themselves and to pressure employers. Artisans and proletarians took to the streets by the thousands in 1890, 1893, 1899, 1900, 1904, and 1906, demanding higher wages and greater control over shop-floor decisions, recruitment, and work processes. Continued mechanization and reorganization of production pushed workers into militancy, as did the growth of unions and national union federations committed to direct action. In general, the larger the community, the higher the incidence of strikes. Although the capital's workers were not themselves the most active strikers in France, they provided models for action through the large Paris-based federations of trades unions. Some of their leaders were committed to revolutionary syndicalism (the use of general strikes and direct action to achieve workers' aims), and unions provided ideological muscle and organizing energy for industrial actions. The Confédération Général du Travail, an association of trades unions headquartered in Paris, called for a general strike on 1 May 1906 in support of an eight-hour working day. Labor organizations in cities all over the country, coordinated by Parisian union officials, stopped work. In the capital, over 126,000 people walked off the job.

Italian cities also served as centers for mass political movements. The long military campaign for a united Italy during the 1850s and 1860s took place against a backdrop of nationalist urban demonstrations and anti-nationalist attacks by defenders of the status quo. Later, food prices, new taxes, and political arrests brought people into the streets to march and to storm city halls. Anarchists led small-scale rebellions in Naples, Pisa, and Florence in 1878. Before 1882, the Italian constitution excluded most men and all women from the electorate, forcing the mass of the population outside organized politics. Major riots took place in 1893 in Naples, Rome, Genoa, and Milan, after news spread that Italian migrants in southern France had been beaten up and murdered by French workers, who considered them to be strike breakers. A range of targets and issues emerged: mobs attacked French consulates and foreigners in Rome; Milanese socialists demonstrated against the evils of international capitalism. Milan erupted into violence in 1898, when troops shot at and killed demonstrators protesting the arrest of socialist organizers. Sympathy strikes soon shut down factories in outlying industrial districts, and suburban workers attempted to march into the cathedral square in the center of town. After strikers built barricades and attacked streetcars, authorities declared a state of siege and bought in troops as well as artillery to take command of the streets. The mayor, who attributed the riots to "the work of rascals" and "the doing of the enemies of order," dissolved the local Chamber of Labor and Socialist electoral groups, and he closed down the radical press. Over 250 people were killed and several thousand people arrested. Their numbers comprised newspaper editors, journalists, and parliamentary deputies. Virtually all the rest were employed male workers, who wanted voting and other political rights as well as the right to demonstrate. In the city, cycles of mass mobilization, police and military repression, and restrictions on public activity produced a boom-and-bust pattern of politics.

A shift toward electoral politics took place in Italy at the end of the nineteenth and early in the twentieth century. Property and education qualifications for men were lowered in 1882 and 1912, enfranchising many new voters who supported an Italian workers' party (Partito Operaio Italiano) and a socialist party. After workers' rights to organize and to strike were legally recognized in 1900, unions multiplied as did formal work stoppages. But while Italian mass politics continued to have a combative edge, increased organization and legal changes led urban populations into electoral politics and officially permitted forms of protest.

Cities were centers of collective action in Britain and Germany too. Urban artisans had a long tradition of organization, and industrial workers followed suit. Widened electorates meant that male workers were an important constituency for politicians, and women's groups of many sorts provided a framework for feminist activities. In Germany, although Catholics demonstrated in 1874 and 1875 against Prussian anti-Church policies, strong government and legal restrictions on socialist activities (particularly during the 1870s and 1880s) meant that cities were the sites of relatively modest amounts of street protests until late in the century. Miners' strikes broke out in the Ruhr towns in 1889 and again in 1910 and 1912. Berlin was the site of conflict between police and socialist workers in 1890 and violent strikes in 1910. Socialists brought thousands of people into the streets to demand reform of the restrictive electoral laws that regulated political participation at the state and local levels. About three-quarters of the disorders reported in the popular German press between 1850 and 1914 took place in cities, despite the fact that even at the end of the period only about 60 percent of the population was urban. Still, in comparison with the events of 1848, urban politics in the second half of the century were disciplined and peaceful.

In Britain, where workers had the right to bargain collectively and to strike after 1825, authorities had far fewer legal grounds for repressing their activities than did their counterparts in France, Italy, and Germany. As more and more workers acquired the right to vote locally and nationally, artisans in many towns gained a political voice through political parties and effective negotiations. Male and female workers joined trades unions, friendly societies, ethnic clubs, fraternal groups, dissenting churches, voluntary societies, and socialist parties. R. J. Morris describes the British town as "an ideal site for creating the social processes and relationships vital to civil society," and he argues that many artisans had discovered how to work within the rules of representative politics and to build alliances with middle-class groups.[26] Electoral politics proved rewarding: positions on city school boards, Poor Law boards, and town councils gave socialists and workers some leverage over local government. Because labor leaders had learned the value of peaceful protest and authorities usually avoided open repression, direct actions – strikes or hunger marches, for example – rarely spiraled into violence. When in 1889 striking London dockworkers gained a reputation for discipline and self-restraint, middle-class opinion swung behind their demands and encouraged a settlement.

To be sure, street demonstrations remained a vital part of local political action in Britain. In Liverpool, Glasgow, and London, ethnic and religious differences ignited sectarian battles. Orange Day parades pitted Protestants against Catholics in Belfast and Liverpool. Between 1910 and 1914, industrial unions mounted mine and railway strikes, a general strike in Liverpool, as well as transport strikes in London and Dublin. British

---

[26] R. J. Morris, "Structure, Culture and Society in British Towns," in Daunton, ed., *The Cambridge Urban History of Britain*, III: 410.

cities were not placid places, particularly in the early twentieth century, when economic troubles, strikes, suffragette demonstrations, and Irish nationalist campaigns coincided. Nevertheless, the truly revolutionary transformation of politics after 1850 was that women and workers gained enough legal and political rights to permit them to agitate openly for more.

As long as class and gender remained barriers to full political participation, supporters of political equality for all adult citizens mobilized to widen the suffrage. Urban feminists, particularly in Britain, demanded both political and social changes in their status. Articulate socialist women such as Margaret McMillan in Bradford, Clara Zetkin in Berlin, and Rosika Schwimmer in Budapest insisted on the linkage of universal suffrage to women's social emancipation. August Bebel's influential book, *Woman under Socialism* (1879), announced that the "complete solution of the Women's Question is as unattainable as the solution of the Labour Question under the existing social and political institutions," linking feminist concerns for political, legal, and sexual equality to reorganization of industry and the state. The fact that socialist parties privileged men's claims over women's and in practice ignored their public feminist commitments did not diminish the scary combination of sex and suffrage. Christabel Pankhurst's slogan of "votes for women and chastity for men" asked for a fundamental reorganization of political and sexual culture, neither of which appealed to British members of Parliament. Yet feminist politics had growing numbers of adherents, particularly in the larger British cities. The Women's Social and Political Union drew 250,000 people to a rally in London's Hyde Park in 1908, and around 40,000 women from multiple suffrage groups paraded in central London in support of the vote in 1911. Led by the Women's Social and Political Union, London suffragettes demonstrated, broke shop windows, and burned golf greens, attempting to coerce Liberal Members of Parliament to authorize votes for adult females.

In Germany, where regional governments barred women from attending political meetings or joining political parties until 1908, women's public agitation for the vote began significantly later than in Britain or Norway. Not until 1902 did a group of Hamburg feminists form the German Association for Woman Suffrage. Berlin activists helped to found the International Women's Suffrage Alliance in that city in 1904. Female activists in Scandinavia also organized effectively to demand the vote. A coalition of socialists and middle-class charity workers founded Stockholm's Women's Suffrage Organization in 1902. Austrian female socialists organized a Women's Suffrage Day in Vienna in 1911, when 20,000 people marched to claim the right to vote.

The complexity and scale of political life testify to the growing power of civil society in Europe during the later nineteenth century, which cities helped to create. Towns provided necessary infrastructures – schools, publishers, churches, factories, meeting rooms, bars, and parks – that brought critical masses of individuals together under a diverse variety of banners. Their dense networks of sociability combined with a mass press facilitated the quick communication of ideas and frustrations, and their styles and forms of governance offered multiple opportunities for political participation and expression of political opinion. Although economics and class identities remained strong motivators, no simple explanation hinging on poverty or class consciousness can encompass the diversity of urban political actions and reactions in the several decades before 1914.

Although governments throughout most of Europe remained hostile to mass political power, the constitutions under which they ruled in 1914, in comparison with those of the early nineteenth century, gave a substantially increased share of adult males a significant say in national as well as local politics. To be sure, great inequalities continued, and the issue of women's place in the political realm remained unresolved, provoking agitation on the socialist and feminist left. But socialist parties abandoned utopian dreams for pursuit of centralized, parliamentary, constitutional, democratic government, and they engaged increasingly in conventional political action. As Geoff Eley argues, "Socialist parties became the torchbearers of democracy in Europe."[27] They drew workers into the public sphere and helped legitimize the ideologies of radical feminism. Coalitions between labor supporters and liberals in London or socialist workers and liberals in Stockholm showed how effective cross-class political alliances could be, an urban lesson central to national politics during the First World War.

The cutting edge of the struggle to expand citizenship and civil society lay in cities, central places for the political conflicts and compromises that transformed the nations of Western and Central Europe. Urban networks acted as conduits for international debates over rights and for the transference of models of action. Urban civil society permitted the expression of diverse viewpoints, while it channeled those expressions into a variety of recognizable forms. During the second half of the nineteenth century, urban political parties took the lead in the expression of political demands, which became focused on legislatures rather than on direct action. Given the scale and complexity of city environments, urban organizations proved to be much more effective than informal crowds as

[27] Eley, *Forging Democracy*, 109.

vehicles for mobilizing and expressing opinion. Cities were incubators of political modernization, as well as of social and cultural change.

BIBLIOGRAPHY

Bairoch, Paul. *Cities and Economic Development: From the Dawn of History to the Present.* Trans. Christopher Braide. Chicago, 1988.

Berlanstein, Lenard. *The Working People of Paris, 1871–1914.* Baltimore, 1984.

Bernhardt, Christoph, ed. *Environmental Problems in European Cities in the 19th and 20th Century = Umweltprobleme in europäischen Städten des 19. und 20. Jahrhunderts.* Münster and New York, 2001.

Chinn, Carl. *Poverty Amidst Prosperity: The Urban Poor in England, 1834–1914.* New York, 1995.

Coddacioni, Felix Paul. *De L'inégalité sociale dans une grande ville industrielle: le drame de Lille de 1850 à 1914.* Paris, 1976.

Crew, David. *Town in the Ruhr: A Social History of Bochum, 1860–1914.* New York, 1979.

Daunton, Martin. *House and Home in the Victorian City: Working Class Housing, 1850–1914.* London, 1983.

Daunton, Martin, ed. *Housing the Workers: A Comparative History.* London, 1990.

Dennis, Richard. *English Industrial Cities of the Nineteenth Century: A Social Geography.* Cambridge, 1984.

Dyos, H. J., and Michael Wolff, eds. *The Victorian City: Images and Realities.* 2 vols. London, 1973.

Eley, Geoff. *Forging Democracy: The History of the Left in Europe, 1850–2000.* Oxford, 2002.

Evans, Richard J. *Death in Hamburg: Society and Politics in the Cholera Years, 1830–1910.* Oxford, 1987.

Fishman, Robert. *Bourgeois Utopias: The Rise and Fall of Suburbia.* New York, 1987.

Gauldie, Enid. *Cruel Habitations: A History of Working-Class Housing in Britain, 1780–1918.* New York, 1974.

Goodman, David, and Colin Chant, eds. *European Cities & Technology: Industrial to Post-Industrial City.* London, 1999.

Gueslin, André. *Gens pauvres, pauvres gens dans la France du xixe siècle.* Paris, 1998.

Hanagan, Michael P. *The Logic of Solidarity: Artisans and Workers in Three French Towns, 1871–1914.* Urbana, 1980.

Hardy, Anne. *The Epidemic Streets: Infectious Disease and the Rise of Preventive Medicine, 1856–1900.* Oxford, 1993.

Hurd, Madeleine. *Public Spheres, Public Mores, and Democracy: Hamburg and Stockholm, 1870–1914.* Ann Arbor, 2000.

Jackson, James H. *Migration and Urbanization in the Ruhr Valley, 1821–1914.* Atlantic Highlands, 1997.

Johnson, Eric A. *Urbanization and Crime: Germany 1871–1914.* Cambridge, 1995.

Jones, Gareth Stedman. *Outcast London: A Study in the Relationship between Classes in Victorian Society.* Oxford, 1971.

Kellett, J. R. *The Impact of Railways on Victorian Cities*. London, 1969.

Köllmann, Wolfgang. "The Process of Urbanization in Germany at the Height of the Urbanization Process." *Journal of Contemporary History* 4 (1969): 59–76.

Koven, Seth. *Slumming: Sexual and Social Politics in Victorian London*. Princeton, 2004.

Lees, Lynn Hollen. *Exiles of Erin: Irish Migrants in Victorian London*. Ithaca, 1979.

Matzerath, Horst. *Urbanisierung in Preussen, 1815–1914*. Stuttgart, 1985.

McKay, John. *Tramways and Trolleys: The Rise of Urban Mass Transport in Europe*. Princeton, 1976.

McLeod, Hugh, ed. *European Religion in the Age of Great Cities, 1830–1930*. London, 1995.

Piety and Poverty: Working-Class Religion in Berlin, London, and New York, 1970–1914. New York, 1996.

Moch, Leslie Page. *Moving Europeans: Migration in Western Europe Since 1650*. 2nd edn. Bloomington and Indianapolis, 2003.

Nolan, Mary. *Social Democracy and Society: Working-Class Radicalism in Düsseldorf, 1890–1920*. New York, 1981.

Olsen, Donald J. *The Growth of Victorian London*. New York, 1976.

Pierrard, Pierre. *La vie ouvrière à Lille sous le Second Empire*. Paris, 1965.

Reif, Heinz. "Städtebildung im Ruhrgebiet: Die Emscherstadt Oberhausen 1850–1915." *Vierteljahrschrift für Sozial- und Wirtschaftsgeschichte* 69 (1982): 457–87.

Reulecke, Jürgen, ed. *Geschichte des Wohnens 1800–1918: Das bürgerliche Zeitalter*. Stuttgart, 1997.

Rodger, Richard. *Housing in Urban Britain, 1780–1914*. London, 1989.

Roth, Ralf, and Marie-Noëlle Polino, eds. *The City and the Railway in Europe*. Burlington, VT, 2003.

Sewell, William. *Structure and Mobility: The Men and Women of Marseille, 1820–1870*. Cambridge, 1985.

Shapiro, Ann-Louise. *Housing the Poor of Paris, 1850–1902*. Madison, 1985.

Stovall, Tyler. *The Rise of the Paris Red Belt*. Berkeley, 1990.

Teuteberg, Hans J., and Clemens Wischermann, eds. *Wohnalltag in Deutschland 1850–1914: Bilder, Daten, Dokumente*. Münster, 1985.

Tilly, Charles, Louise Tilly, and Richard Tilly. *The Rebellious Century, 1830–1930*. Cambridge, MA, 1975.

Tilly, Louise A. *Politics and Class in Milan, 1881–1901*. New York, 1992.

Van de Woude, Ad, *et al.*, eds. *Urbanization in History: A Process of Dynamic Interactions*. New York, 1989.

Weber, Adna Ferrin. *The Growth of Cities in the Nineteenth Century: A Study in Statistics*. Ithaca, 1899.

Wohl, Anthony. *The Eternal Slum: Housing and Social Policy in Victorian London*. London, 1977.

Woods, Robert, and John Woodward, eds. *Urban Disease and Mortality in Nineteenth-Century England*. New York, 1984.

Yelling, J. A. *Slums and Slum Clearance in Victorian London*. London, 1986.

6   Toward the social city

Demonstrating an interest in innovations abroad that was to become an increasingly prominent feature of reformist discourse, a group of Glasgow city officials reported on a trip to Paris in 1866. They had observed there the results of an enormous effort in the area of city planning and reconstruction. Brought about during the preceding decade-and-a-half at the behest of the French emperor, Louis Napoleon, by the prefect of the Seine, Baron Georges Eugène Haussmann, what they saw caused them to gush with admiration. Having gone to the French capital to gather information about the "reconstructions . . . and great works which . . . have been, and still are in progress to improve the sanitary condition, as well as the external aspects of the city," they marveled at a wide range of urban improvements. Impressed not only by a greatly expanded network of sewers and other advances in sanitation and public health but also by new housing and wide boulevards, they voiced embarrassment over what they regarded as the relatively backward condition of their own city. As one of them put it, "We have much to learn from Paris . . . and particularly from modern Paris." Its example, they felt, pointed up the need for urban remodeling and renewal by public authorities in Glasgow too.[1]

In the 1890s, Albert Shaw, an American political scientist and progressive reformer, described with equal admiration the results of innovative municipal administration in many European cities. Europeans, he thought, had effectively tackled the problems that had arisen as a result of urban growth in ways that put Americans to shame. In his opinion, municipal progress had occurred most dramatically in Germany. Germans were displaying locally "more of the scientific method than any other people," applying highly disciplined intelligence to the practical realization of a lofty moral ideal: a conception of the city as a "social organism" in which government promoted the wellbeing of its citizens in every way it could.

---

[1] See Tristram Hunt, *Building Jerusalem: The Rise and Fall of the Victorian City* (New York, 2005), 314–15. See the articles by Harrison and Meller on international visits and exchanges of ideas.

Germany, however, did not stand alone. Elsewhere in Europe too, Shaw observed, local administrators were greatly improving the cities they ran, inviting Americans to imitate their efforts to make urban societies more truly social.[2]

In the second half of the nineteenth century, reformers sought far more energetically and effectively than their predecessors had done to change urban environments for the better. Whether because of high-minded desires to make society more humane and just, or because of fears of nasty consequences for themselves, they responded creatively in numerous ways to the ongoing challenges posed by the rise of the big city. Many of the changes they sought had to do with transforming the physical city, by means of slum clearance, improved housing, the introduction of new sources of energy and means of transport, and other infrastructural innovations. Others, however, had to do with a variety of services that can be grouped under the heading of "social welfare," or the improvement of "human capital." Some changes occurred as a consequence of legislation enacted at the level of national states, but local institutions also served as laboratories in which various programs were tested before being adopted at higher levels. Although city officials took the lead in the overall project of making towns more functional and livable, they were helped by a multitude of private groups, which included women as well as men. The members of these voluntary associations practiced social philanthropy in the tradition praised by Robert Vaughan. Still, while charitable organizations remained quite active, the growth of the public sector in relation to the private sector was unmistakable, with public bureaucracies in control of larger and larger budgets. We now explore various strategies for bringing about urban reform.

Varieties of philanthropic voluntarism

Many members of the middle and upper classes sought to combat social problems in cities voluntarily, making use of social capital that was particularly abundant in urban settings. They contributed time as well as money to trying to help needy individuals, in ways that both predated and supplemented the more bureaucratically oriented efforts of municipal governments. Too often, the ongoing importance of private-sector activity within the overall realm of attempts to improve social conditions is overlooked as historians move toward the end of the nineteenth century, their eyes focused exclusively on the growth of government. Before we turn to this latter story, we need to revisit the terrain on which groups of citizens acted as members of nongovernmental organizations with an

---

[2] Albert Shaw, *Municipal Government in Continental Europe* (New York, 1895), 289–90.

eye to changing cities for the better. Benevolent associations arose much more frequently in urban than in rural areas for several reasons. Not only did cities have greater resources, but it was easier to muster them because of rich traditions of civic-mindedness within a public sphere enlarged by increased literacy and improved means of communication. Moreover, the scale of cities mattered: urban social problems were more difficult to ignore and less susceptible to individual solutions. Voluntary groups helped to prepare the way for the rise of governmental activity, but they also mattered in their own right, as signals of attitudes as well as shapers of local environments. Motives were mixed: many of their efforts reflected fear as much as benevolence, and participation brought gains in social status and, for women, escape from domestic life. But the results were of great urban importance. If we seek to understand attempts to improve urban life during the nineteenth century, urban voluntarism cannot be disregarded. In what follows, we consider giving to the poor and attempts to place it on a more rational basis, philanthropic housing, outreach to young people, and the growing importance of charitable activity as a means of advancement for women.

Providing charitable assistance for the needy stood at the center of private efforts to improve urban life. As the magisterial work of David Owen makes clear, such efforts persisted on a large scale in England during the late Victorian period. He cites an 1895 claim by a Charity Commission established by Parliament "that the latter half of the 19th century will stand second in respect of the greatness and variety of the Charities created within its duration to no other half-century since the Reformation." Whether the late Victorians were actually contributing as large a portion of national income as had been donated in earlier centuries is open to question, but in absolute terms the Commission was right. Since 1875, hundreds of new endowments had been created, and a great deal of money had been given not only to them but also to foundations set up previously. Already in 1885, it was reported that the income from London charities exceeded that of several independent governments, among them Sweden, Denmark, and Portugal.[3] Charitable activity was less striking in Germany and France than in Britain, particularly as a secular phenomenon. In a situation in which both the Evangelical Church and the Catholic Church maintained extensive networks of organizations that were designed both to provide assistance and to strengthen religious faith and in which national bureaucracies were relatively strong, civic-based philanthropy made less of an impression. There was nonetheless a great deal of it, which one can readily see if one looks at particular cities. In Marseille around 1890, more than 150 groups offered assistance to

---

[3] Owen, *English Philanthropy*, 469.

expectant mothers, orphans, sailors, and others deemed in need of it. In Lyon in 1906, there were between 245 and 300 charitable organizations, which spent 50 percent more than municipal agencies that provided comparable services. In Frankfurt am Main in 1901, at least 215 organizations offered help to poor people. In Berlin in 1910, over 1,700 private groups provided all sorts of assistance for the needy, ranging from loans and gifts of money to food and housing. To be sure, many of these entities were religiously based, but most of them were secular.

The enormous numbers of independent groups posed problems that charitable reformers found increasingly worrisome. With so many associations providing assistance, how could one know for sure that help was going to the right people in the right amounts? The danger that some men and women would pretend to be poor in order to gain assistance they did not really need – perhaps approaching several organizations more or less simultaneously – seemed to be all too real. With only so much aid to go around, leading philanthropists felt the need to bestow charitable help "scientifically" in order to maximize its effectiveness.

In this spirit, several Londoners established in 1869 a Society for Organizing Charitable Relief and Repressing Mendicity, which soon changed its name to the Charity Organization Society. Under the long-time leadership of Charles Stewart Loch, its secretary between 1875 and 1914, the COS grew greatly in size and influence. It developed into a network of over forty district committees within the metropolis and became a model for similar societies throughout Britain, with which it communicated through its house organs, the *Charity Organisation Reporter* and the *Charity Organisation Review*. It emphasized bringing order into the world of benevolence, not only by keeping registers of charitable organizations and inspecting and reporting on them but also by evaluating individual applications for relief. One of its strategies involved targeting aid to fit individual requirements. For example, it paid for medical care and rehabilitation, tools for workmen, and school fees for children, focusing on problems rather than just giving money outright. It is best known for the weight it placed on the need to distinguish between the "deserving" and the "undeserving" poor, which reflected traditional thinking about poverty according to which the condition of many of the poor resulted from their moral failings and bad choices, which must not be rewarded. Its views sharply contrasted with what became the dominant view later on, according to which poverty frequently resulted from larger factors over which the poor could exert little control. By the end of the century, these views led reformers to regard the COS as being punitive and ineffective. But its emphasis on the need for accurate information about individuals and groups fostered a casework approach that was to become a central feature in the repertoire of professional social workers. In this sense, it represented modernizing forces in the area of social welfare.

Counterparts to the COS appeared on the continent. Consider, for example, the German Association for Poor Relief and Charity, which emerged in 1880. Unlike the COS, the German Association did not collect information about individual applicants for support. Under the leadership of Emil Münsterberg, a Berlin official who supervised poor relief there, it served instead as an umbrella group for hundreds of other organizations – some public, some private. In 1905, its membership list comprised not only 246 city governments but also dozens of philanthropic groups as well as numerous businesses, which exchanged ideas about how best to combat poverty both through the administration of poor relief and through bestowal of charity. Via its meetings and its publications, it played a major part in accustoming German do-gooders to the idea that effective benevolence entailed acting on the basis of expert knowledge as well as on the basis of generosity. In France, the reformer Georges Picot helped to lead a similar organization, the Central Office of Philanthropic Works. A coalition of secular charities, it opposed older practices of almsgiving, which Picot criticized for what he saw as the harm they did to the character of poor people.

Other changes had to do not just with methods but also with what men and women of good will needed to provide, there being a markedly greater interest in what came to be known as "philanthropic" housing. As we saw in Chapter 5, working-class dwellings stood out increasingly as nasty sore spots on the face of the city, having overtaken defective drainage as the leading source of anxiety about urban environments. For many observers, "the housing question" emerged as the core of the urban problem more generally. Replacing slum dwellings with decent houses or flats that workers could afford to rent became a major objective in the eyes of reformers who wished to make their cities healthier and more conducive to respectable lifestyles.

Many of the residences that one can subsume under the "philanthropic" label came into existence as a result of decisions by employers to construct dwellings for their employees. In France, where several examples of employer-built housing had appeared between the 1780s and 1850, many more employer-based initiatives occurred during the following half century. In 1853, a Society of Workers' Cities was established in the textile town of Mulhouse by a dozen industrialists. They pooled their efforts in order to construct 800 units there by 1867, setting an example that was imitated in other provincial towns during the 1860s and 1870s. As a result of additional efforts by other employers, largely acting as individuals, about 20,000 families lived by 1889 in houses built

Map 6. A housing development for workers around 1910. The Krupp iron and steel firm built model housing for some of its employees in Essen to help ease the shortage of decent accommodation. This map shows the Altenhof Settlement, begun in 1892. By the late nineteenth century, designers of model housing included public parks and individual gardens in their plans, which also featured winding streets and communal buildings. Here we see, among other structures, a store, a produce market, Evangelical and Catholic chapels, a bathhouse, a maternity clinic, and a variety of recreational buildings.
(*Wohlfahrtseinrichtungen der Fried. Krupp AG*, vol. III [Essen, 1911].)

by the men for whom they worked, and in the following two decades the number of such dwellings approximately doubled. Having first arisen in Britain most notably around 1800 in the industrial village of New Lanark in southern Scotland, where the textile manufacturer and socialist intellectual Robert Owen discovered that he could do well in part by doing good, much housing for workers was built later in the century elsewhere. Witness the growth in the 1850s and 1860s of Saltaire, built near Bradford by order of the worsted manufacturer Titus Salt; Port Sunlight, built starting in 1887 by Lever Brothers for occupancy by workers at its soap factory near Liverpool; and Bournville, which arose after 1895 near Birmingham on the initiative of the chocolate manufacturer George Cadbury. In Germany, where a survey carried out by the Prussian state in 1875 showed that of 4,850 employers who participated in the survey 34 percent helped their employees in some way with their housing, the Krupp iron and steel firm stood out for the extent of its building program. By 1873, it owned over 2,000 dwellings. After a pause in construction that lasted about two decades, it resumed its activity in 1893, starting to build three housing estates in Essen, and by 1910 it owned over 6,000 dwellings altogether. Around the turn of the century, many other companies followed Krupp's lead, although not necessarily to the extent of incorporating the curved streets and attractive landscaping that characterized Krupp's newer estates. In all of these cases, even when employer-built housing did not yield an immediate profit, provision was based in large measure less on moral grounds than on calculations having to do with enlightened self-interest. Company-owned housing constituted an essential element in employers' strategies for maintaining both a stable and a dependent work force.

Other construction did conform more closely to philanthropic ideals of disinterested generosity. Two groups having been established in London to promote low-rent dwellings for workers in the 1840s, and an individual effort having been launched here in the 1850s by Baroness Angela Burdett-Coutts, the 1860s witnessed the start of three more programs. All pointed toward improved housing, albeit in multistory buildings of a sort deemed to be sufficient for the lower classes. The first two – the Peabody Trust, funded initially by the wealthy American banker George Peabody, and Sydney Waterlow's Improved Industrial Dwellings Company – fostered construction of flats that were to be leased at below-market prices. While the Peabody Trust was purely philanthropic, Waterlow's company sought to make a profit for investors, but dividends were limited to five percent. Octavia Hill also adopted the "philanthropy and five percent" model. In contrast to the Peabody Trust and Waterlow, however, Hill did not construct new buildings. Instead, she bought and renovated older ones. She then leased flats in them to tenants whom she sought both to help and to control by means of a system of female rent collectors who volunteered to keep an eye on the recipients of her somewhat cramped largesse, much in the spirit of the COS. Inspired by Hill's example, the businessman Gustav Liagre joined with eleven friends to buy two buildings with 240 rooms in the German city of Leipzig in 1883. Managed along the same lines as Hill's, Liagre's buildings received much attention in Leipzig and elsewhere. The Leipzig publisher Herrmann Julius Meyer decided in 1884 to fund nonprofit tenements for working-class families under the umbrella of an Association for the Creation of Affordable Housing, and similar developments occurred in other German cities. In France, the passage of national legislation in 1894 that made low-interest loans available to builders who agreed to limit their profits to 4 percent of invested capital contributed to a doubling in the number of building societies that offered low-cost accommodation. As a result, thirty such organizations existed by the end of that year.

Finally, many urban reformers displayed growing concern over the fate of children and adolescents (i.e., "youth"), becoming increasingly engaged in age-specific efforts to "rescue" members of the cohorts that were destined to become the adults of the future. Reformers employed various methods in order to promote child welfare. One involved establishing institutions for children who had been orphaned or abandoned. A famous example of such an approach can be seen in the Dr. Barnardo Homes for Children, established by Thomas Barnardo, an evangelical preacher who had begun but not completed a course of medical study. The first of these places opened in 1871 in London's East End, and several more appeared in the next few years. They consisted of collections of cottages for homeless boys and girls, to which were added several other establishments, among them schools for poor children and a system for providing foster care for illegitimate infants. Barnardo was in certain respects a shady character. His offenses included not only misrepresenting his own background but also exploiting some of the children under his care in ways that elicited strong disapproval by the COS and others charged with looking into accusations against him. Barnardo's benign impulses were fortunately more widely shared than his questionable ones by other Londoners who became engaged in child welfare work. As a consequence of their efforts, London had in the late nineteenth century about fifty orphanages, and many additional services were provided by a network of Waifs and Strays Societies.

On the continent, one can see among women in Berlin a series of efforts to assist children who remained within working-class families, not only by providing assistance to them through their mothers but also by educating other women in private training centers for work in day-care centers and kindergartens. Note, for example, the establishment of the Pestalozzi-Froebel House in 1882 by Henriette Schrader-Breymann on the foundations of a kindergarten that had been in operation since 1874. Note also the founding of the Social School for Women in 1908 by Alice Salomon as an outgrowth of the Girls' and Women's Groups for Social Assistance, in which she had begun to participate at its inception in 1893. Both of these institutions stand out both in their own right and for their inspirational value for women in other German cities. In France, along similar lines, the reformer Augusta Moll-Weiss established in Bordeaux a School for Mothers which moved to Paris in 1897. Dedicated to imparting the skills needed in order to care for infants and other young children, it provided instruction not only for mothers but also young women who wished to become care givers, teachers, or social workers.[4]

Teenagers – particularly adolescent boys – also attracted closer attention and elicited growing concern. A typical complaint about them appeared in a German pamphlet that posed the question, "What is wrong with our working-class youth?" The author lamented, "Desire and frivolity [and] addiction to amusement and to pleasure . . . in conjunction with the abandonment of piety and contempt for all authority, have intensified rebelliousness among the working-class young to a terribly high level, which is everywhere evident."[5] Efforts with regard to the young focused on the perceived need to improve their character in ways that would benefit society. Seen as being too impulsive and all too likely to challenge behavioral norms, male youths of the working classes who had finished their formal schooling (generally at age fourteen) seemed to require a great deal of ongoing guidance. Otherwise, how were they to resist both sexual temptation and other snares that might prevent them from becoming upstanding and productive grownups? The best-known movements to arise from such motivations were the "boys' brigades," which began in Glasgow in 1883 and then spread to England in 1886, and the Boy Scouts, founded by the former military man Robert Baden-Powell in 1908. In both organizations, older men volunteered to lead youths in a variety of activities. They sought to promote not only the acquisition of ostensibly useful skills (e.g., tying knots and building campfires) but also loyalty to comrades and respect for middle-class values more generally in settings the boys themselves would, it was hoped,

---

[4] Ann Taylor Allen, *Feminism and Motherhood in Western Europe, 1890–1970: The Maternal Dilemma* (New York, 2005), 80.
[5] Ernst Floessel, *Was fehlt unserer Arbeiterjugend?* (Leipzig, 1892), 1–2.

find attractive. The story of efforts to provide guidance for boys in ways that combined instruction with fun can be traced not only at the national but also at the local level. David Pomfret has described a multitude of such efforts in the cities of Nottingham and Saint-Étienne. As he writes, "Volunteers in both cities sought to provide sport and in both cases the emphasis was placed on instilling morality and discipline in young people through the use of militaristic provision formats."[6] In Hamburg, Walther Classen, who had studied to become a Protestant clergyman, made a name for himself as a pre-eminent advocate and practitioner of "youth care" (*Jugendpflege*). He headed up an extensive effort to attract working-class boys and young men to educational and recreational activities there that spawned numerous imitators elsewhere in Germany. Meanwhile, in Hanover, Protestant ladies under the leadership of the conservative Paula Müller tried to encourage young women, particularly of the servant class, to lead upright and virtuous lives. Young females did not pose the same threats of rowdiness posed by young men, but fear that they might bear children out of wedlock or even become prostitutes was widespread. Such anxiety resulted in a series of efforts there and elsewhere to reach out to such at-risk city dwellers. Dozens of girls' clubs and associations for servants were designed to help keep young women on straight and narrow paths.

Despite the fact that the initiatives discussed here failed to fulfill reformers' ambitions, their significance far transcended the meeting of immediate needs. The social sites from which they were launched served both as laboratories and as staging grounds. Within the propitious framework of the city, social experiments led to new methods and strategies that would later be adopted and opened up on a much wider scale, resulting in the growth of social work as a profession and in greater diversity among the people who performed it.

Most notably in efforts to help children and young people, but also in other philanthropic endeavors, upper- and middle-class women became increasingly prominent. In so doing, they used benevolent institutions as vehicles for expanding their influence beyond the domestic realm. Engaging in philanthropy enabled many women – particularly women who lived in cities – to step outside the home and enter, albeit still in a subordinate role, into certain sectors of the public sphere. They thus gained experience and authority that would later help them to move much farther in the direction of equality with males. In Britain, two such women were Baroness Burdett-Coutts and Octavia Hill, mentioned above, and there were numerous others. In Germany, in addition to Henriette

---

[6] Pomfret, *Young People and the European City*, 116.

Schrader-Breymann and Alice Salomon, many more stood out as well. Anna von Gierke, for example, founded the Charlottenburg Youth Center near Berlin and headed a Central Agency for Youth Services that coordinated both volunteer and professional efforts on a nationwide basis. Individual women stand out less clearly in the French case, but there was nonetheless a rich tradition of female participation in charitable activity in that country too.

In all three countries, feminists sought to encourage deployment of what they regarded as characteristically feminine traits in order to make urban society gentler and more humane while simultaneously seeking to raise their own status in ways that did not directly challenge male dominance. Salomon argued with great eloquence in this regard. She asserted that women possessed a number of characteristics that made them more suitable than men for the purpose of overcoming social conflicts. A woman could bring to this task "her mild and considerate understanding . . . her carefulness and conscientiousness, her motherliness [and] the capability of transferring motherly love from the home to the community."[7] The belief that women could contribute more to social improvement by capitalizing on their uniqueness than by seeking to imitate men helped to prepare the way for them to work not only as volunteers but also as paid professionals in later years. Some of what they were to do took place in the private sector. But much of it would eventually involve employment in municipal and state agencies that specialized in social welfare, which became increasingly important as the ultimately limited effectiveness of social philanthropy became clearer and clearer.

Contexts for public intervention

Urban-oriented philanthropy and other forms of voluntarism that centered on cities were paralleled and increasingly overshadowed by measures carried out by public authorities. The relatively small and halting efforts by governmental officials to improve urban conditions during the early phase of urban growth were followed in later years by much more far-reaching and better organized attempts by their successors to deal with urban problems. Reflecting a general movement in Europe during the later part of the nineteenth century away from the emphasis on self-help and laissez-faire espoused by "classical" liberals, a new breed of "social" liberals emerged both at the level of the national state and at the level of what is sometimes referred to as "the local state."

---

[7] Alice Salomon, "Die Frau in der sozialen Hilfstätigkeit," in Helene Lange and Gertrud Bäumer, eds., *Handbuch der Frauenbewegung* (Berlin, 1901), I: 5.

Increasingly aware of the often appalling conditions around them but unwilling to dismiss the city as a monster or a tumor in the manner of romantic and conservative antimodernists, urban leaders – most of whom can be described as middle-class liberals – looked for ways to remedy urban ills within urban settings. With strong support from social scientists and other intellectuals, many insisted with growing intensity on not only the economic but also the social responsibilities of city governments, advocating what was coming to be known as "municipal socialism." Support by middle-class reformers for governmental programs reflected a desire to seek social stability through compromise rather than repression in an era when the numbers of voters were increasing. Their backing for interventionist policies also arose from recognition that the urban environment posed serious threats to public health. In many respects, the advent of big government at the local level reflected the interests, or at least the leadership, of urban elites. It would be wrong, however, to believe that urban administration was controlled by business interests. Toward the end of the nineteenth century, businessmen were increasingly supplanted in local governments not only by full-time politicians but also by "experts" of various kinds from among non-capitalist sectors of the middle classes, among whom scientific social workers played a particularly important part. For all of these reasons, social liberalism asserted itself more clearly and forcefully in the big cities than elsewhere.[8]

Mobilization of opinion in favor of governmental activism resulted to a substantial degree from a combination of social investigations and agitation by men and women who called for specific changes. These individuals frequently acted as members of intellectually and practically oriented pressure groups, which advocated economically and socially interventionist policies. In Germany, the best known of these Organizations was the Association for Social Policy (Verein für Sozialpolitik), which took shape in 1872. In many ways a successor to the Central Association for the Welfare of the Working Classes (discussed in Chapter 4), the association was dominated in its early years by state-oriented economists such as Gustav Schmoller, who criticized the classical economics that had arisen principally in Great Britain. It was joined by the German Association for Public Health, founded in 1873 and led by medical doctors and engineers. These men, supported by additional experts in both organizations, played central parts in alerting other professionals and public officials to the need to combat poor housing as well as poor sanitation.

---

[8] Much of this paragraph and of the rest of this section reworks material that appears in Lees, *Cities, Sin, and Social Reform*, 376–86, into which discussion of developments in countries other than Germany has been inserted.

In Britain, where a Sanitary Institute of London that was established in 1876 soon evolved into a Royal Sanitary Institute, a parallel to the German Association for Social Policy can be seen in the Fabian Society. It was established in 1884 as a forum for men and women, such as Sidney and Beatrice Webb, who advocated an evolutionary form of socialism. The Fabians produced numerous studies that emphasized the desirability of municipal provision of a variety of services. They helped thereby to inspire progressive forces in the London County Council, created in 1888 to administer the metropolis.

In France, where an influential journal had begun to focus on public health in the late 1820s (see Chapter 4), the year 1894 saw the establishment of the Social Museum (Musée sociale). It emerged as the leading example there of what its historian refers to as "parapolitical groups," whose members strove in both the private and the public sectors to propagate and implement the idea of "solidarism." In its meetings and offices, engineers, architects, moderate labor leaders, and social scientists as well as officials and former officials (e.g., the organization's first president, Jules Siegfried, who had earlier served as mayor of Le Havre) met to collect information and to devise and publicize proposals for social improvement, particularly in urban areas. Opposed to socialism in principle, they nonetheless supported not only voluntary self-help but also an expanded role for municipalities. Emphasis on housing reform and public health became increasingly evident, particularly after the establishment in 1908 of a special section of the organization that focused on urban and rural hygiene.

All of these groups and many more helped to produce a climate of opinion that favored not only remedial but also proactive interventions to improve the quality of urban life. Seeing themselves as advocates of the welfare of society as a whole rather than as spokespersons for the interests of particular groups, they all paid close attention to what their members regarded as reforms that were necessitated by the rise of the big cities.

Urban officials operated in an environment in which their range of freedom depended both on legal constraints and imperatives that descended from above (i.e., the non-local state) and on political pressures that arose from below. It was within these fields of force, which varied widely from country to country, that the public interventions on which this section focuses took place.

The powers of municipalities rested on particularly strong foundations in Germany. While their autonomy vis-à-vis state governments came nowhere near the independence that dozens of city states had enjoyed during the Middle Ages, the rights enjoyed by city governments to manage a wide range of local affairs had grown markedly earlier in the century in comparison with conditions in the absolutist states of the early modern period. The crucial step forward in this regard, as we saw in Chapter 4, took place in Prussia in 1808. The sphere within which local communities (*Gemeinden*) that enjoyed urban status could act continued to expand in the course of the century, particularly in the areas of land acquisition and zoning. By the early 1880s, as a result of laws passed by state legislatures, city governments generally enjoyed the right to draw up extension plans for placement of new streets, buy the requisite land, and transfer to the owners of adjacent property the costs of paving, draining, and lighting them. Municipal authorities either already possessed or acquired later a wide range of additional powers too. Rights to regulate heights of and distances between buildings, to zone land for differential use, and to add to the public domain through compulsory purchase figured prominently in this respect. Local officials were not only allowed but in some cases required to exercise their powers, particularly with regard to sanitation. Although higher officials reviewed their performance, they enjoyed considerable latitude to decide in practice on preferred courses of action.

In Britain too, the legal foundations of local government, having been clarified and strengthened by the Municipal Corporations Act of 1835, continued to develop throughout the century. As we have seen, the Public Health Act of 1848 authorized municipalities to safeguard public health through provision of sewerage and clean water and appointment of medical officers. Although some features of this law were compulsory (e.g., the requirement that local boards of health be created in most cities in which death rates were high), most of it was permissive. Cities received the right to enact measures of their own if they chose to do so but were not required to enact them. More control from above was introduced via the Public Health Act of 1875, which subjected both rural and urban sanitary districts to the supervision of a newly created Local Government Board. But most laws that pertained to housing, such as the Torrens Acts and the Cross Acts of the 1860s and 1870s and the Housing Act of 1890, were permissive rather than mandatory. They enabled local authorities to act vigorously against owners of run-down and unclean houses and also to prepare schemes for reconstructing large areas they deemed unsanitary. British cities still did not enjoy the latitude exercised by their German counterparts, but the situation changed significantly in their favor as a result of the passage in 1909 of the Housing and Town Planning Act. It gave urban authorities the right not only to establish patterns of main streets but also to distinguish between industrial and residential areas, to control densities in the former, and to reserve land for public uses.

In France, cities also gained additional powers to influence the urban environment, but more slowly, their latitude still being circumscribed to a great degree by strong central authorities. Although big cities acquired the right to elect their own mayors in 1882, the national government retained the power to suspend both councils and mayors, which it exercised with some frequency. Local governments' rights in the area of planning were correspondingly limited in comparison with those enjoyed by their British as well as by their German counterparts. As a result, "Differential building regulations and zoning . . . do not appear to have entered into the heads of French urban administrators even in the 1890s, apart from the rudimentary banning of noxious industries from populous districts."[9] Change began to take place, however, after 1900. A key milestone in this development was the passage in 1902 of public health legislation that resembled statutes adopted in Britain in the 1870s. It pointed city governments toward more effective regulation of both sanitation and housing.

Although mayors in both France until 1882 and Germany were unelected (being appointed by state officials), men who sat on town councils did depend there as well as in Britain on city dwellers' votes. Again, however, variety prevailed, both among and within nation states. In Germany, although male suffrage was nearly universal and, for those who had the vote, equal at the national level after 1871, only a minority of men had incomes high enough to entitle them to vote at the local level. In most parts of the Empire, both their ability to cast ballots and the weight of their votes depended heavily on the amounts of their taxes in relation to the amounts paid by other voters. Not only in Prussia but also in most other states of the Empire, what really secured the economic influence of the prosperous elites was the division of the electorate into three groups of people, each of which voted on an increasingly unequal basis for one-third of any city's council. Around 1890, the first group generally consisted of no more than the top 2 percent of taxpayers. The second group consisted of the next 8–20 percent, while the third class consisted of the bottom 70–80 percent. As few as 10 percent of urban voters could thus pick two-thirds of city councils, a figure that declined to as few as 5–6 percent by 1914. In Britain, a Municipal Franchise Act, passed in 1869, reduced the length of time during which residents had to pay local taxes in order to vote from two-and-a-half years to one year, allowed tenants to receive credit for taxes paid along with their rents, and also enfranchised widows and other unmarried women. This legislation resulted in municipal electorates that generally included

---

[9] Sutcliffe, *Towards the Planned City*, 136.

18–20 percent of boroughs' populations, which in all likelihood slightly exceeded the percentage of the population entitled to vote in parliamentary elections (from which all women were still excluded). By the late nineteenth century, roughly 60 percent of adult males had the right to cast ballots in local elections, about the same as the percentage that prevailed at the national level. Inhabitants of French cities enjoyed the greatest degree of political equality throughout the period. Universal manhood suffrage was the rule after 1848, although, as in Germany, no women had the right to vote. Effectively nullified by the despotism of Napoleon III during the 1850s and most of the 1860s, the right to vote became more meaningful after 1884 as city councils became increasingly accountable to their citizens.

As we shall see shortly, democratization and the desire to cope energetically with urban problems did not necessarily go hand in hand. Usually, representatives of elites rather than of workers or the lower middle class took the lead in this respect. Their importance can be seen most clearly in German cities, with their quite undemocratic rules for political participation. Indeed, in Britain as well as in Germany, cities were strongholds of liberals whose interest in introducing urban reforms coincided with firm commitments to ensuring the dominance and protecting the interests of men of property. We need to bear this point in mind when we think about the complex interrelationships between urban reform and democratization.

Officials at work

Men who ran or worked for municipal governments sought to improve their cities in a multitude of ways, which we subsume here under two broad headings. On the one hand, much effort went into attempts to upgrade cities' infrastructures and physical spaces. On the other hand, many measures entailed provision of city services, with a view to accumulating and enhancing human capital. Let us consider each of these sets of projects in turn, following in detail the ways in which municipal officials sought to implement their overall goal of expanding their range of action with a view to enhancing life in urban communities.

Architects, engineers, and others in the employ of public authorities sought more and more intensively to impose order on built environments. Reacting strongly against what they perceived as disorderly, unplanned growth, they played key roles in seeking to configure urban space so as to make it more efficient, healthier, and more attractive visually. Although it was often impossible to pursue all of these objectives simultaneously, men who ran or helped to run cities consistently searched for

non-ideological – or at least non-revolutionary – solutions to social problems by making use of the growing powers that lay in their hands.

Some of the most ambitious projects, to be sure, took shape at the
hands of men who answered to national rather than to local officials.
Such was the case in Paris, where the most famous of all of the efforts
to remake large portions of a major city undertaken anywhere during the
century got under way in the 1850s. Begun at the start of the decade at the
behest of Louis Napoleon Bonaparte (soon to declare himself the French
emperor), it accelerated and broadened under the direction of Baron
Haussmann, going far beyond anything attempted by the first Napoleon
or any of the projects launched by others who worked in the Baroque
tradition. By the end of his tenure in 1869 as chief administrator of the
French capital, he had implemented an extraordinary range of plans for
reshaping it both from an aesthetic and from a functional standpoint. As
David Harvey writes, "Urban space was seen and treated as a totality in
which different quarters of the city and different functions were brought
into relation to each other to form a working whole."[10] For reasons not
unrelated to the difficulties posed for authorities by protesters who fought
from behind barricades in narrow and crooked streets in 1848, constructing new boulevards that were broad and straight assumed central importance. Not only did the length of the city's street system increase by
12 percent, but average street width doubled. Haussmann drove most
industry out of the city center, where construction of splendid public
buildings such as the Paris Opera House and also elegant apartment
houses (their facades built according to strict regulations that governed
height) was accompanied by creation of the Central Markets. Municipal
parks also sprang up, their total extent rising from forty-seven to 4,500
acres, while the number of trees along streets and boulevards nearly doubled. So too did the supply of water per day per inhabitant, which also
nearly doubled. But Haussmann's program is best remembered for the
introduction of a feature that was invisible to most city dwellers: a vast
system of sewers, which amounted by 1870 to 348 miles, four times the
total in 1851. Consisting of storm sewers instead of general sewers, the
system did nothing to facilitate disposal of human excrement. That still
had to be removed manually from cesspits. But it did enhance cleanliness of streets, and, along with other achievements of which Haussmann
could boast, it greatly burnished both his reputation and that of his city
as a center of innovation.

Counterparts to the "Haussmannization" of Paris can be seen not only
in a number of French cities – most notably in Lyon and Marseille – but

---

[10] David Harvey, *Paris: Capital of Modernity* (New York and London, 2003), 111.

15. A Paris sewer in 1858. Official visit of the Minister of Interior, General Charles Marie Esprit Espinasse (engraving) by Henry Augustin Valentin. An elaborate system of drains for city streets, built in the 1850s, was one of the most notable results of Baron Haussmann's efforts to improve the infrastructure of the French capital. They quickly became tourist attractions and can still be visited today.

also to some extent in Barcelona[11] and especially in Vienna, the capital of the Habsburg Empire. We focus here on the creation of a broad street known as the Ringstrasse and the buildings that sprang up along it. The Parisian and Viennese cases differed in important respects. The key decisions in the Austrian capital reflected both the will of the Austrian emperor, Franz-Joseph, and the desires of Viennese liberals, who in 1850 had extracted from their ruler new rights to municipal self-government. Also, what resulted in Vienna had more to do with architectural display and less to do with practicality. It stands out nonetheless as an impressive contribution to the history of efforts to remake city centers. The process of change got under way in 1857, when Franz-Joseph decided to order removal of the more than two-mile-long wall that encircled the oldest part of the city (the *Altstadt*). No longer needed for defensive purposes,

[11] An instance of large-scale urban design and construction that bore the influence of Haussmann's example took shape here during the 1860s, under the direction of the engineer Ildefons Cerdà.

it made way for a new thoroughfare that eased the flow of traffic and provided a central site for a string of magnificent buildings. As in Paris, some of what arose, especially early on, expressed imperial values. Witness, for example, a great neo-Gothic church, the Votivkirche, which a contemporary observer described as a symbol of "the rule of the saber and religion,"[12] and also a new arsenal and two new barracks located near railway stations. From them troops could quickly be brought to the capital in case of need to suppress insurrections of the sort that had occured in 1848. But after liberals gained control of the city government in the 1860s, the building process increasingly reflected middle-class rather than dynastic aspirations. The first of the public buildings erected during the period of their hegemony was the Opera House, constructed in the style of the Italian Renaissance. Although the bulk of building activity in the early years resulted in apartments for the well-to-do, starting in the 1870s an impressive array of representational structures also arose. A theater, a main building for the university, a city hall, and a meeting place for the Austrian Parliament were all completed by the late 1880s. In buildings that symbolized its adherence both to secular culture and to self-government, the Viennese bourgeoisie thus proclaimed its ascendancy for all who walked or rode along the Ringstrasse to see and admire.

Elsewhere – albeit on an admittedly less spectacular scale – local officials reconfigured urban space for the most part independently of monarchical rulers. In Britain, the case of Birmingham illustrates well the combination of ideas and tactics that produced effective reform. In that Midlands city, advocates of local improvement, foremost among them the clergymen George Dawson and Robert Dale, preached a "municipal gospel" that helped to prepare the way for the efforts of Joseph Chamberlain. Having made a good deal of money as a successful industrialist, he entered the town council in 1869 and then served as mayor between 1873 and 1876. He dominated the local scene, ending the influence of a coalition of small businessmen and others whose "economy group" had rejected proposals for change they regarded as too costly. In a speech at a local church, Chamberlain asked rhetorically, "How can we tell a man to be good and decent and moral when we find him living in a place that is not fit for a beast to live in, much less a human being?" He continued: "The fact is that in our missions we begin at the wrong end; we attempt to apply remedies to diseases which ought never to exist in the social state at all. What we ought to do is to prevent the disease and then we shall not want the remedy." In the same vein, in a speech to the town

---

12 See Carl E. Schorske, *Fin-de-siècle Vienna: Politics and Culture* (New York, 1980), 30. The quotation appears in a splendid essay on the Ringstrasse.

council, he asserted, "All private effort, all individual philanthropy, sinks into insignificance compared with the organized power of a great representative assembly like this."[13] In this spirit, the city assumed ownership of both its gas and its water works, it set up its first Health Committee for the purpose of supervising disposal of sewage and refuse as well as performing other tasks, and it undertook a great "improvement scheme." The city acquired forty-three built-up acres that were disfigured by narrow streets and were dilapidated and unsanitary, which it leveled with a view to total redevelopment. Construction along the main avenue, the newly laid Corporation Street, began in 1878. It gave rise over the next decade to stately rows of prestigious buildings that reflected the city's importance as a center of commerce. In the meantime, elsewhere in the city, a new Council House was built between 1874 and 1879, a science college was begun in 1875, a new art school began to develop in 1881, and much other construction took place as well. Fittingly, the center of the city also saw, in 1889, the inauguration of a Chamberlain Memorial. Here as in Paris and Vienna, public structures not only served useful functions but also, in their magnificence, proclaimed the greatness of the city more generally.

Let us now look more closely not at individual cities but instead at particular types of infrastructural change – constituent elements of "planning" in the broad sense of the term. Having touched on some of these already, we now consider them in more detail, not only as they took place in a few cities whose individual histories are well known but also in a great multitude of cities whose histories in the areas of municipal government and planning are much less familiar. As we consider such interventions, we turn away from architecture, reverting to more utilitarian projects that were designed to improve living conditions for city dwellers more generally.

Industrial technologies gave engineers the means to make cities healthier by making them cleaner. Provision of increased amounts of pure water stood out in this regard, inasmuch as they made it much easier for people to bathe and to quench their thirsts without becoming sick from waterborne diseases such as cholera or typhoid. Earlier in the century, water had been supplied privately, often via wooden pipes through which water of frequently poor quality moved as a result of the force of gravity. As less porous and more durable materials were used to transport water to more and more destinations (via pipes that eventually reached all buildings, through which the water was driven by central pumping stations), and as improved systems of filtration were introduced, a great

---

[13] Quoted in Hennock, *Fit and Proper Persons*, 141, 143.

expansion of municipal responsibility also took place. Although the measures introduced by Haussmann in Paris in the 1850s and 1860s stand out for their magnitude, the most widespread changes in the third quarter of the century took place in Britain. Between 1845 and 1861, the number of municipally owned systems rose from ten to sixty-one. Between 1855 and 1860, Glasgow embarked on a particularly ambitious scheme. It not only took over the existing water companies but also constructed an aqueduct that enabled it to tap into Loch Katrine, more than thirty miles to the city's north. In later years, the processes of laying down pipe and of municipalization continued unabated, so that by the late 1890s domestic supplies of water were nearly universal in towns and by 1914 most city dwellers got their supplies via public authorities. Germany followed, albeit a few steps behind. Hamburg introduced a system of piped water in 1849, Berlin and Frankfurt am Main did so in 1856 and 1859, and several other cities either did so around the same time or followed suit soon thereafter. Except for Frankfurt, the new systems lay in the hands of private entrepreneurs, but this situation changed subsequently. As a result, by 1900, all German towns with populations in excess of 25,000 had networks of water mains, and by 1907 over 90 percent of all German cities that were served by such systems could boast that their water works were owned by the public. Rapid progress occurred elsewhere as well, eighty-one towns in Sweden having established municipal waterworks by 1909.

These developments not only made it safer for people to drink water but also made possible improved facilities for the disposal of waste, which likewise enhanced public health. Water carried off vast quantities of filth, first from streets and then increasingly from households. It was in Haussmann's Paris that the most spectacular steps forward with regard to sewerage took place, at least in terms of the extent and scale of new tunnels and pipes. Again, however, it was the British who took the lead overall, by building "unitary" sewers for both drain water from streets and human waste. London introduced them in 1848, and its example caught on rapidly. By 1865, forty British cities had constructed such systems. Meanwhile, in the late 1850s, Sir Joseph Bazalgette, the chief engineer of the Metropolitan Board of Works, developed a scheme for ensuring that sewage would no longer flow into the Thames in London, instead being rerouted to a part of the river that lay downstream. Implementation of this plan was completed in 1875. Hamburg, Frankfurt am Main, and Berlin began to build comprehensive sewage systems by 1873. In later years, other cities followed their lead, although they were slow to go beyond draining streets and providing service for businesses. After the turn of the century, city governments displayed greater willingness to provide sewerage for residential dwellings and to clean streets. Under pressure from state governments, they also moved in the direction of sewage treatment plants, which state governments required in return for permitting cities to use rivers for the disposal of water that had been used to carry off feces. French cities began to get in step with British and German ones, Saint-Étienne introducing a comprehensive system in 1854 and Grenoble and Reims following suit by the early 1880s. Substantial progress in this direction did not, however, occur until the passage of legislation in 1894 that compelled property owners to connect their buildings to city-wide networks. Everywhere, sanitary improvement took place slowly and only after many disputes. There were legitimate reasons for fearing that proposed solutions to the pollution problem might not work and that they might in fact increase the danger of contagion instead of reducing it. In addition, property owners frequently resisted being compelled to undergo what they regarded as an unnecessary and costly expense. Still, the overall direction of change is unmistakable.

Middle-class reformers' aversion to dirt, whether on streets or on human bodies, led to other changes made possible by the increased water supply. The quest for personal cleanliness required introduction of possibilities for regular bathing. Since the great mass of city dwellers lacked indoor plumbing, public baths came to be seen as an essential part of efforts to promote personal hygiene. In Britain, stimulated by the passage of the Public Baths and Washhouses Acts of 1846 and 1847, bathhouses became ever more prevalent during the next two-thirds of a century, so that by 1915 there were 343 of them, at least one in all but two towns with populations over 50,000. In Germany, similar developments began only slightly later. Magdeburg, Hanover, and Leipzig made the first moves, in the 1860s. Between 1875 and 1900, nearly every German city built at least one bathhouse. Private initiatives contributed to this process, but some sort of municipal subsidy played an important part too. Sanitary considerations were not always uppermost in the minds of the people who built and ran these baths. In Britain, public authorities regarded them more as centers for leisure-time activity than as facilities designed to promote public health, generally insisting that they at least break even if not turn a profit. In Germany, the bathhouses were quite ornate, and they often included features such as individual tubs and separate dressing compartments that resulted in their being too expensive for use by the people who most needed them. They may be included nonetheless under the broad heading of municipal efforts to use water for the purpose of promoting both cleanliness and health.

Another example of public provision that promoted public health involved earth and air rather than water. Public parks, often referred to as cities' "lungs," helped to combat air pollution or at least to make it possible for city dwellers to escape from it from time to time. Green areas in which urbanites could enjoy not only fresh air and sunshine but also exercise (walking and perhaps renting rowboats for a ride on a pond) fostered physical fitness in ways that went together with having fun. Starting a bit before mid-century in Britain, highly popular parks multiplied fast. Victoria Park, established in the middle of East London in 1842, amounted to over 190 acres of green space in an area that was rapidly being built up with houses and factories. A few years later, a public park was laid out in Birkenhead, across the Mersey River from Liverpool. It served not only as recreational space for city dwellers there but also as an inspiration for Frederick Olmstead, who went on to design Central Park in New York. Movements to create open spaces also gained momentum in Liverpool itself, in Bristol, in Glasgow, and in many other towns, so that by 1902 cities with 500,000 or more inhabitants had on average 6.1 square meters of parks and playgrounds per inhabitant. Despite vigorous efforts by men such as the Essen city councilor Robert Schmidt to promote the creation of parks in the industrial Ruhr area and despite the appearance elsewhere of more green spaces and playgrounds in cities (eighty-four in Breslau, fifty-four in Cologne, forty-six in Hamburg), Germany lagged with regard to park space overall. Its cities with half a million or more inhabitants had only 2.0 square meters per inhabitant. It should be noted, however, that German cities owned far more in the way of forests and woodlands, which amounted in the case of Frankfurt am Main in 1910 to over 8,800 acres. As noted above, the Emperor Napoleon III and Baron Haussmann increased the amount of park land in Paris almost a hundredfold. Later in the century, Bordeaux, Lyon, and Marseille all moved in the same direction, albeit not on as large a scale.

As we already saw in the preceding section, urban reformers displayed growing concern about the quality of housing. To be sure, the results of both philanthropic and public efforts were rather limited. The steps taken toward housing reform were small ones, which met social needs only to a very limited extent. In Britain, municipal authorities used newly acquired powers to condemn unsanitary structures in order to eliminate a good deal of substandard housing, but they replaced little of what they destroyed. In London, between 1872 and 1885 (about the same time as the great "improvement scheme" was being implemented in Birmingham), at least 75,000 people who lived in such dwellings were removed from the central area. Later in the century, major slum clearance projects also got under way in Glasgow, Leeds, and Liverpool. What took the place of buildings that were demolished? In most cases, as in other countries, not nearly enough housing that was priced low enough so that the poor could pay the rent. In order to overcome this problem, some cities built subsidized housing. Liverpool started to do so in 1869, and by 1918 it owned 2,895 dwelling units. Glasgow began to do so in the 1890s, but by 1911 only 0.47 percent of the population there lived in municipal housing, compared with 1.31 percent in Liverpool. The London County Council followed suit after 1900. By 1914, it housed 25,000 people, more than any other municipality, although fewer on a percentage basis than Liverpool.

In Germany, although reformers failed to secure passage of national legislation, city governments implemented various measures on their own, adopting several strategies in response to reformers' pleas for change. One was inspection in order to enforce housing codes that were designed to prevent substandard construction and overcrowding. In 1893, a law in Hessen led to the establishment of housing offices, which supervised dwellings and lodgings in communities with over 5,000 inhabitants, and several other states followed suit. Although such legislation was not passed in Prussia, Berlin and other large cities there established housing departments anyway. Municipal authorities also contributed to the construction of nonprofit housing by cooperative associations. They provided subventions in the form of mortgages, guarantees for loans, reduced taxation, and reduced charges for street building. Some city governments built their own housing. Frankfurt am Main took the lead in 1889 by constructing apartment houses for public employees, and several others (notably Ulm) did likewise. Because of the opposition of property owners who controlled the city councils, the ratio of public to private housing remained extremely small throughout the period. But in this area, as in many others, early initiatives pointed toward the more extensive projects that were undertaken during the 1920s.

Housing reform efforts lagged in France, although some steps there too should be noted. The first legislation that was designed to foster housing construction for people with low incomes, passed in 1894, resulted by 1900 in only 1,400 homes built with loans provided by the law. Around this time, a socialist who belonged to the Social Museum by the name of Georges Picot berated his country's performance in comparison with that of Belgium, which – with a sixth of the French population – had invested five times as much in low-cost housing. Cities were permitted in 1912 to build public housing, but none rushed to do so.

City governments introduced new energy technologies much more vigorously than they promoted changes in the housing supply. Together with water works, gas works and (by around the turn of the century) electrical works seemed to many men from across the political spectrum to be "natural monopolies," which ought to be run as "public utilities." Eliminating wasteful competition of the sort that resulted from laying down multiple gas lines recommended itself as a matter of businesslike efficiency. Growing public ownership of, or at least influence over, such facilities led to use of the term "gas and water socialism" and later the term "municipal socialism" (*Munizipalsozialismus* in Germany), which comprised not only public provision of water, gas, and electricity but also other forms of municipal enterprise. Much of this activity as well as other functions performed by city governments is frequently treated by historians under the heading of "city services." But despite the importance of increased amounts of clean water for the purpose of promoting public health, "service" via the operation of public utilities was not motivated primarily by benevolence. "Municipal trading," as it was known in Britain, certainly worked against the possibility that under conditions of free enterprise businessmen would over-charge customers, but it was not intended to subsidize consumption. Always involving the collection of fees from service users, it reflected the hope of municipal leaders that they could make fair returns on their investments. Funds thus accumulated could then be used for a variety of purposes, including payment for other services that did not yield economic profits. Municipal trading thus contributed to public wellbeing, but it did so in ways that left intact the idea of individual responsibility and permitted capitalists to continue to compete freely in most areas of the urban economy. In short, it represented "socialism" of a very limited sort.

Let us consider the histories of each of these energy sources in turn. Gas, which had first been used to illuminate city streets in 1814 in London and had been introduced in many other cities in the next few decades (fifty-one others in England by 1823, Berlin in 1826, Paris in 1829, Vienna in 1833, and Geneva and Milan in 1845), became available on an increasingly broad scale during the second half of the century. It was used for cooking and heating as well as for lighting in private residences, although not normally in ones inhabited by workers. At the same time, it came more and more under public control. Between 1851 and 1914, when the number of local gas companies in Britain rose from 145 to 831, the percentage of such companies operated by public authorities climbed from 13.8 percent to 37.5 percent. In Germany, where most cities had gas works by the 1880s, municipalization occurred still more rapidly and extensively. About half of these facilities were publicly owned at that time, a figure that rose to about three-quarters by 1913.

In the meantime, starting around 1880, electrical works were also being constructed. Electricity, like water and gas, was first provided by private entrepreneurs, many of whom were later pushed to the sidelines by public authorities. Germany, as a late-comer to the process of industrialization, had invested far less than Britain in steam engines. With its highly developed technical institutes it was thus well positioned to take the lead in the new technology of electrification, its city governments playing a key role as owners and managers of electrical plants. By 1907, municipal ownership in cities with 100,000 or more inhabitants reached 80.5 percent. Although in Berlin electricity was still supplied by a private company, the city received a healthy share of the company's profits. While Britain did not produce nearly as much electricity nationally as Germany did, the number of electricity undertakings there also rose rapidly, from ninety-one to 229 between 1895 and 1900, 71 percent of them in the latter year having been operated by local authorities.

What about other countries? In France, with regard both to gas and electricity, municipal governments did less. Gas was frequently supplied by private companies that enjoyed long-term monopolies, which often gave them the right to provide electricity too. Saint-Étienne stands out as an example of a municipality that offered a wide range of city services, including electricity, during a period of socialist domination there that began in 1900, but its experiment in public ownership came to an end when the socialists fell from power in 1910. On the other hand, in the great cities of the Habsburg Empire – Vienna, Budapest, and Prague – local governments emulated their counterparts in Germany either by taking over energy companies or by moving in that direction. Particularly during the mayoralty of the populist anti-Semite Karl Lueger (1897–1910), public utilities in Vienna were greatly expanded and improved.

Municipal authorities took an interest in electricity in the first place because of the role it could play in the development of mass transit, which also became a key element of municipal infrastructure. The evolution of urban transport – marked not only by the construction of underground railways for steam-driven trains in some of the biggest cities but also by the introduction of electrically powered trolleys more generally – occurred in tandem with movement toward increased ownership and operation by public authorities. In Britain, the number of street railway systems owned by local governments rose between 1875 and 1914 from seven to 171 (nearly 60 percent of the total). The first major city anywhere to municipalize its trams had been Glasgow in 1894, which was followed in 1899 by London. Municipally owned tramways carried 80 percent of all tram passengers and used 81 percent of the electricity required by all tram systems. In Germany, municipalization of street transport lagged in relation to other sectors as well as in relation to what had occurred in Britain; nonetheless, by 1908, nearly 44 percent of the trolley systems in cities with 100,000 or more inhabitants were municipally owned and operated. Public transit remained in private hands in Berlin, but, as in the case of electricity, the city collected considerable funds from the men who provided the service, and it retained the right to purchase the system if it wished to. It also played the leading role in the construction of new lines under ground, two of which were begun in the years 1912–13. In France, private ownership was the rule, resulting in service that frequently failed to take advantage of the latest technology and to satisfy consumers' needs. In Paris, however, concessions to transit companies by governmental authorities (the imperial administration in 1860, the municipal council around 1900) allowing them to operate in particular parts of the city led to extensive regulation both of service and of fares, with an emphasis by the end of the century on the need for running cheap trains for workers.

In the eyes of municipal reformers, maintaining human capital counted for just as much as efforts to enhance urban space and infrastructures. Improved sewers, water supplies, housing, supplies of energy, and means of transportation were basic but insufficient for the purposes they had in mind. Such measures needed to be supplemented, in the minds of urban activists, by direct assistance for targeted portions of the population: the young, the sick, the poor, the unemployed, and others who had particular needs. In what had long been a "mixed economy of social welfare,"[14] social services of many sorts accordingly became more widespread than ever before at the municipal as well as at the voluntary level. They cost a lot of money (some of it raised via "municipal trading," some of it via taxation), but the added expenditures seemed to be justified by the need to foster the fitness of as large a portion of the urban population as possible. One of the most obvious measures of the sort we have in mind here was support for public education, a topic to be treated at greater length in the next chapter. But there were many others, a few of which receive consideration here.

In Germany, with its strong tradition of governmental efforts to protect citizens' welfare (which can be seen most clearly at the national level during the 1880s in the passage of social insurance legislation with respect to sickness, accidents, and old age), municipalities offered a particularly wide array of varying kinds of "protective care" (*Fürsorge*). Made possible in part by the spread of social insurance at the national level, which lessened the burden of caring for the poor, new activities focused on people who were considered to be at particular risk or especially in need of

---

[14] See Michael Katz and Christoph Sachsse, eds., *The Mixed Economy of Social Welfare: Public/Private Relations in England, Germany and the United States, the 1870's to the 1930's* (Baden-Baden, 1996).

help. A much more differentiated and professional assortment of social services arose at the local level than had existed previously.

Welfare work frequently supplemented the efforts of sanitary reformers, with medicalization for the sake of public health proceeding along two complementary paths: expansion in the numbers of places where people could go for treatment and expansion in the numbers of men and women who provided medical services. Municipal hospitals and sanatoria for tubercular patients multiplied considerably. Earlier, church-sponsored and charitable programs for the poor had provided most of the public health care that took place in institutional settings. But starting in 1873, when the Moabit Hospital opened in Berlin, city governments offered medical care to the public in general. Cities' ability to treat patients was strengthened by the Sickness Insurance Act of 1883, which gave sick people who enjoyed coverage (mainly industrial workers) the right to be treated in hospitals as well as at home. Also, city governments employed more and more medical personnel. The first city doctor was appointed in Frankfurt am Main in 1883. His duty was both to look into the design of desks and buildings and to measure the height and weight of 15,000 children. A dozen years later, Wiesbaden began to employ school doctors for regular medical examinations of all children, and by 1913 there were 3,000 school doctors in Prussia. In the meantime, school dental services had also been established. Moreover, under the direction of city doctors, medical offices had become key sites in a widespread network of care givers, who staffed specialized clinics established for the prevention and treatment of various maladies, among them alcoholism, sexually transmitted diseases, tuberculosis, and infant mortality.

The members of an emerging group of nonmedical professionals, most of whom were women, addressed a wide range of risks to infants, youths, orphans, widows, elderly people, homeless people, and other marginalized city dwellers. By providing advice and other services, they attempted to combat threats to social as well as physical health. Under medical supervision, mostly by males, women played an especially prominent role in staffing new centers where mothers were counseled about the care and feeding of newborn children and were provided with cow's milk when they were unable to breast feed. Such centers reflected fears that in the cities low birthrates might lead to urban depopulation and a growing conviction that everything feasible should be done to enable newborns to survive infancy in good health, not only for their sakes but also for the sake of the nation. The first of these centers opened in Munich and Berlin in 1905, and there were seventy-three of them two years later. Day-care centers, of which there were sixty-six in Berlin by 1904, served as another means of utilizing public resources and pedagogical expertise to

safeguard young children. The protection of moral health was especially
evident in the various branches of *Kinder-* and *Jugendfürsorge*, which were
designed for older children and teenagers (in contrast to *Saüglingsfürsorge*,
which was designed for infants). Separate offices for the care of young
people, which a number of cities established, helped to arrange foster care
for orphaned or abandoned children and also served as agencies outside
the criminal courts that could handle youthful law breakers. At the other
end of the age spectrum, old people posed no obvious threat to social
stability. But in an era when old-age insurance still did not cover many
individuals, they constituted a substantial portion of the population that
received poor relief, and poorhouses increasingly became homes for the
aged.

German municipalities also stood out by virtue of their efforts to help
people who lacked jobs, the concept of "unemployment" as a condition
that reflected the economic environment and not just individual unwill-
ingness to work having begun to emerge in the late nineteenth century
in Germany as well as elsewhere. Beginning in the 1890s, urban *Erwerb-
slosenfürsorge* began to entail three sorts of measures. Labor exchanges
publicized job openings. By 1911, local authorities either ran or supported eighty such offices in large and medium-sized cities. Cities also
created public works jobs during hard times, mostly ditch digging and
snow shoveling. The numbers of cities that offered such employment
grew from fourteen in the winter of 1894–95 to fifty-eight in 1908–09.
Finally, there was unemployment insurance. In the absence of protection
at the national level, trade unions provided most of such coverage, but in
1914 sixteen municipalities also supplied it.

Although the record of welfare activity run by city governments is less
immediately impressive in the British case, locally elected and administered Poor Law Unions that coincided partially with the boundaries of
towns provided much public assistance.[15] The Poor Laws served as the
legal underpinning for specialized institutions for children and the elderly
and hospitals for the sick. But British towns also worked to improve their
human capital through institutions and direct investment. While hospitals
remained for the most part "voluntary" operations (i.e., based primarily
on charitable contributions, as well as on fees, with some public support),
more and more of them were municipal institutions, particularly those
specializing in infectious diseases. Public hospitals became much more
common after the passage of the National Insurance Act of 1911, which
both required and financially supported their establishment. Glasgow, for

---

[15] See Lynn Hollen Lees, *The Solidarities of Strangers: The English Poor Laws and the People,
1700–1948* (Cambridge, 1998).

example, soon constructed a "Preventorium" for the purpose of treating patients with tuberculosis. Meanwhile, the Public Health Act of 1872 required medical officers of health in all "urban sanitary authorities" with populations of more than 25,000. Birmingham promptly hired its first MOH, whose presence contributed significantly to Joseph Chamberlain's subsequent efforts to improve conditions there. But the most significant extension of extramural medical care, as opposed to sanitary inspection, occurred as a result of the Education Act of 1907. It required local education authorities to provide for medical examination and treatment of all children between the ages of five and fourteen. Accompanied in some cities by establishment of infant welfare centers, the creation of school medical services marked a major expansion of public responsibility for the health of urban children. Meanwhile, older city dwellers who lacked work received occasional assistance from local governments in the form of temporary employment. In Glasgow, the Corporation repeatedly devised projects that involved road repairs, stone breaking, and peat cutting during half a dozen periods of crisis in the job market between 1878 and 1905. After passage of an Unemployed Workmen Act in 1905, Manchester similarly instituted public works for laborers who had failed to find jobs elsewhere.[16]

Men who governed French cities also recognized the need to offer at least some of their citizens improved medical and social services. Although public funding for hospitals actually declined as a percentage of their operating costs during the nineteenth century, this change reflected in part the fact that poor people were more likely to receive relief at home and not to reside in such institutions than had been the case earlier. Also, decreased support for operating budgets did not prevent city officials from increasing oversight as a condition for the money they did provide. Nor did it reflect governmental involvement in hospital construction. This occurred between 1870 and 1914 with considerable support by numerous cities, among them Mulhouse, Lyon, and Saint-Étienne. Municipalities spent more money in other ways too for the purpose of enhancing public welfare. They supported poor people who lacked food, satisfactory shelter, and medical care, and they also aided infants who were abandoned or malnourished and unemployed workers. The last of these groups, for example, received help in the form of public works jobs in Bordeaux in 1879, in Saint-Étienne in the 1880s, and in Toulouse in 1895. As a result of local initiatives (some of which were compelled by national legislation passed in 1893 and 1905), total spending on

---

[16] It must be pointed out that the inadequacy of local efforts helped to bring about the National Insurance Act of 1911, which established, among other benefits, a scheme of unemployment insurance for the United Kingdom as a whole.

welfare in French communes rose steadily – between 1890 and 1909, from 1.1 million to 2 million francs in Lyon, from 1.2 million to 2.3 million francs in Marseille, and from 431,000 to 1.4 million francs in Toulouse.[17]

Each of these initiatives by town authorities contributed to the growth of both municipal bureaucracies and municipal budgets. Professionalization and specialization in the area of public service proceeded rapidly at the local level. In addition to the workers whom they employed in the various enterprises they ran for profit, city governments hired not only growing numbers of medical personnel but also more and more architects, engineers, jurists, and other experts, as well as a multitude of lower-ranking clerks and manual laborers. The growth of urban work forces was particularly pronounced in Germany. In Dortmund, the number of public employees grew between 1869 and 1909 from thirty-two to about 1,600. Such spectacular increases were unusual. Still, in Mannheim between 1870 and 1906, the size of the municipal work force grew more than five times as much as the size of the city's population (about 2,200 percent compared with 400 percent), and in Leipzig, between 1890 and 1908, it grew twice as much. In Britain, comparable developments took place. The number of municipal officers and employees in Bristol rose from 291 in 1851 to almost 6,000 in 1906. In Glasgow, the corresponding numbers stood at around 10,000 in the 1890s and 15,000 a decade or so later, rising to 34,000 by the 1930s.[18] Smaller but still significant increases in the number of municipal employees occurred in France. While the population of Lyon increased between 1900 and 1912 by only 3 percent, the number of its public employees increased by 25 percent, and in Toulouse, although there was virtually no population growth, the number of public employees increased by two-thirds.

Because of such expansion as well as because of increasing outlays for infrastructure, buildings (e.g., ornate town halls), and welfare, overall municipal expenditures also rose quite dramatically. In Germany, municipal spending grew approximately eleven-fold nationwide between 1870 and 1913. Averaging 4.1 percent per year during the two decades before the First World War, the growth of such expenditure was noticeably more rapid in the cities than at other levels of government (3.2 percent at the national level, 1.7 percent at the state level). In Britain, outlays by local governments, which grew by a multiple of thirty-five between 1870 and 1948, rose during a little less than half of this period from 32 percent of all public spending in 1870 to 51 percent in 1905. Meanwhile, the share

---

[17] For these statistics, see Cohen, *Urban Government and the Rise of the French City*, 209. Cohen's extremely useful book serves as the basis of most of what we have written in this chapter about developments in France outside Paris.

[18] We are indebted for these statistics to Barry M. Doyle, an expert on British local government.

of governmental expenditures accounted for by communes in France grew between 1836 and 1912 from 16 percent to 30.2 percent. In a process in which governmental activity in general became noticeably more expensive, the part played by urban authorities stands out quite strikingly. Cities made a lot of money by charging customers for gas, water, and electricity, which enabled them to cover many of their expenses, but they took out many loans too, rightly viewing much of their expenditure as an investment in the future. Between 1850 and 1910, the indebtedness of local governments in Germany grew approximately fifty-fold. In Britain, whereas local authority debt accounted for just over 12 percent of total national debt in 1874, it amounted to 39 percent in 1896. Building entailed borrowing, which in turn meant that city dwellers had ever greater stakes not only in their own wellbeing but also in the overall financial health of the cities they inhabited. As the powers of government, governmental expenditures, and governmental debt grew at the urban as well as the national level, the links between citizens and both the national state and the local state became much stronger too.

Celebrations of urban achievement

As more and more money was spent by city governments, their reputations as forces for general improvement grew accordingly. Contemporaries expressed great pride at what had been accomplished in their cities. Self-congratulatory celebrations, whether in the form of brick and mortar (e.g., opulent city halls) or books, speeches, and exhibitions, proclaimed that cities had experienced great improvement. Already evident to some extent before 1850 in the thinking of men such as Robert Vaughan, confidence that urbanization could benefit the many and not just the few became much more apparent in later decades. This is not to say that pessimism disappeared. Level-headed social scientists such as Charles Booth, who recommended solving the problem of poverty in East London by removing the poorest of the poor from the city altogether, as well as conservative anti-modernists, who raised their voices most loudly in Germany, expressed a great deal of anxiety about the implications of urban growth was in fact on the rise. But it would be a mistake to let the cries of the critics distract us from recognizing that many others who lived in cities, particularly people who helped to run them, felt quite differently. They took great satisfaction from what they regarded as both the potentialities and at least some of the realities of urban life, in which they had witnessed great improvements.

Many voices echoed the sentiments on which we focused at this chapter's start. Haussmann and others who had continued in his footsteps drew praise quite understandably not only from foreigners but also from fellow Frenchmen, such as the Parisian author Maxime Du Camp. His lengthy survey of life in the French capital, which appeared in nine editions between 1870 and 1905, depicted the city as a vast "body," whose constituent parts all contributed to the wellbeing of the whole. In the French capital, the ordinary citizen could rely with confidence on the smooth functioning of urban institutions: the post offices and the railways, the courts and the prisons, the hospitals and the schools, the banks and the theaters. "Paris," Du Camp wrote, "can rest in peace; while it amuses itself and while it works, while it sleeps and while it wakes, its innumerable guardians arrange the elements of its life without respite and take care of everything so that nothing, whether necessary or superfluous, is lacking." During the 1890s, two inhabitants of Glasgow, James Bell, a former Lord Provost of the city, and James Paton, expressed similar sentiments with regard to their home city. Instead of praising Paris as earlier Glaswegians had done, they emphasized the progress that had occurred in Glasgow itself. Over 10,000 officials and other employees had helped the Scottish metropolis to become "a marvel of ingenious and bold engineering, a highly finished and complex machine." Two decades later, Bell's successor praised an evolving "civic spirit" that supposedly permeated all sectors of the population. Ordinary citizens, he asserted, were "proud of the greatness of their city" and vigorously supportive of town councilors who advocated "large and generous schemes of amelioration and increase of public amenity."[19]

In German cities, well-staffed bureaucracies employed archivists and historians who not only kept records but used them to narrate stories of urban advances. The years around the turn of the century witnessed a great profusion of self-congratulatory writing about municipal successes, a typical example of which appeared in 1902 under the name of the highly successful mayor of Essen, Erich Zweigert. The men who worked under his direction to produce it, like similar officials in many other cities elsewhere in Germany, communicated great pride in the tasks they had performed and the innovations they had recently introduced.[20] On a larger scale, officials from over 100 cities constructed a joint narrative of urban achievement by means of pictures and models as well as reports. At a

---

[19] Maxime Du Camp, *Paris: Ses organes, ses functions et sa vie dans la seconde moitié du 19ᵉ siècle*, 6th edn (Paris, 1875), I: 5, 8, 26; James Bell and James Paton, *Glasgow: Its Municipal Organization and Administration* (Glasgow, 1896), 52–53; D. M. Stevenson, "Preface," in *Municipal Glasgow: Its Evolution and Enterprises* (Glasgow, 1914).

[20] [Erich] Zweigert, *Die Verwaltung der Stadt Essen im XIX. Jahrhundert mit besonderer Berücksichtigung der letzten fünfzehn Jahre: Erster Verwaltungsbericht der Stadt Essen* (Essen, 1902).

time when all sorts of public exhibitions that pertained to technological progress were becoming increasingly common, Germans put on the first such event that focused explicitly on urban developments. The German City Exhibition took place in Dresden during a period of four months in 1903. The more than 400,000 paying visitors who attended it enjoyed an excellent opportunity to learn about the most up-to-date practices with regard to sanitation, model housing, mass transit, fire prevention, and many other aspects of municipal activity. Robert Wuttke, a professor at the Dresden Technical Institute, sought to give the message conveyed by the exhibition an international spin. Writing shortly after it had closed, he asserted that although Germans had learned valuable lessons from foreign countries in the past these countries were "no longer [their] teachers." German cities had "risen to the top" and now led the world with respect to urban planning and management.[21]

Numerous pictures and models of buildings on view at the City Exhibition exemplified civic consciousness via representations of civic architecture, which functioned more generally throughout Europe as a means of expressing and inculcating pride in urban communities. Splendid buildings constructed for public purposes were intended to express public values and to convey public messages. Reflecting a widespread belief among cultural thinkers that architectural styles could favorably influence the psyches of the city dwellers who passed through or walked by them, city halls and other civic structures were designed as statements in stone. Their grandeur proclaimed to city dwellers that civic institutions indeed deserved citizens' respect and loyalty. Public architecture was thus intended to inspire in cities' inhabitants feelings of satisfaction and pleasure with regard to overall developments in the places where they lived. These buildings were not created in a contemporary style. They instead embodied architectural fashions that had first emerged much earlier, during periods when cities had enjoyed much more independence than they possessed around 1900. Looking at one level toward the past, they nonetheless expressed a belief that the cities in which they were located not only harked back to earlier times but also pointed the way toward a happier future. They appeared to demonstrate that the cities in which they arose were working to sustain worthy traditions of urban progress and that old and new could be combined in a potent and admirable synthesis, which ought to serve as a basis for resisting undue encroachment by national governments on municipal prerogatives. City government

---

[21] Andrew Lees, *Cities Perceived: Urban Society in European and American Thought, 1820–1940* (Manchester and New York, 1985), 240–42.

16. The Munich City Hall around 1900. Both the main building, which dated from the 1870s, and its turn-of-the-century extension were constructed in a neo-Gothic style. Their size, grandeur, and central site reflect the rapid increase in the level of services provided by and local pride in city government. The drawing was one of many exhibits at the Dresden City Exhibition of 1903. (Robert Wuttke, ed., *Die deutschen Städte: Geschildert nach den Ergebnissen der ersten deutschen Städte-Ausstellung zu Dresden 1903*, vol. II [Leipzig, 1904].)

and the hope that it could maintain a certain level of autonomy was thus justified not only intellectually but also symbolically.

Our remarks here about representations of the city and about civic architecture, while intended to serve as a reminder of the extent to which urban governments had extended their range of action by the early twentieth century, also lead in a new direction. They point toward the larger realm of urban culture. Here too a wide range of innovative developments requires analysis.

BIBLIOGRAPHY

Adam, Thomas, ed. *Philanthropy, Patronage, and Civil Society: Experiences From Germany, Great Britain, and North America*. Bloomington, 2004.

Allen, Ann Taylor. *Feminism and Motherhood in Germany, 1800–1914*. New Brunswick, 1991.

Ashworth, W. *The Genesis of Modern British Town Planning*. London, 1954.

Beaudoin, Steven M. "'Without Belonging to Public Service': Charities, the State, and Civil Society in Third Republic Bordeaux, 1870–1914." *Journal of Social History* 31 (1998): 671–99.

Bullock, Nicholas, and James Read. *The Movement for Housing Reform in Germany and France, 1840–1914*. Cambridge, 1985.

Cohen, William B. *Urban Government and the Rise of the French City: Five Municipalities in the Nineteenth Century*. New York, 1998.

Conway, Hazel. *People's Parks: The Design and Development of Victorian Parks in Britain*. Cambridge, 1991.

Dawson, William Harbutt. *Municipal Life and Government in Germany*. London, 1914.

Fuchs, Rachel Ginnis. *Abandoned Children: Foundlings and Child Welfare in Nineteenth-Century France*. Albany, 1984.

Gall, Lothar, ed. *Stadt und Bürgertum im 19. Jahrhundert*. Munich, 1990.

Harrison, Michael. "Thomas Coglan Horsfall and 'The Example of Germany.'" *Planning Perspectives* 6 (1991): 297–314.

Hennock, E. P. *Fit and Proper Persons: Ideal and Reality in Nineteenth-Century Urban Government*. London, 1973.

Hietala, Marjatta. *Services and Urbanization at the Turn of the Century: The Diffusion of Innovations*. Helsinki, 1987.

Himmelfarb, Gertrude. *Poverty and Compassion: The Moral Imagination of the Late Victorians*. New York, 1991.

Hofmann, Wolfgang. "Aufgaben und Struktur der kommunalen Selbstverwaltung in der Zeit der Hochindustrialisierung." In *Deutsche Verwaltungsgeschichte*, ed. Kurt Jeserich *et al.* Vol. III. Stuttgart, 1984.

Horne, Janet R. *A Social Laboratory for Modern France: The Musée Social and the Rise of the Welfare State*. Durham, 2002.

Joyce, Patrick. *The Rule of Freedom: Liberalism and the Modern City*. New York, 2003.

Ladd, Brian. *Urban Planning and Civic Order in Germany, 1860–1914*. Cambridge, MA, 1990.

Laski, Harold J., *et al.*, eds. *A Century of Municipal Progress: The Last Hundred Years*. London, 1935.

Lees, Andrew. *Cities, Sin, and Social Reform in Imperial Germany*. Ann Arbor, 2002.

Liedtke, Rainer. *Jewish Welfare in Hamburg and Manchester, c. 1850–1914*. Oxford, 1998.

Linton, Derek S. *"Who Has the Youth, Has the Future": The Campaign to Save Young Workers in Imperial Germany*. Cambridge, 1990.

Melinz, Gerhard, and Susan Zimmermann, eds. *Wien-Prag-Budapest: Blütezeit der Habsburgmetropolen; Urbanisierung, Kommunalpolitik, gesellschaftliche Konflikte (1867–1918)*. Vienna, 1996.

Meller, Helen. "Philanthropy and Public Enterprise: International Exhibitions and the Modern Town Planning Movement, 1889–1913." *Planning Perspectives* 10 (1995): 295–310.

Morris, R. J., and R. H. Trainor, eds. *Urban Governance: Britain and Beyond Since 1750*. Aldershot, 2000.

Owen, David. *English Philanthropy, 1660–1960.* Cambridge, MA, 1960.

Palmowski, Jan. "Liberalism and Local Government in Late Nineteenth-Century Germany and England." *Historical Journal* 45 (2002): 381–409.

Urban Liberalism in Imperial Germany: Frankfurt-Am-Main, 1866–1914. New York, 1998.

Petit, Jacques-Guy, and Yannick Marec, eds. *Le social dans la ville, en France et en Europe (1750–1914).* Paris, 1996.

Petz, Ursula von. "Robert Schmidt and the Public Park Policy in the Ruhr District, 1900–1930." *Planning Perspectives* 14 (1999): 163–82.

Pinkney, David H. *Napoleon III and the Rebuilding of Paris.* Princeton, 1958.

Pomfret, David M. *Young People and the European City: Age Relations in Nottingham and Saint-Etienne, 1890–1940.* Aldershot, 2004.

Reagin, Nancy R. *A German Women's Movement: Class and Gender in Hanover, 1880–1933.* Chapel Hill, 1995.

Reulecke, Jürgen. "Bürgerliche Sozialreformer und Arbeiterjugend im Kaiserreich." *Archiv für Sozialgeschichte* 22 (1982): 299–329.

Roberts, M. J. D. *Making English Morals: Voluntary Association and Moral Reform in England, 1787–1886.* Cambridge, 2004.

Schröder, Iris. "Wohlfahrt, Frauenfrage und Geschlechterpolitik: Konzeptionen der Frauenbewegung zur kommunalen Sozialpolitik im Deutschen Kaiserreich 1871–1914." *Geschichte und Gesellschaft* 21 (1995): 368–96.

Sheard, Sally, and Helen Power, eds. *Body and City: Histories of Urban Public Health.* Burlington, VT, 2000.

Sheehan, James J. "Liberalism and the City in 19th-Century Germany." *Past and Present* 51 (1971): 116–37.

Steinmetz, George. *Regulating the Social: The Welfare State and Local Politics in Imperial Germany.* Princeton, 1993.

Sutcliffe, Anthony. *Towards the Planned City: Germany, Britain, the United States, and France, 1780–1914.* Oxford, 1981.

Tarn, John Nelson. *Five Per Cent Philanthropy; an Account of Housing in Urban Areas Between 1840 and 1914.* Cambridge, 1973.

Trainor, Richard. "Urban Elites in Victorian Britain." *Urban History Yearbook* 1985, pp. 1–17.

Wohl, Anthony. *Endangered Lives: Public Health in Victorian Britain.* Cambridge, MA, 1983.

7   Urban cultures

In an issue of a socialist periodical that appeared in Germany in 1903, an essayist named Lisbeth Stern lauded cities for their creative impact on minds and sensibilities. In her view, urban scenes served as highly stimulating spectacles, allowing artistic activity to take root and flourish much more readily there than in less densely populated areas. "Poetically and pictorially," she wrote, "the big city is equally fruitful." Pointing to the work done by Paris-based authors Charles Baudelaire and Emile Zola as well as that done by the German painter Adolph Menzel, she observed that in an urban setting a great wealth of visual images imprinted themselves on observers' imaginations. "The countless voices of the big city, which blend into a powerful roar," she added, "speak a more meaningful language to the modern artist than nature does."[1] Her celebration of cities as sites for cultural production struck a note that was widely echoed at the time and has been repeated frequently since then. Peter Hall, for example, expresses a similar sentiment when he points to the great metropolises of the world as "the places that [have] ignited the sacred flame of . . . human intelligence and the human imagination."[2] According to such views, cities and culture have been and are inseparably linked.

Cultural life comprises many phenomena and activities. The word "culture" must be used in the plural: cities gave birth to "cultures," rather than "culture." Most important in the eyes of urban intellectuals and elites was what might be called "high" culture, or what the nineteenth-century critic Matthew Arnold began to get at when he referred to culture as the pursuit of knowledge of "the best which has been thought and said in the world." High culture primarily entailed production of and homage to great literature, philosophy, painting, music, and other forms of fine art that had originated in the past, although one might also point, as Stern did, to

---

[1] Lisbeth Stern, "Einige Worte über städtische Cultur," *Socialistische Monatshefte* 7 (1903): 612.
[2] Peter Hall, *Cities in Civilization* (London, 1998), 7; see also 279–88.

examples of outstanding creativity in the present. Many institutions and activities – promoted both by city governments and by voluntary associations – involved spreading appreciation of at least some of this culture downward, from the few to the many. As some museums, concert halls, and theaters opened their doors to wider publics, a multitude of libraries, schools, churches, chapels, and other institutions also helped to promote both enlightenment and "rational recreation" beyond the ranks of social elites. But historians today take a much broader view of what counts as cultural activity, including many aspects of ordinary life beyond the realm of what interested would-be improvers of mass taste. In this connection, we need to consider the growth of a mass leisure industry that drew its audience from all social groups. Music halls and cabarets, dance halls and cafés, department stores, and athletic events offered city dwellers at many levels of the social hierarchy opportunities for self-expression and enjoyment. Although most of the people who migrated to cities did so primarily in order to find jobs, a rich assortment of cultural attractions helped to keep them there. The growth of urban capitalism gave rise to a multitude of businesses that provided opportunities for amusement during leisure hours, and the rise of the big city fostered cultural liveliness and opportunity in many other ways as well.

The rich variety of cultural phenomena that marked the urban scene reflected a complex multitude of fault lines. We need to distinguish between elite culture and mass culture, paying close attention to differences with regard to the social class of intended audiences. But variations among classes were accompanied by important differences within social classes too. Individuals can choose their own favored forms of amusement, and neither wealth nor education correlate tightly with cultural appreciations and leisure activities. Although many members of urban elites used their custodianship of high culture to differentiate themselves from the less privileged, others sought to spread selected cultural forms to the masses to "civilize" them. In addition, certain members of cultural elites, who received some support from among the middle and upper classes, challenged traditional culture under the banner of "modernism." Members of the "avant-gardes," they produced a revolutionary culture, which will also receive attention at the end of this chapter. Meanwhile, popular culture also pointed in a variety of directions. Much of it implied rejection of middle-class norms, in some cases reflecting discontent with the political and social status quo. On the other hand, a good case can be made that popular culture served a compensatory function, providing pleasures that helped ordinary city dwellers to reconcile themselves to the conditions under which they lived. The diverse cultures of European cities embodied not only privilege and efforts to safeguard it but also a greater democratization of pleasure. As a result, more and more city dwellers were able to derive enjoyment as well as material sustenance from urban life. Cultural change was a highly dynamic force, but by enhancing cities' attractiveness it also contributed to urban stability.

Elite elegance

Cultural production and consumption of a particular sort loudly trumpeted the elite status of the urban upper middle classes. Borrowing freely from royal courts and aristocrats' amusements, the wealthy forged a public culture around classical music, opera, theater, and museums, which linked them to European literary and artistic traditions. Participation not only required literacy, money, and fine clothing; it also signaled the acceptance of conservative cultural values and membership in an exclusive club, all of whose members could be seen as possessing "good taste." Such evidence stood out most clearly in cities whose roles as capitals or as regional centers and thus as gathering places for the influential and the well-to-do antedated industrialization. Here, middle-class aspirations were inevitably influenced by the presence of representatives of royal courts and of aristocrats. But it also became apparent in many places whose growth and importance stemmed largely from economic developments that had occurred more recently. Whereas London, Paris, Berlin, Madrid, Munich, Vienna, and Budapest come to mind most readily when we think of urban centers of elegant display, prominent citizens in other towns also sought to add the patina of cultural refinement to their cityscapes and thus to public images of themselves. Simon Gunn argues strongly in his study of "public culture" in Manchester, Birmingham, and Leeds that members of the middle classes there utilized elite culture as a tool for buttressing their positions in local society. "Beyond the fact of property ownership," he writes, "what served to unify the middle class, above all, was culture, conceived from the early nineteenth century as a sphere of consensus and reconciliation. At the art exhibition, the concert hall and the social club, men – and in some cases women – could engage in activities that were deemed to transcend the divisions of sect and party."[3] Newly prosperous businessmen sought through patronage of the arts to counteract any notion that they and other members of their class cared only about making money and thus lacked appreciation of "finer things." Involvement in cultural activity took on value not only as a source of pleasure in its own right but also as a means of establishing bonds among, and supposedly rightful precedence for, members of the cities' leading social sectors.

[3] Gunn, *Public Culture*, 24.

In ways we began to indicate at the end of Chapter 5, merchants, factory owners, and town fathers made their most visible efforts to signal their cultural refinement and status by means of splendid buildings. These were usually sited around impressive squares or along splendid streets, where ensembles of structures invited pedestrians to gaze admiringly at these expressions of urban elegance. City halls (*hôtels de ville* in France; *Rathäuser* in Germany) stood out in the first place as architectural expressions of pride and confidence in the municipalities themselves. They implicitly served as well, however, to enhance the prestige of the men who sat there in positions of authority, most of whom came from or were closely linked to their towns' other elites. A multitude of additional buildings also contributed to the increasingly opulent appearance of city centers, simultaneously testifying to connections among wealth, power, and culture. Some, such as art museums and opera houses, had been designed and established with a view to attracting an upper- and middle-class clientele. But other types of public buildings, such as railway stations and municipal bathhouses, also took on the trappings of elegance. Through architectural style and ornamentation, they reminded members of the lower classes of the benefits they supposedly received from their social superiors. Most of the other structures that deserve mention here arose as a result of private rather than public initiatives. Buildings that housed commercial activities – warehouses, stock exchanges, banks, department stores, and the like – loomed large on the urban scene. They not only constituted vital infrastructure for the forces of capitalism but also carried symbolic weight, suggesting the wealth and worthiness of leading citizens as well as of the institutions they ran. Fancy clubhouses where male members of urban elites met to eat, drink, and talk, gave further indications to passers-by that they deserved the rank they enjoyed.

Although these buildings embodied some of the most centrally important functions in what amounted overall to the creation of a modern society, they did not generally reflect efforts to invent new styles. Architects liked to cloak their buildings with drapery that harked back to earlier times, which were viewed as golden ages of urban civilization. They thus attempted to convey an impression that the men responsible for their construction adhered to traditions of both civic and cultural high-mindedness that stretched back many centuries into the past. Architecturally, the nineteenth century was marked by a series of "neo" styles, each particularly popular during a different part of the nineteenth century but each also still widely apparent to any observer of the urban scene in 1914 – styles that served both to enhance images of cities overall in contrast to nation states and to enhance the images of cities' leading citizens.

Looking back to the period before 1850, we can already see linkages between architectural style, a civic spirit, and high regard for commercial success in the widespread adoption of what came to be known as "neo-classicism." Although this architectural fashion comprised both Greek and Roman elements, the Greek strand predominated. The neoclassical movement spread in part out of a belief that adopting styles first invented in ancient Athens, Corinth, and other city-states would encourage city dwellers to identify their towns with these earlier communities. "To build in the Greek style," writes Tristram Hunt, "indicated a confidence in the values of urban living and the ethic of citizenship. Nineteenth-century civic leaders were determined to emulate that ideal by erecting structures that similarly celebrated the wealth, benevolence and virtue of their cities."[4] Liverpool became especially noted for its collection of Greek revival buildings. One of the most remarkable was John Foster's 1828 Custom House. Boasting an impressive set of Ionic columns and an august portico, it symbolized a synthesis of both commercial success and civic pride. On the continent, to cite just a few examples, construction of a neoclassical Palace of Justice began in Lyon in 1835, work on another one began in Tours in 1840, and several neoclassical town halls were built around this time in outlying parts of Paris. Several decades later, in York, elements of neoclassicism came to the fore in the railway station, where columns that supported the roof over the platforms for passengers were manufactured out of iron in the Corinthian style.

Following the start of the Greek revival, motifs first favored during the period of the Italian Renaissance came to the fore, underscoring even more forcefully the ties between architecture and civic and commer-cial values. Florentine and Venetian precedents served as models that town councilors, urban businessmen, and other members of urban elites eagerly imitated. Sir Charles Barry designed neo-Renaissance meeting places for urban liberals both in London and in Manchester: the Travel-ers' Club and the Reform Club (established after the 1832 Reform Act to provide continuing support for progressive ideals) in the Metropolis and, in the cotton capital, a new Athenaeum building (used for lectures and other cultural purposes) for which he provided a frieze modeled on a Flo-rentine *palazzo*. In the 1850s, one of the most significant civic buildings to appear during the entire century, the Leeds Town Hall, also incorporated neo-Renaissance elements, serving as a reminder that culture, trade, and civic spirit could all co-exist in mutually beneficial ways, and in Glas-gow similarly neo-Renaissance City Chambers were constructed in the 1880s. Meanwhile, in the early 1860s, an article in *The Builder* referred

---

[4] Tristram Hunt, *Building Jerusalem* (London, 2006), 233. Hunt's book has proved useful for much of what we have written here about architecture. See also Gunn, *Public Culture*, 40–43.

to several buildings in Birmingham that echoed Italian styles, asserting that the city "might boast of some excellent examples – both in stone and stucco" of Renaissance architecture. Parisians also looked to Italian models, which helped to inspire the designs for a major library, the Bibliothèque Sainte-Geneviève (1843–50), and a major railway station, the Gare de l'Est (1847–52).

In addition, architects revived the Gothic style, which became ever more popular as the century progressed. During the century's first half, the movement had made its major mark in the area of religious architecture. It gave visual expression to hopes by church builders that their handiwork would contribute to a new age of faith, similar to the Christian Middle Ages. Increasingly, however, it also affected secular architecture, where it reminded city dwellers that during the Middle Ages as well as during classical antiquity and the Renaissance their urban forebears had achieved admirable successes. The Gothic style took a notably secular turn toward mid-century, as one of its chief champions from a religious standpoint, Augustus Welby Pugin, teamed up with Sir Charles Barry to produce the designs for the Houses of Parliament (built 1840–60) in London. Mid-century writings by the cultural critic John Ruskin stimulated desires to apply Gothic principles beyond the religious realm, which produced Gothic-revival town halls in Northampton, Bradford, and Halifax. A quite splendid example of the genre, designed by Alfred Waterhouse, arose between 1868 and 1877 in Manchester, where the town hall covered an entire city block. Pointed arches, numerous statues, and a tower reminiscent of medieval belfries all adorned this magnificent headquarters for the men in charge of leading their city toward a better future. Secular Gothicism lagged on the continent, but it became increasingly perceptible later in the century, in such buildings as the national museum in Amsterdam and city halls in Vienna and Munich, which resembled their counterpart in Manchester.

Finally, beginning after the earlier revivals, there was a revival of Baroque architecture. Linked less to civic traditions than to celebrations of national and particularly monarchical power, this style contributed nonetheless in an impressive way to ornamentation of public spaces. Buildings such as Charles Garnier's lavish Paris Opera, begun in 1861 during the reign of Napoleon III and completed in 1875, and a multitude of banks and other financial institutions as well as governmental structures such as the Palace of Justice in Brussels all stood out as symbols of urban wealth, power, and cultural attainment.

Some of the structures named above and many similar ones served not just as places where people worked but as places where members of the upper and middle classes congregated for pleasure. They went there during leisure hours in order to relax and have fun, but in ways that further burnished the image and reinforced the solidarity of urban elites. In pursuit of cultivation, they sought not only to breathe in architectural splendor but also to experience exposure to other sorts of high cultural production as well. They did so with a view both to improving themselves mentally and aesthetically and to demonstrating that they indeed merited the standing they enjoyed outside as well as inside these cultural centers.

The nineteenth century witnessed a great growth of public museums. Although there were many sorts of collections, the most prestigious ones displayed examples of high art, ranging from sculptures produced in ancient Greece and Rome to paintings produced between the late Middle Ages and roughly the end of the eighteenth century. Some evolved out of private collections whose owners decided to open their doors to broader ranges of visitors than had formerly been admitted, while others grew in large part as a result of private donations to new institutions. Rulers continued to play important parts in fostering museums throughout the nineteenth century, particularly in Berlin, Munich, and other cities in Germany. Here and elsewhere, however, members of urban elites and municipalities also pitched in for the purpose of building up institutions that were viewed locally as well as nationally as ornaments and sources of prestige. Wealthy burghers as well as members of royal and aristocratic families supported these cultural sites by donations of objects and cash as well as by visiting them. Although the British Museum and the National Gallery in London dated back respectively to 1753 and 1824, and although the Old Museum in Berlin and the Glyptothek in Munich (both dedicated to sculpture from classical antiquity) were both finished in 1830, the pace of museum building increased greatly in later decades. In London, a National Portrait Gallery was added in 1856, and the Tate Gallery for British art opened in 1897. Also in the British capital, a huge complex of museums arose in South Kensington. Financed at the outset by profits from the Crystal Palace Exhibition of 1851, it comprised museums for applied arts, natural history, and science. Elsewhere in Britain, where Parliament authorized municipalities to establish their own museums in 1845, progress occurred still more rapidly. By 1891, there were fifty-nine museums or art galleries under local control, among them ones recently established in Birmingham and Manchester. During the next two decades, 151 more appeared on the urban scene, and sixty-two additional ones were established between 1910 and 1920.[5] In

---

[5] For these statistics on Britain, see Frederic Kenyon, "Municipal Museums and Art Galleries," in Harold Laski et al., eds., A Century of Municipal Progress: The Last Hundred Years (London, 1935), 261–62.

Berlin, starting in 1866, a great complex of art museums grew up on the so-called "museum island" in Berlin across from the royal residence, and elsewhere in the city magnificent collections of applied arts and of ethnographic artifacts opened their doors during the 1880s. Major museums were founded in other cities too, among them not only Munich but also Leipzig, Hamburg, and Frankfurt am Main. Between 1900 and 1920, around 210 museums were built in Germany as a whole. In France too, museums open to the public became increasingly apparent on the urban scene during the nineteenth century, particularly during its second half. No single step stood out then as sharply as the opening of the Louvre, with its great collections that had been built up by the kings of France, following the fall of the French monarchy in 1793. But there were a number of significant developments nonetheless. Art museums outside Paris having originated as a result of private efforts by associations of art lovers that began to flourish in the 1840s and 1850s, municipalities became more involved during subsequent decades. Ornate buildings, constructed by city governments, that displayed classic paintings and sculpture opened in Marseille in 1869, Rouen in 1877, and Bordeaux in 1881. Although Parisian museums continued to overshadow those in other parts of the country, provincial cities were by no means inactive with regard to promoting great art.

Other institutions of high culture enabled members of the upper classes to gaze not at objects but at performances and also at one another en masse. Performative culture found expression in three sorts of sites: opera houses, concert halls, and theaters. Opera was centrally significant for urban elites. It provided highly prized opportunities both for seeing elegance and for displaying it. Watching elaborately staged productions of works by Verdi and Puccini and by Mozart and Wagner in opulent surroundings (particularly from seats in private boxes) greatly reinforced images of exclusiveness and superiority among the well-to-do. Members of the upper classes could go to the opera with growing ease as a result of steady construction of new opera houses, whether in Barcelona in the 1840s or in Paris, Vienna, Budapest, and a number of German cities in later decades.

The story is more complex with regard to symphonic music. Here we note increasing opportunities both for members of the middle and upper classes and for others, although sharp differences remained with regard to the matter of who sat where. The number of cities that could maintain standing orchestras remained rather small until fairly late in the nineteenth century. Going to the symphony became easier as more and more cities ran or supported local groups of musicians, for whom new concert halls were constructed. Central Europe, with its strong musical traditions, was particularly impressive in this respect. The Vienna Philharmonic was established in 1842, and it was followed in 1882 by a Berlin Philharmonic. By 1911, 129 out of 271 municipalities in the German Empire provided financial support for musical performances, and seventy of these cities had municipally run orchestras. In Manchester, support for music, which had played an important part in middle-class culture for some time, began to acquire an institutional base in 1849. Charles Hallé, a German pianist, began in that year to conduct a series of occasional Gentlemen's Concerts, which in 1858 were followed by concerts that took place on a more regular basis and were open to a wider public. Birmingham obtained a lasting orchestral series in 1873, and a Leeds Symphony Society was founded in 1890.

Theaters increased in number even more rapidly. Between 1874 and 1913, their numbers tripled in Vienna and quadrupled in Berlin. Paris, which already boasted more than twice as many establishments as its two Central European competitors combined at the start of this period, added to its repertoire much more slowly thereafter (its theaters rising in number from forty to forty-six).[6] In Budapest, the number of theaters doubled between the mid-1890s and 1900. In London, greater ease of obtaining licenses to open theaters, together with the cutting of Charing Cross Road and Shaftesbury Avenue and the formation of Piccadilly Circus, led to rapid expansion of the theatrical world in the fashionable West End, which contained prestigious establishments such as the Lyric Theatre, the Duke of York's Theatre, the Queen's Theatre, and many others.

Throughout the nineteenth century, many of these institutions remained mostly if not entirely out of bounds for the great majority of city dwellers. In theory open to the public, they were in fact generally off limits – or at least difficult to enter – for manual workers and their families. Operatic, symphonic, and classic theater were open only to those who could afford to purchase tickets that cost a great deal more than most people could afford to pay, at least on a regular basis. Entry fees were less of a problem in the case of museums, but owing to pressures exerted by "Sabbatarians" (who wished to limit distractions from attendance at church services) most art museums were closed on Sundays. There was, to be sure, pressure to make high culture available to wider sectors of the urban population. Opening museums on Sundays, reducing or eliminating entrance fees during one or more periods each week, and offering concerts periodically at cut-rate prices contributed to this development. Still, work schedules and incomes – and also lack of what was considered

---

[6] Christophe Charle, "Les théâtres et leurs publics: Paris, Berlin et Vienne, 1860–1914," in Charle and Roche, eds., *Capitales culturelles*, 404.

to be appropriate clothing – tended to keep the mass of the urban population outside the institutions of high culture until late in the century. Thereafter as well, most of their "cultural" life took place elsewhere, as we shall see later.

Before we turn to the themes of cross-class diffusion and popular culture, let us consider other institutions in which members of urban elites went to be by themselves in public. Cities boasted numerous places for pleasure where elegance had less to do with absorbing high culture than with engaging in polished conversation, often lubricated by fine food and drink. Discussing what he calls "clubland" in northern cities in Britain, Simon Gunn writes, "Clubs came to occupy a strategic position in bourgeois culture. They represented an important focus of bourgeois leisure in their own right, while also providing a gateway for middle-class men to other opportunities and pleasures the city had to offer."[7] Here, as well as in London, a wide range of organizations enabled male members of the upper middle classes to associate with one another in semi-public spaces from which non-members were clearly excluded. Some, such as the Reform Club and the Conservative Club in Manchester (both of which opened new buildings in the 1870s), were explicitly based on political ties. Others, such as Birmingham's Central Literary Association and its Debating Society, harked back to the literary and philosophical societies of the eighteenth and early nineteenth centuries. Then too, there was the world of restaurants. The first of these having been invented in Paris in 1765, many more of them appeared in the French capital later. Already by 1825, it was said, more than a thousand were in operation in the French capital. Increasingly, cities boasted multiple places to eat that catered to ordinary citizens as well as to members of elites, but it was expensive restaurants that attracted the most attention in works by travel writers. One of them, Adolphe Joanne, described the Café Riche in the 1870s as one of the "restaurants of exceptional quality, those which one does not enter except with the intention of dining *seriously*, without worrying about the amount of the bill."[8] Although the British were not noted for excellence in the area of fine cooking, by 1900 a substantial area in London that stretched westward from the Covent Garden Opera House was marked by French and other European restaurants. Budapest too, like Vienna, had its share of stylish dining spots, which served Hungarian and Turkish as well as French specialties. But its hundreds of coffee-houses – among which the New York, the Japan, the Hall of Arts, and several others along elegant Andrassy Avenue stood out – deserve particular attention. In a city in which private clubs were not numerous,

[7] Gunn, *Public Culture*, 84.   [8] Quoted in Olsen, *The City as a Work of Art*, 216.

these coffee-houses served as meeting places for members of the middle classes who combined refreshment with cultivated conversation.

Attempts to spread middle-class values

The terrain on which high culture and the culture of elegance took root and blossomed also afforded space for a wide range of efforts that pointed toward cultural diffusion and supposed uplift. Through attempts to spread knowledge and "enlightenment," key prerequisites along with church attendance and sobriety for what Britons called "respectability," urban reformers mounted wide-ranging campaigns to propagate middle-class perspectives and habits among people who, in their view, needed their benevolent guidance. These efforts, which both governments and voluntary organizations promoted, constituted essential elements of what historians sometimes refer to as "governance." This term (reflecting the influence of the French philosopher Michel Foucault) comprises the soft power of informal control as well as power exercised via statutes. Although would-be "governors" of the urban populace often displayed a good deal of condescension, defensiveness vis-à-vis the lower classes was by no means the only – or even the dominant – feature of their efforts. Strivings to spread what counted from reformers' standpoints as "civilization" pointed not only toward promoting respect for bourgeois values (and thus the value of the bourgeoisie) but also toward genuine extensions of opportunity to wider segments of the urban population. Appreciation of high culture was one characteristic, along with church attendance and sobriety, of what the British thought of as "respectability," a prerequisite for full entry into civic life. One important feature of urban culture was undoubtedly cultural democratization, which gained force as a result of widespread efforts to extend some of what was enjoyed by an urban minority to more and more members of urban society. These endeavors were particularly notable in Britain and in Germany, and we shall therefore focus on developments there, with occasional references to parallel trends in France.

Two institutions, both fostered by governments, lay at the heart of efforts to spread knowledge. Public libraries opened new worlds to readers of all ages and statuses. Libraries had long flourished on a small scale in palaces and residences belonging to aristocrats, as well as in monasteries and universities. But they took on much wider importance during the nineteenth century, when they became places to which anyone who wanted to borrow books or read them on the spot could gain access. Following in the footsteps of several towns in the United States, British towns stood out in Europe. In the 1850s, national legislation permitted them to fund libraries and to increase taxes for that purpose. Attracting both private and public support, as town governments poured money into them, municipal libraries rapidly increased in number and size. By the late 1870s, eighty-six of them had arisen. Between 1896 and 1911, the size of the reading public grew dramatically, as library loans doubled. During the same time, public expenditure on library support more than tripled. We are particularly well informed about developments in Bristol, where exponents of liberal culture regarded libraries, in Helen Meller's words, as "positive social institutions dedicated to the 'civilizing' process, with a useful social purpose in raising standards of taste and behavior,"[9] but research comparable to hers would no doubt reveal the presence of similar sentiments elsewhere.

Liberal reformers in Germany, such as the Berlin-based educator Johannes Tews, became similarly engaged in a *Bücherhallenbewegung* (movement to establish halls for books).[10] Striving to imitate reformist efforts in Britain and America, some of them brought about the establishment of their country's first public reading room, which opened in Berlin in 1896. In nearby Charlottenburg the following year, Germany got its first municipally supported lending library that was organized along modern lines. Its collections included serious as well as merely entertaining books, and it was staffed by trained librarians. By 1910 more than 300 other municipalities had followed Charlottenburg's example. Berlin now had, in addition to a principal library with 125,000 volumes, twenty-eight branch libraries, each with 5,000 to 15,000 volumes. As in Britain, supporters of libraries believed that by spreading high culture they helped to forestall disruptive behavior by people who, if left to themselves, were all too likely to deviate from middle-class norms of conduct.

Reading was, of course, predicated not only on the availability of items to be read but also on literacy, which depended on schooling, and in this respect too cities fulfilled crucial functions. Germans were the clear leaders in Europe at all levels of educational provision, from universities and secondary schools down to the level of primary schools, attendance at which had long been compulsory. Leaving aside higher education, for which state governments bore exclusive responsibility, we focus here on the latter two sectors. Although ultimate responsibility for public education of every sort rested in the hands of the state governments, responsibility was in practice shared with local authorities. While the state determined educational requirements and content, municipalities paid teachers' salaries and bore the costs of the construction and upkeep

---

[9] Meller, *Leisure and the Changing City*, 103.
[10] On Tews, see Lees, *Cities, Sin, and Social Reform*, 241–42.

of school buildings. Consequently, there were wide differences between schooling in prosperous suburbs and schooling in newer industrial cities, with class sizes in the latter sometimes being more than 50 percent larger than class sizes in the former. Although great inequalities persisted throughout the period, overall improvements were widespread. These advances reflected vastly augmented expenditures on education, which more than tripled in Prussian localities between 1891 and 1911. Increased outlays led not only to smaller class sizes everywhere but also to a proliferation of new types of schools. In addition to greater numbers of traditional schools (e.g., elementary *Volksschulen* for children from working-class families and classical *Gymnasien* for middle- and upper-class boys that prepared them for higher education), there were more and more vocational schools for workers' children and secondary schools that offered a modern curriculum instead of one that focused on classical languages. Secondary schools for girls helped to fill out a general picture of educational advance in which liberal reformers took great pride, believing as they did in the centrality of education to moral as well as to intellectual progress.

The main features of the French system similarly entailed a mixture of responsibility between national and local authorities. As a result of legislative changes during the 1880s that sharply curtailed the influence of the Catholic Church in the area of education, secondary systems operated under state control, while the primary systems rested in the hands of the municipalities. By the end of the third quarter of the nineteenth century, most city governments had decided to make primary education both obligatory and free of charge, a step not taken by the national government until 1882. Soon thereafter, it assumed responsibility for paying teachers' salaries. Spending on primary education in France as a whole more than quadrupled, although spending by local governments only doubled. Variety among cities persisted, but the general trend was toward centralization.[11]

In Britain, where the voluntary principle had long reigned supreme in the educational area and where public power was correspondingly limited, progress during the period treated here took place on a vast scale. Having done relatively little in earlier years, local authorities moved rapidly under national direction to make up for prior deficiencies. Passage of the Education Act of 1870 by Parliament required election of school boards in areas where voluntary provision was deemed insufficient to meet local needs. These boards were in turn expected to bring about the requisite expansion

---

[11] For these statistics, see William B. Cohen, *Urban Government and the Rise of the French City: Five Municipalities in the Nineteenth Century* (New York, 1998), 107.

of educational opportunity and to establish norms for attendance by children, which generally called for them to be in school between the ages of five and thirteen. This and later legislation led to greatly intensified educational activity in British cities and towns. Not only in London but also in many other cities, newly established school boards moved quickly to expand public education. By 1880, both the number of schools run by local authorities and the number of students in attendance had doubled. In 1902, town councils took over the tasks formerly performed by urban school boards, and they also acquired a good deal of supervisory authority over private schools. They thus gained considerable ability to set educational policy, which they used to expand secondary as well as primary schooling and to offer evening classes for adolescents and adults.

Educational outreach took other forms too. Mounted under the banner of "rational recreation" in Britain, these endeavors were intended to provide wholesome substitutes for lower-class pleasures and practices that were regarded as uncouth and immoral. Some of these undertakings enjoyed strong support among members of town councils or officials who worked for local governments, if not a formal base within the realm of municipal government itself. But many others depended on steps taken by men and women who acted as cultural philanthropists, with a view to fulfilling what they regarded as a duty to help improve lower-ranking citizens.

Take some of the efforts to spread museum culture beyond the ranks of elite city dwellers. Museum directors in Hamburg conducted a vigorous campaign to attract visitors by displaying not only classic art but also local and applied art that embodied fine craftsmanship. Jennifer Jenkins points to the Museum for Art and Industry, established privately in the early 1870s under the leadership of an eclectic collector by the name of Justus Brinckmann. Quickly coming under the jurisdiction of the city, it moved from a private house to a neo-Renaissance public building in 1877, in which it retained its original emphasis on educating local craftsmen. The municipal Art Museum became important slightly later, when Alfred Lichtwark became its director. He believed strongly that museums should help to disseminate *Bildung* (general culture) and that in so doing they could help to strengthen a sense of common culture. A liberal who was decidedly not a democrat, he envisaged efforts to enhance art appreciation as means of civilizing the masses. To do so effectively, however, these efforts had to meet ordinary people to some extent on their own ground, conveying an awareness of art as a multifaceted expression of a whole way of life. Art had to be seen as comprising architecture, furniture, and clothing as well as paintings by great masters. Art of course included painting too, but the painting Lichtwark favored most strongly depicted regional scenes, communicating a sense of rootedness in the local area.

Developments in Manchester also stood out, in no small measure as a result of initiatives by Thomas Coglan Horsfall. The son of a successful manufacturer, he retired from the family business in his mid-forties in order to devote himself to cultural and civic improvement. Influenced by the cultural philosopher John Ruskin, he had concluded that access to works of art could help to "ennoble" the lives of ordinary people and to promote social harmony. Supported by a goodly number of other local worthies, he consequently became the driving force behind the Manchester Art Museum Committee. Owing to its work, an art collection that comprised paintings, prints, and sculptures as well as fabrics and pieces of furniture opened its doors to the public in 1886 in Ancoats Hall, a building on the edge of one of the most run-down areas of the city. Art, the organizers believed, could help to wean workers away not only from vice and crime but also from socialism. From the outset, the museum was intended to serve not simply as a gallery but also as a cultural center in which music and lectures would be made available too, and as a result over 2,000 people visited it each week. Growing awareness of the gap between the organizers' aims and what they could actually accomplish on their own led to recognition of the need for public support, which resulted in a municipal takeover of the museum in 1918, but the burden the town assumed had first been borne by Horsfall and his fellow philanthropists.

Among men and women who acted on a voluntary basis in order to foster cultural betterment, temperance groups also played prominent parts, striving as they did to promote sobriety and broad improvement of character simultaneously. In Glasgow, temperance reformers worked to "clean up" popular amusements by encouraging workers and their families to come to "teetotal" concerts, where music was offered in combination with tea and pastries, rather than alcohol. Their counterparts in Bristol staged not only concerts but also "blameless amusements," among them cheaply priced "penny readings" from literary works. In Dresden, one of the founders of the German Association against the Misuse of Alcoholic Beverages, Viktor Böhmert, pushed for the establishment of a Verein Volkswohl ("association for popular wellbeing"). Founded in 1888, it sponsored seven Volksheime (people's centers) where, although beer was available, it cost a great deal more than non-alcoholic beverages. Dresdeners could find there not only inexpensive food, but also newspapers and magazines and spaces where they could play chess and other games.

The men who established organizations such as Dresden's Verein Volkswohl looked to the examples not just of Britain's temperance reformers but also of British participants in "the settlement movement." This development had gotten under way in East London under the leadership of an Anglican clergyman, Samuel Augustus Barnett, who was the vicar of a parish there, and his wife, Henrietta Barnett. Having given a series of talks at Cambridge and Oxford early in the 1880s in which he urged students to join him and Henrietta in working to spread knowledge and appreciation of the finer things among "all sorts and conditions of men," he, she, and a dozen of them "settled" together in 1884 into a new building known as Toynbee Hall, not far from Barnett's church. Here they served as a nucleus for a larger cadre of fellow "improvers" of the lower middle and the working classes. Through their efforts, evening courses on English and foreign literatures, science, economics, and many other subjects were offered to over 1,000 adult students, and clubs for young people were also organized. The movement spread rapidly, not only in London but also in other British cities, and overseas as well (the most famous of the Barnetts' admirers and emulators having been Jane Addams, the founder of Hull-House in Chicago).

The example of Toynbee Hall appealed to many Germans in addition to Viktor Böhmert, some of whom went much further then he did in trying to make neighborhood centers serve educational as well as recreational purposes. One such German was Walther Classen – like Barnett, a clergyman. Having visited Toynbee Hall during a five-month study tour of British cities in 1900, Classen returned to his native Hamburg hoping to establish a German counterpart in a working-class area in that city. His efforts bore fruit in the founding of an association, the Verein Volksheim, that took the lead in setting up half a dozen "people's houses" during the next ten years. Adults who lived nearby could attend lectures on a wide range of literary, philosophical, historical, and scientific themes, as well as on current affairs and health-related topics, and they could also take part in Sunday expeditions to art exhibitions and musical events. A second individual whose efforts deserve attention at this point was Alice Salomon. Her work as a neighborhood educator began in Berlin in the 1890s, well before she wrote in 1901 about Toynbee Hall, but there is no doubt that she sensed an affinity between what she was doing and what was being done by settlement-house activists in East London (and also at Hull-House in Chicago by Jane Addams, who later became a close friend). Her early efforts as a volunteer evolved by 1908 into an educational institution that trained young women from the middle classes for social work. But it was precisely people in working-class areas whom

Salomon hoped to help – in part by spreading knowledge, if only of a practical sort, via students of hers who were expected to work there.[12]

Many of the reformers who contributed to the "civilizing" project in cities – not only Barnett and Classen, but a multitude of others as well – either held positions within religious institutions or were strongly influenced by religious teachings. Anglicans and Dissenting Protestants in Britain, Evangelicals in Germany, Protestants in France, and Roman Catholics and Jews in all three countries played crucial parts in efforts to spread the mental and moral habits that went along with "rational recreation." To cite one more example along these lines, we point to the Young Men's Christian Association. Established in London in 1844, it quickly spread to Bristol and many other cities in Britain and to Germany as well.

At least in theory, however, clergymen cared most not about such outreach or other cultural activities of a quasi-secular sort but about religious and church-oriented life itself. In this connection, we need to keep in mind that the urban scene continued throughout this period to be marked by religious rituals and practices, a point that recent research has strongly emphasized. Rejecting the view that organized faith retained only marginal significance in a society that was becoming overwhelmingly secular, historians point not only to the ongoing importance of religious outlooks in the area of social action but also to activity within religious communities as culturally significant phenomena in their own right. Although, as Simon Gunn shows, church-going played a particularly important part in the formation of middle-class identity and although workers' formal participation in religious services declined (see the discussion of this subject in Chapter 5), church-related activities still attracted large numbers of women and men across class lines. These activities did a great deal to add brightness to otherwise drab lives. For some, what mattered most were recreational opportunities, such as church-sponsored dances, badminton tournaments, and a variety of musical and other entertainments of the sort promoted in Britain by the Pleasant Sunday Afternoons movement. But, as the important work by Anthony Steinhoff on Strasbourg makes clear, religious culture in a stricter sense remained an essential ingredient of the lives of many, if not most, inhabitants of the city. The sound of bells reached far and wide from the towers of both old and new churches. Lively programs of choral music in which many church-goers participated were accompanied by a thriving culture of religious ritual. Most of the city's residents continued to undergo their faith communities' major rites of passage: baptism, confirmation and first communion

---

[12] On Böhmert as well as Classen and Salomon, see Lees, *Cities, Sin, and Social Reform*, 191–221, 255–317.

(or bar mitzvah), marriage, and burial. Division of the city's schools along confessional lines and the requirement that children receive four hours of religious instruction each week, together with the great growth of confessional associations and newspapers, rounds out a picture of a city in which religious culture remained quite vibrant, helping both to enrich and to unify urban life across class lines.

Finally, to return to the area of municipal provision, we take up once again the subject of urban parks. Having included discussion of them in Chapter 4 in connection with the story of efforts to improve public health, we do not need to narrate their growth here. What deserves emphasis is that urban reformers who sought to establish and enlarge these green spaces did so not simply for hygienic purposes but also for broadly cultural ones. Walking in quiet and attractive surroundings on a Sunday afternoon, particularly in the company of family members, seemed conducive to emotional and moral as well as physical wellbeing. It helped, according to one German observer, to soothe the "often coarse nerves of some groups of city dwellers."[13] Implicit in this assertion was the belief that strolling in parks would encourage respectable behavior and discourage rowdiness. In this sense, park construction too formed a key element in the middle-class project of civilizing the masses and thereby holding in check forces of disruption and possibly of political unrest as well.

Popular culture and mass leisure

Ordinary citizens often preferred amusements that differed markedly from those recommended by would-be improvers. Although certain forms of lower-class play, such as cock-fighting and bear-baiting, had largely been suppressed and although growing percentages of city dwellers were exposed to more schooling and other forms of education, "popular" culture emerged in a multitude of new guises. These differed markedly from what middle-class reformers sought to propagate. As the length of the working day declined for manual laborers throughout Europe and as incomes rose in urban centers, more free time and more money stimulated the rise of an urban-based leisure industry open to all who chose to participate in it. Enhanced opportunities opened up for ordinary people to visit places or otherwise engage in activities in which they enjoyed a culture of their own. This culture was oriented more toward amusement than toward "cultivation." It entailed pursuits of pleasure in an assortment of venues where ordinary city dwellers came together not in order

---

[13] Quoted in Brian Ladd, *Urban Planning and Civic Order in Germany, 1860–1914* (Cambridge, MA, 1990), 69.

to be instructed or "improved" but in order to be entertained or in order to experience recreation. Not all of what comes under consideration here pertained exclusively to members of the lower or lower middle classes. Some of it was shared with members of the middle and upper classes, who certainly did not spend all of their recreational time in public in the pursuit of high culture. Mass culture thus served in many respects to integrate rather than to divide urban society. Almost all of it, however, carried those who enjoyed it beyond the boundaries of what counted, according to traditional and upper-class perspectives, as true "culture."

Many city dwellers liked to walk on city streets. Practiced on fashionable thoroughfares such as Paris's Avenue of the Champs-Elysées or Berlin's Unter den Linden by well-dressed members of the upper classes as a means of being seen by one another and by other passers-by, promenading produced pleasure for others as well. In particular, it offered young people with low incomes a cost-free way to escape from cramped quarters at work and at home and to enjoy both the company of others and the spectacle of the city itself. This became more and more alluring as a result of both the rebuilding of downtown areas and the introduction on city streets first of gas and then of electric lighting. As an observer of central Glasgow wrote in 1901, "Here comes [sic] every night the young persons who have spent the day cooped in shops or warehouses, or offices, and who find sitting at home in dreary lodgings an intolerable torture. On Saturday they come in all the greater number . . . They have no other place in which to spend spare time . . . The lighted street demands no admission money, and so they come in droves."[14] Here, some of what cultural historians, following the poet Charles Baudelaire, refer to as "*flânerie*" (a French word that connotes strolling, in a leisurely and aimless fashion) was practiced as a mass phenomenon.

Among the spectacles that city dwellers gravitated toward indoors, several sorts of venues stood out. Sited along major streets, department stores, with their vast and colorful displays of personal and household goods, beckoned with increasing seductiveness. Places where one could gaze at luxury goods and fantasize about owning them, even if one lacked the means to buy them, they drew people of varied incomes and statuses, offering multiple opportunities to see and be seen. They thus added greatly to the attractiveness of city centers, constituting a vital element of urban culture. These "cathedrals of consumption," as they were sometimes called, grew as a result not only of increases in disposable income and of the rise of consumerism in general but also of other developments.

---

[14] Quoted in Elspeth King, "Popular Culture in Glasgow," in R. A. Cage, ed., *The Working Class in Glasgow* (London, 1987), 144.

17. A department store in Paris around 1890. This photograph shows Au Printemps, one of the great attractions for consumers in the French capital. As a firm, it dated back to 1865. The store shown here was constructed in the late 1880s, after a fire had destroyed an earlier building.

One was the overall tendency toward bigness in the area of economic enterprise. Large scale and rapid turnover permitted lower prices and higher profits than were possible in small family-run businesses. Newspaper advertising, moreover, attracted customers from a wide area, while the availability of plate glass made it possible to open up storefronts visually to sidewalk crowds. The use of gas and then electricity for illumination made it possible both to show goods attractively in large spaces that were far removed from sources of natural light and to extend opening hours.

Although department stores originated in provincial cities in England as far back as the 1830s, the department-store movement took off only after mid-century. In 1852, the merchant Aristide Boucicaut took over a large drapery store in Paris, known as the Bon Marché (a name that implied low prices) and quickly transformed it into a much larger shop, part of whose later history was vividly depicted in literature by Émile Zola in his novel *The Ladies' Paradise* (1883). As its gross receipts grew between 1852 and 1860 from 450,000 francs to 5 million and by 1906 to 200 million, its success helped to inspire competitors and emulators both in Paris and elsewhere. The best known of the other stores in Paris was La Samaritaine (1869), but Au Printemps (1865) was a name to reckon with too. In the meantime, the store À la Ville had opened in Lyon. Also, starting in the 1860s in London, department stores began their conquest of the world of shopping in the fashionable West End, where the linen merchant William Whitely expanded his establishment and renamed it the Universal Provider. In 1909, the American businessman Gordon Selfridge founded a department store he named after himself on Oxford Street. Also around the turn of the century, chains that had begun earlier in smaller cities (Tietz, Wertheim) opened new stores in the German capital. Similar centers of merchandising opened their doors around the same time in Budapest, one of the earliest of them having been called the Parisian Department Store. Everywhere in big cities, small shopkeepers felt understandably threatened as their livelihoods came under attack. Consumers, however, benefited, and not just from enhanced selections and lower prices.

Department stores contributed to at least two other sorts of cultural and social change. By enabling ordinary people to experience a world of high fashion they could otherwise observe only from afar, they promoted cultural democratization across class lines. In addition, they held special significance as a site of liberation for women, at least for women of the middle class. They moved into these public spaces in a way that combined their domestic duties as purchasers of goods for their households with personal pleasure. Collectively, the stores thus became a feminized public sphere. In public places that were eminently safe as well as otherwise suitable for members of "the fair sex," women could not only shop but also meet for lunch or tea with other women. They thus transgressed traditional boundaries that had limited the space in which they could function on their own. Moreover, department stores provided a great many jobs for women from the lower middle and the working classes, who enjoyed new opportunities to work as salespeople.

New kinds of theaters also beckoned with great allure. Entertainers regaled their customers with light music, on-stage dancing, and humorous skits. Some of the Berlin cabarets studied by Peter Jelavich, such as Ernst von Wolzogen's Motley Theater, and the Chat Noir in Paris catered to people with money. Not only local members of the upper classes but also tourists went there in order to have a good time. While consuming good wine in comfortable surroundings, they also consumed satiric songs, monologues, and skits, which targeted sexual standards and behavior, commercial fashions, cultural fads, and political beliefs and figures, although (particularly in Germany) censorship kept overt political attacks within bounds. Similar pleasures could be experienced at *cafés-concerts*, where men and women sipped beverages while listening to pianists and singers. Some of the cabarets and the *cafés-concerts* shared important features in common with upper-class attractions discussed earlier, partaking of a world of leisure-time elegance. But they offered new kinds of amusement that, although sophisticated, were not exactly "refined," and at least some of them extended more hospitality to non-elite sectors of the population.

People in search of light amusement also flocked to music halls. Featuring a great variety of performers – singers, dancers, conjurors, acrobats, and strong men – and offering their customers food and drink, these places provided easily accessible, relatively low-cost entertainment. Having originated in London pubs around mid-century, purpose-built music halls began to appear soon thereafter, the first being the Canterbury Hall in Lambeth. With its gas lighting, lavish décor, open platform stage, and rows of tables to which waiters brought food and drink, it attracted the masses and stimulated competitive emulation. By the end of the 1860s, the capital itself had more than forty music halls. In 1891 in Manchester, 400 establishments were licensed to provide both drink and music. Most of these were quite small, accommodating no more than fifty people at one time, but soon vastly larger ones appeared. One Manchester music hall, opened in 1904, could seat 3,000 attendees. By the turn of the century in France, where the lines between the *cafés-concerts* and the music halls were somewhat blurred, establishments such as the fashionable Folies-Bergère and the Moulin Rouge had been joined by many others of lesser note. They had also extended their reach beyond Paris, and they continued to do so to an ever greater degree in later years. By 1914, there was a Folies-Bergère in Lyon, Le Havre, Rouen, Marseille, Bordeaux, Toulouse, and even Saint-Étienne. In Germany, the earliest equivalent to music halls was to be found in *Tingel-Tangel* saloons (so-called because of the noise made when customers tapped their beer glasses with utensils while listening to songs), which arose already in Bochum in the 1860s. As in Britain and France, purpose-built sites emerged later, one of the first being the Apollo Theater in Düsseldorf (1899), which was followed by similar venues in Essen (1901), Dortmund (1902), and Elberfeld (1904).

Shortly after the turn of the century, movie theaters began to provide yet another way to fill leisure hours other than in a place that offered staged versions of full-length plays. Using camera and film technologies that improved quickly, film makers invented a totally new form of entertainment – one that attracted the masses both because of its novelty and because of its inexpensiveness. First shown in Paris in a Paris café owned by the Lumière brothers in 1895, moving pictures soon moved into buildings dedicated to them alone. While the first "movies" consisted of street scenes, directors soon turned to comedy, fantasy, and horror to attract audiences, and urban theaters proliferated at an extraordinary rate. As a result, there were more than a thousand cinemas in France and more

18. A music hall in East London around 1900. Residents of London's
East End flocked to this and other music halls to hear popular singers
and to see vaudeville artists perform on stage. Ornate facades and bill-
boards invited them into brightly lit rooms. (Walter Besant, *East London*
[London, 1903].)

than two thousand in Germany on the eve of the First World War. In London, where the first films were shown in music halls, there were by 1912 ninety-four purpose-built cinemas and 500 other places showing films. Manchester, by 1914, could boast of almost 100 venues that offered films to the public. Young people in particular flocked to the theaters after work and on weekends.

Many other types of entertainment also beckoned. Not all were available in every city or on offer all the time, some serving as special attractions that helped turn cities into tourist attractions, whether more or less permanently or only temporarily. Few cities other than Paris had places to visit comparable to that city's public morgue or its Musée Grévin, where wax figures depicted horrific crimes and public executions. Nor did any other city rival it with regard to great world's fairs. London had its Crystal Palace Exhibition in 1851, and Barcelona had a great exposition in 1888, but Paris held events of this sort repeatedly – in 1855, 1867, 1878, 1889, and 1900 – attracting to the exhibit halls thousands of exhibitors and millions of visitors (39 million in 1889; almost 51 million in 1900). Performances by circus troupes, on the other hand, took place regularly not only in the French capital but also elsewhere, as in Dortmund, the first city in Germany to construct a building that was reserved for such events. Life in many cities, moreover, was punctuated by local fairs and festivals – for example, in Catholic areas on the continent, by the raucous celebrations that led up to the Lenten season.

Consumers of spectacle could also turn to an increasingly abundant daily press. Rapidly growing numbers of newspapers not only told their readers about places to go and things to see, serving as guides to venues where they might find amusement. They also constituted entertainment in their own right, providing their readers with pictures and with kaleidoscopic, titillating reports about urban scenes and events. Like department stores and music halls, newspapers functioned as theaters of modern life, which they depicted as pulsating with fascinating complexity and endless energy. Having long played important parts in the public life of London and Paris, newspapers continued their rise there and elsewhere during the late nineteenth century. New techniques for rapid printing and the spread of mass literacy stimulated both supply and demand. Expensive newspapers that catered to an upper-class clientele, such as the *Times* of London, were supplemented by much cheaper ones that appealed to a broader sector of the population, such as the *Daily Mail* and *Le Petit Journal*. Then too there were the publications in which words served primarily to explain pictures, such as the *Illustrated London News* and *Le Journal illustré*. Comparable publications appeared in other metropolises as well. Berlin was particularly fertile. Mass-circulation dailies such as the *Berliner Morgenpost*, the *BZ am Mittag*, and numerous others (many of which appeared several times each day) added up to an array of newspapers that ran into the dozens. Here as well as elsewhere, as Peter Fritzsche has argued, "The newspaper report of the events itself constituted part of the eventfulness of the city,"[15] as people flocked to areas where copies of newspapers were posted in public. Smaller cities could also take pride in their journalistic offerings. Manchester had not only its prestigious *Manchester Guardian* but also much cheaper papers, among them the *Manchester Evening News*. By 1891, it claimed a circulation of 152,000, probably the largest for any evening paper in Britain.

Beyond the realm of commercial entertainment – whether on stage or on paper – city dwellers engaged in a variety of pursuits in which observation of others mattered less than interaction with them. Urban men and women came together with friends and colleagues in a more active fashion, also for the purpose of having fun. In a growing number of commercial venues – and here class boundaries remained very much in place – they spent time socializing with one another.

For amusement, many city dwellers went out to drink and to dance. The most popular place for having a good time was the neighborhood tavern. Pubs and beerhouses in Britain, cafés in France, and *Kneipen* in Germany served as places where men and women went not only to drink but also to talk, to laugh, and (in Britain) to play darts or (in France) to read newspapers. Charles Booth described taverns as playing toward the end of the nineteenth century "a larger part in the lives of the people than clubs or friendly societies, churches or missions, or perhaps than all put together."[16] Numbering in the tens of thousands in Britain as a whole, they were particularly widespread in industrial cities. In Manchester in 1892, over 3,000 establishments were licensed to sell alcoholic beverages. Paris had more drinking places in 1900 than any other major city in the world (27,000 cafés, not counting wine shops and cabarets), but the frequency of such establishments was greater in Lille, which had at least a dozen cafés per thousand inhabitants. Stricter licensing laws in Germany resulted in lower numbers of drinking places there (a little under three per thousand inhabitants in Bochum in 1898), but the large numbers of workers who frequented them meant that they fulfilled vital functions for urban populations nonetheless.

New sorts of places where workers could both drink and dance spread at the end of the century. By the 1890s in Britain, charity balls and

[15] Fritzsche, *Reading Berlin*, 14.
[16] Quoted in Douglas A. Reid, "Playing and Praying," in Martin Daunton, ed., *The Cambridge Urban History of Britain*, vol. III (Cambridge, 2000), 768.

upper-class assemblies in hotels were being supplemented by "shilling hops" and dancing classes held in a variety of public buildings. In Bochum in 1877, twenty-seven taverns permitted dancing as well as drinking, and by 1914 Düsseldorf had about eighty establishments where dances were held regularly. In the 1880s in a working-class suburb of Paris, Saint-Denis, 20,000 adults had access to twenty places where they could go to dance, at least five of which catered to single customers. Small, dark, and located near boarding houses or brothels, they were closely linked to the world of prostitution. Later, however, music for dancing was added to the Sunday afternoon offerings at cafés, in the hope of making them attractive as settings for family recreation.

Music making by amateurs, much favored by members of the middle and upper classes, was also an important part of mass culture. Although working-class use of musical instruments was, owing to their cost, relatively rare, workers made music with their voices in large numbers. In Germany, an Association of Workers' Choral Societies, which had its headquarters in Berlin, linked a vast number of local groups (2,818 of them by 1913) that fostered class solidarity along with sociability. No comparable organization existed in Britain, but numerous groups of working-class singers made themselves heard in individual towns. In Bristol, where the establishment of workers' choral groups originally reflected middle-class efforts to promote religious conversion and temperance, the movement took on a life of its own, transcending such agendas. The late 1890s and the early years of the twentieth century witnessed the establishment there of several choirs named after the districts of the city in which they operated, one of which was a successor to a Railwayman's Choir. Around this time, Glasgow had at least half a dozen socialist choirs, among them the Orpheus Choir, the William Morris Choir, and various Clarion Choirs.

Finally, there was the lure of sports, both professional and amateur, which claimed the time and the physical energies of more and more city dwellers. Reflecting in part a spirit of competitiveness that was endemic in urban environments, events one attended or in which one took part that produced winners and losers appealed greatly to all sorts of city dwellers. In addition to athletic teams linked to schools, others were sponsored by churches and by employers, but teams tended increasingly to identify themselves with geographic areas: urban neighborhoods at the amateur level or entire cities at the professional level. As regards either spectatorship or participation, various sports grew in popularity. Football, horse-racing, cricket, rugby, cycling, rowing, all deserve mention. Football (known as soccer in America) occupied pride of place in Britain. Having originated as a game played, like rugby and cricket, largely by middle- and upper-class amateurs, it became increasingly popular in industrial towns in the 1880s. An upsurge of enthusiasm for the sport among city dwellers led to formation of a professional Football League. It linked twelve teams in the industrial north, almost all of which were affiliated with cities that had populations in excess of 80,000 inhabitants. A Southern League and a Scottish League came into existence shortly thereafter. By 1911, almost all of the thirty-six towns in Britain with populations of 100,000 or more had professional teams. By this point also, 6 million spectators, most of whom were workers, attended contests in which these and other teams were engaged. As Richard Holt has written, "In essence football clubs provided a new focus for collective urban leisure in industrial towns or cities that were no longer integrated communities gathered around a handful of mines or mills."[17] At the same time, football and other athletic activities continued to broaden their appeal to people who welcomed the opportunities they provided both for physical exercise and for sociability.

Much influenced by the British example, would-be improvers of popular life in France and Germany also sought to encourage sport, which many of them regarded as a key to national vigor and competitiveness. Except for cricket, they promoted much the same range of athletic practices and events as their counterparts across the English Channel, albeit with more emphasis on gymnastics, which required less space than football. The leading Frenchman in this effort was Pierre de Coubertin, through whose efforts a Union of French Athletic Societies was established. The number of football, rugby, and athletic clubs that operated under its umbrella grew from around 200 in the late 1890s to over 1,600 by 1914. In the working-class suburb of Ivry, near Paris, the town council subsidized at least seven athletic clubs by 1903, some of which doubtless competed against similar clubs that were based in other towns. In a massive study of half a dozen cities in northern Germany, Stefan Nielsen shows that by 1900 in these places 875 gymnastic and sports associations had been founded, Hamburg having led the pack with 434. Churches, employers, youth groups, and trade unions played important parts in this development, but neighborhood and municipal affiliations became increasingly significant, with local governments doing more and more to encourage athletic activity in public spaces.[18]

How did the growth of the leisure industry shape social and political history? Some evidence indicates that popular culture functioned as an important element of efforts to counteract middle-class hegemony not only in the cultural area but also in the broader realm of social and political relations. In Germany, leaders of the Social Democratic Party and affiliated trade unions supported workers' libraries, choirs, and sports'

---

[17] Holt, *Sport and the British*, 167.   [18] Nielsen, *Sport und Großstadt*, 207.

groups. All of these organizations were intended to help build up a Social Democratic workers' subculture, in which members of the movement would achieve a heightened sense of solidarity and purpose. The record of workers' participation in activities sponsored by such institutions in Berlin shows that this subculture was indeed widespread. Similar evidence with regard to Bristol points to efforts by Labour leaders there to use culture as a means of mobilizing workers. The Bristol Co-operative Education Committee, for example, sponsored programs of historical lectures and discussions that were clearly intended to serve as anti-capitalist propaganda. Meanwhile, a socialist sports federation was established in France in 1908, and French cafés continued to serve as centers of agitation for radical workers. On the whole, however, popular culture tended not to encourage but to undercut popular rebelliousness. Apart from the fact that much of what was sponsored by socialists suggested a desire to appropriate high culture for workers rather than to replace it (a point made effectively by Vernon L. Lidtke in his study of Germany), developments that reflected the tastes and desires of workers themselves also had a dampening effect on political radicalism. As Gareth Stedman Jones argued some time ago, what he referred to as "a culture of consolation" tended to divert people from directly challenging the social and political status quo. Moreover, mass entertainments frequently brought people together in public spaces across class lines – for example, in the case of sporting events, giving them reason to put aside differences in order to support local teams. For many reasons, the growth of urban recreations went hand in hand with the growth of urban stability.

Avant-gardes

Other alternatives to elite culture took shape among artistic experimenters who self-consciously rejected what they regarded as overly conservative taste. Many of their works have long been celebrated by cultural historians as examples of high creative achievement.[19] Members of "clusters of pioneers" (to coin a term that roughly translates the contemporary

---

[19] We can scarcely begin to do justice to the story of these developments here. Others have treated them extensively elsewhere. For a brief overview, see Edward R. Tannenbaum, "Revolution in the Arts," in his *1900: The Generation before the Great War* (Garden City, 1976), 354–413. For a lengthier overview, see Butler, *Early Modernism*. For specialized studies of particular themes and places, see the works listed below in the Bibliography by Clark and Gluck on Paris, Hughes on Barcelona, Paret on Berlin, Jelavich on Munich as well as Berlin, Jenkins on Hamburg, Schorske on Vienna, Lukacs on Budapest, and Hanak on both Vienna and Budapest. For examples of works by individual artists and architects, readers can turn either to books about them, which offer rich assortments of illustrations, or to Google Images on the internet. Unfortunately, dates of origins are not given there, and much of what was produced by people mentioned here appeared during the interwar years, which witnessed a continuation of trends that had begun earlier.

French term used in the title of this section) intended to displace inherited standards of beauty and to forge new criteria for aesthetic excellence. The French phrase for much of this project was *épater le bourgeois* ("rattle the middle class"), which a vast number of creative artists and writers sought to do by producing cultural artifacts that struck traditionalists as highly offensive, usually on stylistic but sometimes also on moral grounds. Judged by censors and men who ran art academies or officially sponsored exhibitions to be lacking in some combination of aesthetic appeal, intelligibility, and decency, these works struck most "respectable" people as being strange or worse. At the same time, although their creators sometimes drew on elements of popular culture in fashioning their wares, they intended to distance themselves from the masses as well as from the established arbiters of artistic propriety. Many regarded themselves as members of a new elite, who had moved beyond the tired forms of traditional culture and risen above the banalities of mass culture. Their enthusiasms initially impressed only a small circle of fellow innovators and a few wealthy consumers who took satisfaction in being able to appreciate the newest trends in cultural production. But from the standpoint of later cultural historians who saw in their work the roots of "modernism," these avant-gardes laid the groundwork for the best in twentieth-century writing, music, and art.

Innovative creativity manifested itself in many forms. It appeared in the literary arts and the performing arts: poetry, fiction, theater, and musical composition. It appeared also in painting, sculpture, architecture, and interior design. In all of these areas of cultural production, new styles emerged with increasing rapidity, challenging not only established standards but also recent fashions that were forced to give way to or at least to jostle for position with their successors.

Many of these styles cut across the boundaries that marked the divisions between the various areas of creative activity. Around the middle of the century, "realism" emerged both in literature and in the visual arts as a reaction against fantastic and idealistic views of the world and of life that were exemplified in works by romantics. Members of the realist movement emphasized faithfulness to what was contemporary and true or at least plausible, turning away from historical and mythological themes in favor of depicting the world as they knew it. At its most extreme, as naturalism, the realist movement migrated toward an emphasis on what most people viewed as sordid and depressing if not disgusting, whether in the countryside or, increasingly, in the city. (Zola is worth mentioning again in this context. Most of his novels are a great deal grittier than *The Ladies' Paradise*.)

Movements that began later reacted against realism as well as against continuations of what the realists had already rejected. (Although historians talk about a succession of styles, simultaneity of competing styles, even as some lost ground to others, was a basic fact of cultural life.) Practitioners of impressionism in painting, which began in the 1860s, and several later tendencies asserted themselves vigorously on the cultural scene.

Impressionists and post-impressionists and, after the turn of the century, cubists, expressionists, and futurists all rejected realist modes of portraying nature and developed new ways of rendering perceptions and communicating sentiments. They believed that the creative artist had a higher calling than accurate depiction. He or she should not try to compete with a camera or with a newspaper reporter. Depending on his or her inclinations, the task at hand was to capture the essence of appearances in ways that took account of their changeability, to reveal underlying structures that lay beneath observable surfaces, or to use pictures or words as vehicles for expressing chaotic emotions. By the eve of the First World War, some artists were expressing themselves in abstract works, which bore no discernible relationship to a world of recognizable objects. Art Nouveau, a term that originated in the 1890s in France but is also used in English, and its German equivalent, *Jugendstil* ("youth style"), pertained to architecture and the applied arts as well as to painting. Less prominent in canonical histories of art than the "isms" referred to above, this style left its mark on a variety of artifacts – from sumptuous portraits to private homes and pieces of furniture and jewelry – in which sinuous lines and delicate decoration figured prominently. What would later become known as modern architecture began to appear too, particularly in factories but also in some other structures. Buildings constructed in this style stood out for their linear functionalism and simplicity. Anticipated by the Crystal Palace built in London in 1851, the newer architecture made extensive use of glass and steel while avoiding the kind of useless decoration that appeared on the facades of buildings of the sort discussed at the start of this chapter.

The cultural producers whose works exemplified these styles frequently gathered in urban centers. They benefited from the overall urban milieu, with its manifold sights and sounds and its constant hurly-burly, as well as from opportunities to interact with others who shared their outlooks. Modernism, however, came to the fore in a relatively small number of places. London does not stand out in this regard. One can talk about the Bloomsbury Group, formed in 1904, which included the novelists Virginia Woolf and E. M. Forster, the painter Vanessa Bell, and art critics who sympathized with artistic modernism, but nothing else requires mention here. For the most part, other cities in the United Kingdom were similarly infertile. The main exceptions were Glasgow, which experienced around 1900 an outburst of creativity in the area of interior design, best exemplified in the work of Charles Rennie Mackintosh, and Dublin, the home of the poet William Butler Yeats and the scene of an Irish literary renaissance more generally in the early twentieth century. For the most part, however, historians of aesthetic modernism must look elsewhere.

In Western Europe, Paris, Barcelona, Brussels, and Milan all experienced exciting innovations in the realm of creative art. The French capital enjoyed pride of place, certainly among these four and arguably among all cities with regard to cultural novelty and productivity. Although its citizens had witnessed the rise of the Eiffel Tower, a marvel of modern engineering, in connection with the world's fair of 1889, Paris was not particularly noted for modern architecture. In other respects, however, the city pulsated with artistic creativity, much of which centered on the cafés of Montmartre. Painters came here from nearby studios to rub shoulders with one another and other members of the avant-garde who were known since mid-century as "Bohemians" because of their alternative lifestyle. They also combined forces in order to exhibit their works after being denied the opportunity to do so in officially sponsored venues. Paris gave birth to and long nourished impressionism. It was invented by Edouard Manet and others in the 1860s and sustained in later years by famous painters such as Pierre-Auguste Renoir and Camille Pissarro. They depicted many facets of life in and around the French capital colorfully and sympathetically. (Among representatives of later schools, Georges Seurat and Henri Matisse also deserve special mention.) Not only Frenchmen but also foreigners, such as the American Mary Cassatt and the Spaniard Pablo Picasso gathered in Paris to develop their skills and show their wares. Another foreigner who contributed to artistic modernism in Paris was the Russian-born Igor Stravinsky. He wrote three ballets to be performed there in 1911, 1912, and 1913. The last of them, *The Rite of Spring*, aroused great hostility because of the jarring quality of its music and because of its apparent celebration of violence, which aligned it with a good deal of expressionism.[20]

Other cities also fed the torrent of artistic innovation. Barcelona, the birthplace of the painter Picasso and a place where he began his study of art before his move to Paris, experienced an artistic revival that resulted in part from the return there of others who had gone to France for visits, most notably the painters Santiago Rusinyol and Ramón Casas. They and other advocates of Spanish *modernisme* congregated at The Four Cats café. Barcelona also served as the setting for buildings designed by Antoni Gaudi, an architect whose inventive flair defies stylistic categorization,

---

[20] See Hall, *Cities in Civilization*, 201–38, for further analysis of the Parisian case.

19. Modern architecture in Vienna around 1910. The Postal Savings Bank, designed by Otto Wagner and built between 1904 and 1912, has a curved glass roof and a glass tiled floor to let natural light penetrate the central space at all levels. An early example of architectural modernism, the building achieved elegance through its simplicity of design and its use of structural materials, such as polished steel rivets, as decoration and did not depend on applied ornamentation.

although it has been compared with works of abstract expressionism. His most notable building was the Sagrada Familia cathedral, begun in 1882 and finished only in 1930, four years after his death. In Brussels, Victor Horta designed private dwellings encrusted with curvilinear shapes, such as the Solvay house, and larger structures, such as the House of the People and the Innovation Department Store, all in the Art Nouveau style. Milan, meanwhile, attracted attention as the center of futurism, an artistic style that celebrated speed and modernity, for example in Umberto Boccioni's "Dynamism of a Cyclist."

In Central Europe, Vienna, Munich, and Berlin all vied for cultural pre-eminence. The capital of the Habsburg Empire, long renowned for its leadership in the arts as well as (until 1866) for its political dominance in the region, experienced an explosion of creativity during the closing decades of the century. It bore fruit in the writings of Arthur Schnitzler,

Karl Kraus, Robert Musil, and Hugo von Hofmannsthal, whose works paralleled Sigmund Freud's in their emphases on the irrational. Among painters, the most famous were Gustav Klimt, who memorably embedded images of upper-class women in richly decorative backgrounds, and Oskar Kokoschka, whose portraits, executed with broad brushstrokes, expressed a strong sense of turmoil and tension. Modernism became apparent architecturally in buildings such as Otto Wagner's Postal Savings Bank and in many structures designed by Adolf Loos, among them not only private houses but also the Kärntner Bar. In the area of musical composition, Anton Bruckner, Gustav Mahler, and Arnold Schoenberg all challenged earlier traditions.

In the German Empire, the capital of Bavaria was Vienna's main rival until the closing decades of the century. Long nurtured by the Wittelsbach dynasty, the arts there reached new heights in the 1890s. Progressive painters such as Franz von Stuck, who exemplified *Jugendstil*, showed their canvases in a series of Munich Secessionist Exhibitions, the name of which indicated their rejection of dominant styles. Expressionist artists came together after the turn of the century as members of a group that called itself The Blue Rider. The best known of these artists, Wassily Kandinsky, had come from Russia, as had Alexei Jawlensky. Paul Klee had come from Switzerland, and Gabriele Münter had come from Berlin. Only Franz Marc was a native of Munich, but all of these painters found a congenial home there. Despite censorship that forced experimenters underground, new currents in the area of dramatic art were also widespread, asserting themselves in private theaters and in cabarets. Highly critical of prevailing religious, political, and sexual mores, dramatists such as Frank Wedekind challenged middle-class moral standards as well as stylistic conventions.

To the north, the Prussian-German capital witnessed the birth of numerous movements that contributed to what became its cultural as well as political primacy among German-speaking cities. Justly enamored of their burgeoning museums, Berliners could also take pride in an upsurge of innovative painting. The foremost German impressionist, Max Liebermann, led the way in the 1890s. He started a Secession that functioned in the same way as its counterpart in Munich, only to be left behind by a group of younger painters, many of whom had first come together in Dresden under the name Die Brücke (The Bridge). In 1911, Ernst Ludwig Kirchner, Erich Heckel, Max Pechstein, Emil Nolde, and other expressionists formed a New Secession, which served as an umbrella for much more radical departures from traditional standards than those carried out by Liebermann. These younger painters produced angular, boldly colored, stridently simplified images of people and the natural world. The

20. Berlin street scene in 1913. The expressionist artist Ernst Ludwig Kirchner painted this picture of pedestrians in the German capital. Elegant, almost identically dressed men and women scurry past one another without engaging in conversation or any other form of contact. The gaze of the viewer turns the women into objects of consumption, similar to goods in the shop window, located on the right edge of the painting.

dramatist Gerhart Hauptmann, whose work was staged by the innovative director Otto Brahm, produced socially critical plays in the recent tradition of Henrik Ibsen, while lyric poets – the naturalist Arno Holz and the expressionist Georg Heym in particular – dealt still more specifically with urban themes. Like naturalist and expressionist painters, they implicitly criticized urban poverty and anomie, even as they drew inspiration from contemplating the urban scene. In a more positive spirit, Alfred Messel and particularly Peter Behrens designed buildings that marked important steps in the early development of modern architecture.

Despite the challenges they posed to inherited standards of good taste and acceptable style and despite their efforts to shock "respectable" members of the bourgeoisie, producers of avant-garde culture in fact already received a good deal of favorable attention and support from wealthy patrons during the years considered here. Long before its post-1918 efflorescence and acceptance, modernist culture was taken up by people who belonged to a culturally progressive segment of the upper middle class. As Peter Gay has shown, although the "Victorians" and their immediate descendants have long been denigrated by many partisans of modernism as conservative philistines, enough of them were receptive to modern tendencies to give modern movements a significant boost before the First World War. He writes, "The chasm separating traditionalists from subversives did not place a united bourgeoisie on one side and an aggressive anti-bourgeois phalanx on the other . . . For the most part, it was the commitment, or the conversion, of cultivated bourgeois to the unconventional that would make the principal difference in the rise and triumph of modernism."[21] Rich Jews stood out. The French banker Isaac de Camondo shifted from collecting Renaissance paintings and eighteenth-century furniture to collecting paintings not only by impressionists but also by Vincent van Gogh and Paul Cezanne. The Berlin industrialist Eduard Arnhold displayed similar tastes, accumulating a collection that included works by many men, sculptors as well as painters, who were working to revolutionize European taste. Such collecting was facilitated by Paul and Bruno Cassirer. Cousins of Jewish origin, they displayed modern works of art in their gallery in Berlin and further encouraged modernism in their capacity as art publishers. And to cite one more example that pertains to Berlin, a work of modernist architecture such as Peter Behrens's turbine factory could not have been built except for the fact that the people who ran the German General Electric Company (hardly a hotbed of hostility to the bourgeoisie!) commissioned it. Here and in other big cities, money spent by Jewish and non-Jewish members of the

---

[21] Gay, *Pleasure Wars*, 197.

upper middle classes enabled them to position themselves as members of a modernist aristocracy, whose rank was based on their emerging reputations as people who favored aesthetic experimentation.

The modern culture that found favor among progressive patrons differed markedly from both the traditional high culture favored by most of the well-to-do and most of what we have discussed under the heading of "popular culture." It is worth pointing out, however, not only that some of it reworked popular culture in Europe (whether rural in the form of folk songs drawn on by modern composers or urban in the form of cabaret culture) but also that there were complex connections between modernism and interest in what artists regarded as primitive cultures overseas. For instance, Picasso, Matisse, and Kirchner all incorporated African masks or other elements of folk culture in Africa, which they had seen in museums in Europe, into many of their paintings. Such examples point toward the larger theme of contacts between Europeans and non-Europeans, which greatly facilitated and were facilitated by urban development.

BIBLIOGRAPHY

Abrams, Lynn. *Workers' Culture in Imperial Germany*. New York, 1991.
Adam, Thomas. *Buying Respectability: Class and Philanthropy in American, Canadian and German Cities From the 1840s to the 1930s*. (Unpublished manuscript.)
Bailey, Peter. *Leisure and Class in Victorian England: Rational Recreation and the Contest for Control, 1830–1885*. London, 1978.
Popular Culture and Performance in the Victorian City. Cambridge, 1998.
Berlanstein, Lenard. *The Working People of Paris, 1871–1914*. Baltimore, 1984.
Blau, Eve, and Monika Platzer, eds. *Shaping the Great City: Modern Architecture in Central Europe 1890–1937*. New York, 1999.
Butler, Christopher. *Early Modernism: Literature, Music, and Painting in Europe, 1900–1916*. Oxford, 1994.
Charle, Christophe, and Daniel Roche, eds. *Capitales culturelles, capitales symboliques: Paris et les expériences européennes, XVIIIe–XXe siècles*. Paris, 2002.
Clark, T. J. *The Painting of Modern Life: Paris in the Art of Manet and His Followers*. London, 1985.
Crossick, Geoffrey, and Serge Jaumain, eds. *Cathedrals of Consumption: The European Department Store, 1850–1939*. Aldershot and Burlington, VT, 1999.
Fritzsche, Peter. *Reading Berlin: 1900*. Cambridge, MA, 1996.
Gay, Peter. *Pleasure Wars*. New York and London, 1998.
Gluck, Mary. *Popular Bohemia: Modernism and Urban Culture in Nineteenth-Century Paris*. Cambridge, MA, 2005.
Gunn, Simon. *The Public Culture of the Victorian Middle Class: Ritual and Authority and the English Industrial City, 1840–1914*. Manchester, 2000.

Haine, W. Scott. *The World of the Paris Café: Sociability Among the French Working Class, 1789–1914*. Baltimore and London, 1996.

Hanak, Peter. *The Garden and the Workshop: Essays on the Cultural History of Vienna and Budapest*. Princeton, 1998.

Haxthausen, Charles W., and Heidrun Suhr, eds. *Berlin: Culture and Metropolis*. Minneapolis and Oxford, 1990.

Hill, Kate. *Culture and Class in English Public Museums, 1850–1914*. Aldershot and Burlington, VT, 2005.

Hitchcock, Henry-Russell. *Architecture, Nineteenth and Twentieth Centuries*. 4th edn. New York, 1977.

Holt, Richard. *Sport and Society in Modern France*. London, 1981.

Sport and the British. New York, 1989.

Hughes, Robert. *Barcelona*. New York, 1992.

Jelavich, Peter. *Berlin Cabaret*. Cambridge, MA, 1993.

Munich and Theatrical Modernism: Politics, Playwriting, and Performance, 1890–1914. Cambridge, MA, 1985.

Jenkins, Jennifer. *Provincial Modernity: Local Culture and Liberal Politics in Fin-de-Siècle Hamburg*. Ithaca, 2002.

Jones, Gareth Stedman. "Working-Class Culture and Working-Class Politics in London, 1870–1900: Notes on the Remaking of a Working-Class." *Journal of Social History* 11 (1974): 460–508.

Kidd, Alan J., and Ken Roberts, eds. *City, Class, and Culture: Studies of Cultural Formation and Social Policy in Victorian Manchester*. Manchester, 1985.

Lees, Andrew. *Cities, Sin, and Social Reform in Imperial Germany*. Ann Arbor, 2002.

Lidtke, Vernon L. *The Alternative Culture: The Socialist Labor Movement in Imperial Germany*. New York, 1985.

Lukacs, John. *Budapest 1900: A Historical Portrait of a City and Its Culture*. New York, 1988.

McLeod, Hugh. *Piety and Poverty: Working-Class Religion in Berlin, London, and New York, 1870–1914*. New York, 1996.

Meacham, Standish. *Toynbee Hall and Social Reform, 1880–1914*. New Haven, 1987.

Meller, Helen. *European Cities, 1890–1930s: History, Culture, and the Built Environment*. Chichester, 2001.

Leisure and the Changing City, 1870–1914. Boston and London, 1976.

Merlio, Gilbert, and Nicole Pelletier, eds. *Munich 1900: Site de la modernité*. New York, 1998.

Nielsen, Stefan. *Sport und Großstadt 1870 bis 1930: Komparative Studien zur Entstehung bürgerlicher Freizeitkultur*. Frankfurt a. M., 2002.

Olsen, Donald. *The City as a Work of Art: London, Paris, Vienna*. New Haven, 1986.

Paret, Peter. *The Berlin Secession: Modernism and Its Enemies in Imperial Germany*. Cambridge, MA, 1980.

Rappaport, Erika Diane. *Shopping for Pleasure: Women in the Making of London's West End*. Princeton, 2000.

Rearick, Charles. *Pleasures of the Belle Epoque: Entertainment and Festivity in Turn-of-the-Century France*. New Haven, 1985.

Schorske, Carl. *Fin-de-Siècle Vienna.* New York, 1979.

Schwartz, Vanessa. *Spectacular Realities: Early Mass Culture in Fin-de-Siècle Paris.* Berkeley, 1998.

Sheehan, James J. *Museums in the German Art World: From the End of the Old Regime to the Rise of Modernism.* Oxford and New York, 2000.

Sherman, Daniel J. *Worthy Monuments: Art Museums and the Politics of Culture in Nineteenth-Century France.* Cambridge, MA, 1989.

Steinhoff, Anthony. "Religion as Urban Culture: A View from Strasbourg, 1870–1914." *Journal of Urban History* 30 (2004): 152–88.

Weiner, Deborah E. B. *Architecture and Social Reform in Late-Victorian London.* Manchester, 1994.

8   Imperial and colonial cities

In May of 1886, Queen Victoria opened the Colonial and India Exhibition in what was described as "one of the finest and most successful spectacles of recent years." The Queen's carriage, the carriages of her family and attendants, and their military escort paraded through West London to the site of the exhibition, where she walked into the India Court through the elaborately carved Gwalior Gate, a "triumphal arch" donated by the Maharajah Scindia. Oriental carpets, palm trees, and flowers decorated her path. After a quick tour, she entered the giant Prince Albert Hall, where a "choir of hundreds" performed "God Save the Queen," with one verse translated into Sanskrit, India's ancient language, in a bizarre tribute to South Asia. Musical odes to empire then followed. The Prince of Wales explained that the exhibition was designed to give Britons a chance to see "the marvelous development which, under your beneficent rule, their brethren and fellow subjects [had] attained throughout so many portions of the globe." The "deeply moved" Queen expressed her hopes that the exhibition would encourage trade, promote peace and industry, and "strengthen the bonds of union which now exist in every portion of my Empire." After a flourish of trumpets, the firing of cannons, and a prayer, she marched out of the hall to the tune of "Rule Britannia." Empire had officially come to London.[1]

For the price of one shilling, people in the imperial capital could tour reproductions of Britain's global outposts. The exhibition proved wildly popular. Over a million visitors had entered it by late June, attracted by the chance to see the whole of the empire in one afternoon. The India sections included a bazaar filled with working artisans in their stalls, as well as a "jungle" complete with a stuffed elephant, tiger, peacock, boar, python, and cheetah, hiding from one another and the hunters in hot pursuit. The South Australia Court attracted much attention with a panorama of a bush scene complete with aboriginal inhabitants, pioneer

[1] *Illustrated London News*, 8 May 1889, 472; *The Graphic*, 8 May 1886, 487.

settlers, emus, kangaroos, and exotic birds. For the most part, displays stressed the "traditional" or primitive character of the colonies, whose products and people contrasted markedly with British modernity. Yet visitors could also see how British migrants had transformed the ends of the earth. Paintings of Australian cities – Melbourne, Adelaide, Brisbane, and Perth – lined entrance hall walls, and the Canadian exhibitors took pains to send agricultural machinery, stoves, and pianos manufactured in their towns.

Visitors to the site received mixed messages about the nature of the imperial world. On the one hand, they saw pictures of mostly rural places, where people far distant and far different from themselves produced "raw" materials or hunted and fished for a living. On the other hand, the exhibition itself illustrated the efficacy of sophisticated global networks of trade, migration, communication, investment, manufacturing, and cultural influence organized through cities. Londoners had initiated the event through letters and cables sent in 1884 from the imperial metropolis to British governors in their colonial capitals. A transatlantic and transpacific flow of people and products resulted, bringing thousands of English-speaking, western-dressed, colonial subjects to London and then home again, port-city to port-city. The exhibition made clear the popularity of the imperial connection and its visible imprint on the British metropolis.

This chapter first explores the imprint of empire on European capitals and then examines the networks that linked them to colonial cities. It next turns to colonial cities themselves, comparing them with cities in Europe. City dwellers overseas had to contend with many of the same problems faced by their counterparts in London, Paris, and Berlin. Some of the results of their efforts were similar, but many were quite different. Similar technologies were increasingly used around the world. Nonetheless, assumptions about municipal services and the rights of citizenship varied greatly between Europe and its colonial outposts. While the political world of the European metropolis was being reconstructed around a growing commitment to equal rights, the assumption of racial difference shaped the organization of colonial towns in Asia and Africa. Although networks of communication and transportation tied imperial and colonial cities together, permitting rapid flows of people, goods, and ideas, double standards of administration and admission created barriers within colonial cities for individuals and groups. Nevertheless, these cities were dynamic networks, difficult to control. The experience of urban life had many unintended consequences, which undermined European power in the longer run.

Variations on an imperial theme

Cities may be seen as having enjoyed "imperial" status according to one or more of several criteria. The term "imperial cities" refers most commonly to the capitals of countries that possessed overseas colonial empires, such as London, Paris, Berlin, Brussels, The Hague, Madrid, Lisbon, and Rome after 1911, and such cities are at the center of our discussion here of developments in Europe. But cities could also count as "imperial" by virtue of being capitals of multinational empires within Europe itself. In this sense, Vienna (the capital of the Austrian part of the Habsburg Empire) and St. Petersburg (the capital of the Russian Empire) were imperial cities too. In addition, Paris during the period of European-wide rule by Napoleon I, London (on the basis of British control of Ireland), and the German Empire that was established in 1871 (which included areas where Polish, Danish, or French was spoken) should also be considered in this group. A third criterion was based on connection to overseas empires via international ports. London and Lisbon count again in this respect, but so do Liverpool, Hamburg, Amsterdam, Rotterdam, and Marseille. Imperial networks were not bounded by land directly controlled by one political center. Nor were imperial connections strictly limited to present time. To suggest a fourth meaning for the term, Rome's imperial status rested in large part on its historic and symbolic importance, which was based on centuries of memory and a rich architectural legacy. When Europeans thought about imperial cities, multiple images overlaid one another. The great cities of Europe gained imperial status on several grounds, and therefore could have simultaneously different sorts of relationships with other settlements, both within and outside Europe.

In 1893, the *Pall Mall Gazette* asked which cities could be deemed "imperial." In its opinion, only Rome, London, Paris, Constantinople, Vienna, Delhi, and "perhaps" Moscow deserved the title. Neither great national power nor the possession of colonies was sufficient. To qualify, a city also had to have "antiquity and world interest," as well as intellectual or cultural influence on an imperial scale. In addition, true imperial cities also had to have grand public buildings and avenues for parades. *The Builder*, the leading British architectural review, recommended that parts of London be rebuilt in Roman style. The city needed triumphal arches, domes, columns, wide streets, and huge, open spaces where monarchs could be celebrated.[2] Despite London's undoubted imperial status,

---

[2] L. Griffin, "An Imperial City," *Pall Mall Gazette* 56 (1893): 657; "Imperial London," *The Builder* 72 (1912): 13.

contemporaries felt that it needed to be still further highlighted by appropriate public spaces and structures.

European architects and politicians commonly linked imperial rank to urban design, expecting emulation of past models to enhance present images. Imperial cities had to look the part, which meant resembling ancient Rome. A proper imperial public building would be gigantic and classical in its decoration, like the Colosseum. Long, straight streets would allow the viewer to see it from a distance and be overwhelmed by its size and beauty. Neo-Roman building forms, decorations, and statuary multiplied in European capital cities during the nineteenth century, as governments proclaimed themselves the heirs of ancient empires. While town fathers favored imitation of ancient Greek, medieval, and Renaissance architecture as a means of identifying themselves with leaders of earlier cities, rulers and leaders of national governments proclaimed themselves the heirs of Roman emperors. European rulers used an architectural rhetoric of ancient empires in their capital cities to reinforce their claims to power. The messages sent by classical references were sufficiently positive and clear that republican as well as monarchical regimes drew on them freely when seeking to assert their countries' prominence in the wider world.

Let us consider developments in several cities beginning with Rome itself. After Italian armies incorporated it into Italy in 1870 and it became the new capital, the government began to modernize the city by revitalizing symbols of its imperial heritage. In 1881, Francesco Crispi, a future prime minister, defended the expensive master plans and the need for governments to "perpetuate themselves in marble and in monuments." When presented with both ancient and modern wonders, he predicted "posterity can say we were great like our fathers."[3] National Avenue connected Trajan's Forum and the ancient Baths of Diocletian, and along its course were set the new Bank of Italy, a National Exhibition Hall, and the National Museum of Antiquities. Archeologists uncovered and mapped parts of the ancient city, creating in 1911 a public walkway for tourists. A gigantic, white marble monument frosted with neoclassical columns and statues built in honor of the first king of the newly unified Italian state, Victor Emmanuel, proclaimed that Rome was once again an imperial city where the present matched the past.

Vienna also relied heavily on its architecture to signal its imperial status. In the city's center were the palaces of the Habsburg emperors and

---

[3] Quoted in David Atkinson, Denis Cosgrove, and Anna Notaro, "Empire in Modern Rome: Shaping and Remembering an Imperial City, 1870–1911," in Driver and Gilbert, *Imperial Cities*, 47.

21. The Victor Emmanuel Monument in Rome in 1911. Dedicated to the king during whose reign modern Italy was formed, this neoclassical monument made of white marble uses images of ancient and modern empires to glorify the Italian state. Started in 1885 and shown here when it was dedicated in 1911, by which time Italy had an empire of its own, this "Altar of the Nation" dominates central Rome because of its site and its size.

the Austrian aristocracy. Neoclassical forms and statues decorated the facades of old and new Baroque buildings. By the late nineteenth century, even banks and other commercial buildings imitated their style. Every year thousands of Europeans chose to visit "imperial" Vienna. Visitors toured richly decorated palaces and Baroque gardens. They watched the changing of the emperor's military guard and walked along the Ringstrasse to see the neoclassical parliament and art museum. Guidebooks told travelers what to see and where to find it, while postcards captured picturesque scenes based on the city's imperial image.

The story of the links between architecture and empire in nineteenth-century Paris is more complex. Empire itself had two different sets of meanings: first, the vast European empire of Napoleon I, which greatly expanded French power but then disappeared for good after military defeat in 1815; second, a set of overseas territories, many of which were lost during the later eighteenth century but then replaced during the nineteenth and early twentieth centuries under various regimes. Successful imperial references in Parisian architecture were linked to Napoleon I and his triumphs, and most incorporated neoclassical designs. Napoleon built three memorials to his army and its victories: the gigantic Arc de Triomphe, finished in 1808; a Roman-style temple, now the Madeleine church; and the Vendôme Column, a copy of Trajan's monument made partially from cannons captured in the battle of Austerlitz. In 1836, the July Monarchy erected an Egyptian obelisk in the Place de la Concorde, hoping that references to Napoleon's invasion of Egypt would erase the memory of the guillotine which had operated in the same space during the 1790s. Louis-Philippe also brought Napoleon's body back to Paris in 1840 and ordered that a tomb be built in a military complex known as the Invalides. Memorials to the first empire occupied key sites in central Paris, and the redrawing of the Parisian map by Baron Haussmann gave them even greater prominence.

The conquest of overseas territories during the nineteenth century left few permanent marks on the cityscape in the French capital. Seeking to capitalize on nostalgia for Napoleonic glory, Kings Charles X (1825–30) and Louis-Philippe (1830–48), sent soldiers into north Africa, hoping that military victories would solidify public support for their monarchies. While the army slowly conquered Algeria, it had to fight a bloody, guerilla war. Atrocities it committed were reported in the French press and were hard to celebrate. During the 1850s and 1860s, Napoleon III proclaimed the Second Empire and tried to expand French control of territory in Europe and abroad, but the costs of his efforts were high and he enjoyed only modest success. Jennifer Sessions argues that "colonial warfare proved incompatible with the straightforward triumphalism of nineteenth-century monuments."[4] The violence and difficulty of conquest undermined plans to use military images to celebrate colonial rule. Ten renamed streets and modest bronze reliefs of an Algerian battle on a statue of the duc d'Orléans were the net results in Parisian public space of the long Algerian campaign. The Third Republic simplified the problem of public symbolism of empire by deciding that statues in Paris would commemorate heroes of the French Revolutionary period and not anyone living. They avoided the issue of which controversial generals to commemorate by focusing on heroes linked directly to the birth of the modern French nation, whose successes were clear.

When George IV ordered the improvement of London during the 1820s, he and his architects took Augustus's rebuilding of Rome as their

---

[4] Sessions, "Ambiguous Glory," 101.

guide, designing new streets, a park, and neoclassical government buildings, and the trend continued. Palatial quarters for the Colonial, Foreign,
and India Offices, decorated with statues of the continents and imperial
heroes, were built in the 1860s and 1870s. When the Sultan of Turkey
visited London in 1867, 2,500 people welcomed him at a state ball in
the Durbar Court of the India Office. Its golden marble floors, gas lighting, and glittering, fan-shaped windows made it a favored spot for state
receptions. The War Office, Admiralty, and Board of Trade also moved
into enormous, neoclassical structures near the end of the century.

As Britain's empire grew, so did London's celebration of imperial
heroes. In Trafalgar Square, where Lord Nelson stood proudly on his
Roman-style column with British lions at his feet, public subscriptions
from "a grateful country" paid for statues of Sir Henry Havelock, who had
defeated Indian rebels in 1857, and Sir Charles James Napier, conqueror
of the Sindh province in Pakistan. Nearby in Carlton House Terrace, John
Franklin, the Arctic navigator, and other victors of campaigns in India
were immortalized in bronze. Although the image of empire was mainly
male and military, another sort of imperial tribute was added in 1911,
when George V and Kaiser Wilhelm II unveiled a monumental statue
of Queen Victoria, portrayed as Mother of the Empire. Surrounded by
helmeted versions of Britannia and surmounted by a winged image of
Victory, the queen looked serenely toward Whitehall and the Admiralty
Arch. It was, in the words of the *Illustrated London News*, "a great imperial and national ideal wrought in marble." Moreover, the statue was the
focal point for a new processional road between Buckingham Palace and
Trafalgar Square, intended for royal parades and imperial celebrations.[5]
The leap from monarchy to empire, formally made in 1877 when Victoria became Empress of India, had found yet another expression in urban
space. By the early twentieth century, empire was publicly represented
and celebrated in London, as well as woven into its economic organization
and political institutions, in a multitude of ways.

Cultural expressions of empire were similarly numerous and varied.
Moreover, there was no single European pattern. Although the celebration of empire was Europe-wide, its national incarnations differed
markedly, as did European governments and nation-states. While empires
occupied a large place in national imaginations, representations of them
took on the colors of the cultures that shaped them.

Empires marked urban cultures as well as architecture, institutions, and economies. Imperial ceremonies and objects provided good

---

[5] Tori Smith, "'A Grand Work of Noble Conception': the Victoria Memorial and Imperial
London," in Driver and Gilbert, *Imperial Cities*, 31–32.

entertainment, as the opening in London of the Colonial and India Exhibition in 1886 illustrated. Crowds flocked to see emperors and empresses in action all over Europe in events designed to increase support for colonialism. Empire as theater shaped Parisian cultural life. Empire went on display and became entertainment. Both Charles X and Louis-Philippe sought to drum up support for the Algerian campaign through public ceremonies – masses at Notre Dame, state funerals at Invalides, parades, and illuminations. Indirect advocacy of empire was more successful. French painters won prizes for "oriental" scenes in the annual Salons, and the Louvre museum opened an Egyptian collection in 1827, which housed artifacts seized there by Napoleon I after his invasion. Todd Porterfield sees in this display of Egyptian mummies and artifacts clear efforts to make empire a national project. The French state portrayed itself as the caretaker of civilization in the Near East and a worthy successor to Napoleon I in its ability to strengthen the nation.[6] Napoleon III continued this merging of the national and the imperial, using a modernizing Paris as a backdrop for the Second Empire's culture of display. As the century progressed, empire turned more and more into entertainment for Parisians. World's fairs put colonies on show, bringing to Paris villagers from Dahomey, dancers from Cambodia, and merchants from Tunisia to act their parts in front of strolling tourists. Visitors to the 1889 exposition could walk down a model of a Cairo street complete with dirt, noise, donkeys, and drivers. Fairs sold the illusion of knowing the empire along with images of colonial backwardness and French modernity. The cultural complexity, sophistication, and varieties of Asia and Africa were reduced to a few simple settings of "traditional" sites and exotic people. Exhibitions encouraged Europeans to imagine their empires in simplistic, self-serving ways.

It is important not to equate attendance at a celebration of empire automatically with support for it. We know little about how audiences perceived these ceremonies and exhibits or how similar events elsewhere influenced public opinion. Parisians held many different political positions and did not hesitate to attack the government's policies in the press or more informally. The same point can be made about residents in other imperial cities. Jonathan Schneer argues that Londoners held "diverse, even conflicting, understandings of imperialism," and he finds many ways in which the metropolis permitted people to work for change in colonial policies.[7] Early in the century, campaigners against the slave trade and slavery had enjoyed a high public profile, petitioning, parading, and denouncing the treatment within the empire of human beings as property.

[6] Porterfield, *The Allure of Empire*, 82, 86.   [7] Schneer, *London 1900*, 14.

22. The Colonial Exposition in Marseille. An international fair that took place in Marseille in 1906 was widely advertised in and outside of France by means of images that highlighted exhibits there from French Africa and Indo-China. In this poster, travelers from French overseas territories sail into the city's harbor to begin their visit to the city, inviting Frenchmen and other Europeans to make the voyage there as well.

Later, Governor Eyre, who ordered and then defended the murderous British response to a small riot in Morant Bay, Jamaica, in 1865, was burned in effigy in the capital and opposed by prominent Liberals. Militant Irish nationalists argued against British rule in multiple settings, as did South Asian Londoners. An international Pan-African Conference brought delegates from around the world to London in 1900 to challenge the premises of European imperialism and racism. Such voices were important and had sizable audiences. Nevertheless, support for empire seems to have been widespread in London, until at least the end of the Boer War in 1902.

Cityscapes and city cultures expressed the influence of empire in multiple ways. By the end of the nineteenth century, the redrawing of European maps and the conquest of foreign spaces meant that most Western, Central, and Southern European capitals headed either continental or overseas empires, and sometimes both. As central places for exchanges of administrators, information, investment, and goods, they became highly charged symbolic sites. Public buildings evoking the Roman empire suggested the kinship of present rulers to historic conquerors, as well as the wealth derived from imperial connections. Meanwhile, politicians used urban ceremonies and celebrations that made reference to control over overseas territories to reinforce loyalty to imperial states. Imperial references enriched urban culture, as colonial goods swelled the tide of urban consumption. Using the example of London's global connections, Felix Driver concludes that "if the imperial city was at the center of the world, the empire was now at the heart of the urban experience."[8]

Networks of connection

Although architectural style was an important signal of imperial status, focusing on it alone misses a wealth of imperial connections expressed through urban institutions – banks, scientific societies, government departments, businesses, department stores, for example – whatever their design. Empires required multiple sorts of services and generated long-distance exchanges.

Empires can be conceptualized as series of overlapping networks – political, economic, personal, cultural – which channeled exchanges along a variety of paths. Cities acted as nodes in these vast webs, which stretched far beyond national borders. Zoë Laidlaw, who has studied imperial connections in the British Empire, argues for the international centrality in this process of London, which served as a "hub of imperial activity and imagination."[9] Its newspapers, companies, banks, scientific societies, and philanthropic groups reached out from the capital to colonial towns around the world, initiating dialogues with similar institutions. Cities served as gateways between Europe and the rest of the world via their sites on rivers and seas. Relationships with other places, rather than regional location, are central to the identity of larger towns and cities. To analyze Amsterdam in 1850, one needs to look at Batavia (present day Jakarta); similarly, to understand Batavia, one has to know of Amsterdam.

The easiest way to understand the multiplicity of urban networks is through the analysis of port cities, which are transit points on the interface of land and sea. Via roads and railways, they are linked to a broad hinterland. Port cities served in our period as markets for goods, destinations

---

[8] Driver, *Imperial Cities*, 3.   [9] Laidlaw, *Colonial Connections*, 17.

for migrants, sites for industrial production and the processing of raw materials, and prime locations of political, social, and financial services. Via rivers or seas, they reached out to much wider networks of places in their forelands, other ports with which they exchanged goods, people, services, and information. Cultural differences – for example, of language, religion, dress, diet, or political ideology – flowed into ports, making such cities hybrid places. In addition, their high proportions of foreign born signaled a level of international connection and awareness that differentiated them from their smaller, landlocked neighbors.

By anyone's reckoning, in the nineteenth century London was the world's largest and greatest imperial metropolis and the world's largest port. By walking its streets, visitors could see, hear, and touch evidence of the British capital's many colonial connections. Ships sailed and steamed from around the world up the Thames, importing both the exotic and the ordinary. Warehouses surrounded the East India and West India docks on the Isle of Dogs, where stevedores unloaded sugar, tea, Jamaican rum, Ceylonese cinnamon, and Egyptian cotton. They carted and stacked bales and casks, to be counted and stored before being whisked out again to factories and distributors. Around the docks in Limehouse, St. George in the East, and Southwark lived thousands of sailors, laborers, and watermen, who worked long hours riverside. Irish, Chinese, Indian, Cockney, and African laborers crowded into the area's dingy pubs and eating houses after work. When the author Sir Arthur Conan Doyle wanted detective Sherlock Holmes to confront an exotic enemy, he sent him to a back alley near London bridge, where he visited an opium den, run by a Malay. In 1881, over 6 percent of London's population was foreign born.

Also consider the German port, Hamburg. Its relatively large size (it had almost a million inhabitants in 1910), which exceeded that of most European capitals, can only be explained by its international ties. A city-state within the German Empire, the city drew in hundreds of thousands of people yearly because of its trading activities and coastal site. Hamburg merchant families regularly apprenticed their sons to overseas branches of their firms in the West Indies, Mexico, or Africa, and older businessmen knew much more about London or American towns than they did about Berlin. In a reverse migratory flow, merchant families from London, New York, and Douala in Cameroon sent their sons for a time to this great city on the Elbe River, not far from the North Sea. The politics of empire, as well as the weight of international trade, dictated these exchanges. German shipping firms based in Hamburg had become the largest in the world by 1910. Hundreds of thousands of Eastern European and Russian migrants came yearly to take passage on North German Lloyd or the Hamburg–America Line. New docks that opened in the 1890s signaled favored destinations – Asia, Africa, Australia, India – in their names. The city's foreign-born population also reflected its international shipping ties.

The geography, as well as the intensity, of these overseas links changed over time, along with political relationships and with technology. As ships became larger and transport cheaper, coastal towns such as Whitehaven in northwest England or Bristol on the southwest coast, both prosperous in the eighteenth and early nineteenth centuries, lost out to towns which invested more in their harbors. The building of railways channeled exporting to a few favored ports, bypassing smaller centers, as did the shift from sailing ships to steamships. London and Liverpool emerged as giants in the shipping and passenger trades, their positions reinforced by massive investment in large wet-docks and railway lines. Southampton on Britain's south coast became a major passenger port for international travel after the railway to London opened.

One of the strengths of sea transport is the flexibility of routes, which are cheap and easy to change. After the abolition of the slave trade and the loss of some of France's American possessions, the importance of Bordeaux and Nantes along the Atlantic coastline declined in favor of Marseille and Toulon, which handled trade with Algeria. As political relationships and technology changed, cities had to rework their international connections to keep up with the world around them. By late in the nineteenth century, passengers from Western Europe to Asia had multiple choices of inter-urban routes, the fastest being a railway journey to Marseille and then steamer travel via the Suez Canal to an Indian port, Shanghai, or Sydney. Sharp competition among the numerous long-distance passenger lines based in Hamburg, Rotterdam, or London meant that travel times and fares declined.

Active exchanges between European countries and overseas areas increased greatly during the nineteenth and early twentieth centuries as a result of acquisition of colonial possessions. The Dutch, in addition to their control of Java and nearby islands, gained Dutch Guiana and Curaçao. Although their colonies in Latin America had declared independence in the decades between 1810 and 1830, Spain retained control of Cuba and Puerto Rico and acquired two colonies in Northern Africa: Spanish Morocco and Rio de Oro. The Congo, owned by King Leopold II, passed to the state of Belgium in 1908, and Italy moved into Libya, Eritrea, and part of Somaliland. French possessions in Africa extended from Algeria, Morocco, and Tunisia through the enormous territories of French West Africa and French Equatorial Africa; the government of the Third Republic approved the military takeover of Indochina as well. Portugal acquired Mozambique, Angola, and Guinea in Africa, and the German Empire took possession of Tanganyika, Rwanda, Burundi, Cameroon, Togo, and German South West Africa, as well as islands in the South Pacific. As a result of steps too numerous to recount here, territories subject to the British crown extended by 1902 around the globe from Australia and New Zealand through Malaya, Burma, India, and large parts of Africa to Canada and the Caribbean.

Economic networks bound cities together both within and among empires. Because of its role in the international financial system, London was truly the world's capital. London merchant bankers provided much of the credit for world trade, and the Bank of England managed the gold standard, which enabled the trading nations of the world to arrange multilateral payments easily among the many international banks located in major imperial and colonial centers. British capital exports, which flowed through the London Stock Exchange, financed much of the development of Latin America, Russia, the Middle East, and East Asia. Moreover, countries that had difficulty paying their international debts borrowed from British bankers. A circle of exchange, guaranteed in gold, passed through the City, London's financial district, and stretched around the globe.

London's financial elite, very rich "gentlemanly capitalists," carried out the business of empire. Offices of trading companies and international agency houses lay along narrow, winding streets, near joint stock banks and insurance firms. Within a few minutes' walk, a trader could telegraph current prices, purchase stock, insure a cargo, discount a foreign bill of exchange, and still have time to rush to a directors' meeting. Newspapers printed on Fleet Street announced the arrival of ships from Singapore, Sydney, and Shanghai and the sailings of colonial officials and troops to their new postings. In 1890, the Penang Sugar Estates Ltd. occupied a small office, where one clerk, a secretary, and a director worked. From a distance, the tiny headquarters ran six large sugar plantations and a sugar refinery on the Malay peninsula, employing several thousand people: managers and an engineer from Scotland, field workers from south India and China. Their sense of the business came via letter from their plantation manager based near the town of Penang; they wrote to him twice a month, sending information on London sugar prices, Glasgow refining machinery, potential Scottish employees, and West Indian production methods. Their investment protected by land titles, control of the purse strings, and access to colonial officials, they made basic decisions about marketing and expansion from their headquarters in the British capital. Information and supplies sailed regularly from London in return for profits, which arrived in the form of bills of exchange, redeemable at the office of a City bank. It was a typical, international firm, its daily routine undramatic and unnoticed, run through an intercity network of ships, cargoes, telegrams, and letters.

Other much smaller British towns also had strong colonial ties. The case of the Scottish town of Dundee during the nineteenth century shows how extensive and complex imperial economic relationships could be. Dundee businessmen began the factory production of jute in the 1830s, using a raw material grown in rural Bengal, which was exported through Calcutta to Dundee. After the fiber was spun and woven into burlap by Scottish and Irish women and children, it was made into bags and then sold to suppliers of Australian wool, United States cotton and grain, Caribbean sugar, and Javanese coffee. Anyone who wanted to ship bulky, loose items used burlap packaging. Unfortunately for Dundee, British and Indian entrepreneurs soon realized that jute could be processed more easily and cheaply in Calcutta. Jute had been grown for centuries in Bengal, and local people were so skilled in its spinning and weaving that the export of burlap was that region's major industry. It was an easy step to move from hand production to a machine-made product. Calcutta factories, financed by British and Indian capital and supported by London banking, insurance, and shipping services, took over major world markets, and by 1910 they dwarfed Scottish competitors. Although the factories were located in South Asia, Anglo-Indian international management firms with offices in London, as well as in Calcutta, controlled most of the mills until the 1920s, when Indian capitalists moved in aggressively. Capital, equipment, and organization had a solid British base. Calcutta producers used the multiple resources of Dundee, which supplied most of the managers, engineers, and overseers for Calcutta mills, and which trained Indian assistants in jute production at the Dundee Technical College. Not only were several of the Calcutta factories financed by Dundee capital and controlled in Scotland, but a regular flow of letters and visits linked the two cities and their industrialists with each other and with London. The jute story is one of networks and exchanges, not one of Indian deindustrialization under pressure of British competition. In this case, T. Stewart Gordon argues that "imperial policies ended up helping Calcutta rather than Dundee."[10]

After their military conquests, Europeans used whatever were the most advanced communication and transportation technologies in order to consolidate their empires. Ports, post offices, telegraphs, steamship lines, and railways followed their arrival, creating new channels for the flow of information, goods, and people. When the Marquis of Dalhousie served as governor of India, he set out to modernize the country, claiming in

[10] Gordon, *Jute and Empire*, 5.

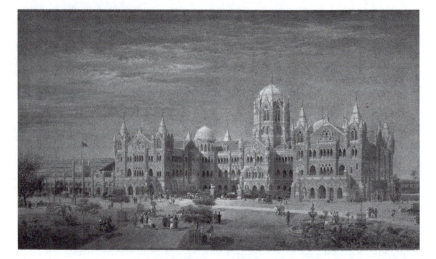

23. The Victoria Railway Station in Bombay. The Indian colonial government erected huge brick buildings, which mixed Gothic with other indigenous historical styles, to serve as schools, administrative centers, and transportation hubs in central Bombay. This picture was painted in 1878 by Axel Herman Haig.

1856 to have introduced "three great engines of social improvement, which the sagacity and science of recent times had previously given to the Western nations – I mean Railways, Uniform Postage, and the Electric Telegraph."[11] The net impact of these changes was to increase the speed and volume and to lower the cost of exchanges between Europe and its colonies. Even when not commercially profitable, these investments were deemed politically necessary, and substantial subsidies in the form of land concessions, land and ocean floor surveys, diplomatic help, government contracts, and direct funding followed from decisions to link colonies to metropolises. Daniel Headrick identifies electricity as a "web of power" that greatly helped Europeans to consolidate their hold over their empires. By making telegraphy possible, it permitted almost instantaneous contact between imperial cities and their colonies. Headrick also sees political gains following from the telegraph: rebellions were easier to defeat, and orders from Europe were easier to transmit to subordinates, although enforcement of those orders remained a major problem.[12] The net impact of these new technologies was to reinforce the importance of the larger cities, whose status as transportation hubs and as centers

---

[11] Quoted in Headrick, *Tentacles of Progress*, 64.   [12] Ibid., 98, 110.

of communication greatly increased their significance as administrative centers.

Since railways and telegraphs moved from point to point, they forced choices of destinations. Capitals, ports, and key production sites were the earliest beneficiaries. Within the British Empire, such investments went first to India, then to Australia, Canada, and New Zealand, and finally to less important colonies. The French worked outward from Paris to Algeria and then to other African colonies. Annoyed by the sluggish pace of overseas communications, English and French governments funded underwater telegraph cables, as soon as they could after the new technology became available around 1850. Construction of telegraph trunk lines between the chief cities of India began in 1853, with communications open among Calcutta, Agra, Bombay, and Madras by 1855. Mid-century rebellion in India energized British attempts to set up speedy, secure communications between Britain and South Asia. Building on land lines from European cities to Constantinople, British engineers extended that system to Baghdad and on to the Persian Gulf at Fao, where it joined an undersea cable to the town of Gwadur and then went on to Karachi and the towns of British India. The French had opened telegraph offices in key towns in Algeria by 1861. After 1864, using a land line that went from Paris through Spain to Cartegena, an undersea cable to Oran, and then a land line to Algiers, officials in Paris could communicate easily with their subordinates in Algeria. By the 1880s, Saigon in Indochina and several West African ports also had cable links to Paris.

Imperial intercity connections fostered not only material exchanges but also new ideas and the creation of new cultural forms. The spread of Christianity within empires illustrates this process. Heavy use of imperial resources and networks had, of course, been made early on by Spanish and Portuguese priests traveling from Europe to the Americas, who helped to build Baroque churches in missions from California south through Latin America. The resulting religious practices combined European and indigenous beliefs and rituals in new, unorthodox ways. Priests sent by the Paris Foreign Missions (Missions Etrangères de Paris) founded Roman Catholic communities in the towns of China and Southeast Asia, and they reported regularly to their French superiors. Some of their Asian converts went to Paris for training in the priesthood. In the process, all became multilingual and multicultural. British evangelical groups – the Church Missionary Society and the London Missionary Society, as well as groups run by the Church of England, the Methodists, and the Baptists – had offices, directors, and small staffs based in London. They corresponded with colonial missionaries, who served in churches throughout the empire and returned periodically to

England for conventions and home leave. After 1819, the Rev. Dr. John Philip was the London Missionary Society director in Capetown, supervising and visiting its clergy in the Eastern Cape. In the longer run, the incorporation of black and Asian Christians as missionaries and preachers reshaped church practices and triggered debates about equality, citizenship, and gender relations that were unanticipated and often unwelcome to European Christians. Power, as well as the forms of belief, was at issue.

Cultural exchanges included far more than religion, of course, and the flows moved more than one way. Well before the late nineteenth century, European diets changed greatly as a result of the addition of tea, sugar, maize, and potatoes. Cotton clothing, paper books, and gunpowder had transformed the ways that people dressed, communicated, and fought. Already by the eighteenth century, the European cultural landscape was deeply influenced by the heavy stream of travel accounts, paintings, books, and objects – looted as well as purchased – that flowed from Asia, Africa, and the Americas into European cities. Many buildings (such as the Royal Pavilion in Brighton) incorporated Egyptian, Chinese, and Indian designs, reworking them in novel directions. By the end of the nineteenth century, every country within Europe had incorporated multiple influences from colonized territories. In European cities, ethnographic museums opened to show off foreign objects which were thought to represent human nature and the wide range of its diverse cultures. Explorers and archaeologists sent home chaotic collections of masks, pots, clothing, totem poles, and weapons, which curators were supposed to organize and explain to European audiences. In return, Europeans exported their own material culture, plants, and animals. These global movements produced culturally hybrid societies, whose most sophisticated expressions were located in towns and cities.

The creation and transmission of knowledge was a key part of the imperial enterprise, and both metropolitan and overseas institutions shaped this process. Zoë Laidlaw argues that after 1830 the British Colonial Office changed its strategy for controlling dependent territories: an information revolution brought vast quantities of statistics, maps, and descriptive accounts to London. A new set of professionals – surveyors, scientists, and bureaucrats – created and processed these materials and shaped the exercise of colonial rule.[13] Education also was part of this information revolution, particularly in the French empire. The French state operated secondary schools, or *lycées*, in colonial towns, such as Saigon or Algiers, where bright boys (both European and indigenous) studied the same liberal arts curriculum as was available in Paris. Although no European

---

[13] Laidlaw, *Colonial Connections*, 203–04.

government invested very much in technical education in its African colonies, training in engineering was available in Calcutta, Pune, and Madras by the 1860s, and the Khedive of Egypt, using French contacts, opened several small colleges where men intending to work for the state could get advanced scientific education. For medical education, wealthy colonial subjects went to Paris, Amsterdam, or Edinburgh. To study law, British subjects throughout the empire went to London's Inns of Court.

The spread of botanical knowledge depended on the international movement of individuals who travel within imperial networks. As empires expanded, so did plant transfers to the botanic gardens of Paris, Leyden, and London. The French state in the early seventeenth century established a royal garden for the study of medicinal plants, which later expanded to include a botanical school and various units for the study of particular colonies. Today it is known as the Jardin des Plantes. Kew Gardens on the outskirts of London became a research site in 1772, when Joseph Banks, who had botanized in the Pacific with Captain Cook, became its director. During the nineteenth century, the staff of Kew Gardens ran a global network of botanical transfers: information, seeds, and plants traveled world wide. British colonies around the globe maintained botanic gardens, where Kew-trained scientists worked to breed and hybridize plants and to improve imperial agriculture. The Dutch government sent an Amsterdam professor of natural history to start a research garden on Java in 1815. Although the Parisian scientists were less active in the nineteenth century than their Dutch and English counterparts, the French government also set up a colonial garden on the outskirts of Paris in 1899, which supplied plants throughout the French empire. The staff of the National Museum of Natural History published reports on tropical agriculture, and the French Ministry of Colonies set up a school of tropical agronomy for administrators and would-be emigrants. Metropolitan gardens and research institutes functioned as knowledge banks on which colonial officials could draw at will. At the same time, scientists in botanic gardens outside Europe, particularly those in Singapore, Buitenzorg on Java, and Barbados, produced important discoveries about the cultivation of quinine, sugar, and rubber. The creation of new botanical knowledge emerged from a dense network of exchanges that brought metropole and colony into a close relationship.

World globalization, when measured in terms of exports and international investment, reached a level by 1914 not to be exceeded until the 1980s. Industrialization triggered an enormous expansion of trade and capital flows among the countries of the world, which was channeled through cities and their networks of exchange.

Urbanism overseas

During the years between 1850 and 1914, as Europeans took over most of the African continent and large parts of Asia, they used cities as their bridgeheads. Algiers and Hanoi grew with the influx of French administrators, as did the new town of Dakar in Senegal, which became the capital of the French West African Federation in 1902. Cairo and Alexandria passed from Egyptian to British oversight when Her Majesty's government imposed financial, and later political, authority over the Khedive. Sections of central Shanghai passed to European control after Chinese military defeats. Colonial towns had several different functions for their imperial masters. The most important centers – for example, Batavia in the Netherlands Indies, Calcutta and, later, New Delhi in India, and Saigon in Cochin-China – were capitals of colonies. Ports, such as Bombay, Haiphong, Lagos, and Colombo, attracted European businesses and merchants, particularly after railways made trade with inland areas easier. Europeans' wish to escape tropical heat produced hill stations and vacation towns. Plantation agriculture and mining areas required service centers where food, mail, and transport could be found. The expansion of European empires thus led directly to a new wave of urbanization, expressed most obviously through a consolidated network of capital cities, ports, and subsidiary towns.

Colonial cities differed greatly in size. Most of the very large ones at mid-century were in India – Calcutta, Madras, and Bombay – their size a function of the territorial power and trade of the East India Company. The typical colonial town in Africa or Australia had only a few thousand residents. Not until the end of the century did many colonial towns break the 100,000 mark. Most of the new towns founded by European states or commercial companies were small when compared with the oldest imperial cities of Asia and Africa, such as Peking, Constantinople, and Cairo. The most important new settlements grew quickly. Around 1800, Sydney had only 2,500 residents, but it boasted 53,000 in 1850. Singapore, which dated from 1819, had reached 81,000 by 1860.

The term "colonial city" covers a broad range of places and urban types. It expresses the political linkage of towns to an overseas capital and their function as instruments of colonization. A simple typology of European colonial settlements provides some helpful distinctions. First, we must distinguish between older, pre-colonial settlements and newer towns. Second, we must distinguish areas where there were few European immigrants from settler societies. Islamic areas from northern Africa through the Middle East and South Asia, China, and the coasts of East Africa and the Indian Ocean had well-developed urban networks centuries before

Table 5 *Large cities in Asia and Africa, 1800–1900*

City	1800	1850	1900
Peking	1,100,000	1,650,000	1,100,000
Calcutta	200,000	413,000	1,085,000
Constantinople	570,000	785,000	900,000
Shanghai	100,000	250,000	837,000
Bombay	175,000	575,000	780,000
Cairo	263,000	256,000	595,000
Sydney	2,500	53,000	485,000
Hong Kong	–	15,500	192,000
Singapore	–	81,000	185,000
Saigon	–	6,000	175,000
Capetown	14,000	–	148,000

Source: Tertius Chandler and Gerald Fox, *Three Thousand Years of Urban Growth* (New York and London, 1974), 324–443; Goerg and de Lemps, "La ville européenne outre-mer," 379, 388, 420, 422; Mayne, *Fever, Squalor, and Vice*, App. 1.

Europeans used guns and ships to conquer them. Such towns tended to be relatively large and well-sited; few disappeared as a result of European conquest. Europeans could seize or buy a particular settlement, or they could look for relatively empty territory and move in with the permission of a local ruler to start a new community. In either case, local people made up most of the population. In other parts of the world, particularly Australia, New Zealand, and North America, where urbanization was either weak or non-existent and population density low, most towns were new. Their residents were initially long-distance migrants. European influences were far heavier, understandably, in the latter case than in the former. When cities are grouped in this way, the strongest differences emerge between the pre-colonial settlements in urbanized territories such as Egypt, India, and Vietnam, and new cities with settler populations.

Societies in Asia and in the Middle East had been urbanized for hundreds, if not thousands, of years. Their architecture and street patterns had arisen long before any Europeans were in residence. Neighborhoods that grouped specific trades or ethnic groups grew up around market places, mosques, and temples. Muslim Cairo grew from a walled, medieval city, sand-colored and unpaved. Informally segregated by ethnicity, religion, and occupation, its inhabitants lived in tiny, separate neighborhoods, which were barricaded against outsiders. Greeks, Jews, Armenians, and Coptic Christians had their own quarters in the northwest of the older city, while poor migrants, former slaves, and unskilled

Table 6 *Types of colonial cities*

	Nonsettler colonies	Settler colonies
Pre-colonial cities	Cairo Delhi Hanoi	Algiers
New cities	Dakar Madras Batavia (Jakarta)	Sydney Melbourne Capetown

laborers settled on the fringe of the built-up area and in eastern districts. People worked, lived, and shopped close to their homes, walking on foot to places where they needed to be. Streets were narrow, short, and shaded by overhanging balconies. Two cemeteries, whose shrines, monasteries, tombs, and schools drew people there for festivals and recreation, served as the major open spaces. By the nineteenth century, Cairo was very large – over 250,000 inhabitants in 1850 and around 690,000 in 1910 – but its organization after 1870 was that of a dual city. The Egyptian Khedive Ismail, intent on modernizing Cairo according to the Parisian model, left the old city intact, adding straight streets, parks, gas lighting, and piped water to a new district near the Nile. By the time the Suez Canal opened in 1869, the new city had acquired the technologies of a European capital, but only for part of its inhabitants. The modernized, European quarter lay like a foreign frosting on top of a dense Egyptian cake. As two European observers wrote early in the twentieth century, "European Cairo . . . is divided from Egyptian Cairo by a long street that goes from the railway station past the big hotels to Abdin [palace] . . . It is full of big shops and great houses and fine carriages and well-dressed people . . . The real Cairo is to the east of this . . . and is practically what it always was."[14]

In contrast, European migrants could plan entire towns as they wished in lightly settled lands, such as Australia, or places where there were few cities, such as southern Africa. They laid out and named the streets, put their own European-style civic and religious buildings in central areas, and divided the land among themselves. This pattern can be seen clearly in Capetown. The Dutch East India Company founded Capetown in 1652 to serve as a provisioning stop for its ships on their way to Asia. Soon known as the tavern and brothel of the two oceans, the city became

---

[14] Augustus Lamplough and R. Francis, *Cairo and its Environs* (London, 1909), xv; quoted in Abu-Lughod, *Cairo*, 98.

invaluable to the British Navy after its conquest in 1806. A fort and military parade ground, flanked by markets, stood near the harbor. Poor workers and sailors lived near the port on low-lying land, while the rich settled higher ground on the mountainsides. Segregation was economic, rather than racial. Immigrants, mostly Dutch, British, and German with their slaves from the Indian Ocean area, made up almost the entire population; virtually no Africans lived in the town in the early nineteenth century. In 1840, the population of around 20,100 was divided in official racial classifications into two groups: whites (54 percent) and colored, the term used for non-European, often mixed-race populations (46 percent). Thousands of Indonesians, Sinhalese, Malagasies, and South Asians had been brought there as slaves, but they stayed on as free laborers and artisans after emancipation, intermarrying with one another and with the local population. Capetown's settlers were racially diverse and thoroughly multicultural.

In most colonial towns outside of Australia, New Zealand, and Canada, the vast majority of the inhabitants were not of European origin. Ethnic mixes, however, varied widely. To be sure, in Algiers, Muslims constituted about 20 percent of the population in 1866 and 22 percent in 1911, while French, Italians, Maltese, and other Europeans made up the rest. But the numbers of European settlers in Asian towns were far lower. In the early twentieth century, Europeans constituted about 3 percent of Calcutta's population, 7 percent of Batavia's, and 4 percent of Hanoi's. Even these proportions exceeded those for small market towns in Asia. European migrants to the colonies clustered in capitals and port towns, where the demand for professionals or for merchant services was high. Small towns of the Malay peninsula had only handfuls of European and Eurasian residents, perhaps only half of 1 percent of overall population. The rest were Chinese, Tamil, and Malay. Chinese migrants made up about 75 percent of Singapore's population around 1900, and almost 25 percent of those living in Batavia. Gender mixes varied too. Immigrants to Asian, African, and Australian towns tended to be male from the later eighteenth through the mid-nineteenth century. The arrival of increasing numbers of European and Asian migrant women in the second half of the nineteenth century shifted gender balances, permitting more male migrants to marry and increasing the number of children. In the meantime, people of Eurasian, Eurafrican, and mixed Asian descent had multiplied.

Colonial cities, much more than their European counterparts, were plural societies, hybrid in culture, and stratified according to race. As a result, however, of their pre-colonial heritages, colonial towns differed enormously. Towns from Casablanca east through Java and south of the Sahara had strong Islamic roots, visible in their mosques, schools, and law courts. In contrast, Benares and Madurai attracted Hindu pilgrims and worshippers to their many temples and sacred sites. Chinese culture pervaded the cityscapes of Hong Kong and Singapore. Hué, the seat of the Nguyen dynasty in central Vietnam, had as its core a walled palace compound, modeled on Peking's Forbidden City. Along the coast of the Indian Ocean, trade shaped the ports, drawing in multilingual and multicultural populations of merchants and sailors. Places such as Mozambique City and Mombasa bore the marks of long-term occupation by Arabs, Swahilis, and Portuguese. In contrast, Chinese, Malay, Portuguese, and Dutch influences shaped the food and architecture of Malacca. All were pluralist societies in which political, economic, and social power was concentrated in the hands of people culturally and ethnically different from the indigenous populations. Only in Australia, New Zealand, and North America was the British influence pervasive.

Despite great differences among colonial cities, there was an underlying theme in ways they were designed by their European masters. Governments intended colonial cities to justify the imperial enterprise. Infrastructures and buildings brought "modernity" to "traditional" societies. Forts, government houses, and law courts embodied colonial authority. Neoclassical, Renaissance, and Gothic styles put a European stamp on public buildings, while railways and electric lights signaled technical expertise. Capital cities, in particular, had the function of symbolizing imperial power through spatial design and architectural magnificence. Whatever the outer areas looked like, the central administrative and colonial business district copied European forms. After conquest, newly French Saigon featured tree-lined boulevards, hotels, an opera house, a neo-Renaissance city hall, and a Romanesque cathedral – all of which embodied the "civilization" being offered to the Vietnamese. The British government intended New Delhi to be visibly imperial, a reconciliation of East and West, which would announce British determination to continue to rule India. Built between 1911 and 1931 and designed by the architects Edwin Lutyens and Herbert Baker, New Delhi took its street names from both British and Indian rulers, but its street design was decidedly European. Officials lived here in hierarchically arranged palaces and spacious bungalows, around which opened parks and other green spaces. Its central road, the Kingsway, twice as wide as the Avenue des Champs-Elysées in Paris, led uphill to the gargantuan, pink stone Viceroy's House, which combined a neoclassical dome and colonnades with carefully subordinated South Asian architectural forms. A parliament building, not even included in the original design, lay downhill, shunted onto a side street. The old city sat dwarfed and trapped between British residential districts and the new military cantonment.

24. The City Hall in Saigon. Finished around 1910 under the direction of French authorities, it shows the strong influence of the neo-Renaissance style that was highly popular in the design of civic architecture in Europe. Located on a central boulevard near the Roman Catholic Cathedral and Post Office, it lay in the heart of the colonial city. (Photograph by authors.)

Because of costs and colonial demography, such calculated colonial displays were possible only in a few carefully selected places. While capital cities seemed to require an assertion of a European presence in their public spaces, smaller towns of limited political importance got much less architectural attention. In any case, it was impossible to maintain a cultural neo-Europe in the absence of significant numbers of European settlers. Small, simple buildings lined the main streets of market towns throughout Asia and Africa, their hybrid designs testifying to the mixed origins of populations and cultural traditions. Paved roads, post offices, and police stations gave only quiet notice of a colonial presence, easy to overlook in the midst of coffee shops, street traffic, and children playing.

The relationship between European and colonial cities overseas can be pictured in several ways. Those who emphasize the logic of capitalist production model the connection in terms of economic dependence: metropoles supply finished goods while employing professionals and artisans, whereas towns and regions of the periphery use low and unskilled labor to provide cheap goods and raw materials, remaining comparatively undeveloped. This stark division is too simple, as the examples of Dundee and Calcutta demonstrate. In any case, a city's contribution to the global economy can change over time, as can the location of manufacturing and the composition of a local labor force. New technologies could be bought and installed in colonies, as well as in metropoles. As the history of the last half-century has shown, international divisions of labor have not been static. Although colonial governments thought of colonies as economic resources for European nation-states, they had only limited control over the markets and the people who worked in them. Wealthy Chinese, Indians, and Arabs continued to operate family businesses and trade internationally, consolidating local positions of power.

A more useful economic concept that helps describe colonial cities is that of dualism. European trading networks in Asia and Africa were superimposed upon agricultural economies and small-scale units of production. Exporting on a large scale required massive reorganization of land and labor markets, which destabilized social hierarchies and residential patterns and led to migration and an influx of foreign entrepreneurs. Towns became the places where the linkage between new and old took place. Both could be observed on their streets, where this dualism was expressed in spatial terms. Algiers had a modern port and a central commercial area superimposed upon the spatial organization of the Arab-Ottoman town. Local artisans and most of the Muslim population lived in a warren of alleys and dead-end streets of the Casbah, while European residents, for the most part, moved into new suburbs or rebuilt central areas. This physical dualism accentuated the inequality resulting from the political and economic inequalities intrinsic to colonial rule.

Empires were as much political enterprises as they were cultural and economic ones. Therefore, a wider set of interactions and results need to be taken into account when analyzing colonial cities. Because of the widely varied periods and circumstances under which colonies were acquired, they tended to have different forms of government, which reflected the political ideas at different times in the home countries and varying judgments about the resident populations. In general, the more European settlers present, the more local political rights granted.

Consider first the forms of municipal government, which varied according to region and date of acquisition. Both the French and the British governments, as well as their chartered companies, granted substantial rights of self-government during the eighteenth and early nineteenth centuries to propertied elites in larger towns in the Caribbean and in the Americas. The legal rights of towns in France were extended progressively to their counterparts in the French Antilles and the islands of Saint-Pierre-et-Miquelon and to appropriately screened electors. During the eighteenth century, the British exported their legal traditions to American and Caribbean colonies along with political forms, such as elections, legislatures, and town corporations. Boston and Philadelphia had elected city governments. Kingston, Jamaica, became a self-governing corporation in 1802, although its autonomy was suppressed after a rebellion in 1865. Slaves and women were denied political representation, however, so that political institutions represented only a minority of the residents.

Outside the Americas and the Caribbean, there were a few other places where the power of local merchant communities induced colonial authorities to delegate some powers of self-government. The East India Company permitted municipal councils to be set up in Bombay, Calcutta, and Madras. It also worked out consultative committees of merchants and administrators in Penang and Singapore, which became elected bodies during the 1850s. The French state set up municipal councils in four coastal Senegalese towns – St. Louis, Gorée, Dakar, and Rufisque – between 1872 and 1887. Bordeaux merchant firms with offices in Senegal ports pushed for these rights. Since these Senegalese towns, atypically, had universal male suffrage for those literate in French and the right to elect a deputy to the national legislature, their governing structure was similar to that of a French commune. Willingness to permit towns some amount of self-government was greatest where populations included significant numbers of European settlers. Sydney became an incorporated town in 1842, when taxpaying heads of households got the right to vote for a mayor and a municipal council with wide local powers over city spaces and sanitation. Both in the timing and in the legal forms used, British towns served as its model.

These areas were exceptional, however, in their rights of self-government, if compared with the entire range of colonial towns. Soldiers generally ran new colonies in Australia, Africa, or Southeast Asia after their conquest. More elaborate structures of government which usually did not include elected institutions, followed later. Many cities were considered too central to British authority to permit any steps toward truly representative government on the basis of election. The Dutch East India Company and the Dutch government kept a tight hold on the towns and port-forts of its colonial empire. Colonial bureaucrats ran Indies towns until the early twentieth century, keeping power out of the hands of residents. In Lucknow in India after 1862, ten British officials nominated by the central government managed the town with the aid of five unofficial members, two Muslims and three Hindus. The council collected taxes, arranged for clean streets, and set sanitary rules. Neither Cairo nor Hong Kong had rights of self government. During the later nineteenth century, the French state backed away from assimilating members of indigenous elites who adopted French language and culture, turning to the idea of "association," which called for unequal rights for those who were not French citizens. In most of Senegal and French Africa, municipal councils were only consultative; French officials appointed their members, who were usually wealthy merchants, and gave Africans only one or two representatives. Both British and French designs for municipal government involved keeping non-Europeans in the minority, a task easily accomplished through nomination of members or by restrictions on voting rights according to property and/or race. In matters of governance, therefore, most colonial cities in Asia and Africa differed greatly from their European counterparts. Except in a few settler colonies, most of them British, colonial governments denied adult males the political rights which had come to be the hallmark of political modernization in Europe.

The growing influence of ideas about racial differences during the nineteenth-century expansion of European empires helped to account for this result. European imperialists boasted of a "white man's burden" of ruling and uplifting "primitive" peoples whom they ought to "civilize" through the export of European knowledge, culture, and technology. Colonial cities, which housed the institutions through which European civilization could be communicated, were central places in this process. Yet there was a contradiction inherent in the urban colonial cultural project. While colonial cities exhibited the trappings of a European modernity, they did not offer them to all their residents.

In European political culture and law after the French Revolution, rights were not race based. People born on British soil in British colonies were all subjects of the ruling monarch, and had the same legal status. The French empire can also illustrate this point. Colonial subjects who assimilated to French culture, accepting the French language, education, and mode of life, were thought qualified for citizenship and political privileges. African residents of the four communes of Senegal could vote in French Parliamentary elections, if they were literate in French and met other standard requirements. In Algeria, Arabs who were willing to give up their status as Muslims could become naturalized French citizens. Slavery was formally abolished within the British Empire in 1838 and in Danish and French colonies in 1848. Yet laws were unevenly enforced, and there was much slippage between the letter of the law and the reality on the ground. Moreover, there was a tension between legal rights on the one hand, and science and popular attitudes on the other, which shaped exchanges between imperial cities and their colonial counterparts. In practice, as well as in theory, colonial administrators viewed colonial populations and their cities as culturally and racially different from and inferior to those in the metropoles, and they sometimes resisted the application locally of laws passed by European legislatures.

European anthropologists helped to construct the view of non-European populations as racially and intellectual inferior. They represented the world's populations in terms of an evolutionary racial tree topped by the Anglo-Saxons, along whose trunk lay various Asian groups, and at whose roots lay Bantu and other African populations. Belief in European superiority increased during the second half of the nineteenth century. According to Catherine Hall, in Britain between 1830 and 1860 images of a human family whose younger members could be educated into equality were "displaced by a harsher racial vocabulary of fixed differences."[15] Biological determinism replaced belief in the possibility of cultural diffusion.

The need to govern urban populations forced colonial administrators to think hard about means and ends. What goals would be pursued and who would achieve them? Veena Oldenburg comments that the British were determined to rebuild Lucknow into a safe, clean, and loyal city after the end of the India Mutiny in 1858. No more political challenges would be tolerated, and European residents were to be assured of protection from disease as well as from assault. Such aims, applicable well beyond northern India, required a high degree of control over the behavior and attitudes of urban populations as well as over physical environments. At

[15] Hall, *Civilising Subjects*, 440.

the same time, imperial government was supposed to be cheap, a goal inconsistent with the rulers' political and environmental aims.

Improved sanitation became a challenge and a test of European imperialism after the 1850s, as public health campaigns accelerated, which firmly linked the problems of death, dirt, and disease. Common views of older colonial cities stressed their filth and chaotic appearance. As late as 1917, W. H. McLean described a smaller Egyptian town as a "rabbit warren with narrow winding streets . . . evil smelling and littered with garbage."[16] As standards of comfort for middle- and upper-class Europeans rose, colonial settlers wanted to live in similar circumstances, and they lobbied for new infrastructures in their cities. Professional planners and architects saw new colonial towns as laboratories for urban improvement, where there were few barriers to innovative design. At the same time, ideas about racial and cultural difference led colonial officials to see obstacles to the export of some European technologies and particularly to their providing them for non-European populations. Colonial administrators tended to be cultural conservatives, lacking faith in the ability of local people to appreciate changes and thus reluctant to tamper with existing habits. The idea that Asians and Africans might not be interested in particular rights or technologies quickly slid into assertions that they would not be able to maintain them or use them appropriately. For Europeans, possession of advanced technologies signaled cultural superiority. Those who lacked machines perhaps did not deserve them.

French administrators in Morocco illustrate this position well. Hubert Lyautey, Resident-General of Morocco from 1912 to 1925 and a veteran of urban planning in Madagascar and Vietnam, wanted to modernize Morocco and develop the colony economically in the interests of French imperial power, but he distinguished between those who would be given the benefits of modern urbanism and those who would not: "Touch the indigenous cities as little as possible. Instead improve their surroundings where . . . the European city rises, following a plan which realizes the most modern conceptions of large boulevards, water and electrical supplies, squares and gardens, buses and tramways."[17] The implementation of his goals produced a dual city, a "traditional" area of Arab residence whose architecture and culture were to be preserved and a European district given the newest technologies and a complete array of government services.

---

[16] W. H. McLean, "Local Government and Town Development in Egypt," *Town Planning Review* 7 (1917): 93.

[17] Quoted in Wright, *The Politics of Design*, 79.

Recognition of infrastructural needs in the colonies and the search for the money to pay for them forced decisions upon colonial officials that moved beyond governmental form to issues of technology and social access to it. How would water be supplied, to whom, and at what cost? What kinds of public health measures and sanitation were appropriate? The answers to these questions illuminate the unequal nature of colonial urban society.

Municipal services operated on a restricted level for several reasons beyond the prejudices of colonial officials. First, there were fiscal reasons. The power of the purse generally lay with European administrators, who were supposed to cover costs with locally generated revenues. But most urban residents were poor and could pay little for any given service. Local councils had relatively little power, in any case. As a result, the potential was quite low for raising local taxes in colonial cities. Second, acceptance of active municipal government grew much more slowly during the second half of the nineteenth century in colonies than in Europe, where it was pushed by competition between political parties, pressures largely absent in the colonies because of the lack of elections. In the colonies, citizens quarreled sharply about the extent to which municipalities should undertake public projects. Third, quarrels still raged about methods for preventing diseases. While the goal of a sanitary city could be widely accepted, people fought about which strategies were best. In the colonies, these problems were compounded by the cultural gaps between rulers and ruled. The task of sanitizing every colonial city and all of its territory took more political and financial resources than imperial governments were willing to devote to it.

A brief look at the problem of providing adequate water and waste disposal systems reveals some common difficulties. While riverside sites offered the easy, but potentially lethal solution of dumping and dipping, other locations required wells, aqueducts, canals, and reservoirs. Although older colonial cities had water and drainage systems in place, they regularly needed maintenance and expansion, which colonial authorities tended to neglect. The demand for water increased not only with town growth but also with rising standards of cleanliness and with the invention of water-closets to flush human waste. In Jakarta, although authorities dug wells, the water table was so high and pollution so widespread that supplies were contaminated. Piped water went mainly to European areas. In Hong Kong, the colonial government provided hilltop reservoirs to hold rainwater and pipes, which carried water down to the town. Nevertheless, the population expanded so much faster than the water supply that in the late nineteenth century city dwellers received on average one-tenth of the daily water allowance available in London, and no water was available for sewage disposal. In contrast, Calcutta had ample supplies: pumps and aqueducts transported water to hydrants throughout the city and to a relatively few houses whose owners agreed to pay for connecting pipes. Epidemics combined with spreading awareness of the links among sewage, water, and cholera induced the municipality to fund new waterworks and a network of underground sewage pipes, installed first in European areas. Much of the town's water passed through sand filters, which removed bacteria and other pollutants. Provision of water and sewers spread to predominantly Indian areas in the city during the 1880s and 1890s, but rich and poor had different levels of service. The worst-provided used unfiltered river water and left their wastes on the street. In comparative terms, Calcutta had done more to provide for public health than had Hamburg in the 1890s. Nevertheless, the city's wealth and technical savvy did not effectively solve the problem of sewage disposal. Calcutta pumped its sewage into a local river, its government rejecting other solutions as too expensive.

The cost of sanitary reform imposed an ever-present constraint for municipal authorities: good colonial government was supposed to be cheap and self-financing, but sanitation was expensive, and it did not produce profits. When New Delhi was constructed after 1912, the government spent vast sums on buildings but economized on sanitation. The government of India provided ample water and waterborne sewage disposal for public buildings and employees' residential areas in New Delhi, but not in the old walled city where most inhabitants lived. There, armies of sweepers collected waste each morning from the streets and drains, while a parade of rubbish carts shifted it to landfills outside the walls. As long as the stink did not reach European noses, it was tolerated. Rajnarayan Chandavarkar argues that effective sanitary reform in India would have required dangerous meddling in the habits of local people, and "as they [colonial administrations] knew only too well, the key to the enjoyment of their political kingdom lay not in social engineering but in salutary neglect."[18]

Nevertheless, neglect had its limits. If empires were to remain secure, soldiers had to survive and so did the settlers and administrators sent to far-flung corners of the world. Appalled by high death rates from epidemic diseases in the tropics, the British government appointed sanitary police and medical officers of health to work with officials in India who rebuilt urban military bases after the 1857 mutiny. These cantonments – new towns in effect – created sanitary space, according to the most advanced public health ideas of the time. High sites and wide, paved streets allowed

---

[18] Chandavarkar, *Imperial Power and Popular Politics*, 241.

air to circulate; separate markets and canteens offered European goods and kept soldiers out of the nearby city. Easy to clean, brick barracks and spacious bungalows tended by servants kept dirt at bay. Plentiful supplies of clean water benefited both gardens and residents. When death rates plummeted, the model of a separate, racially segregated space for Europeans gained popularity. In the absence of exact knowledge of how particular diseases spread, doctors recommended isolation from bad air, contagious bodies, and tainted soil as the best available general protection. The leap to blaming cities and their poor residents for infection was easily made well after germ theory, pharmacological discoveries, and medical research provided more satisfactory explanations.

Despite the availability by 1900 of good scientific evidence on the transmission of malaria and its deterrence, doctors in colonial towns still disagreed over the best methods of its prevention. By 1900, three different modes of combating malaria had medical support: 1) ingestion of quinine, an effective anti-malarial agent that could be taken regularly; 2) elimination of the anopheles mosquito and reduction of exposure to all mosquitoes; 3) segregation of populations. Even though the third method was the least effective, racist attitudes were sufficiently strong that it had influential adherents. In 1914, Dr. W. J. Simpson, the leading British specialist in tropical medicine, recommended that there be at least 300 yards of open land between areas where Europeans lived and the houses of Africans and Asians because "the diseases to which these different races are respectively liable are readily transferable to the European and vice versa."[19] Noting that British officials often used images of infection to describe race relations in Africa, Maynard Swanson links the ideas of a "sanitation syndrome" to the "creation of urban apartheid."[20] Extensive efforts to segregate urban populations in the interests of public health were made in Freetown, Capetown, Port Elizabeth, Kano, Duala, and Dakar, but despite great economic and political costs they were ineffective. The objections of wealthy Africans and of a few colonial governors blocked forced relocations in Accra and Lagos, where the provision of free quinine and mosquito eradication provided easier and more humane alternatives. Despite medical arguments in favor of segregation, limitations on colonial power and opposition by Africans, as well as by a few influential Europeans, made racial separation virtually impossible to implement. In any case, the large number of Africans in colonial towns made segregation too expensive for colonial administrators, who were intent upon spending as little as possible on their overseas possessions.

[19] Quoted in Curtin, "Medical Knowledge," 611.
[20] Swanson, "The Sanitation Syndrome," 387.

Town governments, threatened by opposition, took on the task of maintaining public order. Strong police forces or colonial armies were on call to stop riots and discourage rebellions. Remembering the loss of their north Indian urban bases in 1857, the British government built army cantonments, or barracks, on the edge of larger cities so that they had soldiers ready to hand. Large police forces made up of migrant Sikhs kept the peace in the towns of the Malay peninsula. They stopped factional fights between Chinese secret societies, pursued runaway indentured workers, and harassed young men loitering on the streets. During the 1890s, a series of major riots and strikes so alarmed Bombay authorities that they tripled the size of their armed mounted police and gave policemen the power to ban a wide range of public behaviors. After major riots between Hindus and Muslims, the police gained the power to block processions and ceremonies, to stop loud drums and music, and to control places of entertainment. Street life that had formerly been left to neighborhood leaders to control now came under the gaze of public authorities. Prashant Kidambi argues that "industrial urbanization began to generate new problems of social control" in the towns of British India late in the nineteenth century, giving rise to intrusive policing and to added conflict between police and the poor.[21] Limitations on numbers and resources, however, suggest that colonial police lacked the power to impose consistent discipline on local populations. Instead they intervened selectively to keep the peace.

Unintended consequences

The contours of colonial rule in the towns of European empires varied over time and place, and the ways in which it was experienced differed according to an individual's race, class, gender, and political outlook. While many people had access in the cities to improved communications and transportation services and simple improvements in public health, fewer benefited from the expensive, sanitary infrastructural reforms installed primarily in European neighborhoods. Men had more contact with both the costs and the benefits of imperial rule than did females who were more confined to domestic spaces, which remained largely untouched by colonial governments. Imperial administration employed significant numbers of educated males, although non-Europeans were generally limited to subordinate positions. The poor and the politically

---

[21] Prashant Kidambi, "'The Ultimate Masters of the City': Policing Public Order in Colonial Bombay, c. 1893–1914" (paper presented at the Eighth International Conference on Urban History, Stockholm, August, 2006), 27.

hostile felt the weight of colonial policing differently than did those who had money and who were loyalists or discreet about their opinions. In any case, the disciplines that came with colonialism fell most harshly on plantations and mines, not on city streets or neighborhoods. Within colonial societies, urban populations were relatively privileged. No simple division between European oppressors and non-European victims can be made.

Even where Asian and African city dwellers did not have formal political power, they had many informal ways of influencing officials. Colonial cities, like European ones, had active civil societies within which ideas were presented and criticized. Newspapers, schools, chambers of commerce, clubs, and religious organizations provided forums for discussion and the expression of opinion, as did civic ceremonies. Groups could parade, petition, or actively protest particular policies. Power was exercised in many forms, and its distribution was both unequal and unstable. Brenda Yeoh calls "the colonial urban landscape" a "terrain of discipline and resistance," arguing that even where power relations were "asymmetrical," they were open to negotiation.[22] She shows how the Chinese of colonial Singapore effectively asserted their control over public space by methods ranging from non-compliance to negotiation to riot. The pluralist nature of colonial societies generated multiple voices on any given issue, and imperial rulers could not control the perceptions and responses of their subjects.

Imperial authorities had many different aims, but a common denominator was the maintenance of formal imperial rule. The failure of that enterprise in the decades following the Second World War resulted in large part from the growth of cities throughout the empire. Their civil societies supported the nationalist organizations and trades unions which launched effective resistance to imperial regimes. More generally, the people educated in urban schools and exposed to the social and political criticisms expressed in town newspapers learned to cross cultural borders. As their horizons widened, so did expectations and, eventually, political demands. The mobilization of people for collective ends occurred in colonial cities as well as European ones.

The export of European styles, goods, and technologies left the mark of European modernity on towns far distant from London, Paris, and Lisbon. The common use of English, French, Spanish, and Portuguese opened international cultural channels, while steamships and railroads promoted long-distance migration. The growing ease of travel was not matched by a relaxation of the tension between the value systems that

[22] Yeoh, *Contesting Space*, 10.

Europeans espoused at home and abroad. Cities, it could be argued, intensified conflicts between the colonizers and colonized peoples. As sites of economic exchange where markets were given relatively free rein and where local people attended European schools, they both promised and also blocked access to a wider world. The language of racial difference co-existed uneasily with texts that spoke of nationalism, equal rights, and democratic rule. The disciplines of colonial authority operated side by side with growing urban civil societies composed of literate, mobile, often multilingual individuals, who operated effectively in different cultural arenas. Well-developed urban networks of exchange were open to those who could pay or who could qualify for admission, despite colonial authorities' insistence on racial differences. By mixing the imperial and the colonial, the global and the local, the towns of European empires undermined the basic division on which imperial governance was based. Their civil societies showed "civilization" in action, not as a distant goal to be bestowed by foreign rulers. The network of connections among imperial and colonial cities ought, therefore, to be seen as transforming both sorts of urban places, widening horizons while undermining the forms of political dependence.

Intercity networks had unintended impacts in Europe too. The circulation of knowledge ran along a two-lane highway. European cities were influenced by colonial people who moved there. Even before the mass migrations of the later twentieth century, a steady trickle of young males sailed to Europe to study or work. Their presence changed political dialogues in Paris, Oxford, London, and Berlin, and some became active in Europe as well as at home. Dadhabai Naoroji, a Parsi born in Bombay, shuttled back and forth between the Indian subcontinent and London from the mid-nineteenth century into the early twentieth, working in both places for reform in India. A town councilor and member of the Legislative Council in Bombay, he served briefly as prime minister in the princely state of Baroda. In London, Naoroji, who was able to vote, was elected to Parliament as a Liberal in 1892. An advisor on Indian issues to well-known Liberal and Radical politicians, he became the public face of Indian nationalism, helping to establish the British Committee of the Indian National Congress. Slightly later, when Nguyen Tat Thanh, later known as Ho Chi Minh, left his home village in Vietnam, he traveled first to Hué to study and then on to Saigon in 1911 to look for work. Signing on as a sailor, he traveled to Boston, New York, and London, before moving to Paris in 1919. With the aid of socialists and the radical French press, he articulated powerful demands for Vietnamese independence, drawing on familiar democratic, egalitarian discourses developed in Europe and the Americas. The future founder of the Vietnamese Communist

Party found his political voice through international dialogues and cultural exposures, which occurred as a result of his movement among cities. Urbanism, although it supported empires, eventually undermined them as the unintended consequences of exported modernity spread among city dwellers, whatever their race, religion, or gender.

BIBLIOGRAPHY

Abeyasekere, Susan. *Jakarta: A History*. Rev. edn. Singapore, 1989.
Abu-Lughod, Janet. *Cairo: 1001 Years of the City Victorious*. Princeton, 1971.
   Rabat: Urban Apartheid in Morocco. Princeton, 1980.
Broeze, Frank, ed. *Brides of the Sea: Port Cities of Asia from the 16th–20th Centuries*. Honolulu, 1989.
Çelik, Zenap. *Urban Forms and Colonial Confrontations: Algiers Under French Rule*. Berkeley, 1997.
Chandavarkar, Rajnarayan. *Imperial Power and Popular Politics: Class, Resistance, and the State in India, c. 1850–1950*. Cambridge, 1998.
Connell, John, ed. *Sydney: The Emergence of a World City*. Oxford, 2000.
Cooper, Frederick, and Ann Laura Stoler, eds. *Tensions of Empire: Colonial Cultures in a Bourgeois World*. Berkeley, 1998.
Curtin, Philip D. "Medical Knowledge and Urban Planning in Tropical Africa." *American Historical Review* 90 (1985): 594–613.
Dossal, Miriam. *Imperial Designs and Indian Realities: The Planning of Bombay City, 1845–1875*. Bombay, 1991.
Driver, Felix, and David Gilbert, eds. *Imperial Cities: Landscape, Display, and Identity*. Manchester, 1999.
Goerg, Odile, and Xavier Huetz de Lemps. "La ville européenne outre-mer." In Jean-Luc Pinol, ed., *Histoire de l'Europe urbaine*, vol. II. Paris, 2003.
Gordon, T. Stewart. *Jute and Empire: The Calcutta Jute Wallahs and Landscapes of Empire*. Manchester, 1998.
Gupta, Narayani. *Delhi Between Two Empires, 1803–1931: Society, Government, and Urban Growth*. Delhi, 1981.
Hall, Catherine. *Civilising Subjects: Metropole and Colony in the English Imagination, 1830–1867*. Oxford, 2002.
Hamer, David. *New Towns in the New World: Images and Perceptions of the Nineteenth-Century Urban Frontier*. New York, 1990.
Headrick, Daniel R. *The Tentacles of Progress: Technology Transfer in the Age of Imperialism, 1850–1940*. New York, 1988.
Home, Robert. *Of Planting and Planning: The Making of British Colonial Cities*. London, 1997.
Idowu, H. O. "The Establishment of Elective Institutions in Senegal, 1869–1880." *Journal of African History* 9 (1968): 261–77.
King, Anthony D. *Urbanism, Colonialism, and the World Economy: Cultural and Spatial Foundations of the World Urban System*. London, 1990.
Laidlaw, Zoë. *Colonial Connections, 1815–1845: Patronage, the Information Revolution, and Colonial Government*. Manchester, 2005.

Levine, Philippa. *Prostitution, Race, and Politics: Policing Venereal Disease in the British Empire*. New York, 2003.

Lewandowski, Susan J. "Urban Growth and Municipal Development in the Colonial City of Madras, 1860–1900." *Journal of Asian Studies* 34 (1975): 341–60.

Mandy, Nigel. *A City Divided: Johannesburg and Soweto*. New York, 1984.

Mayne, A. J. C. *Fever, Squalor, and Vice: Sanitation and Social Policy in Victorian Sydney*. St. Lucia, 1982.

Metcalf, Thomas R. *An Imperial Vision: Indian Architecture and Britain's Raj*. Berkeley, 1989.

Mitchell, Timothy. *Colonising Egypt*. Berkeley, 1988.

Morris, Jan. *Stones of Empire: The Buildings of the Raj*. Oxford, 1983.

Murphey, Rhodes. "Traditionalism and Colonialism: Changing Urban Roles in Asia." *Journal of Asian Studies* 29 (1969): 67–84.

Nas, Peter J. M. "The Origins and Development of the Urban Municipality in Indonesia." *Sojourn* 5 (1990): 86–112.

Oldenburg, Veena Talwar. *The Making of Colonial Lucknow, 1856–1877*. Princeton, 1984.

Papin, Philippe. *Histoire de Hanoi*. Paris, 2001.

Pasquier, Roger. "Villes du Senégal au XIXe siècle." *Revue française d'historire d'outre-mer* 47 (1960): 387–426.

Penny, H. Glenn. *Objects of Culture: Ethnology and Ethnographic Museums in Imperial Germany*. Chapel Hill, 2002.

Port, M. H. *Imperial London: Civil Government Building in London, 1851–1915*. New Haven, 1995.

Porterfield, Todd. *The Allure of Empire*. Princeton, 1998.

Prochaska, David. *Making Algeria French: Colonialism in Bône, 1870–1920*. Cambridge, 1990.

Ross, Robert, and Gerard J. Telcamp, eds. *Colonial Cities: Essays on Urbanism in a Colonial Context*. Dordrecht, 1985.

Sessions, Jennifer E. "Ambiguous Glory: The Algerian Conquest and the Politics of Colonial Commemoration in Post-Revolutionary France." *Outre-Mer* 94 (2006): 91–102.

Schneer, Jonathan. *London 1900: The Imperial Metropolis*. New Haven, 1999.

Statham, Pamela, ed. *The Origins of Australia's Capital Cities*. Cambridge, 1989.

Swanson, Maynard W. "The Sanitation Syndrome: Bubonic Plague and Urban Native Policy in the Cape Colony, 1900–1909." *Journal of African History* 18 (1977): 387–410.

Turnbull, C. M. *A History of Singapore, 1819–1988*. 2nd edn. Singapore, 1989.

Wright, Gwendolyn. *The Politics of Design in French Colonial Urbanism*. Chicago, 1991.

Yeoh, Brenda S. A. *Contesting Space: Power Relations and the Urban Built Environment in Colonial Singapore*. Kuala Lumpur, 1996.

Conclusion

Between the start of the Industrial Revolution and the start of the First World War, the biggest cities in Europe became much bigger than ever before and the proportion of European population accounted for by city dwellers swelled dramatically. London grew between 1750 and 1914 more than ten-fold, from 676,000 to well over 7 million inhabitants, and the populations of dozens of other cities soared at a similar pace. Even places that grew only half as fast increased in size enormously. Some of this growth reflected an increase in the European population as a whole, but the urban sector expanded much more rapidly than did non-urban areas. Between 1800 and 1900, the percentage of Europeans living west of the Russian Empire who resided in "big" cities (towns that numbered 100,000 or more inhabitants) more than quadrupled. As a result, cities became much more important in the countries where they were located.

We have sought to show where and why they expanded so dramatically and how and why their expansion mattered. Instead of writing urban history as a collection of local histories, we have used London and Manchester, Paris and Marseille, Berlin and Munich, and many other cities, as windows through which one can look at large-scale processes that shaped the making of modern Europe and its global position.

Cities ought to be seen as a "third force" in modern European society, occupying a large space between individuals and nation-states and mediating contacts between them. Cities provided the infrastructures of civil society: the schools that produced literacy, the newspapers and libraries that provided information, and the organizations that linked individuals one to another. Although civil society extended beyond city limits, its centers of creation and diffusion lay in the towns, which were major sites for capital investment, centers of political power, and centers of cultural production. The strategic positions of cities in a variety of networks empowered city dwellers – as workers and writers, voters and volunteers, consumers and critics – to promote the processes that modernized Europe during the long nineteenth century. Cities reflected, shaped, and also diffused the intellectual, financial, cultural, and human capital that supported industrialization, democratization, commercialization, and state formation.

Life in cities and the positions occupied by cities in Europe changed quite markedly during the century and a half that followed 1750. Not only in terms of size but also in terms of physical, economic, social, and political structures, the urban worlds of the mid-eighteenth and the early twentieth centuries differed vastly from one another. At the start of our period, cities were relatively self-contained. In many cases, walls built in earlier centuries sharply separated towns from their hinterlands. Manufacturing was largely done by artisans who worked in small firms or as sub-contractors for merchant-entrepreneurs. Many artisans on the continent still enjoyed a great deal of protection from competition as a result of the persistence of monopolistic guilds. The absence of unified, national governments on the Italian peninsula and in German-speaking territories, as well as the weakness of the Dutch state, meant that towns in large parts of Europe enjoyed substantial independence. In France, local *parlements* and local memory kept alive resistance to monarchical rule, and in Britain, royal charters and customary rights shielded incorporated towns from central authority in legally defined ways. Within towns, power was firmly in the hands of propertied families of high status. Most workers lacked the right to vote and, often, even citizenship in their towns of residence. In cities, the impact of rapid technological development, state growth, and democratization had yet to be felt.

One hundred and fifty years later, each of those three forces had decisively transformed European cities. City walls had been almost entirely demolished, railroads had further undermined urban self-containment, and technological developments more generally had greatly stimulated urban manufacturing. A whole host of additional changes had further contributed to the transformation of urban economic life, and in place of craft guilds trade unions had emerged as the major vehicles for workers' assertions of their rights as workers. As states consolidated their power at national levels, urban independence had been greatly curbed, but city government had gained a great deal of power to act for their inhabitants on matters of local concern. Meanwhile, rights to participate in the electoral process at the local level had been expanded to include most adult males.

Urban growth during the later nineteenth century brought many new issues to the fore. With the expansion of the metropolis came problems relating to scale, internal governance, and cultural identity. Could settlements with hundreds of thousands or even a million or more inhabitants function effectively as cohesive communities? What infrastructures would be necessary to keep them orderly, safe, and clean? How would increasingly diverse sets of residents relate to one another, particularly when leisure time increased? How would a mass male electorate deal with the issues of social inequality and cultural difference? Urban governments and residents still wrestle with these problems. Nevertheless, the combination of effective state and city bureaucracies, commercial leisure culture, and the technologies and wealth of the second industrial revolution provided resources with which to begin to tackle them.

We have emphasized the 1850s as a turning point in the urban history of Europe. That date serves as a rough marker for the important shift in towns from a period of heightened disruption to an era of greater stability. During the preceding century, the combined forces of industrialization, demographic change, political mobilization, and political revolution had disrupted many relatively stable communities. Suspicion of royal incompetence, clerical corruption, and foreign threats unsettled public opinion at a time when international wars raised taxes and prices. Unruly urban crowds along with dissatisfied liberals and radicals were determined to limit the power of monarchical regimes or replace them entirely. Urban patterns of proto-industrial manufacturing gave way in parts of Britain, Belgium, and France to factory production, whose scale and technological base transformed their settings and whose low-cost products threatened other cities' markets. As steam engines belched coal smoke and migrants squeezed into unrenovated or makeshift housing, death rates rose, and workers' quality of life deteriorated. Meanwhile, population growth and railroads brought into many cities hordes of newcomers who needed food, jobs, and housing, pressuring economic networks, which had to readjust to disrupted trade, new technologies, and market changes. The part-time amateurs who staffed local governments were overwhelmed.

While the particular combinations of such problems varied among European towns, all were touched in some fashion or another by them. Contemporary exposure of conditions in a few notorious places, for example Manchester and Lille, forced recognition of similar problems elsewhere and of their increasing scale. When the possible trajectories of both political and economic changes were taken into account, the urban future looked bleak indeed to people who valued social and political order.

In contrast to the previous decade, the 1850s saw the return of political stability under mostly conservative regimes and more prosperous economic times. Although cities had their own local timetables of change, they generally responded to the political and economic weather of their states and regions. The reconstruction of Paris ordered by Napoleon III, who wanted to be remembered as the man who found the French capital stinking and left it sweet, demonstrated with great fanfare the effectiveness of large-scale urban activism. Clean water, effective drainage, green parks, and new housing (at least for the wealthy) were provided by state investment in alliance with the private market, while costs to dispossessed individuals had little political impact. Meanwhile, urban doctors and sanitary reformers in several countries argued successfully for improved sanitation, which helped to lower death rates substantially in the second half of the century. As medical knowledge increased, so did the willingness of local governments to expand hospital provision, vaccinate children, and filter water supplies.

The spread of industrialization to other parts of Europe after 1850 helped to employ that region's increasing population and generated resources which could be tapped by local and central governments. In the four dozen cities that had crossed the quarter-million mark by 1910 (and in many dozens of others that had crossed the 100,000 mark), new wealth in combination with the availability of relatively cheap steel and electricity permitted the introduction of mass transit systems, elevators, high-rise buildings, and telephones. Increased revenues gave cities funds to hire professional staff and to invest in citizens' wellbeing. The growth of national bureaucracies had its parallel on the municipal level. Mass electorates and trade unions also increased pressures for change. Even if women's claims for representation were largely ignored, maternalist demands for improved family support were not, producing in the cities a range of services from infant care centers and free medical check-ups to school meals. Although the teeth of urban poverty still remained sharp, the adept could use a range of urban institutions, charitable funds, and state insurance to supplement what they earned in the labor market. European cities were far from being miniature welfare states, but the range of social services within them increased greatly during the nineteenth century.

Growing prosperity contributed not only to practical improvements but also to expansion in the cultural realm. Although elites continued to dominate in the area of high culture, considerably larger sectors of the urban population now enjoyed access to museums and libraries, as well as to public schools. For those who could pay, theaters, cabarets, department stores, wax museums, and professional sports also beckoned; for those who could not, wide streets, riverside walks, and public parks afforded places to relax and entertain themselves. The means of modern leisure, which were invented for city dwellers, helped greatly to enrich popular culture.

European cities were marked by great dynamism and diversity. Rapid growth was at first chaotic. It was accompanied both by environmental and social problems of great magnitude and by sharp conflicts among contending groups, which sometimes spilled over into political revolutions. Increasingly, however, urban dynamism and diversity pointed toward urban improvements. Cities posed great challenges, but they also fostered a multitude of efforts to improve the quality of urban life. For cultural as well as administrative, technological, and medical reasons, life in European cities became a great deal better by the end of our period than it had been previously. Whereas the costs urbanization imposed had seemed earlier to many observers to outweigh the benefits it conferred, urban development later on had a much more favorable impact on the lives of city dwellers. The problems that had arisen in connection with rapid growth had been by no means fully solved. For example, high levels of pollution and of poverty continued to blight cityscapes. Nonetheless, a great deal had been done to justify the expectations voiced by optimists such as Robert Vaughan.

In the twentieth century, city dwellers and their leaders had to confront a whole host of new problems. In both world wars, urban networks were called on to help mobilize national populations into the service of the state. Urban institutions had to direct new divisions of labor and flows of resources into war efforts. During the First World War, many city dwellers (particularly in Central Europe) had to cope with extreme shortages of food. During the Second World War, in Britain and the Netherlands as well as in Germany, aerial bombing led to widespread destruction of urban centers. Thereafter, as rebuilding was taking place, even greater damage occurred as a result of the rising use of automobiles. Demolition of buildings for road construction occurred on a vast scale. Even so, traffic congestion as well as air pollution continued to worsen. Finally, as a result both of economic growth and of declining birth rates, European cities have become markedly more multi-ethnic. Movement of workers and their families from one part of Europe to another and from former colonies has proved essential for urban vitality. The need to assimilate foreigners, however, has posed great cultural and political challenges. How these problems, as well as other problems of the post-1914 period, have been perceived and addressed is too broad a question to answer here.

Although, in a book about "the making of modern Europe," we have necessarily focused on cities *in* Europe, European cities cannot be understood in isolation either from one another or from cities beyond Europe itself. In line with B. J. L. Berry's apt comment that "cities are systems within systems of cities," we wish to re-emphasize ties of the sort that linked places such as London, Marseille, and Amsterdam to places such as Capetown, Hanoi, and Batavia (Jakarta).[1] These networks of connection had profound impacts both on European metropoles and on their colonial offshoots, greatly contributing to urban growth both in Europe and elsewhere and also influencing urban life in many other ways. Since 1914, as expansion in Europe has slowed down, movement into cities has accelerated in Asia, Africa, and Latin America, producing megacities more than twice as large as London. This development points up the ongoing relevance of the European experience in the past. The story of urban growth in Europe between 1750 and 1914 matters not only as a chapter in the history of Europe itself but also as a basis for comparison with a global process that continues unabated elsewhere.

[1] B. J. L. Berry, "Cities as Systems within Systems of Cities," *Papers and Proceedings of the Regional Science Association* 13 (1964): 147–63.

Appendix A
The growth of selected large cities in Europe, 1750–1910

Cities	1750	1800/01	1850/51	1880/81	1910/11
Amsterdam	219	201	224	326	574
Antwerp	43	62	88	169	302
Barcelona	70	115	175	346	587
Belfast	–	37	103	208	387
Berlin	113	172	419	1122	2071
Birmingham	–	74	233	437	840
Bordeaux	64	91	131	221	262
Bradford	–	13	104	194	288
Breslau	52	60	114	273	512
Bristol	45	64	137	207	357
Brussels	55	66	251	421	720
Bucharest	–	–	120	–	341
Budapest	–	54	178	371	880
Cologne	44	50	97	145	517
Copenhagen	79	101	129	235	559
Dresden	60	60	97	221	548
Dublin	125	165	272	250	305
Düsseldorf	–	10	27	95	359
Edinburgh	55	83	202	295	401
Essen	–	4	9	57	295
Frankfurt a. M.	38	48	65	137	415
Genoa	72	91	120	180	272
Glasgow	–	77	357	587	1000
The Hague	40	38	72	118	281
Hamburg	90	130	132	290	931
Hanover	–	18	29	123	302
Leeds	–	53	172	309	453
Leipzig	30	30	63	149	590
Lisbon	213	180	240	242	435
Liverpool	–	80	376	553	753
London	676	1117	2685	4770	7256
Lyon	115	110	177	377	460
Madrid	123	160	281	398	600

(cont.)

(cont.)

Cities	1750	1800/01	1850/51	1880/81	1910/11
Manchester	–	90	303	462	714
Marseille	88	111	194	360	551
Milan	123	135	242	322	579
Munich	30	40	110	230	596
Naples	324	427	449	494	723
Nuremberg	30	30	54	100	333
Palermo	124	139	180	245	342
Paris	560	547	1053	2269	2888
Rome	157	163	175	300	542
Rotterdam	46	53	90	153	427
Sheffield	–	31	135	285	465
Stockholm	60	76	93	169	342
Stuttgart	–	18	47	117	286
Turin	60	78	135	254	427
Vienna	169	247	444	1104	2031

The table refers to all cities in Europe outside the Russian Empire in 1910 that had 250,000 or more inhabitants. Numbers are in thousands. Numbers for 1750 come from Tertius Chandler and Gerald Fox, *3000 Years of Urban Growth* (London, 1974), 18. Numbers for later years come from Brian Mitchell, *European Historical Statistics, 1770–1970*, 2nd edn (London, 1981), 86–88. As Mitchell explains, in some cases his numbers pertain to years other than the years indicated above (when censuses were taken slightly earlier or slightly later). In most cases the numbers pertain to areas within officially defined boundaries, although in a few cases (Antwerp, Brussels, London, Rome) he included suburban areas in his tabulations. The fact that for a few cities the numbers for 1750 are higher than the ones for 1800/01 may be accounted for by differences between Chandler and Fox's and Mitchell's criteria for determining size or by differences between the criteria used in the sources on which they rely. But the fact that in some cases cities did in fact decline in size as a result of the international wars that beset much of Europe for over two decades starting in 1792 should also be borne in mind.

Appendix B
General works on individual cities

This appendix lists books of a fairly general sort about almost all of the cities listed in Appendix A. In most cases, the volumes may be described as urban biographies, in the sense that they deal with many aspects of a city over long periods, but some deal with relatively short periods, and, in the absence of general works about a city in English, some deal with special aspects of a city's history. Titles that were not published in English, French, German, Italian, or Spanish have been excluded. In all cases (particularly those of Berlin, Hamburg, London, and Paris), they represent an extremely small portion of writings about these places.

Amsterdam

Mak, Geert. *Amsterdam*. Trans. Phillip Blom. Cambridge, MA, 2000.

Antwerp

Isacker, Karel van, and Raymond van Uyten, eds. *Antwerp: Twelve Centuries of History and Culture*. Antwerp, 1986.

Barcelona

Hughes, Robert. *Barcelona*. New York, 1992.

Belfast

Beckett, J. C., *et al. Belfast: The Making of the City, 1800–1914*. Belfast, 1983.

Berlin

Large, David Clay. *Berlin*. New York, 2000.
Masur, Gerhard. *Imperial Berlin*. New York, 1970.
Ribbe, Wolfgang, ed. *Geschichte Berlins*. 3rd edn. 2 vols. Munich, 2002.

Birmingham

Gill, Conrad, and Asa Briggs. *History of Birmingham.* 2 vols. London, 1952.
Hopkins, Eric. *Birmingham: The First Manufacturing Town in the World, 1760–1840.* London, 1989.

Bordeaux

Figeac, Michel, and Pierre Guillaume, eds. *Histoire des Bordelais.* 2 vols. Bordeaux, 2002.

Bradford

Koditschek, Theodore. *Class Formation and Urban Industrial Society: Bradford, 1750–1850.* New York, 1990.

Bristol

Little, Bryan D. G. *The City and County of Bristol: A Study in Atlantic Civilisation.* London, 1954.

Brussels

Dumont, Georges-Henri. *Histoire de Bruxelles: Biographie d'une capitale.* Brussels, 1999.

Budapest

Lukacs, John. *Budapest 1900: A Historical Portrait of a City and its Culture.* New York, 1988.

Cologne

Ayçoberry, Pierre. *Cologne entre Napoléon et Bismarck: La croissance d'une ville rhénane.* Paris, 1981.

Dublin

Cosgrove, Art, ed. *Dublin through the Ages.* Dublin, 1988.

Düsseldorf

Weidenhaupt, Hugo, ed. *Düsseldorf: Geschichte von den Ursprüngen bis ins 20. Jahrhundert.* 4 vols. Düsseldorf, 1988–90.

Edinburgh

Cosh, Mary. *Edinburgh: The Golden Age.* Edinburgh, 2003.

Rodger, Richard. *The Transformation of Edinburgh: Land, Property, and Trust in the Nineteenth Century*. Cambridge, 2001.

Essen

Borsdorf, Ulrich, ed. *Essen: Geschichte einer Stadt*. Bottrop, 2002.

Frankfurt am Main

Palmowski, Jan. *Urban Liberalism in Imperial Germany: Frankfurt-am-Main, 1866–1914*. Oxford, 1998.
Roth, Ralf. *Stadt und Bürgertum in Frankfurt am Main: Ein besonderer Weg von der städtischen zur modernen Bürgergesellschaft*. Munich, 1996.

Glasgow

Devine, T. M., and Gordon Jackson, eds. *Glasgow*. 2 vols. New York, 1994.
Maver, Irene. *Glasgow*. Edinburgh, 2000.

Hamburg

Jenkins, Jennifer. *Provincial Modernity: Local Culture and Liberal Politics in Fin-de-Siècle Hamburg*. Ithaca, 2002.
Klessmann, Eckhart. *Geschichte der Stadt Hamburg*. Hamburg, 2002.

Hanover

Mlynek, Klaus, and Waldemar R. Rohrbein. *Geschichte der Stadt Hannover*. 2 vols. Hanover, 1992–94.

Leeds

Fraser, Derek, ed. *A History of Modern Leeds*. Manchester, 1980.

Lisbon

Couto, Dejanirah. *Histoire de Lisbonne*. Paris, 2000.

Liverpool

Muir, Ramsay. *A History of Liverpool*. Liverpool, 1906.

London

Porter, Roy. *London: A Social History*. London, 1994.
Rudé, George. *Hanoverian London, 1714–1808*. Berkeley and Los Angeles, 1971.
Schneer, Jonathan. *London 1900: The Imperial Metropolis*. New Haven, 1999.
Sheppard, Francis. *London, 1808–1870*. Berkeley and Los Angeles, 1971.

Lyon

Latreille, André, ed. *Histoire de Lyon et du Lyonnais*. Toulouse, 1975.

Madrid

Parsons, Deborah L. *A Cultural History of Madrid: Modernism and the Urban Spectacle*. Oxford and New York, 2003.

Ringrose, David R. *Madrid and the Spanish Economy, 1560–1850*. Berkeley and Los Angeles, 1983.

Santos, Julia, *et al.*, eds. *Madrid: Historia de una capital*. Madrid, 2000.

Manchester

Kidd, Alan. *Manchester*. 3rd edn. Edinburgh, 2002.

Marseille

Temime, Émile. *Histoire de Marseille: De la Révolution à nos jours*. Paris, 1999.

Milan

Storia di Milano. 16 vols. Milan, 1953–62.

Tilly, Louise A. *Politics and Class in Milan, 1881–1901*. New York, 1992.

Munich

Bauer, Reinhard, and Ernst Piper, eds. *München: Die Geschichte einer Stadt*. Munich, 1993.

Bauer, Richard, ed. *Geschichte der Stadt München*. Munich, 1992.

Naples

Galasso, Giuseppe, ed. *Napoli*. Rome, 1987.

Lancaster, Jordan. *In the Shadow of Vesuvius: A Cultural History of Naples*. New York, 2005.

Nuremberg

Pfeiffer, Gerhard, ed. *Nürnberg: Geschichte einer europäischen Stadt*. Munich, 1971.

Palermo

Cancila, Orazio. *Palermo*. 3rd edn. Rome, 1988.

Paris

Favier, Jean. *Paris: Deux milles ans d'histoire*. Paris, 1997.

Harvey, David. *Paris, Capital of Modernity.* New York and London, 2003.
Higonnet, Patrice. *Paris: Capital of the World.* Trans. Arthur Goldhammer. Cambridge, MA, 2002.
Marchand, B[ernard]. *Paris, Histoire d'une ville (XIXᵉ–XXᵉ siècle).* Paris, 1993.

Rome

Boriaud, Jeans-Yves. *Historie de Rome.* Paris, 2001.
Nicassio, Susan Vandiver. *Imperial City: Rome, Romans and Napoleon, 1796–1815.* Welwyn Garden City, 2005.
Vidotto, Vittorio, ed. *Roma capitale.* Rome, 2002.

Sheffield

Hey, David. *A History of Sheffield.* Lancaster, 1998.

Stockholm

Hurd, Madeleine. *Public Spheres, Public Mores, and Democracy: Hamburg and Stockholm, 1870–1914.* Ann Arbor, 2000.

Stuttgart

Borst, Otto. *Stuttgart: Die Geschichte einer Stadt.* Stuttgart and Aalen, 1973.

Turin

Castronovo, Valerio. *Torino.* Rome, 1987.
Storia di Torino. 8 vols. Turin, 1997.

Vienna

Csendes, Peter, and Ferdinand Opll, eds. *Wien: Geschichte einer Stadt.* 3 vols. Vienna, 2001–06.
Johnston, William M. *Vienna: The Golden Age, 1815–1914.* New York, 1981.
Schorske, Carl. *Fin-de-siècle Vienna.* New York, 1979.

Index

NEW APPROACHES TO EUROPEAN HISTORY